CHINESE IN AMERICAN LIFE

Some Aspects of Their History,
Status, Problems, and Contributions

CHINESE IN AMERICAN LIFE ❧ ❧ ❧ ❧

Some Aspects of Their History, Status, Problems, and Contributions

BY S. W. KUNG

University of Washington Press • *Seattle*
• *1962*

To my parents

Mr. and Mrs. Wu-Kan Kung
龔梧根先生龔梧根夫人

Foreword

It is a well-known fact that there are about fourteen million Chinese living abroad. Those residing in the United States constitute an important part of these "overseas Chinese." Their history, their status, their problems, and their contribution and achievements, especially in the past few decades, deserve the earnest attention of all public-spirited Americans and Chinese.

Unfortunately, few serious attempts have been made in recent years to search for and to present such desired information. By providing up-to-date material regarding contemporary Chinese immigrants and Americans of Chinese ancestry, the author, Dr. S. W. Kung, renders in this new book a valuable service in meeting an urgent demand.

Although the book is entitled *Chinese in American Life,* the scope of its contents also includes studies of the Chinese in Southeast Asia, as well as in Canada and Latin America, thus enabling us to obtain an over-all impression of the Chinese overseas. The frequent references to the Chinese in Hawaii are certainly useful and timely. It is there that racial prejudice is at a minimum. That a senator and a representative of Chinese and of Japanese ancestry, respectively, were elected to Congress in 1959 shows that the Orientals there are thought of as equals. They do not need to worry that they will ever be considered second-class citizens. Those who are skeptical whether the Chinese on the mainland of the United States can be assimilated into American society need only take a close look at the experience of its youngest state.

The important material and findings contained in this book represent the result of serious research pursued by the author over a period of several years. The value of the book is further enhanced by the well-selected footnotes, by some thirty explanatory tables, by fifteen noteworthy tables in the appendix, and by the selected bibliography and index. Such a publication could very well be used as a source book, a textbook, or a reference book on overseas Chinese and on immigration law or policies.

Dr. Kung has collected a wealth of material about many so-called "old immigrants" who have sacrificed themselves in the true Chinese tradition for the benefit of the next generation. They are immigrants who have added some riches to American culture. His studies also reveal that in recent years Chinese scholars in America have made numerous contributions to science and to humanity. The names of Chinese scholars mentioned in the study as having made such contributions are most impressive. They naturally include the two young physicists Dr. Tsung-Dao Lee of Columbia University and Dr. Chen-Ning Yang of the Institute for Advanced Study at Princeton, who have attracted world-wide attention because they were the recipients of the Nobel prize. But there are many others who have made notable contributions and deserve public recognition and appreciation.

Other facts revealed by the study are that Chinese immigrants, including engineers, scientists, teachers, doctors, and nurses, as well as laundrymen and restaurateurs, have rendered valuable service in meeting demands; and that, in turn, they have received many benefits from this country of their adoption; that Americans have much to learn from the Chinese civilization, especially in moral and spiritual values; and that the annual immigration quota of 105 for Chinese is exceedingly small and is not equitable because the standard country-of-birth formula used for European quotas has not been applied to the Chinese quota.

In order to understand Chinese immigrants and Chinese-Americans thoroughly we should make a comprehensive study of their problems. The Chinese are here to stay, and it is to the good of everybody concerned that they should be understood, not just by the scholars but by the general public. As Dr. Kung has rightly stated, he would feel very happy if some of the problems discussed by him could be used as a basis for additional study.

I had the pleasure of being associated with Dr. Kung in the years 1931 and 1932, when I was Director of the Bureau of Foreign Trade of the Chinese government, while he was, first, chief of the research department, and later editor of the *Chinese Economic Journal*. As a student of international trade, Dr. Kung has a unique interest in the subject of overseas Chinese. The annual remittances sent to China by the Chinese abroad constituted for many years very important items in China's balance of international payments, second only to the merchandise export. It is for this reason that we found it was necessary to pay special attention to the life of the Chinese abroad. After he left the bureau, Dr. Kung taught in a number of colleges in Shanghai. He has written several books on international trade and on the world immigration problem. His connections with the Bank of China and, as a member, with the Foreign Exchange Stabilization Board, Central Bank of China, have given him much first-hand information for his studies of the Chinese abroad.

Such being the nature of this book and the qualifications of its author, it should be welcomed by Americans and Chinese, as well as by institutions concerned with contemporary Chinese and Chinese-Americans in the United States and in other areas having large numbers of Chinese residents. It is my considered opinion that a perusal of its pages will appreciably increase one's understanding of the overseas Chinese and of Chinese-American relations.

> P. W. Kuo, Ph.D., LL.D.
> Founder and Trustee Emeritus, China Institute in America, formerly President, National Southeastern University, Nanking, China.

Washington, D.C.
March, 1961

Preface

The author's interest in the subject of the overseas Chinese dates back to 1931, when he was with the Bureau of Foreign Trade, in Shanghai, as head of its research department, where a great deal of attention was being paid to the problem. Since 1939, he has made several trips to both North and South America, to Europe, and Southeast Asia, with the view of making firsthand contacts with the Chinese. The question always raised in his mind, as he made his survey, was this: What are the factors that have made the majority of the Chinese in those regions do fairly well, with all the odds against them almost everywhere?

The twin subjects of Chinese immigrants and of Americans of Chinese ancestry, the author realized, had not been fully examined. To be sure, in the second half of the nineteenth century, much was written pro and con about either accepting or excluding the Chinese, praising them as though faultless—which they are not—or condemning them as a race beyond the scope of salvation. Such bias and inconsistency much confused the public, resulting in the very grossest illogical generalities. In preparing this book, the author had no intention of dwelling at length upon the history of the Chinese immigration into this country. Rather, the aim has been to bring up to date the material for the study of contemporary Chinese immigrants and of Chinese-Americans in the United States. The author understands that many interesting aspects of the problem cannot be covered fully in a single volume. He will feel, therefore, amply rewarded if his efforts in this book serve to provide bases for further research.

The classification of Chinese-Americans and Chinese immigrants into different groups is certainly a delicate one. There are native-born and foreign-born Chinese-Americans; native-born of mixed parentage; first generation Chinese-Americans or immigrants; also persons of the second, third, or even fifth generation. There are those immigrants and their descendants who may be termed "old," since they came before the repeal of the Chinese Exclusion Act; and those that may be termed "new"—the ones who, while actually present in the United States, adjusted their status by taking advantage of the existing immigration laws. Again, "new immigrants" came to this country under the McCarran-Walter Act, the Refugee Relief Act of 1953, and later legislations. A number of them may represent simply the offspring of the second, or of a later, generation of the "old immigrants." There are those native born and reared in this country, as well as foreign born, who have been assimilated into American life; others, perhaps because of their different cultural backgrounds or because they experienced discrimination, have been rather more slowly absorbed. A few are trying hard to preserve their own way of life. On the other hand, before World War II a number of American-Chinese, especially if well educated, went to China to obtain employment, for the reason that in this country many fields requiring skill and training seldom were open to those of oriental ancestry. Some Americans still think that a Chinese is a Chinese, regardless of whether he was born in this country. The opening of occupational opportunities, the raising of social status, the increasing Chinese contribution in American society, the vast improvement in attitude toward Chinese which is reflected in the laws of the land, the gradual lessening of racial discrimination, but above all the repeal of the Chinese Exclusion Act, were made possible principally by World War II. In a true sense, we can only make our study of the life of Chinese immigrants and of Chinese-Americans richer and more interesting by considering the period since the beginning of that war. Therefore, when in the text classification according to origin or nativity has to be made, it serves merely for convenience in grouping. At any rate, it does not matter whether people came from the province of Kwangtung, whence most of the "old immigrants" came, or from other parts of China. In the course of several more decades, the great majority of the Chinese in America will consist of native-born and naturalized citizens. As time passes, there will be less and less point in making group distinctions.

Carey McWilliams has stated that the Chinese are one of the few ethnic groups that have made important contributions toward the culture of California. Yet few treatises are available in making the story known. Perhaps an account of the life of the Chinese in California and elsewhere in the early days would be highly interesting towards evaluating the contributions made by the Chinese. On the other hand, when we discuss the contributions made by the Chinese since World War II, it is almost certain that a number of worthy cases must have escaped the author's attention. The establishment of criteria for determining exactly who have made positive contributions would be difficult indeed. One thing is certain: the "old" and the "new," the "native born" and the "foreign born"— all have accomplished much.

The author has received much assistance from friends—in the United States, Canada, Latin America, Southeast Asia, Hong Kong, and Taiwan—whose names are too numerous to mention. He is greatly indebted to Dr. P. W. Kuo, chairman of the Chinese Advisory Committee on Cultural Relations in America and a former president of the National Southeastern University; to Dr. C. F. Remer, professor of economics at the University of Michigan; and to Professor John M. MacGregor, chairman of the department of law in the graduate school of business administration, New York University, for reading the manuscript and for offering many helpful criticisms. He is indebted also to Dr. Anthony Koo, a professor of economics at Michigan State University, for suggestions on "Fallacies in the Official Statistics on Chinese Immigration"; to Professor Kwei Yu of the National Taiwan University for some information on litigation and court decisions; to Mrs. William Wilmet, an attorney at law, on the present status of Chinese immigration; to Dr. Maurice T. Price, a sociologist of many years' standing, on the Chinese community and the characteristics of Chinese population; to Dr. H. D. Fong of the United Nations in Thailand on "Chinese Abroad"; to Professor James O. Wettereau, assistant chairman of history, New York University, on Chapters 3 and 4 concerning history of Chinese immigration; to Professor Ralph W. Gilbert and Dr. Eugene Shen, psychologists, on the subjects of prejudice and discrimination; and to Mr. K. Y. Pao, formerly United States representative of the China Merchants' Steam Navigation Company, on matters related to the shipping trade. Mr. Ferris Luboshez, an attorney at law, expended much effort in collecting material and in making possible the author's analysis of the "Relief of Chinese Nationals through Private Legislation." Mr. T. C. Tsao, a senior research engineer of the Electronic Research Laboratory at Columbia University, has been most helpful on "intellectual migration." The author's appreciation is expressed to Miss Edith Lowenstein, editor of *Interpreter Releases,* American Council for Nationalities Service, who has made numerous suggestions for improvements in both form and content on Chapter 5 and 7, in relation to problems of Chinese immigration and court decisions. She suggested a number of modifications in interpretation and presentations which have been adopted. Any opinions expressed in the study are necessarily the responsibility of the author.

I am thankful for discussions on several specific subjects with

Dr. Howard G. Brunsman, chief of the Population Division of the Bureau of the Census; Mr. E. A. Loughran, associate commissioner of the Immigration and Naturalization Service; with the Federal Bureau of Investigation; with the Federal Bureau of Prisons; Bureau of Narcotics; National Office of Vital Statistics; Office of Health Statistics; Department of Health, Hawaii; and with the Canadian Bureau of Statistics. Appreciation must also go to my wife and to Miss May-Sun Wang who have helped me all around in improving the manuscript.

S. W. Kung

Rego Park, New York
March, 1961

Contents

1. The Chinese Abroad 3

2. Characteristics of the Chinese Population
   in the United States 30

3. Free Immigration (1820-82) 64

4. From Exclusion to Repeal (1882-1943) 80

5. Recent Status of Chinese Immigration 106

6. Relief through Private Legislation 132

7. Litigation, Court Decisions, and the Problem
   of Illegal Entry 148

8. The Problems of the Second-Generation Chinese 165

9. Occupational Adjustment 179

10. The Chinese Community 197

11. Contributions and Achievements 228

12. Conclusions 253

Appendix 265

Notes 281

Bibliography 329

Index 345

CHINESE IN AMERICAN LIFE

Some Aspects of Their History,
Status, Problems, and Contributions

1

The Chinese Abroad

Although this treatise deals primarily with the Chinese in the United States—their life here, their history in this country, their difficulties, their accomplishments—nevertheless it may not ignore the fact that they are to be found almost everywhere in the world, a great majority of them in Southeast Asia. The Chinese abroad are usually termed "overseas Chinese," or *hua-chiao,* which means Chinese sojourning abroad. Generally in Southeast Asia, census officials consider Chinese in the ethnographical sense. However, each country applies its own rules in determining ethnic and cultural grouping, and the term Chinese is often interpreted differently. Though Chinese born in the United States are legally citizens, the census lists them also as a separate racial group. We are concerned with the ethnic Chinese. We shall not deal with those who merely come and go, such as students, visitors, and governmental officers.

The Chinese have now for many centuries been in Southeast Asia: in Malaya, Singapore, Borneo, Vietnam, Indonesia, and the Philippines, long before the British, French, Dutch, or Spanish occupied those places. This is evidenced by journals, accounts of travel, and other writings depicting Chinese pilgrims and priests or showing Chinese influence. Traditions say that even in prehistoric times the Chinese had infiltrated into Alaska, North America, and Mexico. The Immigration Commission records that the first Chinese arrived in the United States in 1820, and that a total of eleven came between 1820 and 1840; but according to report a Chinese person lived in New York as early as 1807. However, we know definitely that in 1847 three Chinese students came to the United States, one of whom in 1852 became naturalized.[1]

By about 1850 a considerable Chinese immigration began. Their migration to the United States, Australia, Hawaii, and Southeast Asia was greatly accelerated by the wanton devastation wrought by the Taiping Rebellion (1850-64). Since then, the Chinese have

been to a marked degree an emigrating people, at least until restriction and, eventually, exclusion blocked their way.

Because the Chinese immigrants have been almost everywhere
in this world, they have had to cope with various problems in the
countries in which they live. There were sparsely populated areas
with natural resources and therefore little competition with the
natives in Malaya, Indonesia, the Philippines, and other parts of
Southeast Asia when the Chinese first moved there. So Chinese
labor built the great rubber plantations and tin mines in Malaya,
and Chinese enterprise contributed greatly to Singapore's becoming
one of the world's great ports. The rapid economic progress in the
United States mainland and Hawaii enables the Chinese to participate
in the great opportunity offered to them. The competition is, however, very keen and the discrimination frequent. In Peru, in Jamaica, and in other parts of Latin America, there were less competition and less restriction suffered, and these factors explain
why Chinese have been able to make great headway in business.

The countries in Southeast Asia before World War II, with the possible exception of Thailand, were under the control of colonial governments. The Chinese prospered economically in such areas by acting as liaison between the Europeans and the natives; however, they
were mostly considered "second-class citizens" even though they had
been born in the country in which they lived. One of the significant
effects of the war was the creation in that part of the world of many
independent countries. The emergence of many youthful nations found
the Chinese even less happy. Their most urgent problem was assimilation, for the Chinese are often accused of being race-conscious, of
shunning citizenship, and of failing, thus, in loyalty to their adopted
country. Without doubt the Chinese are satisfactorily assimilable; the
widespread intermarriages among *hua-chiao* and the natives demon-
strate that. Nor do religious differences present a knotty problem.
The question is whether the Chinese are really wanted.

Racial prejudice against the Chinese and other Orientals is, however, demonstrated fully in Australia and New Zealand, where it
is extremely difficult for Chinese immigrants to gain admission.
In Hawaii there is little prejudice, since Orientals, economically
and politically, are on a par with other races. The fact that in 1959
an American of Chinese and one of Japanese descent were elected,
respectively, a United States senator and a member of the House of
Representatives is ample demonstration of equality. In Latin America, since the racial question has never been considered important,
the Chinese do not suffer. Negroes and American Indians also enjoy
equal status with immigrants from other lands. In Hong Kong there
also seems to be less prejudice against the Chinese, chiefly because

of the overwhelming majority of Chinese residents as well as the proximity of their homeland.

Finally the quality and character of the average Chinese immigrants must carefully be considered. Being clannish and cooperative among themselves, they think of ways to avoid trouble. They are individualists, mind their own affairs, and are little inclined toward politics; they are for the most part intelligent, frugal, and industrious. Such characteristics sometimes bring them into disfavor with the natives. As Dr. Eduard I. Hambro has stated: "Perhaps these very qualities, as well as their high rate of reproduction, contribute to the widespread resistance to the admission of any large numbers of Chinese immigrants."[2]

For convenience in study and in order to group Chinese immigrants according to their present status, the Chinese abroad may be classified as: (1) Chinese in the mainland United States and in Canada, (2) Chinese in Hawaii, (3) Chinese in Latin America, and (4) Chinese in Southeast Asia and in Hong Kong. There are Chinese in Australia, New Zealand, and Europe as well as in Japan and Korea, but we shall exclude them from our analysis.

To assist our study of the Chinese in the United States, we think it useful to give certain highlights, as it were, of the Chinese abroad—their history, their present status—and to discuss a number of special features relating to Chinese immigration.

Early History of Chinese Immigration

Since Chinese civilization goes back more than four thousand years, the Chinese have had ample opportunity to utilize many forms of communication with the rest of the world. Chinese have journeyed in considerable numbers, by land and by sea, from very early times, for various purposes, such as commerce, religion, travel for its own sake, and the pursuit of knowledge. Their journeyings took them particularly into Southeast Asia, bordering closely on China. In early days, however, the Chinese abroad proved to be more or less temporary residents, and therefore they were not in the modern sense immigrants. Some two thousand years ago, according to Chinese history, vessels were sailing from southern China to Indo-China and to the Malay Peninsula; conversely, during the first and second centuries B. C. , people of Southeast Asia frequently made voyages to the Celestial Empire. Near the end of the fourth century, a number of Chinese monks traveled to India to study Buddhism.

The Tang dynasty (618-906) marked a new era in Chinese expansion into Southeast Asia, because the Tang ruler embarked full sail on foreign conquest. Many territories, such as Amur, Korea, most of Inner and Outer Mongolia, Chinese and Russian Turkestan, Tashkent, Samarkand, Bokhara, Fergana, and Annam, hitherto unknown to the Chinese rulers, acknowledged themselves to be under the suzerainty of Tang.[3] As a result of these expansions, trade assumed a greater importance than it had in the past. Hindus, Arabs, and Persians went to China to trade; Christian travelers, together with devotees of other faiths, received sympathetic toleration. During the seventh century, Chinese pilgrims in great numbers visited holy places in India and in Ceylon. Several chose the sea route instead of the overland way preferred by their predecessors through Tibet and Nepal.

After the fall of the Tang, the great dynasties were Sung (960-1279), Yuan or Mongols (1280-1368), Ming (1368-1644), and Ch'ing, the Manchus (1644-1912). Throughout all those years, with only occasional interruptions, many Chinese were living in Southeast Asia. Long before the Dutch settled there, China had established lucrative trade with what was to become the Netherlands East Indies; likewise in Malaya, the Chinese had established settlements many years before its occupation by the British; in the Philippine Islands, Chinese residents had already become very influential before the Spaniards took possession. In Burma, in Indo-China, and in Siam, where the Celestial Empire had, in addition to its commercial intercourse, a strong political influence, Chinese immigrants had been well settled for many centuries.

Apropos of all this, we should observe with special interest the hitherto unprecedented naval activity of the Chinese in Southeast Asian waters from 1405 to 1433, under the command of that renowned eunuch, Admiral Cheng Ho. His powerful navy executed no fewer than seven highly successful ventures to Southeast Asia, penetrating as far as the coasts of Arabia and Africa. When he returned home after each expedition, he left many of his men behind on those distant shores. As a result of Cheng Ho's naval operations, many countries had been compelled to pay homage to the Ming emperor. Thus, for many years after, China succeeded in extending her mercantile interests through the seaboard states lying to the south.

With the fall of each dynasty, as Chinese history reveals, numbers of people fled as political refugees; when the last strongholds of the Sung dynasty were seized by the Mongols, some two hundred thousand faithful officers and their followers went aboard ship for Indo-China and contiguous regions. One reason for the Ming Emperor's sending Cheng Ho abroad so many times was to discover the whereabouts of the dethroned emperor of the once all-powerful Mongols.

Sometimes military invasions of distant foreign soil were initiated more for the purpose of apprehending notable political refugees than for any other reason.

Although there is historical evidence of migration during various earlier dynasties, it is safe to assert that large-scale emigration did not begin until the outbreak of the Taiping Rebellion (1850-64), when many people in the southern part of China suffered great hardships. It was in that period of economic stress that the Chinese began to go abroad in numbers, even though the Manchu throne did everything possible to discourage actual emigrations. Much less did the emperors adopt any positive emigration policy. In point of fact, the throne condemned every Chinese person living abroad. Section 225 of the imperial legal code asserted that emigration was illegal and that Chinese emigrants were punishable as traitors. It is sanguinary evidence of the Manchu policy that in 1740 the Dutch massacred several thousand Chinese in Batavia without the Emperor's caring even to inquire about the matter, to say nothing of proposing intervention.[4]

The Manchu rulers did not regard the emigrants as true sons of China, but instead chose to assume that they were defying the imperial prohibition. The rulers' attitude is partially explained by many of the political refugees' having fled abroad during and soon after the fall of the Ming dynasty. Furthermore, a number of those refugees formed a secret society with the avowed purpose, as shown by the pledge, of recovering the mainland from the so-called Manchu intruders. The existence of political refugees probably accounted, then, for the policy of nonintervention practiced by the Manchu dynasty.

The Manchu throne's complete ignorance of, and utter stupidity toward, the Chinese living abroad may be clearly perceived in a conversation reported between Captain Dupont, the representative of William B. Reed, the first American minister plenipotentiary to China, and Viceroy Tien-Hsian Tan, in the course of negotiations preceding the signing of the Treaty of Tientsin (1858). When Captain Dupont suggested sending Chinese consuls abroad to further the interests of the Chinese in the United States, as these were rich enough to make it worth while for the emperor to protect them, the viceroy made the foolish remark that the wealth of his emperor was beyond computation and there was no reason to consider the support of those subjects who, without permission, had left the borders of their fatherland.[5]

One year, however, after the signing of the Treaty of Tientsin with Great Britain, the imperial government announced officially

that Chinese would be permitted to go abroad for permanent settlement, an action reluctantly taken as a result of the military defeat
suffered at the hands of the British. The Manchu ruler thus had
been forced to recognize a *fait accompli,* since Britain and several
other nations had already been recruiting Chinese laborers.

Later, the fact that the Chinese abroad had—before and after the
fall of the Manchu regime—contributed generously, financially or otherwise, toward the successful establishment of the Republic of China
automatically raised their status in the opinion of the new Chinese
republic. The Bureau of Overseas Affairs, whose director holds the
rank of a cabinet member, was established to supervise the welfare
of the "overseas Chinese." In addition, they were granted the privilege of choosing a representative to Parliament. For many years the
Chinese abroad have greatly assisted the establishment of schools
and hospitals in China and have contributed to many other good
causes. From 1937 to 1945 they made very sizable donations to assist the Chinese government in its war against the Japanese invasion.

Before the occupation of the mainland by the Communists, remittances to China from the Chinese abroad became, indeed, an important source of invisible income in China's balance of international
payments; these remittances became, in fact, the principal item on
the credit side after merchandise exports. To quote one authority:

> The chief factor in the payment of China's growing imports of goods and
> silver has at all times been remittances to China from Chinese abroad. China
> has exported the skill of her merchants, the dexterity of her handicraftsmen,
> the strength of her laborers. The ties which bind her people abroad to their
> homes in China have brought it about that the chief factor among China's
> credit items in her international balances, after merchandise exports, have
> been remittances from her people overseas.[6]

Distribution and Settlement of Chinese

It is generally recognized that the Chinese show greater reluctance
to leave their native shores and to establish homes in distant lands
than do the people of Western nations. Yet true also is the saying:
"Wherever the ocean waves touch, there are overseas Chinese."
Though the Chinese have spread to all parts of the world, the total
number abroad is nevertheless relatively small compared with the
overwhelming numbers of European emigrants, especially during
the period of 1820 to 1930.

Just how many Chinese may be living abroad at any one time would
be difficult to estimate; authorities have differed considerably. Professor C. F. Remer, in an attempt to calculate the amount of remittances from Chinese abroad between 1871 and 1921, arrived at
the following figures, based on studies made by seven authorities:[7]

1871-84	2,000,000
1885-98	4,000,000
1899-1913	7,000,000
1914-21	8,000,000

Because the United States and Canada take a census periodically, in those countries the figures of the Chinese population are comparatively accurate. In Southeast Asia correct estimates prove difficult for a variety of reasons: the Chinese have been residing there for at least a thousand years; many countries are closely connected with China both by land and sea; and many cities have a large number of Chinese residents. Since the definition of the Chinese race is open to question, the difficulty in correctly interpreting their number is understandable. The taking of a complete and correct census is indeed required and will depend on the cooperation of all people concerned.[8] Thus some Southeast Asian censuses should not be accepted without reserve. The Indo-China census of 1936 listed only 326,000 Chinese; but according to Professor Chen the Chinese there numbered about a million, perhaps more. He cited the fact that at least 200,000 Chinese went to Indo-China by land routes for a period of seven to eight years after the outbreak of the Sino-Japanese War in 1937 without ever being noticed by French authorities. Indeed, there are many routes other than the regular ones. Before World War II, the usual routes of Chinese migration were by sea.[9] Victor Purcell assumes that in 1947 there were 8,505,000 Chinese in Southeast Asia; that is, 5.4 per cent of a total population of 156,597,000.[10] A recent estimate by various authorities put the total number at approximately 10,991,307.[11]

An estimate of population in any country, without a reliable census including vital statistics and figures on immigration and emigration, is always confusing, and therefore subject to a wide range of interpretations. Take the case of Chinese in Thailand. What is the numerical proportion of ethnic Chinese to Thai? What is the approximate number in a given year? Authorities differ in their estimates, each taking a different period and a different method of calculation. Sir John Bowring, an English diplomat and author, estimated that in the year 1857 the kingdom of Siam had 1,500,000 Chinese settlers, 200,000 of whom were in Bangkok and environs.[12] According to M. Gaston Rautier, the Chinese formed about a third of the population of Siam, which, shortly before 1890, was about 10,000,000.[13]

Large numbers of Chinese emigrated annually to Siam, thus swelling the Chinese ranks there. Hans Mosolff pointed out that in 1918-19 70,000 went to Siam from China, and that from 1918 to 1928 over 900,000 Chinese left home for Siam. He estimated that 25 per cent of the country's population was pure Chinese.[14] Richard Kiliani, an Indian scholar, suggested 2,000,000 to 3,000,000 for 1926; while Y. Tateyania believed 2,500,000 was the figure at the beginning of World War II. Another writer, Wilhelm Credner, estimated 2,000,000 about 1932. His figure was challenged by Erik Seidenfaden, who suggested 2,500,000 instead. Professor Kenneth P. Landon, a scholar familiar with Thailand, estimated the Chinese as 1,500,000 in 1939 and 1,600,000 in 1943. Skinner accepted Credner's figure as the maximum and said that he believed, "While the total Chinese population will in all probability continue to rise during the next decade, the proportion of the total population formed by all ethnic Chinese may be expected to continue the decline evident since 1947." His estimate in 1955, therefore, was only about 2,315,000, or 11.3 per cent of the total population in Thailand.[15]

Other writers on the subject are inclined to think the figures should be higher. Su-ching Chen calculated that the total increase in the Chinese population of Thailand from 1888 to 1938—half a century— must have been more than 4,000,000. Victor Purcell's estimate in 1947 was 2,500,000, or probably less.[16] The figures arrived at by the Chinese government were: 1,500,000 for 1916 to 1934, 2,500,000 for 1934 to 1948, and since 1948 around 3,500,000. Mullender, a French writer, put it from 3,000,000 to 4,000,000 in 1950.

A brief review of the estimates made by the various authorities and observers will show that it is difficult to arrive at a figure for any one time. We are not sure whether sufficient allowance has been made for illegal entry, the corrected birth and death rate, and the number of immigrants and emigrants. In one point, however, authorities agree: there are always more Chinese than the census reveals. The Thai law holds that all children born in Thailand are Thai nationals. The Thai woman who marries an alien acquires the nationality of her husband. An unfortunate coincidence, that each of the four censuses closely followed government action, greatly increased the Chinese' anxiety and uneasiness caused by unavoidable noncooperation with the census-takers.[17] In addition, the census definition of a Chinese is inexplicit. A man is considered a Chinese if his father was a Chinese national, so that only the first and second generations are of the parent race. One tends to agree with Landon: "A Chinese is so, either by birth or by sympathy."[18] To estimate the number of Chinese in Thailand and elsewhere, one must take a realistic attitude. If one should assume a range of 15 to 20 per cent of the total population, he would be approximately correct.[19]

For a number of years the Chinese government has published its official estimates of the number of Chinese abroad. Owing to the difficulty of obtaining all figures for any particular year, the numbers estimated from country to country must necessarily be only an approximation. Though unavoidable, this is unsatisfactory. The drawback is obvious when the figures for the Chinese in the United States in 1957 have to be based on the 1950 census. The same situation is true in Canada, after the census of 1951, and in Malaya, Singapore, or Hong Kong, where more Chinese reside than appear in the figures presented by the Chinese government.[20]

Growth of Overseas Chinese Population, 1946-57

1946	8,700,804
1947	8,484,820
1948	8,721,204
1949	10,779,013
1950	11,093,979
1951	12,126,874
1952	12,536,206
1953	13,330,192
1954	13,472,311
1955	14,126,723
1956	14,207,749
1957	14,405,040

Source: *Overseas Chinese Year Book, 1958* (Taipei, Taiwan: Overseas Chinese Affairs Commission, 1959), p. 37.

Special Features of Chinese Immigration

What contributions have the Chinese abroad made, politically, economically, culturally, or otherwise? True, the Chinese abroad, especially before World War II, have been unable to offer much in comparison to the contributions of exceptional European immigrants. No Chinese scientist received the Nobel prize until late in 1957. Not until after World War II did many "new immigrants" arrive, to augment the third and fourth generation Chinese, the "old immigrants." Among them were many scholars who contributed greatly to the welfare of the United States. On the other hand, it has been well recognized that the overseas Chinese as a group have always been industrious, thrifty, law-abiding, and trustworthy. In California, in Hawaii, in British Columbia, and elsewhere, the Chinese have contributed much to economic development. In Southeast Asia they accomplished much toward the progress and prosperity of otherwise savage and barren areas. To a large extent, the Chinese who went abroad were farmers and laborers; until about 1941 very few scholars were among them. These emigrants were handicapped by the lack of an organized governmental plan to guide or assist them; their only help came from their families or friends. Since most of the immigrants were without much means of support, survival went to the fittest only. Even after having become well settled in the new land, many still had to face governmental restrictions and the discriminatory acts of the local population. Before the turn of the twentieth century and even after it, Chinese were often murdered, and sometimes massacred. The inhuman treatment received by many Chinese coolies who went to Peru and to Cuba shocked the civilized world, leaving an ugly mark on the history of Chinese immigration.

But despite all handicaps and hardships, the Chinese moved into Southeast Asia. Under the circumstances, it is not surprising that very many left wives and children at home. Their ambition was to save as much money as possible in order to return eventually to China to lead comfortable lives. Fortune, though, did not always favor them; often they had to remain a very long time before they could return, even for a visit. It was common, indeed, to hear in the villages of South China songs like this one:

> Flowers shall be my headdress once again,
> > For my dear husband will soon return from a distant shore.
> Ten long years did I wait
> > Trying hard to remember his face
> As I toiled at my spinning wheel each lonely night.

Not until the beginning of the twentieth century did many women and children go abroad to join their husbands and fathers. Meanwhile there occurred an interesting phase of Chinese immigration in Southeast Asia: marriage between Chinese and the natives of countries in which they settled. From these marriages have come children of mixed blood. [21]

In spite of the fact that many of these mixed-blooded Chinese had lived years in the countries of their birth, even after several generations they tended to remain Chinese in their customs, religion, and culture. Usually their fathers educated them well, occasionally sending them to study in China. They passed on the special qualities of keenness and industry possessed by their forebears. This mixed group the natives of Southeast Asia ordinarily accept as they would men of common blood; therefore, they do not dislike them as sometimes they do the pure Chinese. In several countries, especially in the Philippines and in Thailand, some of the present leaders have emerged from this group.

We often hear that, at one period or another, there have been in Southeast Asia so-called anti-Chinese movements. Since the Chinese concentrate their efforts in economic activities, occasional conflict is bound to occur. Some tendency on the part of the natives toward showing dislike and distrust is consequently perhaps unavoidable. Such an anti-Chinese demonstration, in the opinion of one writer, has been the result more of the fears of colonial governments than of the feelings of the natives themselves.[22] For one thing, before the coming of the Western powers, although the Chinese had been for more than a thousand years in those regions, few records indicate any large-scale conflicts. As a matter of fact, the Chinese have rendered many useful services to the natives, such as contributing to progress by the development of natural resources. Only after the occupation by the Dutch and Spanish of their respective holdings in the East Indies and in the Philippine Islands were there massacres of the Chinese. Thus the responsibility of colonial governments would appear to be evident.

Furthermore, restrictions and discriminatory acts against the Chinese in many countries have been mostly governmental. The imposition of immigration quotas and of excessively high poll taxes are wholly governmental and tantamount to strangling Chinese immigration. The discriminatory legislation usually includes a prohibition against carrying on specific businesses and employing more than a given percentage of nonnative laborers—Chinese. The Philippine government has forbidden Chinese residents to engage in retail trade, and the Indonesian government has long imposed discriminatory acts against Chinese business activities. The present status of *hua-chiao* in Indonesia is very precarious, going from bad to worse as time passes. True, the restrictive policy has occurred elsewhere, such as in Vietnam and in Thailand, where the practice of certain trades and businesses are forbidden to Chinese. Many states in America have enacted legislation to limit certain professions to citizens. Quite apart from the responsibility of colonial governments for the instigation of anti-Chinese troubles, Chinese interests in foreign lands have not been protected in proportion to to the protection given to nationals of other races. Had the Ming and Manchu dynasties paid due attention to Chinese nationals abroad, and had they given them continuous diplomatic protection instead of adopting a foolish policy of recriminatory prohibition while taking an attitude of indifference toward Chinese overseas, the history of Chinese immigration might have been altogether different. On the other hand, we must admit that the rise of nationalism in various countries would probably have created anti-Chinese prejudice and trouble for the Chinese. We have now to investigate two of the most shameful transgressions against the human rights of the Chinese abroad, namely, the coolie trade and repeated massacres of the Chinese in foreign lands.

Though the average Chinese may have fared well economically and in other ways, the history of Chinese immigration is full of catastrophe. Any status earned was paid for by sorrow and bloodshed. Life was indeed hard for the earlier Chinese immigrants.

In the early period of immigration to the Philippines and to the Dutch East Indies, thousands of Chinese fell victims to ruthless massacres perpetrated by Spanish and Dutch colonial officers, though the Chinese had been there before the arrival of the Europeans. At first the Chinese were welcomed by the Spaniards, who seemed to take a liking to them. The rapidly increasing numbers of the Sangley, however, and the fact that they had under control much of the trade and commerce of the islands aroused the jealousy and suspicion of the Spaniards. In the beginning they attempted to segregate the Sangley, but, failing in that, resorted to brutal killings. That Spanish hatred followed Spanish friendliness within a few years makes the reversal of feeling all the more striking. The mischief began when Chinese oarsmen, who had been so cruelly treated that they felt forced to rise in rebellion, murdered Dasmarinas, the Spanish governor of the Philippines. Thereupon, the entire Philippine Archipelago awaited tensely the expected attack by the Great Ming Emperor—but no attack came. This pusillanimous attitude on the part of the Celestial Empire tempted the Spaniards to brutality. In 1603 they proceeded to massacre no fewer than 23,000 Chinese. Again in 1660, and once more in 1756, they slaughtered considerable numbers. In 1775 they expelled 2,000. Such actions formed the typical Spanish pattern for several hundred years.[23] Undoubtedly the attitude of indifference maintained by the Celestial Empire was at least partly responsible for those tragedies.

Another of the very largest and most savage massacres, in which thousands of unoffending Chinese died, occurred in Batavia in 1740. The Dutch, after they had occupied Batavia in 1619, recognized and appreciated the nearly continuous residence of the hard-working, law-abiding Chinese settlers and believed that their sterling qualities would assist materially in promoting a prosperous Batavia. They employed every means to induce the Chinese to reside there. Practices both fair and foul were used. The Dutch carried out a whole series of piratical raids on the coast of Fukien and Kwangtung, resulting in the forcible deportation to Batavia of a great many Chinese.[24] By 1720 the Chinese in Batavia numbered about sixty thousand. As by that time the bulk of trade and business had come into the hands of the Chinese, the Dutch, beginning to worry about the consequences, imposed restrictive measures to limit competitive commercial activities. The strained relations that inevitably followed provoked the dreadful massacre of 1740. Bernard H. M. Vlekke gives a graphic account of what happened.

In that year . . . the government decided to deport all superfluous Chinese to Ceylon and South Africa. When the embarkation began, a rumor spread among the Chinese that they were to be thrown overboard in midocean! Armed groups of Chinese gathered in the neighborhood of the city and began to attack the outposts. The government promptly ordered a search for weapons in all Chinese houses. When the search started, fire broke out and then the government lost control. Sailors, soldiers, Dutch citizens, and their Indonesian slaves rushed out into the streets and began to kill the Chinese wherever they met them. Several thousand died in the catastrophe. The government seemed helpless or unwilling to stop the massacre.[25]

The Manchu throne declined to interfere after the massacre at Batavia though the Dutch expected retaliation. Fear of retaliation was all the more justified by the fact that the Manchus were just then at the very height of their military power.

In 1782, 10,000 to 11,000 Chinese lost their lives in Cholon and Saigon, Indo-China. Many shops and much property of Chinese residents were looted and destroyed.[20] In 1828, about one thousand Chinese miners on Sungai Ujong were massacred by the Malays, not because they were Chinese but because they had amassed treasure.[27] In 1857, 3,500 Chinese were either killed or driven out of Sarawak by James Brooke after the Chinese had started a revolt against him.[28]

Within the past two decades there have been sporadic instances of the killing of Chinese immigrants. During the Japanese invasion of Hong Kong and Southeast Asia in 1942, many Chinese were murdered. In Singapore alone, 5,000 or more Chinese perished in the purge immediately after the surrender of that fortified port.[29] Even before the close of World War II, the Chinese in Indonesia suffered large casualties. Between June 6 and 8, 1946, 600 Chinese were killed west of Tangerang River by the Indonesian army because of the alleged cooperation between the Chinese and the Dutch. More than 1,500 Chinese dwellings were destroyed. On September 18, 1946, 329 Chinese are said to have been killed by the Indonesians, and in January, 1947, another 250.[30]

Indeed, if we make a fuller study of the history of the Chinese abroad, in addition to what we have examined in this section as well as in the section following on coolie trade, we shall have no hesitation in stating that the history is full of tragedy, even of catastrophes.

The Coolie Trade

The coolie trade, as Professor MacNair refers to it, forms a chapter of history in which no one could take pride.[31] To some extent, it is said to be very similar to contract labor, in that the laborer signs a contract of his own free will. Actually that is not so; for, though apparently the contract is a legal document, a vast number of Chinese laborers, being quite illiterate, may easily have been subjected to fraud. Some of the Chinese agents for the contractors—variously called "runners" or "crimps"—made use of every means of deception in persuading farmers or laborers.

The coolie trade may be said to have begun about the year 1845, when a French steamer fully loaded with Chinese coolies sailed from Amoy and steamed direct to North Africa. Two years later, in 1847, 800 laborers sailed from Amoy to Cuba. After that the coolie trade flourished. Many coolies were exported to Cuba, Peru, Chile, and other countries in South America, while voluntary emigration to California and to Australia likewise increased. From 1847 to 1874 half a million coolies, it has been estimated, went abroad. At first the coolies sailed mostly from Hong Kong, but after the port prohibited coolie-carrying vessels they embarked at Macao. In Hong Kong and in Macao prisonlike labor camps known as "barracoons" housed coolies prior to their embarkation. These barracoons were barnlike structures of varying size. Once the coolie was inside and the gate had closed behind him, he was no longer a free man. His only hope of freedom was to survive the contract period of from five to seven years.

Coolie trade on a large scale began with Peru. The Peruvian congress, on November 17, 1849, passed an immigration law making possible the introduction of Chinese. This statute, which became the basis for the immigration of Chinese into that country, gave to two Peruvian capitalists—for four years—the exclusive privilege of importing Chinese. As a matter of fact, in October, 1849, seventy-five Chinese coolies had already been brought into Peru. From 1850 to 1859, 13,000 Chinese arrived, mostly from the Portuguese port of Macao.

Chinese Arrivals in Peru

1850-59	13,000
1860-70	38,648
1871-74	35,599
	87,247

Source: Watt Stewart, *Chinese Bondage in Peru:* Durham, N.C.: Duke University Press, 1951, p. 73.

Since the importation of Chinese coolies was being managed by capitalists, little attention was paid to their comfort on the long voyage of some 9,000 miles, requiring on the average 120 days, between Macao and Callao; thus the mortality rate in the years (1860-63) ran extremely high, ranging from 22.5 per cent to 41.5 per cent. Later conditions improved somewhat, so that between 1864 and 1870, of the 35,417 coolies who had sailed from Macao, 33,164 reached Peru alive—a mortality rate just short of 7 per cent.[32]

After the coolies had arrived at their final destination, the employer seldom considered their physical fitness or aptitude for the performance of their work. The unfortunate coolie had to labor at four pesos a month. Indeed, abuses and flagrant treatment actually drove many to suicide; the hostile Peruvians, inflamed by various bloody incidents, killed many others. There was a dissenting body of Peruvians who criticized openly the inhuman treatment of the coolies and demanded the repeal of the immigration law. As a consequence, in 1856 the law was repealed. But a new law was passed over a veto by the president of Peru; early in 1860 the country again brought coolies from Macao.[33]

In the interim between the repeal in 1856 and the repassing of the law in 1860, Macao continued as a coolie trade center, but sent coolies only to Cuba. Not until 1874, after repeated world condemnation of the coolie traffic of Macao, did the governor of the colony officially announce that no more coolies destined for Peru or elsewhere would be permitted to embark at Macao. Thus on March 27 of that year, the coolie trade came to an abrupt stop.

When the coolies became determined not to go abroad against their will, at times they took matters into their own hands. In the third quarter of the nineteenth century, ten or more incidents of violence occurred, in which coolies had killed the captains or other officers of the vessels and set themselves free. Several unsuccessful attempts to free themselves resulted only in the severe punishment or death of the insurgent coolies.

The Celestial Empire had, as usual, been turning a deaf ear to what was going on in Macao and neighboring cities. Nevertheless, before the termination of the coolie traffic in Macao, two governmental investigating commissions had been ordered to proceed separately, one to Peru and one to Cuba, to study the condition of the coolie laborers in those countries. Dr. Yung Wing, the first Chinese ever to be graduated from an American college (Yale), spent some time in Peru in September, 1874. A few months earlier, a commission had been dispatched to Cuba. It consisted of Lan-pin Chen, A. Macpherson (commissioner of customs at Hankow), and A. Huber (commissioner of customs at Tientsin).[34] The members remained in Cuba from March 17 to May 8, 1874.

Both commissions were, of course, fact-finding ones. Dr. Yung's report contained all the necessary testimony of many Chinese persons, supplemented by detailed accounts of eyewitnesses, who furnished particulars in regard to time, place, and precise names of persons. The report was illustrated by two dozen photographs of Chinese coolies, showing how badly their backs had been lacerated by the lash. The commission in Cuba listened to stories told by 2,500 Chinese, collected 1,176 depositions, and received eighty-five petitions supported by 1,655 signatures.[35] The result of the inquiry was revealed: at least 80 per cent of the entire number of coolies under investigation had been either decoyed or kidnapped.

Since the closing of coolie traffic at Macao in 1874, there have been attempts, with varying success, to recruit Chinese contract laborers for work abroad. A far different kind of recruiting of Chinese labor was the contribution of manpower—some 150,000—to the allied forces by the Chinese government during World War I. That contribution served a vital purpose in the war effort, facilitating victory.

The Chinese in Canada

A review of the life of the Chinese immigrants in Canada reveals a situation parallel to that of the Chinese immigrants in the United States. The famous gold rush of 1849 induced numerous Chinese to come to the United States; the discovery of gold in British Columbia nine years later attracted Chinese and other people to Canada. Whereas Chinese laborers had contributed much to the building of the Central Pacific, their compatriots between 1881 and 1885 provided sweat and toil for the completion of the Canadian Pacific.[36] At first they were welcomed and accepted as equals, but soon they were discriminated against and mistreated. As a result, each country passed a Chinese Exclusion Act. The Chinese settlers had all emigrated from the same districts in China. In their new homes they engaged in the same kind of work; their ways of life were about the same. The immigrants in both regions concentrated in two localities: California and British Columbia.[37]

The first Chinese immigrated to Canada about 1858. The finding of gold during that year in the Fraser River Valley tempted thousands of miners from California; with them came a number of Chinese. Before long, the Chinese began to go to Canada direct from China. By 1863, the total Chinese population in British Columbia was about 2,500. The census of 1891 gives the Chinese in Canada as 9,129. Practically all of them were in British Columbia. However, during the 1884 session of the British Columbia legislature, the Select Committee of the Assembly estimated the Chinese in British Columbia as between 15,000 and 18,000; the majority had been brought by contractors to build the railroad.

As early as 1864, an attempt to secure action against the Chinese was tabled in the Legislative Assembly at Victoria. When, however, about 1886 an economic recession occurred in British Columbia, resentment against Chinese labor became inevitable. The Chinese had already begun to be absorbed into many occupations in which they were competitive against the white laborer. Their willingness to accept lower wages caused dismay. In 1888, a special tax, to be imposed on all Chinese residents of British Columbia was levied by the legislature. The act was, however, held unconstitutional by the supreme court of that province because it interfered with the authority reserved to the Dominion Parliament with reference to the regulation of trade and commerce, the rights of aliens, and the treaties of the Empire.

The first debate on the Chinese question occurred in 1878 in the Dominion House of Commons. After this debate a number of legislative bills to restrict and to exclude the Chinese were introduced by the members from British Columbia, and this led to the passage of legislation in 1885 requiring Chinese laborers to pay a head tax of $50.00. A ratio of one Chinese immigrant to every fifty tons of tonnage was also provided. This first federal restriction act did not satisfy British Columbia. More pressure was put upon the House; as a result, the 1900 Act increased the amount of the tax to $100, and in the 1903 Act to $500 a head. For three years after the 1903 Act, Chinese arrivals virtually stopped; but in 1907, the number increased suddenly to 1,542, reaching 4,667 in 1910 and 6,227 in 1913. The result of the higher tax per head, contrary to the expectation of British Columbia and the federal authorities, was that Chinese servants became a sort of monopoly. Wages of Chinese domestic servants of the better class doubled and later even tripled. This unexpected demand prompted the Chinese to pay the tax willingly. The renewed agitation against oriental immigration went on in the course of a continuous influx of Chinese after World War I. This development led to the Immigration Act of 1923, which admitted only forty-four Chinese up to 1947, when it was repealed. Only eight merchants were actually admitted during the entire exclusion period, but their families were nonadmissible.

Hostility against Chinese eventually died down after World War II, and the Chinese Immigration Act and other restrictions were repealed on May 14, 1947. Those Chinese already there might be naturalized; by becoming citizens, they would be permitted to send for their wives and unmarried children under eighteen. More than 22,000 Chinese received citizenship certificates from 1947 to 1959 by virtue of the Canadian Citizenship Act of 1947, though a number of them had been naturalized; in 1941, 2,055; in 1945, 8; in 1946, 83.[38] Since the Citizenship Act, the number of naturalizations have increased. The years 1951 and 1952 showed the largest number of certificates issued, being 3,006 and 2,984, respectively.

There have been changes in immigration procedure since 1957; at that time, Chinese Canadians could sponsor the admission of their spouses and children, but now when they bring fiancées in, they no longer need a return ticket in case the marriage does not take place, nor must the bride wait thirty days to get married. However, there have remained other acts that discouraged new Chinese arrivals into Canada, such as age limits for dependents joining relatives. There is no Chinese or Japanese quota, but the Canadians have denied the Chinese Benevolent Association's request that for five years a minimum of 500 intellectual refugees be permitted to enter annually.

Permitting wives, children, and other dependents of Canadian citizens of Chinese origin to enter Canada resulted naturally in the admission of women and girls. The number of females has equaled the number of males only since 1956. Because relatives were allowed to enter Canada as a result of the change in the administrative procedures in 1957, the trend of more males being admitted was reversed, and between 1957 and 1959, there were twice as many females admitted as men, 54 per cent of these of the childbearing age (20-44). This circumstance would tend to rectify the Canadian Chinese' abnormal sex ratio.

The character of Chinese immigrants entering Canada seems to be changing. In 1959, of the intended occupations of 463 Chinese immigrants, 159 or 34.3 per cent were of the professional class, including twenty-nine physicians and surgeons, eighteen teachers and professors, and thirty-two engineers. The Chinese immigrants are fifth in the number of professionals, preceded only by British, Dutch, German, and French. Professional men and women among the Chinese Canadians are increasing, as many of the second or later generation begin to enter institutions of higher learning, some going to universities in the United States. Others are laborers, vegetable farmers, domestics, laundrymen, cooks, and waiters. Many are businessmen of various kinds, in grocery stores, food stores, and exporting and importing houses. There are Chinese physicians, nurses, lawyers, professors, and scientists working independently for the government or in colleges. Two of the contributors to the premiere edition of the *Encyclopedia Canadiana* are Chinese Canadians. Mention may be made of the political sensation caused by the decisive defeat of the incumbent minister of defense by a Canadian Chinese, Douglas Jung, M. P., in the parliamentary election of June, 1957. Jung, the first Chinese to be so elected, is a lawyer, thirty-three years of age at the time of his election, a former paratrooper in World War II, a graduate of the University of British Columbia School of Laws. In 1958 he was re-elected.

The Chinese spokesmen in Canada are the Chinese Benevolent Association of Vancouver and Ontario. The former, established as early as 1888, about four years after the completion of the Canadian Pacific, was most helpful in assisting the laid-off Chinese railway workers when in the 1890's their need was most acute. They have done much in the interest of fair and equal treatment of Chinese immigrants. The Chinese Community Center Association of Ontario spent $1,500 advertising in three Toronto dailies against the alleged claim in May, 1960, that 11,000 Chinese had illegally entered Canada since 1950. In these advertisements, they listed a number of accomplishments of the Chinese Canadians.

The Chinese in Latin America

Most of the Chinese settlements in Latin America in the middle of the nineteenth century had originated with the importation of coolies. Since the African slave trade had been abolished, Cuban and Peruvian planters had turned to China for cheap workers. When the Portuguese closed the port of Macao to coolie trade in 1874, the traffic was dead. Chinese labor joined the Cuban rebels in the "Ten Years' War" against Spain (1868-78) and thus brought coolie importation there to a standstill.

Only a few coolies returned to China. Those who chose to remain adjusted to becoming free farm laborers or engaged in some other occupation. The absence of Chinese women was conspicuous everywhere except in Jamaica, where their admission was permitted. The Chinese who married native girls made good husbands; they were industrious and fond of their families. The mixed-blood offspring, however, soon spoke the native language and could in no way be considered Chinese, unlike the emigrants to Southeast Asia, where the children usually followed their father's way of life.

Among all Chinese settlements in Latin America, those in Cuba are the largest, numbering about 33,000, approximately one third of whom reside in Havana. The Chinatown of Havana, known as the *barrio de los chinos,* occupies some nine blocks not far from the capital. There is scarcely a town or large village without at least one Chinese resident. No segregation exists there, no restriction of property rights.[39] In addition to operating laundries and restaurants, the Chinese in Cuba have established hotels and theaters. Also they have a good share of the grocery and dry goods businesses. They are dealers in Chinese medicine and fruit. They are barbers, tailors, farmers, and gardeners. They endeavor to carry on businesses of their own.[40]

About 12,000 Chinese are scattered among the cities of Mexico. The earliest immigrants came in 1864. Most Chinese there, now engaged in small businesses, have established hotels or operate perfume shops, curio stores, shoe stores, and laundries. A few Chinese merchants, considered wealthy, are holders of real estate, operators of factories, and department stores.

The Chinese became well acquainted with Panama because of the Isthmus of Panama Exposition. Chinese laborers were utilized from 1903 to 1914 in the construction of the Canal and railways. Starting soon after the completion of the Canal and continuing for many years thereafter, they have been occupied in various retail trades and have held a lion's share of the business. Almost all the towns have Chinese grocery stores, restaurants, coffee shops, and dry goods stores.

The Chinese settlement in Jamaica is perhaps one of the richest in the Caribbean region. Not only are most of the Chinese well-to-do, but the settlement is properly organized. In Kingston and other towns the Chinese own most of the grocery stores, occupying the choicest locations at the street corners. They control about 40 per cent of the wholesale business in addition to operating department stores and bakeries; ice cream, aerated water, and coconut-processing plants, one of which is among the largest factories in Jamaica. In many countries the Chinese find social life outside of business negligible, but social life in Jamaica is the great exception. They have started a recreation club of their own, where they mingle socially with other members of the community. The Chinese population is estimated at about 13,000.

The economic status of overseas Chinese in Peru is as good as any in Latin America. The number of Chinese there has dropped sharply, however. From the highest count of about 80,000, during the period of contract labor migrations between 1849 and 1874, the Chinese population has declined until now it is between 22,000 and 23,000, more than half of whom live in Lima.[41] There are several reputable Chinese firms, each with a capital of over a million dollars, operating a wide variety of commercial activities ranging from wholesale and retail farming to import and export trade; the Chinese find farming the most profitable occupation. Some large-scale Chinese haciendas were leased from the Spanish landowners. Also, the Chinese own most of the shoe shops, department stores, grocery stores, and hotels. There are two Chinese newspapers in Lima and one Chinese school.

Though Brazil and Argentina are the largest countries in South America, their Chinese populations are very small. In Argentina there are only about 250, most of them in Buenos Aires. They keep curio shops and glassware shops and operate in the tea business. In Brazil the Chinese used to number only about a hundred; but since 1950 the number has increased to slightly more than five thousand, mostly in São Paulo and Rio de Janeiro. Those recently arrived operate factories and engage in import and export trade. A flour mill and a small cotton mill have been functioning for several years. In 1953 a vegetable oil mill was started in Rio Grande as a joint enterprise with the Brazilians. Other Chinese are engaged in farming.

In both Colombia and Ecuador the Chinese are getting along very well with the natives and enjoy a high economic status. The Chinese in Colombia, about one thousand altogether, firmly entrenched in cities like Cali, Buenaventura, and Barranquilla, are engaged in all kinds of gainful occupations including trade and farming. There are 3,100 Chinese in Ecuador. In the main commercial port of Ecuador, Guayaquil, the Chinese own the largest rice mill, which employs several hundred native workers. The Chinese community supports a Chinese school and a Chinese chamber of commerce.

There are also a number of Chinese in Trinidad, Chile, Venezuela, Costa Rica, and Nicaragua, where they are chiefly engaged in business. The Chinese there appear to be good businessmen, no matter what their previous occupations may have been. The Chinese in general get along well with Latin Americans. They have many things in common: both groups are sentimental, mindful of the private feelings of others, and appreciative of the good life.

The Chinese in Southeast Asia

Nothing gives the overseas Chinese greater happiness than to work tirelessly in order to be able to forge ahead and attain financial success, with eventual independence. The ambition of the average overseas Chinese is to develop business acumen. They work hard, live thriftily and modestly, save as much as they can. The spirit of mutual aid, often confined to the family or to the clan, has contributed much to the success of the Chinese abroad. With the possible exception of those in Malaya and Singapore, few Chinese engage in governmental affairs or attempt to influence politics.

Rags-to-riches is not merely fictional in the experiences of the overseas Chinese; it is an often repeated reality.

Most of the overseas Chinese have for many generations been in Southeast Asia. The influx of immigrants, a higher birth rate, and comparatively low mortality have been responsible for the phenomenal increase of the Chinese population. With the exception of Burma, where they are outnumbered by Indians, the Chinese form the largest of the minorities in Southeast Asia. In Singapore more than 76 per cent of the population is Chinese; in Malaya, about 40 per cent; in British Borneo, approximately 25 per cent; and in North Borneo, about 20 per cent. The Chinese are urban dwellers. In the three big cities—Singapore, Penang, and Kuala Lumpur—more than 80 per cent of the Chinese live in the well-developed and densely populated region forming a strip about seventy to a hundred miles wide running down the west coast from Penang to Singapore. In Thailand more than 40 per cent of Chinese immigrants live in Bangkok or its vicinity. Thus several cities in Southeast Asia are virtually Chinese: at Cholon, Vietnam, almost everything is Chinese, with pagodas, theaters, restaurants, and dragon symbols, so emblematic of China. In Phnom Penh, the capital of Cambodia, one third of the population is Chinese. At one time there was a rather prosperous colony in the busy port of Haiphong.

For several decades there has been a gradual increase of Chinese female immigrants; fewer Chinese males leave their wives in China, and as a result there are fewer intermarriages with the natives. Today in Indonesia, Sarawak, Brunei, and British Borneo, about two thirds of the Chinese are native born. The recent increase in the younger generation in Singapore owing to the improvement in the sex ratio, with over 50 per cent being twenty-two years of age or younger, has been remarkable.[42]

The Cantonese, who formed the bulk of the immigrants to the United States, Canada, and Latin America, are a minority within a minority in many of the countries of Southeast Asia.[43] The Hokkien of Fukien, the Swatow, and the Hakkas of Kwangtung have supplied the bulk of Chinese immigrants for many generations. The emigrants from Hainan, Foochow, and other parts of China have provided the remainder. The Chinese in Southeast Asia, like all other Chinese abroad, have relied heavily on the associations, formed many years ago, for protective welfare and assistance and even for diplomatic help. The Chinese organization is usually composed of representatives from all the Chinese groups. Its officers are normally chosen according to the group distribution among the whole Chinese population. In Thailand, British Borneo, and elsewhere the Chinese maintain their own speech-group associations. The Chinese

Chamber of Commerce in Bangkok has performed useful functions for the Chinese community. This organization is composed of representatives from all the Chinese groups in Thailand. Thus about 60 per cent of the officers are Teochins from Swatow. There are five speech-group associations: Teochins, Hakkas, Cantonese, Hainanese, and Hokkiens. All these associations are formally registered with the government.

The intensification of the nationalist spirit has moved a number of countries to become embroiled with the Chinese population. In the Philippines, for example, the Chinese have long been blamed for faults in local economy. For a long time, unpleasant feeling has existed between the Philippine government and Chinese residents, evidenced by the Retail Trade Nationalization Law of 1954, aimed solely at the Chinese retail merchants, with the ultimate purpose of forcing Chinese out of the retail business. The Thai government since 1948 has adopted a policy to encourage greater participation by ethnic Thai in the economic fields. The campaign may be relaxed at one time, only to be revived more vigorously at another. Skinner says, "No Chinese alien could be sure that his means of livelihood would not be threatened."[44] The Chinese immigrant in Thailand must register with the government and carry a special card of identity. The registration fee is now 200 baht.[45] In Indonesia the position of the Chinese is even more untenable. Restrictions against the Chinese, especially in trade, have made them suffer since the majority of them are small independent entrepreneurs, skilled artisans, foremen, and clerks.[46] The special alien head tax, amounting to about $130 every three years, in addition to an income tax, retroactive to January 1, 1957, affects Eurasians and most Chinese. Many Chinese banks have been placed under governmental control since late 1958, while Dutch banks were controlled over a year before. A number of Chinese schools and trade enterprises are also under state control.

In September, 1956, orders were issued by the government of Vietnam, making it illegal for noncitizens to own or to do business in eleven important trades, such as transport and many lines of retail trades. Another decree was that all Chinese born in Vietnam automatically became citizens. The question whether *hua-chiao* will be loyal to the country in which they live has troubled the government. The right to tighten citizenship requirements cannot be disputed. The government has also the right to urge minorities to become citizens. On the other hand, events have proved that the Chinese are indeed assimilable; for a number of decades integration has been quietly proceeding. Many Chinese who have settled in their adopted land have married natives of that land and have acquired the customs, language, dress, and even the religion, gradually merging completely with the natives, except perhaps where their names might identify their race. There is no question that other Chinese in Southeast Asia have also been moving in the direction of assimilation, although some may feel that this is being done reluctantly and grudgingly. The fact that Chinese in Malaya and Singapore have lately participated in politics with remarkable enthusiasm indicates that they are casting their lots with the land that adopted them. It is evident that if the Chinese in Southeast Asia were treated as equals by the governments concerned, the rate of Chinese assimilation would be much accelerated.[47]

The average Chinese business establishment in North or Latin America is generally on a small scale, but not so in Southeast Asia. In many countries there the Chinese have a firm grasp on both wholesale and retail trade; they keep stores in the interior villages and in the cities. Almost everywhere in Southeast Asia the Chinese seem to be doing the same kinds of business: they are owners of rice mills or operators in tin mines or rubber plantations; they are proprietors of many branches of light industry; they are artisans or workers. As the result of their thrift and industriousness, the laborers become merchants, and the merchants in turn soon branch out into various spheres of activity. In the Philippines, Malaya, and Thailand the Chinese have become bankers.[48] They make excellent physicians, dentists, architects, and engineers—they form the backbone of the middle class. Some are moneylenders, and these are often accused of being usurers.[49] A number of Chinese in Southeast Asia, and possibly a few elsewhere, have been reputed to be millionaires.[50] Their unique position in the past had a great deal to do with this. Some had served as captains or lieutenants in the old days when the Dutch ruled the East Indies. Others had been appointed tax collectors. Also a common practice was for the Chinese to apply to the sultan or king for a certain tract of land for cultivation; thus they came eventually to own much fertile soil. There was plenty of chance for getting rich quickly. Besides, the vast, virgin land afforded unusual opportunities for the hard-working, farsighted Chinese pioneers to make fortunes.[51]

But to become a millionaire today is a task next to impossible. World War II, the Japanese occupation, the ultranationalism manifested on the part of some newly independent nations, the civil war in Indonesia, the jungle fighting, and, above all, price fluctuations in tin and rubber—all have worked against the interests of Chinese in Southeast Asia. Only through perseverance, hard work, and patience are they still able to control a share of the economy larger than their numbers would lead one to expect. The opportunities are now less striking, and competition is keener almost everywhere. In spite of the unfavorable situation, however, the Chinese plan to start businesses of their own as soon as they can.

Just exactly how important the economic status of the Chinese abroad is, no one knows. The Chinese business investments and their profits made in various countries may be used as a yardstick. Professor Remer in 1932 estimated that the Chinese holdings abroad were about the same as foreign holdings in China.[52] The large amounts of remittances to China from overseas Chinese showed that the Chinese abroad have about two and a half billion dollars of business investments, and that two thirds of the annual overseas remittances actually represent interest and profit, while the balance is the actual saving out of salaries and wages. If we accept Professor Remer's study as a basis, after the lapse of more than a quarter of a century the Chinese business investment abroad should be considerably more than it is, in view of the high return of the investment in Southeast Asia. On the other hand, Southeast Asia's occupation by the Japanese during World War II, and the current uncertain political situation in some of the countries, resulting in the outflow of capital, have tended to reduce the value of Chinese holdings. Nevertheless, since the Chinese abroad are living mostly in Southeast Asia, and since it is easier for the Chinese to make money there, it is almost certain that most Chinese holdings abroad are in that area.

Another study of Chinese business investment in Southeast Asia was made by Helmut G. Callis before the Japanese occupation.[53] He estimated that in or around 1936 the Chinese business investment in Southeast Asia totaled about $630,000,000. The following is the breakdown:

Area	Business Investment
Philippines	$100,000,000
Netherlands Indies	150,000,000
British Malaya	200,000,000
Thailand	100,000,000
French Indo-China	80,000,000

Callis maintains that Chinese capital ranks probably next to the British in Malaya, the American in the Philippines, the Dutch in the Netherlands East Indies, and the French in Indo-China; but in Thailand, the Chinese investment probably equals all the other foreign investments put together. Callis admits that his estimate is rough and conservative. Compared with the study made by Professor Remer, the figures suggested by Callis are too low. But a more comprehensive and up-to-date survey of this subject is not to be had.[54]

The Chinese in Hong Kong

Because of its proximity to the mainland, most of the population of Hong Kong is Chinese—in the neighborhood of 99 per cent. The 1931 census gave the population of Hong Kong as 849,473. During the Japanese occupation (1941-45) it was greatly reduced; but after the Japanese surrender, people poured in again from the Chinese mainland, raising the total population in 1947 to 1,800,000. The Communist seizure of the mainland in 1949 further stimulated migration until in 1950 the population rose to 2,360,000; by the end of 1960, it reached the peak of 3,014,000.[55] The majority of the Chinese residents had come from Kwangtung and, to a lesser extent, from Fukien province. Beginning in 1949 many people from Shanghai and from other parts of China have established themselves in Hong Kong. Cantonese is the *lingua franca,* but Hakka, Chinchow, Kuo Yu (the national language or Mandarin), and Shanghai dialects are widely heard.

Since World War II, but more particularly after the occupation by the Communists of the mainland of China in 1949, a great deal of capital has flowed into Hong Kong in search of profit and safety. The bulk of it has gone into real estate and the establishment or expansion of various industries formerly unknown. Apart from shipbuilding and ship repairing, iron foundries, and rolling mills, foremost among Hong Kong's industries is cotton textiles. In November, 1959, there were twenty cotton mills in operation, equipped with more than 400,000 spindles. The bulk of the capital for the mills had been supplied by the Chinese from Shanghai and its vicinity. In addition to the cotton mills, many other industries have been set up. In order of importance they rank approximately as follows: clothing, enamelware, and metal products; electric torches, batteries, bulbs; paints; foodstuffs; beverages; tobacco; footwear. Most of these products are for export.

Hong Kong is still famous as an entrepôt; in fact, it shows promise of becoming the clearing center for the whole of Southeast Asia. Hong Kong is the starting point for vast emigration—to the United States, Canada, Latin America, and Southeast Asia. The demand for skilled labor in the Brunei oil fields and in other developments there, and in Dutch New Guinea, has been met by Chinese from Hong Kong. Since the political and economic situation in Southeast and Far East Asia is none too stable, Hong Kong is at least a temporary haven for capital fleeing from many countries. The real estate boom, resulting in the construction of many apartment houses, hotels, office buildings, and other impressive structures, indicates that there is always capital available for commercial projects.

Brief mention must be made also of the Chinese in Macao, since the two ports, Hong Kong and Macao, are both adjacent to the mainland and since they are the only ports of consequence in the Far East belonging to Western powers as colonies. In 1934 Macao had a total population of about 160,000, the Chinese numbering about 150,000. After the occupation of the mainland by the Communists in 1949, the population reached a peak of 260,000; but it soon receded so that in 1953 it had fallen to 187,000, of which only 4,000 were non-Chinese. The population in 1957 was estimated at 250,000, at the ratio of 95 per cent Chinese. Macao is known to be the last port in the Far East that was the center for supplying Chinese coolies to such countries as Cuba, Peru, and South Africa.

Our brief account of the Chinese abroad indicates that the problems facing them differ in various countries. The Chinese may be happy in Jamaica or in Peru, but in many other places they consider their status far from satisfactory. Though economically they may have led a fairly good life, socially it has not been a happy one. Discrimination is often countered with passive resistance; hostility may thus engender ultranationalism, completing the vicious circle. Certainly the Chinese cannot have the most favorable attitude toward a country that does not consider them as equals. Overcoming the difficulties will require cooperation on both sides. Those who wish to settle permanently should realize that it is to their advantage to be naturalized and to participate in politics.

On the whole, it must be said that the overseas Chinese, whose forefathers had been predominantly farmers and laborers, were a group of adventurers; yet they possessed the qualities of keen observation, industry, thrift, and perseverance. They still have a lively respect for cooperation as an efficacious means of progress. Despite their frequent setbacks, despite discrimination in all its infinite varieties, they have forged forward. In the opinion of one competent writer, "They have prospered exceedingly, a fact which may be accepted as a vindication of their methods—and worthy of consideration by the standards of the 'Sermon on the Mount' in relation to modern imperialism."[56]

2

Characteristics of the Chinese Population

in the United States

The history of immigration has revealed that the earlier Chinese immigrants were from the laboring classes, that they worked in the United States on railroads, in mines, on farms, and as domestic servants—in fact, they appear to have been jacks of all trades. Nearly all of them had come from the six districts of Kwangtung Province. At first, they had been received with enthusiasm, but rather soon American miners viewed them with hostility as competitors. The fact that Chinese were satisfied with low wages, and willing to perform any menial jobs, invariably put the white laborers at a disadvantage. After the completion of the transcontinental railroad in 1869, because of riots, expulsion, and even lynchings, the Chinese were forced to seek employment that brought them into little, if any, direct competition with their white coworkers. The solution to a great extent appeared first to be in the laundry and later in the restaurant business. For many years, indeed, those seemed to be the only trades that the Chinese might follow. Eventually, however, after the first or second generation had either died or returned to China, those born in this country, or here from a very early age, attended school (as few of their forebears had been able to do) and gradually prepared themselves for much more advanced and lucrative employment. Yet, because of discrimination, Chinese professional men were unable to make their own way. Not until the beginning of World War II, when both manpower and skill were badly needed, did Chinese engineers and scientists first work in government agencies, and later with American companies.

Nor can the false impression that the Chinese are specially adaptable to laundry and restaurant occupations be completely dispelled. When, for example, Tsuyee Pei was chief of the Chinese technical mission stationed in Washington early in the 1950's, he was often addressed as Dr. Pei. After repeated denials that he was a Ph. D. , he was informed that there were only two categories of Chinese in

30

this country, laundrymen and Ph. D.'s, and that he would, therefore, have to belong to one of them.

Characteristics of the Chinese in the United States are slowly but steadily changing. Benefiting by social, economic, and political progress since World War II, they have become able to make a decent living and to give their children a good education. Their courage, patience, and, above all, their hard work have enabled them to withstand whatever discrimination they have encountered. Professionally and economically they are better off. The repeal of the Exclusion Act in 1943 afforded them at least a sense of equality with respect to immigration regulations, though there still remain technicalities differentiating to some degree European and Asiatic immigrants. Moreover, with the arrival of more and more females, the ratio between the sexes greatly improved. After the Chinese had become eligible for naturalization, thousands became citizens; their voting potentiality is now superior to what it was at any time in the past. Twenty years ago the majority were launderers or restaurateurs; today the number of professional men may be estimated in the thousands. Because socially the Chinese are having wider relationships outside their own race, time will tell how successful they may become as integrated members of the American community. Quite wisely the Chinese have begun to show an interest in governmental affairs, knowing well that it would be a mistake to avoid participation in politics. Already many Chinese have been active in party affairs, even providing candidates.

The 1960 census revealed that the total Chinese population in the United States increased 58.2 per cent from 150,005 (Hawaii included) in 1950 to 237,292 in 1960. During the past decade, the Chinese rate of growth exceeded that of all other groups, including Indian (46.5 per cent), Filipino (43.7 per cent), Japanese (42.3 per cent), Negro (25.4 per cent), white (17.5 per cent), and all other (18.5 per cent). California still has the most Chinese of any state or about 40 per cent of the United States as a whole.

This increase is due to laws enacted since the McCarran-Walter Act of 1952 which have admitted 27,502 Chinese immigrants between 1951 and 1960. There has been a steady return of Chinese-Americans since the Communists took over the mainland China. Increases by birth have also helped to boost the number of Chinese in this country.

The Chinese seem to prefer to live in cities. About 75 per cent are concentrated in California, Hawaii, New York, and Illinois, and more than half of them in twelve cities.

The increasing number of Chinese will probably have important implications; family life will be more wholesome owing to a normal sex ratio; more and more Chinese will start businesses outside

Chinatowns, where decline will be somewhat slowed by newcomer's businesses; the number of Chinese in white collar jobs will increase; more Chinese will attend college.[1] But will the concentration of Chinese in New York and in San Francisco revive the possibility of prejudice and discrimination against them?

On the other hand, the Chinese in Hawaii have fewer problems than those on the mainland.[2] Their rate of increase has been normal during the past decade. The Chinese in Hawaii are unique, fascinating, and deserving of special attention. The Chinese laborers were the first Orientals to come on a large scale to Hawaii to help build its economic strength. They gradually worked out a better economic adjustment as they achieved economic success and they also raised their social status. At the turn of the century, educated Chinese also came to Hawaii. Their strong traditional motivation toward intellectual betterment stabilized their position. They achieved distinction as lawyers, physicians, dentists, bankers, and businessmen. Therefore, for several decades the Chinese in Hawaii have been quite happy economically, socially, and politically. In almost every respect, they were equal with any other ethnic group, including the Caucasians.

Sex Distribution

For more than a century, decade after decade, the sex ratio of the Chinese population has never been a normal one. The census of 1960 showed that there were 135,549 males and 101,743 females, or about 1.3 to 1, which is still below normal standard.[3] This ratio includes the state of Hawaii. So far as the mainland of the United States is concerned, the sex ratio is even less normal, or 139.4 males to 100 females. Nevertheless, it must be noted that the great disproportion in the sex ratio has improved since 1920, as revealed by Table 1 on the following page.

This table shows that in 1890 the ratio between the two sexes reached the fantastic figure of 2,678.9 males to 100 females, almost 27 males to one female. The Japanese, when they began to migrate in considerable numbers to the United States in 1900, had a sex ratio as high as 2,369.6 males to 100 females. In 1950, the ratio sank to 117.8, but, in 1960 there were more Japanese females than males. Though a preponderance of male immigrants in the early years is certainly to be expected, the abnormality is startling. The extremely slow adjustment of the unbalanced sex ratio over a number of decades may have been caused by the fact that for a Chinese-American to bring his wife and children from China is always difficult, sometimes impossible. Furthermore, conditions prevailing

before the repeal of the Exclusion Act in 1943 made it necessary
for Chinese immigrants to leave their families at home.

TABLE 1

CHINESE POPULATION OF THE UNITED STATES BY SEX, 1860-1960

Census Year	Total	Male	Female	Excess of Males	Per cent of Total Male	Per cent of Total Female	Males per 100 Females
1860	34,933	33,149	1,784	31,365	94.9	5.1	1,858.1
1870	63,199	58,633	4,566	54,067	92.8	7.2	1,284.1
1880	105,465	100,686	4,779	95,907	95.5	4.5	2,106.8
1890	107,488	103,620	3,868	99,752	96.4	3.6	2,678.9
1900	89,863	85,341	4,522	80,819	95.0	5.0	1,887.2
1910	71,531	66,856	4,675	62,181	93.5	6.5	1,430.1
1920	61,639	53,891	7,748	46,143	87.4	12.6	695.5
1930	74,954	59,802	15,152	44,650	79.8	20.2	394.7
1940	77,504	57,389	20,115	37,274	74.1	25.9	295.3
1950	117,629	77,008	40,621	36,387	65.5	34.5	189.6
1960	237,292	135,549	101,743	33,806	57.1	42.9	133.1

Source: United States Census, 1930-60.

This ratio in 1960 suggests that the trend will lead to a more
normal ratio within the next two or three decades. Thus, according
to the Immigration Service reports of Chinese immigrants admitted
between 1948 and 1959, there is a surprising preponderance of females: 22,291 females to 12,564 males, which is a ratio of 177.4
females to 100 males. The liberalization of immigration laws to
admit wives and children as nonquota persons certainly has had
considerable influence. It is significant that the majority of the
females have been under the age of thirty-nine. Lastly, many of
the "new immigrants"—those under the Refugee Relief Act of 1953
and under recent legislation—have brought their families with them.
This trend will probably continue in the foreseeable future.

Tabulating these data according to areas, we observe that since
1850, a somewhat more normal ratio has existed in California, the
stronghold of Chinese immigration, than in any other state (except
Hawaii). In 1960 there were 127.8 males to 100 females, whereas
for the whole country, the ratio was 133.1. New York State, with
the third largest Chinese population in the decade 1900 to 1910 and
the second largest since 1920, has a higher ratio of males per females than average. There is no doubt that the ratio improved considerably after 1930, but it may take several decades to reach an
equal balance between the two sexes. Needless to say the practice
of intermarriage of Chinese with native Hawaiians and later with
other races in Hawaii has led to that newest state's having a more
normal ratio than even California. For example, in the 1950 census,
the ratio is 111.2 and in 1960, the ratio has been improved to 105.5.

Among typical metropolitan areas in 1960, Honolulu was the least unbalanced in its ratios, with 105 males per 100 females, followed by Sacramento (120 males), and San Francisco (130.3). Los Angeles had 129.3 males, Chicago 165.3, and New York City, 169.7. All these ratios showed an improvement over those of 1950.

It will be seen that the highest ratio of males to females was found in the censuses of 1880 and 1900. There were more Chinese in the United States during those three decades than in the rest of the time since Chinese first entered this country, with the exception of the decade after 1950. As a consequence, the deficiency in the number of females made the sex ratio in the three decades mentioned above startling. However, one effect of the Exclusion Act was that many Chinese left the United States permanently. Since there were not many newcomers to replace these emigrants, beginning in 1920 the sex distribution has improved.

Marital Status

The excess of Chinese males over Chinese females in the United States indicates that Chinese males who had married before leaving their homeland lived virtually the lives of bachelors after arriving here. Many of the unmarried Chinese males who came to the United States had no opportunity to marry: in 1890 Chinese married men numbered only 26.1 per cent of the total number of Chinese men in the United States, unmarried Chinese males, 69 per cent, and widowed or divorced Chinese, 4.9 per cent. The situation has improved decade by decade, especially since World War II (see Table 2, page 35).

The percentage of married Chinese females, ranging from 57.4 to 69.1 in the decades between 1890 and 1950, may be considered quite normal as compared with the total number of married women in the United States. That the Chinese ratio was slightly higher than that of the rest of the population from 1890 to 1930 may have been caused by the fact that Chinese marriageable women seldom remain single. The lower percentage of Chinese single women is attributable to the Chinese tradition of marrying at an early age. It is curious that the percentage of Chinese widows is distinctly lower than that of Americans. Chinese divorces are fewer, as custom frowns upon them. But the large proportion of unmarried Chinese males remains a startling fact. The ratio, to be sure, is improving, but in 1950, 36.9 per cent were still unmarried. The recent influx of female immigrants and the large number of war brides of World War II will in time ameliorate the situation.

TABLE 2

MARITAL STATUS OF CHINESE POPULATION IN THE UNITED STATES, FIFTEEN AND OVER, 1890-1950

Census Year		Total	Single Number	Single Per Cent	Married Number	Married Per Cent	Widowed Number	Widowed Per Cent	Divorced Number	Divorced Per Cent	Unknown Number	Unknown Per Cent
1890	Male	102,322	70,625	69.0	26,720	26.1	550	0.5	13	0.1	4,434	4.3
	Female	3,074	993	32.3	1,951	63.5	85	2.8	3	0.1	42	1.3
1900	Male	83,633	48,997	58.6	31,794	38.0	1,310	1.57	19	0.02	1,513	1.81
	Female	3,204	778	24.3	2,157	67.3	259	8.1	3	0.28	7	0.02
1910	Male	64,394	34,330	53.3	26,449	41.1	1,139	1.8	45	0.1	2,431	3.7
	Female	2,955	680	23.01	2,016	68.22	229	7.75	5	0.17	25	0.85
1920	Male	49,818	23,096	46.4	24,782	49.7	1,355	2.7	66	0.16	519	1.04
	Female	4,407	962	21.8	3,046	69.1	371	8.4	15	0.41	13	0.29
1930	Male	51,519	25,108	48.7	23,868	46.3	1,349	2.6	112	0.3	1,082	2.1
	Female	8,169	1,904	23.3	5,574	68.2	631	7.7	37	0.52	23	0.28
1940	Male	48,633	21,352	43.9	25,790	53.0	1,314	2.7	177	0.4	0	0.0
	Female	12,463	4,163	33.4	7,155	57.4	1,070	8.6	75	0.6	0	0.0
1950*	Male	62,784	23,157	36.9	36,484	58.1	3,143†	5.0	0	0.0	0	0.0
	Female	28,397	8,005	28.2	18,341	64.6	2,051	7.2	0	0.0	0	0.0

*Figures for 1950 are for individuals fourteen years old and over.
†Divorced included.
Source: United States Census, 1890-1950.

Age Composition

Three or more decades ago, in the Chinatowns of San Francisco, New York, and other cities, males predominated. The community thus was unique and unnatural from the sociological point of view. To be sure, not all of them were bachelors, but the wives and families of many of them were in China. Meanwhile, very few marriages took place with native Americans. Such a heavily male community could not continue indefinitely. In the course of time, the first and second generations of Chinese immigrants had become very aged or had died. As more Chinese women and children appeared, the community took on a robust color of healthy existence. The small proportion of aged women is only natural, since most of the female immigrants were either of childbearing age or were children. While the number of males between fifteen and forty-four fluctuated moderately from 1910 to 1950, up to 1940 the number of those forty-five and over declined, and youngsters under fifteen increased. Further reduction in percentage of aged males is virtually certain.

TABLE 3

PERCENTAGE DISTRIBUTION OF THE CHINESE POPULATION
IN THE UNITED STATES BY AGE GROUP, 1910-50

Age Group	1910 Male	1910 Female	1920 Male	1920 Female	1940 Male	1940 Female	1950 Male	1950 Female
0-14	3.9	39.5	7.6	43.1	15.3	38.0	19.2	31.2
15-44	47.1	50.2	45.7	46.6	53.3	49.2	49.1	55.8
45 and over	49.0	10.3	46.7	10.3	31.4	12.8	31.7	13.0

Source: United States Census, 1910-20; 1940-50.

The larger number of female immigrants, 1950 to 1960, further swelled the percentage of women. Of the 17,331 Chinese females admitted, 84 per cent were under forty-four. In addition, more Chinese males departed: 2,893 males as against 1,194 females.[4] No doubt the trend of the Chinese in the United States is to constitute a more wholesome and more evenly distributed immigrant popu-

TABLE 4

AGE OF CHINESE IMMIGRANTS ADMITTED (MINUS EMIGRANTS DEPARTED), 1950-60

Age Group	Male	Per Cent	Female	Per Cent
0-14	2,903	26.0	2,524	15.0
15-44	5,069	46.0	12,046	69.0
45 and over	3,073	28.0	2,761	16.0
TOTAL	11,045	100.0	17,331	100.0

Source: Annual Report of the Immigration and Naturalization Service, Washington, D.C. (hereafter referred to as Annual Report), 1950-60.

lation as a result of the gradual disappearance of abnormalities in age and sex distribution.

Birth and Death Rates

The Chinese fertility in Hawaii in 1932, and again in 1940, was comparable with that of the Portuguese and other Caucasians. Since World War II the Chinese have followed the upward trend of whites and nonwhites in the Islands. The Chinese corrected birth rate, however, was mostly below that of all other races. The Japanese fertility according to the census of 1950 was the lowest. Meanwhile, the rate of the Chinese in the continental United States has been most unusual. In 1940, the Chinese birth rate was the lowest among all races, being 14.5 per cent against 19.4 per cent. In 1950, it showed a most spectacular rise, tripling to 43.9 per cent, so that it was second only to that of the American Indian.

TABLE 5

LIVE BIRTHS AND BIRTH RATES ADJUSTED FOR UNDERREGISTRATION
BY SPECIFIED RACE IN THE UNITED STATES, 1940-50

Race	Number		Per cent	
	1940	1950	1940	1950
All races	2,558,647	3,631,512	19.4	24.1
White	2,198,911	3,107,638	18.6	23.0
Nonwhites	359,736	523,874	26.7	33.3
Negroes	341,577	497,503	26.5	33.1
Indian (American)	14,022	15,671	42.0	45.8
Chinese	1,123	5,139	14.5	43.9
Japanese	1,905	3,458	15.0	24.5
All other	1,109	2,103	22.0	19.1

Source: United States Department of Health, Education, and Welfare, Public Health Service, Vital Statistics of the United States, 1950, Vol. I, p. 79.

Since 1951 the Chinese have continuously maintained a high birth rate though the percentage has been slightly less than the former peak (1949, 1950). The dearth of Chinese women in their most fertile age, twenty to twenty-nine years, before World War II, was responsible for the low birth rate.[5] From 1950 to 1953 the rate was considerably higher than that for the whole United States. Since 1954 the Chinese rate has gradually lessened and has slowly approached the prevailing United States rate. There is no sign that in the near future the Chinese birth rate will go much lower.

On the other hand, if we take into consideration younger children per 1,000 women of twenty to forty-four, to determine the fertility rate as shown below, we find a somewhat diverse answer. Although the number of children under five increased more than three times between 1940 and 1950, and the number of women of twenty to forty-

four increased 2.6 times, the rate of children per 1,000 women increased only from 595 to 714. The number of Chinese children per
1,000 women in 1930 was as high as 1,051; that is, more than 100
per cent higher than among the whites. Evidently any attempt to
determine the fertility rate from the number of children in terms
of women of the fertile-age group is unrevealing. The larger number
of children in relation to women of twenty to forty-four in 1930 may
be explained by the fact that Chinese wives of Chinese-Americans
had been rendered inadmissible to the United States by the Act of
1924, which was not modified until the very year of the census.
Therefore, many women stayed in China without joining their husbands.

Year	Women 20-44	Children under 5	Children under 5 per 1,000 women
1930	5,502	5,781	1,051
1940	7,345	4,375	595
1950	19,077	13,628	714

Source: United States Census, 1930-50.

The death rate of the Chinese in the United States, based on figures
from 1933 to 1950, was high.[6] In 1940, the death rate per 1,000 population of the United States was only 10.8, whereas the Chinese death
rate was as high as 15.3. During 1948 and 1949, the rate was de-
clining, when more Chinese immigrants were admitted than departed,
while the birth rate jumped to almost 100 per cent higher than that of
the year 1947. The Chinese birth rate continued to increase after

TABLE 6

BIRTH AND DEATH RATES PER 1,000 CHINESE POPULATION
IN THE UNITED STATES, 1950-58*

Year	Birth Rate	Death Rate
1950	36.2	7.6
1951	33.9	8.3
1952	32.1	8.2
1953	30.2	7.9
1954	28.1	8.3
1955	27.4	7.2
1956	28.1	7.7
1957	26.7	7.8
1958	25.7	7.3

*For number of births and deaths between 1950 and
1958 see Appendix Table 8, Registered Live Births and
Deaths for the Chinese in the United States, 1933-58.
    Source: Vital Statistics of the United States, 1950-
58. See also Table 12 (p. 45), Estimate of Chinese Population in the United States, 1951-59.

1948; the trend of the Chinese death rate, however, is toward a gradual decline. In fact, beginning in 1955, the decline has reached a point which is lower than the rate that has been maintained by the United States.

The leading causes of death among the Chinese are diseases of heart, malignant neoplasms, and vascular lesions affecting the central nervous systems, but tuberculosis ranks surprisingly high.[7] Between 1950 and 1958, the highest death rate from that disease was in 1950: 81.3 per 100,000, or more than three quarters of one per cent of the Chinese in this country. The situation is improving; the number of cases decreased almost yearly, until it reached its lowest ebb, 4.6, in 1958. All the time the Chinese population was increasing. Still if the rate is compared with that of the mainland United States, it is abnormally high. In 1956, 1957, and 1958, the Chinese rate was estimated at 28.2, 32.6, and 24.6; whereas in the same years the rate for the mainland United States was only 8.3, 7.8, and 7.0. The ratio is about four to one. The crowded living conditions in Chinatown are responsible for much of the tuberculosis. Many of the buildings there are unsuitable for residential purposes. It is possible the disintegration of some of the very crowded Chinatowns may be accelerated because of the higher rate of tuberculosis.

Native and Foreign Born

Again, the excess of Chinese males in this country reflects the vastly higher percentage of the foreign-born Chinese as compared to the native-born Chinese. The practice of leaving families home in China brought those of foreign or mixed parentage as high as 97.3 per cent in 1900, improving slightly in 1930 to 86 per cent. The ratio of foreign born in 1950, 47 per cent, compared with 48.1 per cent in 1940 and 58.8 per cent in 1930, was by no means a marked improvement. The admittance at the close of World War II of a number of Chinese G.I. brides, fiancées, and children helped to maintain a somewhat high ratio of foreign born. Those born in this country usually remained and married Chinese. With the increase of the birth rate since 1948, and because most of the deaths of Chinese were among the foreign born, it is estimated that in 1970, the native-born Chinese will be in the neighborhood of 70 per cent of the Chinese population in the United States, and by 1980, this rate may increase to 80 per cent.

From the point of view of potential suffrage, the number of Chinese-Americans has increased considerably since 1930. Though the census of 1950 gave actually 55,050 or 47 per cent of foreign born, yet—owing to naturalization of a number of Chinese—the citizenship status had increased accordingly.[8] This is one of the factors one must take into consideration in estimating the suffrage potential. In fact 14,133 Chinese were naturalized between 1954 and 1960. The trend is for more and more naturalization, regardless of the fact that for a number of years there will still be many foreign-born Chinese-Americans. Beginning in 1860, many Chinese who had acquired the right to reside in the United States permanently under the Refugee Relief Act of 1853 and under later legislations gradually became eligible for naturalization.

TABLE 7

POTENTIAL VOTING CHINESE POPULATION, BY CITIZENSHIP, NATIVITY,
AND SEX, IN THE UNITED STATES, 1930-50

| | Both Sexes | | | Male | | | Female | | |
	1930	1940	1950	1930	1940	1950	1930	1940	1950
Citizen	30,868	40,262	84,904	20,693	25,702	54,918	10,175	14,560	29,986
Alien	44,086	37,242	32,236	39,109	31,687	21,807	4,977	5,555	10,429

Source: United States Census, 1930-50.

The early Chinese immigrants came as laborers, working on the railroads, on the farms, in the mines; they were necessarily concentrated in rural districts. Now the situation has been entirely reversed; in fact the proportion of urban residents has increased from 75.9 per cent in 1910 to a high of 95.5 per cent in 1960.

TABLE 8

CHINESE IN THE UNITED STATES, BY NATIVITY AND SEX, 1910-50

	Total	Per cent	Male	Per cent	Female	Per cent
1910	71,531	100.0	66,856	100.0	4,675	100.0
Native	14,935	20.9	11,921	17.8	3,014	64.5
Foreign born	56,596	79.1	54,935	82.2	1,661	35.5
1920	61,639	100.0	53,891	100.0	7,748	100.0
Native	18,532	30.1	13,318	24.7	5,214	67.3
Foreign born	43,107	69.9	40,573	75.3	2,534	32.7
1930	74,954	100.0	59,802	100.0	15,152	100.0
Native	30,868	41.2	20,693	34.6	10,175	67.2
Foreign born	44,086	58.8	39,109	65.4	4,977	32.8
1940	77,504	100.0	57,389	100.0	20,115	100.0
Native	40,262	51.9	25,702	44.8	14,560	72.4
Foreign born	37,242	48.1	31,687	55.2	5,555	27.6
1950	117,140	100.0	76,725	100.0	40,415	100.0
Native	62,090	53.0	36,256	47.3	25,834	63.9
Foreign born	55,050	47.0	40,469	52.7	14,581	36.1

Source: United States Census, 1910-50.

Those in the rural districts can be subdivided into nonfarm laborers and farm laborers. Both in the north central area, and in the

TABLE 9

CHINESE POPULATION IN THE UNITED STATES, URBAN AND RURAL, 1910-60

Census Year	Total	Urban	Per cent	Rural	Per cent
1910	71,531	54,331	75.9	17,200	24.1
1920	61,639	50,008	81.1	11,631	18.9
1930	74,954	65,778	87.7	9,176	12.3
1940	77,504	70,226	91.6	7,278	8.4
1950	117,629	109,434	93.0	8,195	7.0
1960	237,292	226,577	95.5	10,715	4.5

Source: United States Census, 1910-60.

West, the percentage of those living in rural districts is about the same as the average in the whole United States. It is only in the South that there are considerably more rural nonfarm, as well as rural farm Chinese (about three to one against the average) and consequently fewer urban dwellers.

The trend of Chinese preferring to live in the urban areas has been very consistent as can be seen by the 1960 census in that only about 4.5 per cent of Chinese were not living in the cities. Again it is in some of the southern states, such as Arizona, Mississippi, South Carolina, that more than 30 per cent of Chinese live in rural areas. The foreign-born Chinese have followed the trend of the native born in residing in urban localities. In the past there were always more foreign born than native born living in the country. According to the 1950 census, the gap has been almost closed.

Needless to say, those in the rural districts received lower incomes than did those in the urban. The median income of Chinese living in the rural, nonfarm regions in 1949 was $1,463, but only $862 in the rural farm districts, against the $1,820 for those living in the urban areas.

Distribution of Population by States

The early Chinese immigrants practically all congregated in California, but because of discrimination against them, many Chinese gradually moved out of the state. By 1869, the Central Pacific had had its last spike driven home. The cessation of construction deprived hundreds of employment. Meanwhile the mining frontier had been invaded by throngs of fortune-seekers, first because of the California gold rush and then in 1858 because of the discovery of the gold fields of Colorado. A definite pattern kept repeating itself. Though a town could be built almost overnight, it could in a day become a ghost town. "Discovery, boom, and bust" formed the pattern, to be repeated in Montana, Utah, Washington, and Wyoming. As many Chinese immigrants had become mineworkers in California,

it was only natural that they should move to nearby mining territories. The difference between the majority of frontiersmen or
European immigrants, moving from east to west, and the Chinese
from California, moving largely from west to east, is striking.

Thus out of 17,000 Chinese miners listed in the census of 1870,
California had about 9,000; the remaining 8,000 were working in
Idaho, Oregon, Nevada, and Montana, with a very small number
in Utah, Washington, and Wyoming. As long as the mining frontier
existed, Chinese miners were present. Chinese population in California has ranked first in number throughout the history of Chinese
immigration, with Idaho next on the list in 1870 and Oregon important
between 1880 and 1910; Nevada, Idaho (1880-90), Washington, and
Montana ranked among the first ten states from 1870 to 1890, at
about which time the last American frontier disappeared. Chinese
miners in great numbers drifted away toward the East, so that by
1900 New York, Massachusetts, Pennsylvania, and Illinois ranked
high. New York for the past five decades has ranked second, with
Illinois and Massachusetts rivals for third. Among other states in
the first ten (1920-60) were Washington, Oregon, Pennsylvania, Arizona (11th in 1960), New Jersey (11th in 1950), Texas (from 1940 to
1960 only), and the District of Columbia, which barely squeezed into
its position by 1950, and dropped to twelfth place in 1960. Michigan
managed to rank ninth by the last census.[9]

Some of the states like Montana, Idaho, Wyoming, Nevada, and
Colorado have for several decades been gradually deserted by the
Chinese because of the disappearance of the mining frontier and the
massacres that took place in the late nineteenth century. Since Hawaii has a Chinese population of 38,197 (1960), it has thus taken the
place of New York, the state having, since 1920, the second largest
Chinese population after California. However, this ranking may
soon change; not too many new immigrants settle down in Hawaii,
as they do in New York and California. These three states will be
the stronghold of Chinese residents for a great many years to come.
The Chinese spread to all portions of the United States, but chiefly
to California and New York. Only the state of Kentucky showed a
decrease in Chinese population in 1960. The following table shows
that, though the percentage of Chinese in all regions considerably increased from 1940 to 1960, the majority of Chinese, like the Japanese, are congregated in the West and especially in Hawaii and in
California.

Though Chinese are to be found in many cities in the United States,
the 1950 census revealed that only seventy-one cities have a hundred
or more, twenty-six of these cities in California. In view of an increase of 58.2 per cent of Chinese from 1950, no doubt the latest

census will show more cities with a hundred or more Chinese.

TABLE 10

CHINESE POPULATION IN THE UNITED STATES, BY REGIONS AND DIVISIONS, 1920-60

	1920	1930	1940	1950	1960
Regions					
Northeastern	12,414	17,799	19,646	28,931	53,654
North Central	6,721	8,078	6,092	10,646	18,413
South	3,900	4,194	4,926	10,468	16,839
West	38,604	44,883	46,840	67,584	148,386
Geographic Divisions					
New England	3,602	3,794	3,238	4,684	8,527
Middle Atlantic	8,812	14,005	16,408	24,247	45,127
East North Central	5,043	6,340	4,799	8,454	14,750
West North Central	1,678	1,738	1,293	2,192	3,663
South Atlantic	1,824	1,869	2,047	4,755	8,555
East South Central	542	743	944	1,763	2,307
West South Central	1,534	1,582	1,935	3,950	5,977
Mountain	4,339	3,252	2,853	3,750	5,966
Pacific	34,265	41,631	43,987	63,834	142,420
TOTAL	61,639	74,954	77,504	117,629	237,292

Source: United States Census, 1920-60.

TABLE 11

CHINESE POPULATION IN THE UNITED STATES BY CITY, 1930-60

	1930*	1940*	1950**	1960[†]
San Francisco, Calif.	16,303	17,782	24,813	36,445
New York, N.Y.	8,414	12,753	18,327	32,831
Los Angeles, Calif.	3,009	4,736	8,067	15,443
Oakland, Calif.	3,048	3,201	5,531	5,264
Chicago, Ill.	2,757	2,013	3,334	5,082
Sacramento, Calif.[‡]	1,366	1,508	2,885	5,551
Seattle, Wash.	1,347	1,781	2,650	4,076
Boston, Mass.	1,595	1,383	2,101	3,592
Washington, D.C.	398	656	1,825	2,632
Stockton, Calif.[††]	991	1,052	1,825	2,291
Portland, Ore.	1,416	1,569	1,467	1,869
Philadelphia, Pa.	1,672	922	1,242	1,810
TOTAL	42,316	49,356	74,067	116,886

*Chinese population for cities of 100,000 or more.
**Figures shown for cities of 10,000 inhabitants or more with ten or more Chinese.
[†]Subject to possible revision prior to publication in the state reports PC (1)-B, General Population Statistics, Bureau of the Census, Washington, D.C.
[‡]In 1930, the population of Sacramento was 93,750.
[††]Stockton had a population of 47,963 in 1930; 54,714 in 1940; and 70,853 in 1950.
Source: United States Census, 1930-60.

From a comparison of the totals in Tables 10 and 11, it can be seen that the percentage of Chinese living in twelve cities were 55 per cent in 1930, about 63 per cent between 1940 and 1950, and, in

1960, 58 per cent of the total Chinese population in the mainland United States. Almost half of this number of Chinese were concentrated in four of the large cities between 1940 and 1950, whereas in 1960 the proportion was about 45 per cent. With the inclusion of Hawaii in the 1960 census, it was shown that the cities of Honolulu (with its 30,138 Chinese), San Francisco, and New York together have slightly over one third of the Chinese population in the United States.

The 1960 census reported that there were 237,292 persons of Chinese ancestry. What the future trend of Chinese population will be is dependent upon a number of factors. Taking into consideration the natural increase and the volume of immigration, there were 21,413 Chinese unaccounted for from a comparison between the 1950 and 1960 censuses. Among these, many failed to report to the census taker since a number were probably smuggled in and therefore tried every means to evade being discovered. The projection of Chinese population trends is of course reliable only to the extent that the assumed birth and death rates are correct. In addition, the estimated volume of immigrants and emigrants ought to be assumed as approximate. According to our estimate, the 2 per cent annual natural increase in births over deaths will be maintained for some time; we make this surmise after recognizing the increase in the Chinese female population in the United States as a whole. We also have to consider the trend of lower birth and death rates of the Chinese in Hawaii. It is difficult, however, to estimate the volume of immigration for the sixties or afterwards, since the census interval between 1950 and 1960 saw several important immigration laws enacted that resulted in the admission of a large number of Chinese immigrants. There is no assurance that the next decade will see a similar influx. It can be stated confidently that there will be less emigration in the foreseeable future. We have also to take into account the derivative citizens admitted. Those who have confessed previous illegal entry to the Immigration Service and have had their records straightened will certainly be counted by the census taker as new additions to the population. Also, there may still be a number of Chinese who for obvious reasons wish to avoid the census taker as much as possible, adding to the uncertainty of the estimate.

The decade of 1960 will probably see a less spectacular increase in the Chinese population as compared with the ten year period since 1950. It is estimated that by 1970 the Chinese population in the United States may reach a figure of approximately 310,000, or an increase of about 30 per cent over that of 1960.[10] But in relation to the population of the United States as a whole, the percentage of Chinese will be just a little short of 0.15 per cent. Without including

Hawaii, the percentage of 0.1 per cent has been maintained since 1900. From 1870 to 1890 it was about 0.2 per cent; in 1860, slightly more than 0.1 per cent.

TABLE 12

ESTIMATE OF CHINESE POPULATION IN THE UNITED STATES, 1951-59

Year	Number	Natural Increase*	Volume of Immigration**
1951	143,629†	3,682	523
1952	147,834	3,536	755
1953	152,125	3,397	800
1954	156,322‡	3,103	2,014
1955	161,537‡	3,264	1,707
1956	166,661‡	3,407	4,226
1957	174,458‡	3,310	4,840
1958	182,778‡	3,400	3,193
1959	189,506‡	3,500 (estimate)	5,931

*Birth rate minus death rate.
**Immigration minus emigration.
†This figure derived from adding (1) census of 1950 or 117,629 (2) 21,413 unaccounted for between 1950 and 1960 census (3) natural increase of 1950 or 3,972 and (4) volume of immigration of 1950 or 615.
‡Including those who acquired derivative citizenship: 98 in 1954; 153 in 1955; 164 in 1956; 170 in 1957; 155 in 1958; and 287 in 1959.
Source: United States Department of Health, Education, and Welfare, Public Health Service, Vital Statistics of the United States, 1951-58; Annual Report. 1951-59.

Crime and Criminals

Relationships between crime and immigrants have been studied by capable authorities for a good many years. "Damn the foreigner" has been a saying, as though foreigners were responsible for most of the crimes committed. Nevertheless, records show that the foreign born have no more tendency to crime than do the native born. Age may be of some significance. The foreign born have a larger proportion of adults; but younger people commit more crimes. Another fallacy is that, if not the first generation of foreigners, then the second commits serious offenses. So far, such sweeping statements lack statistical support.[11]

Though some Californians of the old days probably would not agree that crimes committed by the Japanese and the Chinese were slight in relation to crime in the state as a whole, yet they were. Tong feuds were, of course, a different matter. Otherwise, Chinese crimes were confined mostly to petty offenses.[12] Professor Walter G. Beach, in his studies of oriental crime in California between 1900 and 1927, revealed that there were 2,037,794 arrests of which

3.5 per cent were of Chinese, 0.9 per cent of Japanese.[13] That an exceedingly small percentage of crimes involved the Japanese was perhaps the result of the Japanese' leading normal family lives. The absence of women and the lack of family life, plus the crowded state of things in Chinatown, led the Chinese to resort to such vices as gambling and opium smoking. The majority of arrests were for offenses committed against city and state ordinances.

As to more serious crimes, the records of both Chinese and Japanese offenders in California are better than might have been expected, certainly not worse. Indeed, only a very small percentage of offenses (1900-27) actually belong in the category of crime. Out of a total of 71,626 arrests of Chinese, only 1,028 or 1.44 per cent were for serious charges leading to the death sentence or terms in state prisons. Parallel arrests of Japanese in the same period were 17,727; 382—or 2.2 per cent—were for serious offenses. Professor Beach came to this conclusion: "The oriental serious offenses in relation to total oriental offenses are low—lower than the average for the state as a whole—and that the absolute total of oriental serious offenses is but a small fraction of the entire number of such offenses committed by men of all races in the state."[14]

Since 1934 the Federal Bureau of Investigation has released racial statistics on persons arrested.[15] Through more than a quarter of a century (1934-59), we should be able to observe the trend of crime committed by the Chinese in the United States. The bureau has, however, repeatedly cautioned readers not to use the published figures unreservedly for purposes of comparison. Thus in 1958 a uniform crime index is employed for the first time; therefore, the crime rate presented in 1958 is not comparable to the rates presented in previous publications.[16] Since 1952 the bureau has published analyses obtained from fingerprint arrest cards on age, sex, and race data, and therefore they cannot be compared with fingerprint data published previous to 1952, when the police generally could prepare the full complement of reports required.

Comparison is all the more difficult because the population figures are based on the census year. The crime rates from 1950 through 1957 were obtained by measuring the crime figures for the years against the 1950 decennial census. The figures presented in the 1958 and later issues, however, are the current estimates for that particular year. Thus they are not comparable with those presented in 1951-57 or in any previous year, with the exception of the years 1930, 1940, and 1950, when the general census of the whole United States was taken. The yearly average of arrests of Chinese between 1955 and 1957 was 253. However, in these three years, the arrests did not include the San Francisco Police Department figures, thus making the arrests of Chinese in these three years conspicuously smaller, since San Francisco has the largest segment of the Chinese population in the United States: 36,445 in 1960, against 237,292 for the whole United States.[17]

Arrests of Chinese for Serious Offenses

During 1958 the *Uniform Crime Report* followed the recommendation of a special consultant committee of experts in making changes in form and content. The serious offenses now consist of criminal homicide, or murder, and nonnegligent manslaughter. These serious offenses are differentiated from manslaughter caused by negligence, such as in traffic accidents; forcible rape; robbery; aggravated assault; burglary; larceny; and automobile theft. These also are considered grave. The public necessarily reports fully to the police.

From 1934 to 1960, there were a total of 20,663 Chinese arrested, among whom 2,587 had committed serious or the so-called Part 1 Offenses, and 18,076 the less serious or Part 2 Offenses. For offenses against persons, there were 922 arrests; against property, 1,665. The most serious offenses against persons—murder and nonnegligent manslaughter—totaled 115 arrests, which are fewer than one half of one per cent (0.44) of all serious crimes. Prior to 1952, there was no such distinction made between murder and death attributable to gross negligence. All we know is that between 1952 and 1960 there were only nine arrests of Chinese on the charge of murder.

Among the serious crimes, offenses against property are increasing, especially that of larceny. This comprises a total of 870 arrests of which 289 occurred during 1959-60. The past three years have witnessed large numbers of auto thefts, or half the total of the last twenty-seven year period, 206 cases. Burglary increased from twenty-four arrests in 1959 to fifty-six in 1960. In fact these three offenses accounted for 80 to 90 per cent of all serious crimes in the last two years. However, in terms of 100,000 population, the Chinese arrest rate for larceny, burglary, and auto theft is still lower than that of the white population and the country as a whole.

Because of these increases, the Chinese arrest rate for all the serious crimes has been increasing faster than the Chinese rate of population in both 1950 and 1960. Yet the Chinese rate remained lowest of all during 1940, 1950, and 1960, while the total U.S. population and white arrest rate for all serious crimes increased rapidly from 1950 to 1960. We might add that during 1940, homicide, rape, and assault arrest rates rose for the Chinese race, but decreased significantly during 1950 and 1960, so that in both years they were lower than those of the white and the total arrest rate.

For the first time, the F.B.I. in 1960 has presented arrests by race in rural areas as well as for cities. In 1960 there were only 31 rural Chinese arrests compared with total arrests of 368,615, and 308,589 for white population. True, the number of Chinese living in rural areas has been very small indeed; still the Chinese rate is exceedingly low. There were no cases of criminal homicide and only eight Chinese arrests were for serious crimes against the total arrests of 68,863; of these, whites were responsible for 56,483.

Another means of assessing the relative criminality of the Chinese in the United States would be to count the actual number of prisoners received from the courts. They are the ones actually convicted, and hence may be said to be "criminal" in the eyes of the law. The Chinese rate of commitment had been high during the 1930's because of large numbers of Chinese violators of narcotic laws and of immigration acts. The past decade, however, has seen a decrease of Chinese prisoners receiving federal sentences. From 1931 to 1960 (1942 not available), Chinese prisoners totaled 2,075, averaging about seventy-two a year. Since 1949 the average has declined to fifty-five a year. In the three years 1958-60 the number became notably smaller, forty yearly. In spite of these decreases, the Chinese rate of commitment was still twice as high as the whites in 1960.

Arrests for Other Offenses

Minor offenses are usually designated misdemeanors. The terms, however, are confusing, since they often overlap. Thus, what in one state in the United States may be considered a felony may in another state be considered a mere misdemeanor and vice versa. Many offenses that are merely infractions of regulations have slight social or moral consequences. Indeed, it would be rash to say that drunkenness, vagrancy, disorderly conduct, or violations of municipal ordinances have much threatened the welfare of our society. The offenders themselves may be abnormal; but certainly, apart from a cultural definition, they are far from being criminals (although drunkenness may lead to auto accidents or to impulsive acts).

Arrests of Chinese for the less serious crimes, also known sometimes as Part 2 Offenses, from 1934 to 1960 amounted to 18,076. Almost a third of them were for violations of narcotic drug laws. The next most frequent cause of arrest was for gambling; these arrests accounted for about one fifth of the total. Next to these, drunkenness causes 1,792, or 10 per cent of the arrests, while vagrancy caused 1,049, or 5.8 per cent. Charges of disorderly conduct and of being a suspicious person were about 3.5 per cent each.

Violators of Narcotic Drug Laws

The violators of narcotic drug laws accounted for 5,897 arrests of Chinese out of the total number of 20,663 (1934-59). This ratio of almost one third of the total arrests involves unlawful possession, sale, or use of narcotic drugs. Federal offenses are not included. The arrests were very noticeable from 1934 to 1941. In fact, 4,204 arrests of Chinese were made during these eight years. About 90 per cent (465) of the total of 519 federal prisoners sentenced during the same period were arrested because of violations of narcotic drug laws. The United States Department of Justice does not release information on types of offenses committed, but the data released by the San Francisco and Los Angeles police departments indicate that the percentage of actual addicts to violators as a whole was about one out of four. It is to be noted that the actual arrests have been greatly reduced in recent years; thus, between 1958 and 1959 the average was only forty-three arrests yearly, compared with about six hundred arrests a year between 1934 and 1937; it would appear that the frequency of those offenses may soon be reduced to insignificance. The trend seems to coincide with the report of the Bureau of Narcotics—which deals with federal offenses—that the number of Asiatic addicts, most of them Chinese, has lately decidedly decreased (1953-58).[18]

Gambling

The gambling offenses, which were responsible for 4,117 arrests between 1934 and 1960, show no visible sign of abatement, except that the absolute number was conspicuously reduced during the years 1952 to 1957; it averaged about twenty-three arrests a year. These figures are not to be interpreted at their face value since the Federal Bureau of Investigation figures did not include the police reports in San Francisco from 1955 to 1957. The number of arrests thus increased to 341 in 1958 and to 723 in 1960. Beginning in 1959 figures include for the first time the arrests in Hawaii—there we have more than 38,000 Chinese—it is too early to evaluate the trend. However, there seems to be rather widespread gambling indulged in among a large number of Chinese in the United States. A Chinese loves to play four or eight rounds of mah-jongg with members of his family, other relatives, or friends. Bridge or poker for stakes is more often played by the native born. As long as there are people who want to play games of chance, there are always professionals happy to accommodate them. The lack of recreational outlets for the middle-aged or elderly people in Chinatown is another reason for gambling as a means of obtaining psychological gratification. More than three quarters of a century ago, the police in San Francisco had already declared that gambling was a natural passion with the Chinese. The lottery and fan-tan games have long been popular among the people of the province of Kwangtung where almost all the earlier immigrants came from, bringing the habits with them. In Boston, New York, and in many other cities, a raid on Chinatown by the police on Saturday night was a common occurrence. There were always gambling implements to be seized. Those who were arrested included innocuous players and the professionals behind the game. There were a great number of repeated offenses. The Chinese seemed usually to prefer to pay their fines instead of going to prison. Had there been no alternative to prison, curbs on gambling might have brought some results.

Drunkenness

Next to gambling offenses in frequency, drunkenness caused 1,792 arrests. It is worth while to mention that about 90 per cent of such arrests were made between the years 1945 and 1959. As a matter of fact, half of these occurred in 1958-60, while only twelve arrests were made each year between 1934 and 1944. It may be stated that arrests of Chinese for intoxication have become somewhat noticeable only since World War II. Few arrests for drunkenness were made before 1943. The San Francisco police records show that between 1944 and 1955, of the 682 arrests of Chinese, 483 were of the foreign born and that about half of those arrested were forty-five years of age or older. One explanation is that the unbalanced sex ratio persuaded many bachelors or other men who were alone to resort to drink or gambling as an important way of procuring excitement and recreation. To the older people who are isolated in Chinatown, drinking is a form of discharging a complex sickness that may have been caused by medical, domestic, moral, or spiritual factors.

Vagrancy

This is an offense that has been subject to arrest for many years, and 40 per cent of Chinese arrests in 1934-41 were due to vagrancy (vagabondage, begging, and so forth). Few charges have been pressed against either Chinese or other Orientals for professional begging. Since the Chinese consider frugality as good conduct, their personal appearance is often neglected, and especially the foreign born are likely to be picked up as vagrants. Of the 981 arrests of Chinese in San Francisco between 1941 and 1955 for vagrancy, 806 were of the foreign born and only 175 were of the native born. The 1956-60 arrests, the records of which are limited to oriental races only, still show a preponderance of the foreign born.

Offenses of Chinese Women

Women commit fewer crimes than men, and Chinese women even fewer than other women, since they are outnumbered by Chinese men and have less chance to exercise overt aggression. The *Uniform Crime Report* gave, from 1935 to 1940 only, separate lists of arrested Chinese males and females. In those six years a total of forty-six Chinese women were arrested; nineteen for narcotic violations; five for gambling; and seven for prostitution, other sex offenses, and vagrancy. Only one woman was arrested for homicide. Between 1934 and 1960 (1942 excepted), forty Chinese women sentenced to federal prisons were received from the courts; of these, twenty-five were native born. There were nine years without the conviction of a single Chinese woman.

Criminality Classified by Nativity

During our period of review, there were about two foreign born to every one federally sentenced, native-born Chinese prisoner. The narcotics and immigration violators and also an exceptional number arrested for gambling were mostly foreign born. From 1943-49, foreign-born prisoners were especially numerous, 481 against 203 native born; this imbalance has lessened to 355 against 220 in recent years (1950-60). The diminishing of narcotic violations since 1952 will decrease the number of foreign-born Chinese prisoners; however, as the 36,359 Chinese immigrants since 1944 will certainly have troubles in adjusting, it will be difficult to reduce the number of foreign born arrested for other offenses.

Juvenile Delinquency

The *Uniform Crime Report* does not offer any statistics on the ages of Chinese arrested nor does the *Federal Prison* offer any breakdown. It has long been known that oriental youths have not been a problem to the police. Articles have appeared asking why there is such a low rate of juvenile delinquency among Chinese-American teenagers. Representative Arthur G. Klein of New York submitted to the House on July 29, 1955, five articles prepared by the *New York Post,* dealing with the New York Chinatown. The statement was made that during 1954 only nine Chinese teenagers were delinquents out of a total of 7,700 delinquents brought into the Children's Court in New York City. In submitting these articles Congressman Klein says:

There have been many myths about Chinatown. Sensation-seekers and writers of trashy fiction have done their worst to give Chinatown a bad name. The facts are quite the reverse of their sordid pictures. New York's Chinatown, while picturesque and colorful and worthy of a visit from the out-of-towners, is a community of Americans of Chinese descent, most of them citizens, possessed of a great tradition and with admirable human and social qualities. Its members follow a way of life that deserves to be known, applauded, and emulated. The sober virtues of respect for parents and teachers, of a stable and loving home life, of the desire to learn, and of peaceful adjustment are predominant in New York's Chinatown. I am proud to be the Representative in Congress of the district that includes these fine men, women and children.[19]

The Chinese family system helps make the low delinquency rate possible. At the earliest possible age a child is encouraged to know his responsibilities, that whatever he does will reflect upon his parents, his ancestors, and his friends. The growing child is treated with warm affection, but with firmness. He is made to appreciate the dignity of a good home.

Much juvenile delinquency is made possible by the heterogeneity of racial origins within the American group. A high rate of delinquency was found in a section of Honolulu with a heterogeneous population, but in the adjoining area occupied entirely by Japanese, the rate was low. By contrast, the Chinese in San Francisco have some delinquency trouble. Professor Rose Hum Lee in her study, between 1943 and 1949, of 225 cases of juvenile delinquency among Chinese boys and girls in San Francisco, found that their overt antisocial activities resulted from cultural conflicts between parents—of foreign-born or mixed nativity—and native-born children, from broken homes, and from longing for self-expression.[20]

Observe, however, that a low juvenile delinquency rate is not a monopoly of Chinese teenagers. Japanese, Koreans, and Filipinos have the same low rate. Oriental parents usually have greater control over their children, whose welfare and conduct are keenly watched. The prime cure for juvenile delinquency is found in the home.

In summary, a small proportion of all aggressive crimes against persons—such as homicide, rape, and assault—are committed by the Chinese. In fact, for all serious crimes, the rate for Chinese is the lowest in the country as a whole. If gambling and violations against narcotic drug laws were excluded from consideration, then in 1940 and 1950, the Chinese rate for all offenses was the lowest; and in 1960 it was the lowest with these two offenses. This is because for both whites and the population as a whole, the crime rate has been increasing much faster than the population. The Chinese crime rate is also increasing faster than the population, but at a much slower pace.

The largest number of arrests of Chinese between 1934 and 1960 was for violations against narcotic drug laws. This is an offense against public health, which may breed other crimes. The strictness of law enforcement together with social disapproval in Chinatown may have been responsible for the decrease in arrests. Gambling, drunkenness, and vagrancy are the next most frequent causes of arrest, mostly committed by foreign-born adults confined to Chinatown, still adjusting to a new way of life. Excepting professional gambling and violations of narcotic drug laws, all these offenses represent nuisances rather than crimes.

It seems reasonable to conjecture that a major factor in the low crime records of the Chinese in America is their continuing involvement with an interrelated Chinese community extending beyond the family. Also, the greater majority of Chinese-Americans have strong motivations to gain what seems to them of paramount importance—security. This goal, with the plentiful opportunities offered in America, may be another reason for the low Chinese crime rate.

Mental Illness

Statistical data on the mental illnesses of Orientals are scanty. Chinese are subject to the same mental illnesses as are other persons, and are sometimes admitted for hospital care; but the rate is considered comparatively low. In 1933 only eighty-four Chinese were admitted to state mental hospitals.[21] The number increased to 336 in 1939. A total of fifteen Chinese were deported between 1939 and 1958 because of mental and physical defects. Yet the Chinese as a group are less tense in facing problems; accepting life as it is, they are less vulnerable to mental suffering.

Deaths among the Chinese owing to mental disorders were few, nineteen during nine years, 1950-58. World War II surely caused maladjustments and personal disorders among the ex-servicemen's families, since some marriages had been in haste and cultural backgrounds had been different. The same dislocations were present among wives who had been long separated from their husbands.

Chinese suicides, 1950-58, numbered 362, or about 40 a year. Of these 302 were males and 60 females. This rate is almost two and one half times above that in the whole of the United States, which is about one person in 100,000. No official figures are given on the Chinese or Japanese prior to 1950, so a comparison with the earlier figure is not possible. One explanation is that with the mainland lost to the Communists, old people planning to return to China are unable to do so. Life is hard for others because of family separation. It is possible that some suicides were mentally ill. Further study is needed to determine the true causes of suicide in this troubled world.

Religion

The four great religions of China are Taoism, Buddhism, Mohammedanism, and Christianity. Of these, Taoism has perhaps the fewest professed followers. Christianity is comparatively a newcomer; its effects are pronounced, but its numerical strength not at all impressive. It takes partial responsibility for the introduction of Western culture; its contribution to education in China has been only one of many. A number of Chinese immigrants in North America and in Southeast Asia, when interrogated by census takers, gave as their religion Confucianism, which Chinese do not recognize as a religion. (The idols of Confucius in the temples are placed there merely to show respect for his greatness.)

The early European colonists imported a variety of faiths and sects into the new land, playing an important part in molding American culture. The religions brought in by the Chinese have had quite negligible influences. The vast majority of Japanese immigrants were adherents of Buddhism, whereas the Chinese worshipped many gods and goddesses. The religion of the early Chinese immigrants may be said to have been a fusion of the popular aspects of Buddhism and Taoism. Perhaps they observed certain rites in the temples at fixed times of the year, and occasionally burned joss. It does not appear that their religion seemed significant to them. Nevertheless the early Chinese laborers built many temples throughout California, of which there remain about twenty, largely for the enjoyment of tourists. The one in the San Francisco Chinatown is considered authentic. It is interesting that the most famous temple in Los Angeles is the Kong Chow Temple, dedicated to the god Kuan Ti, a military hero in the days of the Three Kingdoms (A. D. 220-65). He represents valor and loyalty, which the Chinese respect.

On the West Coast, Christian churches have not failed in their missionary endeavors: first the Presbyterian, then a score of years later the Baptist, then the Methodist, the Congregational, and last the Episcopal. San Francisco was the first city of Protestant activity in behalf of the Chinese, and today it still claims to have the largest number of Chinese religious groups. Nearly all Chinese churches in San Francisco date back to the late nineteenth century. The Chinese Presbyterian Church, organized in 1852, remains the most active. The early churches in San Francisco rendered great service to the Chinese, such as teaching them English, providing Sunday schools, acting as their spokesmen, and as their protectors against violence. The most important work, however, performed by the Christian churches was the establishment of so-called "rescue homes" in an effort to solve the serious problems of concubinage and prostitution, especially in the early days of Chinatown, when the vast majority of the inhabitants were single males. The Christian women, in fact, were very gravely concerned over the plight of Chinese girls imported for immoral purposes. In almost every home-mission history one reads glowing accounts of the women who participated in this rescue work.

Not until the beginning of the twentieth century did the Roman Catholic Church undertake the task of proselyting; now the number of Chinese Catholics in the United States is increasing rapidly, perhaps because the structure and the ritual are readily accepted by the Chinese, particularly by the foreign born. Chinese are members of many non-Chinese Catholic churches.

The precise number of Chinese Christians in the United States is not ascertainable, but all the data point to a low percentage. It is estimated that less than eight per cent of the Hawaiians of Chinese ancestry had become Protestants. In the continental United States, the percentage is probably even smaller. A rough estimate put the number of Chinese Protestants at from 7,500 to 7,700 (1953).[22] By adding the 5,000 Roman Catholics and all the Christians in Hawaii, the total comes to perhaps 17,000 or about 7.5 per cent of the total Chinese population in the United States. A large proportion of Chinese church members are young people, with students and professional persons predominant. The Chinese congregations are mainly English-speaking. Restaurant and laundry workers do not attend these churches as a rule. Their long hours and their characteristic attitude of indifference toward religion are very likely the reasons—a great many Chinese adhere to the conviction that as long as they are thinking rightly and doing rightly they require little religion for the salvation of their souls. Unlike the Japanese, they are not particularly attracted to Buddhism. Since 1955, however, Chinese Buddhists in Hawaii have begun to organize temples; the first was organized in the lovely Nuuanu Valley, and two years later a second one was dedicated in the heart of the Honolulu business section.

On the other hand, some evidence indicates an increase of Chinese Christians. Dr. Lin Yu-tang's return to Christianity is but one of many examples of educated Chinese who have accepted the faith, or in their mature years reaffirmed it. Another obvious fact is that many of the Chinese immigrants stranded here because of the Communist occupation, as well as those who arrived under the Refugee Relief Act of 1953 (or later acts), had been graduated from missionary schools in China, or at least in some way had participated there in Christian work. They would be ready converts. In time the younger generation, largely by reason of mingling with their non-Chinese acquaintances, very likely will become Christian. As a matter of fact, in a survey of one hundred and twenty-eight Chinese college graduates—members of the Rho Psi fraternity—seventy-seven (or 60.1 per cent) replied that they were Protestants, six that they were Roman Catholics, and forty-five that they had no religion whatever.

Education

The traditional respect for learned men in China has no doubt

left its impact upon the Chinese in the United States. Early immigrants had of course very little schooling, but they usually gave their
children the very best education available. The 1950 census revealed
that out of 62,820 male pupils, 7,825 or 12.5 per cent were graduated
from high school and 7,665 had one to three years. The number of
college graduates was 4,955 or 7.9 per cent. Those who attended
college from one to three years amounted to 4,885. Female graduates
from high school numbered 6,420 or 23.1 per cent out of a total of
27,795, whereas female college graduates numbered 2,180 or 7.8 per
cent. Those who did not complete college numbered 2,625. In both
respects, the women were slightly more than the equals of the men.

What the census report did not indicate was that many Chinese
take postgraduate studies. The number of Chinese who in recent
years have attained the Ph. D. has increased tremendously. Of the
1,124 who were on college faculties for the academic year 1959-60,
there were 498, or 44 per cent who had a Ph. D. , an Sc. D. , or an
M. D. The degrees obtained by 146 Chinese, according to a 1956
survey made by the Rho Psi fraternity, are here listed.

Highest degree attained	Number of college graduates	Percentage
Doctor	54	37.0
Master	45	30.8
Bachelor	47	32.2

Of these 146 college graduates, two held five degrees and two, four
degrees. Thirty-nine had three degrees, and thirty, only one. Forty-
eight of these college graduates have published scientific articles in
journals and in magazines; seven of them are authors of books; and
two have written monographs. Twelve have secured patents of one
kind or another, and six have received scientific awards.

On the other hand, one should take into consideration that many of
the older Chinese immigrants had little or no education.[23] In the
censuses of 1940 and 1950 unschooled males and females outnumbered those with schooling by about three to one. As we have indicated previously, earlier immigrants were practically all males. The
females had the larger percentage of illiterates as well as of those
unable to speak English (1910-30). Just how many Chinese in this
country speak or write the Chinese language well, we do not know.
It is hardly necessary to say that the Chinese immigrants who came
here with their families, or sent for their families later, are able
to speak Chinese, as are their children. On the other hand, Chinese
born in this country are usually less able to grasp even the speaking
of the language than those who came from China. The "old immi-

grant" families and their youngsters usually speak Chinese at home and may attend Chinese schools after their regular school hours. It is the youngster of the "new immigrant" family that speaks little Chinese even at home. The explanation is that the parents in the so-called "new immigrant" families usually are both working and therefore can afford little time to give enough Chinese language training to their children. Another interpretation is that most of the "old immigrants" tend to be more conservative and think it wise and proper to have their children know something about Chinese culture, especially the Chinese language.

Occupation and Employment

It has become almost axiomatic that a Chinese in this country is either a restaurant worker or a laundryman; but such a statement expresses only part of the truth. The earlier Chinese workers in California were railroad laborers and miners; they were employed as domestics; they tilled the soil on the farms. In the census of 1870, of the 46,274 persons in all occupations 3,653 were launderers and laundresses, while only 66 were restaurant keepers. Laundry occupation gradually became more important until in 1900 its workers numbered 25,483. As for restaurants, Chinese native dishes were first widely known with the arrival in 1898 of Viceroy Li Hung-chang, the Chinese premier, who passed through the United States on his return from Russia to China. He made chow mein and chop suey popular with Americans. Although the laundry operatives, owners, and managers head the list in the 1920 census—with 12,559 out of 45,614 in all occupations—cooks, waiters, and restuarant keepers followed closely with 11,438. Since then these two employments have dominated the occupational field.

For several decades employment available to the second and third generations of Chinese-Americans was very limited, regardless of their college education or other training. A relatively small number of young men and women with proper education returned to China to pursue their vocations; others had to content themselves with inferior positions. Only during and after World War II, with the shortage of trained personnel, did Chinese college men and women begin to secure proper and diversified employment. Meanwhile, more and more Chinese attended college. Consequently the number of engineers, scientists, doctors, nurses, and lawyers increased many times over what it had been twenty or thirty years ago.[24]

Table 13 affords a comparison of the 1940 and the 1950 censuses. The number of Chinese professional and technical men and women increased significantly from 2.8 per cent in 1940 to 7.1 per cent in

TABLE 13

MAJOR OCCUPATION GROUPS OF EMPLOYED CHINESE IN THE UNITED STATES, 1940-50

	Number		Per cent	
	1940	1950	1940	1950
Total Employed	36,992	48,409	100.0	100.0
Professional, technical, and kindred workers	1,028	3,455	2.8	7.1
Farmers, farm managers, managers, officials, and proprietors	7,966	10,170	21.5	21.0
Clerical, sales, and kindred workers	4,172	7,722	11.3	15.9
Craftsmen, foremen, and kindred workers	457	1,390	1.2	2.9
Operatives and kindred workers	8,252	8,275	22.3	17.1
Private household workers and service workers	13,318	15,200	36.0	31.4
Farm laborers, unpaid family workers, farm foremen, and laborers	1,562	1,489	4.2	3.1
Occupation not reported	237	708	0.7	1.5

Source: United States Census, 1940-50.

1950. The Chinese thus evidenced a progress decidedly greater than did the Japanese or the Filipinos.[25] Today, more and more Chinese college graduates become university instructors and enter industrial corporations. Again, we refer to the fields of specialization of 158 college graduates and undergraduates appearing in the Rho Psi fraternity survey of 1956.

Field of Specialization	Number of Graduates
Engineering	96
Social Science	29
Pure Science	20
Medical Science	7
Agriculture	3
Architecture	2
Language	1
Total	158

Only 19 per cent of the graduates and those still attending college have specialized in the social sciences; the other 81 per cent are engineers, chemists, physicians, and scientists. The colleges from which they were graduated or are still attending are listed below:

Massachusetts Institute of Technology	31
Cornell University	23
University of Pennsylvania	17

University of Wisconsin	10
Harvard University	9
Columbia University	7
New York University	7
University of Illinois	5
Other colleges	49
Total	158

Income

The median annual income of the Chinese in the United States in 1949, according to the 1950 census, was $1,799. Chinese in the West received the better median income of $1,906, whereas in the South the median was only $1,528.

TABLE 14

INCOME OF CHINESE IN THE UNITED STATES IN 1949 (14 YEARS AND OVER)

Without income	29,665
Less than $ 500	6,315
$ 500 to $ 999	7,405
$1,000 to $1,499	7,385
$1,500 to $1,999	7,720
$2,000 to $2,499	8,040
$2,500 to $2,999	4,340
$3,000 to $3,999	5,560
$4,000 to $4,999	2,115
$5,000 to $5,999	1,155
$6,000 and over	1,420
Income not reported	9,495
TOTAL	90,615

Source: United States Census, 1950.

This median was very low compared to Hawaii's $2,964. The reason for the discrepancy is that in Hawaii there was little discrimination against the Chinese, so that they could from the beginning plan to become doctors, lawyers, or engineers. That the Chinese on the mainland United States gained comparatively little headway until after World War II indicates too short a time had elapsed for them to make a proper showing in 1949. Undoubtedly, Chinese incomes are improving as the Chinese are admitted to more remunerative positions. The 1956 Rho Psi fraternity survey reveals the annual incomes of 103 college graduates in the United States.

Income	Number of college graduates	Per cent
$12,000 and above	15	14.6
10,000 to 12,000	24	23.3
7,000 to 10,000	59	57.3
5,000 to 7,000	5	4.8

Hawaii's Chinese

The first Chinese came to Hawaii as laborers under contract. In 1852 the Royal Hawaii Agricultural Society engaged Captain Cass to bring in Chinese laborers in accordance with provisions in the Master and Servants Act. First came a contingent of 180; later in the year, 100 more. Since the Chinese were considered "quiet, able, and willing men," the plantation owners were well satisfied with the experiment.[26] Consequently between 1852 and 1864, 700 additional Chinese laborers were brought into the Islands, and during the next twenty years the number of Chinese laborers admitted into Hawaii increased rapidly: from 62 in 1875 to 3,652 in 1880, and to 4,295 in 1884. By 1886 there were 20,000 Chinese in the Islands, of which one fourth were plantation laborers.[27]

TABLE 15

CHINESE IN HAWAII, 1853-1960

Census Year	Number	Per cent of Total Population
1853	364	0.5
1860	816	1.2
1866	1,306	2.0
1872	2,038	3.6
1878	6,045	10.4
1884	18,254	22.6
1890	16,752	18.6
1896	21,616	19.8
1900	25,767	16.7
1910	21,674	11.3
1920	23,507	9.2
1930	27,179	7.4
1940	28,774	6.8
1950	32,376	6.5
1960	38,197	6.0

Source: Andred W. Lind, Hawaii's People (Honolulu: University of Hawaii Press, 1955), p. 27. Advance Reports: Hawaii General Population Characteristics, 1960 Census of Population, Bureau of the Census, Washington, D.C.

The problem of race relations in Hawaii is most fascinating, for the racial composition is heterogeneous; in 1950 the Orientals constituted 57 per cent, but the rate declined in 1960. The largest racial element is the Japanese, with 32.1 per cent. Other important segments are: Caucasians (31.9 per cent), Filipinos (11 per cent), Chinese (6.0 per cent). Other races constitute 19 per cent. One of the important recent changes in the composition of population in Hawaii is that,numerically, the Orientals are increasing, but in terms of total population, they are losing ground. Though the Chinese population in Hawaii increased 18 per cent, from 1950 to 1960 or 32,376 to 38,197, Japanese increased 10.2 per cent and Filipino, 13.1 per cent, yet the total population in Hawaii increased more, or 26.6 per cent. As a matter of fact, the downward trend of the Chinese population has been noticeable since 1900 and declined to its lowest percentage in 1960. The Chinese birth rate has been low for several decades. Fewer Chinese immigrants settled in Hawaii and Chinese and Japanese migrated to the mainland, especially to California. The Caucasians moved to Hawaii due to business and other reasons. When Hawaii's admission to the Union caused its economic expansion, many Caucasians were especially prompted to settle there.

The Chinese immigrants, as soon as their contracts had expired with the plantation owners, customarily established themselves in trade. First perhaps they were peddlers; later they opened retail shops and eventually branched out into other kinds of business. The conditions suitable to business were so fully utilized by the Chinese that the later immigration groups could hardly expect to share the advantages to the same extent. As in Southeast Asia, the Chinese usually became the owners of the retail and wholesale establishments. They have also qualified in many professional positions; moving from a low of 0.5 per cent of all professionals in 1910 to 5.7 per cent in 1940 and 10.7 per cent in 1950, they have surpassed all other ethnic groups except the Caucasians. In the class of managers, officials, and proprietors, the Chinese share was 20.1 per cent in 1950, compared to 18.5 per cent for Caucasians, 15.1 per cent for the Japanese, and 3 per cent for the Filipinos.

Next to the Caucasians, the Chinese have a larger proportion of college-trained men and women than does any other ethnic group. According to the census of 1950, 5.1 per cent of the Chinese had four or more years of college education, as compared with 7.9 per cent among the Caucasians, 1.7 per cent among the Japanese, 0.9 per cent among the Hawaiians, and 0.2 per cent among the Filipinos.

The median income for the Chinese male in 1949 was $2,964, which is the highest figure of all ethnic groups, including the Caucasians ($2,856). In the top income bracket, from $5,000 to $10,000 and over, the Caucasians still enjoyed a slight advantage over the Chinese, who in turn surpassed all other groups.

It is significant that among females of fourteen or over the Chinese received the highest median income, $1,887, followed by Caucasians with $1,551; Japanese, $1,207; Hawaiian, $999; Filipino, $548; and all races, $1,247.

That the Chinese in Hawaii enjoy better than average income is not without good reason. Chinese are well established in all leading professions, including law, medicine, dentistry, architecture, and engineering. The Chinese run two banks in Honolulu and operate many businesses—such as real estate, investment, contracting—out of proportion to their numbers. This is largely due to their tendency to secure better-than-average education. The lack of racial prejudice in Hawaii has contributed to the welfare and prosperity both of the Chinese, and of other ethnic groups.

A glowing example of business sagacity and success is Hawaii's Mr. Chinn Ho, the grandson of a rice farmer who came from China. Besides being the first oriental president of many important Hawaiian business institutions, he is the founder of the Capital Investment Company, which has ten subsidiaries operating across the Pacific from Hong Kong to California, dealing in investments and real estate.

In the postwar period the increasing fertility rate among the whites in the West has been matched by a similar tendency among the Chinese in Hawaii. For several decades before 1950 the Chinese corrected birth rate has been very closely comparable to that of the Caucasians, though always slightly lower. The American environment has affected the Chinese group in Hawaii to a very large extent.[28] But available statistics disclose that between 1951 and 1959 the Chinese birth rate was temporarily arrested, whereas the Caucasian rate still showed a marked tendency to rise year by year. The birth rate of Caucasians in 1951 was 2,912; it advanced to 3,722 in 1954 and to 4,942 in 1959, while during the same period the Chinese rate was 830, 844, and 780.[29] The Chinese death rate is also low by the Western standard, averaging 237 each year between 1951 and 1959.[30] This low rate is to be expected, since Hawaii's population is made up of a large number of young people.

The population abnormalities of the Chinese in Hawaii have now largely disappeared. In 1920 more than 36 per cent of the Chinese were between the ages of thirty-five and sixty-four, but in 1950 the percentage was reduced to 29 per cent, with a slight excess of males more than seventy years old. The practice of intermarriage with the native Hawaiians until about the decade of 1910 explains the fact that the sex ratio of Chinese in Hawaii is always more normal than in any other state.

Like many other Chinese abroad, the Chinese in Hawaii tend to prefer to live in the city. In 1950, 82.5 per cent were residents in Honolulu, compared with only 49.6 per cent of the total population. In 1920, however, only 56.9 per cent of Chinese had been city residents. The latest census revealed that only 6 per cent of Chinese were living in the rural area of Hawaii.

On the basis of the 1950 census, 82.1 per cent of adult Chinese were United States citizens, whereas only 50.1 per cent were citizens in 1930, and 5.9 per cent in 1910. Although the 38,000 Chinese are a mere 6 per cent of the population in Hawaii today, nevertheless they are generously active in the island's life, economy, and local government, both in elective and appointive positions. To mention but a few, the treasurer of Hawaii, Raymond Y. C. Ho, and Honolulu's chief of police, Dan Liu, are both of Chinese ancestry, as are the chief executive officers of two of Hawaii's four counties. Six of the eighteen cabinet-rank officials under Republican Governor William F. Quinn are Chinese-Americans or Chinese-Hawaiians, and also many members of both houses of the state legislature. Herbert K. H. Lee, a Democratic candidate for governor, is the president of Hawaii's last territorial Senate. The recent election of Hiram L. Fong to the United States Senate proves that for the first time America has enfolded its people of Polynesian and Asian ancestry in its warm embrace.

3

Free Immigration (1820-82)

The history of California from 1820 to 1882 has an important bearing on the history of Chinese immigration into the United States during that period. From California's admission to the Union in 1850 until a century later when it was the second largest state, the Chinese immigrants contributed their full share to its spectacular growth. After the discovery of gold at Sutter's Mill some time in 1848, Chinese laborers from the province of Kwangtung, along with other pioneers from all quarters of the globe, made a rush into the state. Labor shortage caused the people to welcome the arrival of the Chinese and to praise them. Since cheap white labor was extremely scarce, the Chinese became largely responsible for the completion of the Central Pacific Railroad. They did many other jobs usually disdained by the whites.

More Chinese arrived year after year in the United States—by 1875 there were more than 100,000 on the Pacific Coast alone. When the antiforeign movement in California became intense, it is not surprising that the Chinese bore the brunt of it. The aroused animosity was partly due to the fact that the Chinese, conspicuously different in appearance, customs, and language, adhered tenaciously to their own way of life. Also, their low standard of living and their willingness to accept trifling wages seemed to many a native laborer an actual menace. When organized labor concentrated its ill will on the Chinese, Californians tried to pass bills of restriction in the state legislature; failing in that, they successfully urged their senators and representatives in Washington, D. C. , to keep introducing bills of restriction. A permanent exclusion act was passed, and subsequently oriental immigration was ended by the Quota Act of 1924.

During the anti-Chinese movement, the Californians claimed exclusive understanding of the oriental problem, since they had by far the largest proportion of the Chinese population in the United States. Any sympathy in the East toward the Chinese aroused bitter resentment in the West. Moreover, throughout the last forty years of the nineteenth century there appeared many writings on the Chinese question; lectures, debates with their claims and counterclaims (according to the particular interest or bias of the speaker), added to the turmoil of special pleading. An impartial study would have had few listeners or readers. The relationship between China and the United States was seriously disturbed until the Sino-Japanese conflict, when anti-Chinese agitation died down.

Influx of Chinese

Even before the news that gold had been discovered in California reached Hong Kong in the spring of 1848, Chinese had come to America. Immigration statistics in the United States show that forty Chinese had arrived, but because no complete records of the Chinese became available until the 1860 census, the number of Chinese in the United States was not, for several years at least, recorded accurately. As to exactly when real immigration began, authorities differ. Professor Maurice R. Davie states that immigration on a large scale began in 1854.[1] On the other hand, Doctor H. F. McNair believes that it began in 1852, at which time the Chinese may be estimated at more than 18,000.[2] Professor Mary Roberts Coolidge and others state that in 1851 a comparatively large number of Chinese had arrived in California: 2,716 recorded by the San Francisco customhouse; 7,520 as released by the Chinese Six Companies; and about 10,000 as estimated by several American authorities.[3] As a matter of fact, H. H. Bancroft has stated that by February 1, 1849, there were already fifty-four Chinese in California and by January 1, 1850, the number had risen to 791, passing the mark of 4,000 by the end of 1850.[4]

According to the report of the Immigration Commission published in 1911, only 42 Chinese immigrants came to the United States in 1853, whereas 13,100 came in 1854. Compared with the record of more than 20,000 Chinese arrivals at the San Francisco customhouse during 1852, one wonders how such impressive discrepancies could be possible. As to discrepancies after 1852, they may be due to the use by various officials of different methods of recording, to a difference in the area covered, or to changed bases of computation.

Meanwhile, during more than thirty years of free immigration, the decade of 1868 to 1877 witnessed the largest continuous influx of Chinese, with more than 130,000 arrivals against fewer than 60,000 departures. The influx between 1873 and 1876 was especially large.[5]

As far as the number of Chinese actually on the Pacific Coast is concerned, the estimates computed by Mary Roberts Coolidge are perhaps the best available for the period of free immigration. Her figures were made on the basis of Chinese arrivals and departures at the San Francisco customhouse, minus a death rate of 2 per cent annually.[6] They are higher than those of the census report. Since the census figures cover the whole United States, no doubt those for 1860 and 1870 are low. The number of Chinese increased yearly after 1868 until it reached over 111,000 in 1876. Undoubtedly this marked increase intensified the anti-Chinese feeling during those years.

At the time of the California gold rush, there were additional reasons for the Chinese to seek employment abroad; chiefly, perhaps, the ruin and resulting poverty in the southern portion of China, aftermath of the terrible Taiping Rebellion. The horrors of war, with the consequent devastation, plundering, and famine, had driven many of the people to seek a living in Macao and in Hong Kong. There the contract coolie trade flourished, so that thousands were shipped off to Peru, Cuba, and other countries. Meanwhile, voluntary emigration to California and to Australia swelled.

Consequently, unlike the mixed motives—religious, political, adventurous, and economic—that impelled the forefathers of America to cross the Atlantic, the motive of the Chinese immigrants was mostly economic. Some of the Chinese who came to California in pursuit of gold returned in a year or two to China, spreading their reports of riches. Thus the name in Chinese for California is "Golden Mountains."[7] There is no doubt that, like other immigrants, the Chinese were also sellers of labor at a better market.

Whereas the Chinese in Kwangtung had been prompted by the devastation of war to venture elsewhere, the effective demand for labor in California made their presence worth while.[8] In addition, railroad and steamship companies were powerful influences promoting Chinese immigration.

The Chinese who came early to America were nearly all from Kwangtung. Since Canton, the capital of Kwangtung, is situated near Hong Kong and Macao, and since trade in the early days flourished between the westerners and the Cantonese, it was natural that the name Cantonese should be applied to those people who emigrated from that area. As soon as the typical immigrant had gained a foothold somewhere in California, members of his family and other relatives immediately followed. Even today, so-called Cantonese form a majority of the Chinese in the United States.

From Total Praise to Bitter Reproach

For the first few years at least, the arrival of Chinese laborers was hailed, and they were warmly welcomed both by the people of California and by state and county officials. The Chinese were seen to be reticent, decent, industrious, thrifty, and adaptable to various kinds of employment—ready and willing to perform labor uncongenial to the Caucasian; indeed the Chinese became well-nigh indispensable. The fact that they had behind them an organization that made it possible for an employer to secure any number of workers by negotiating with a single "contractor" placed Chinese labor in a comparatively advantageous position.[9]

Once a Chinese had gone to work, he almost invariably "saw his job through," even agreeing to do the most unpleasant tasks, readily satisfied with low wages, cooperating with his employers. With the acute scarcity of unskilled labor and with the Chinese totaling about 25 per cent of the foreign-born population of California (1860-80) and outnumbering any other group of immigrants,[10] the Chinese soon filled in as general laborers, domestic servants, cooks, and gardeners; some became carpenters, others employees in factories and workshops, making boots and shoes, cigars, and clothing. The majority went into the mines; several thousand labored in the construction of the Central Pacific Railroad, the first of the transcontinental railroads fostering an influx of Asiatics.

Although the Chinese were openly praised and were in many quarters considered to be desirable, as early as 1852 they found opposition in the mining camps. After the Mexicans, the Chileans, and later the Frenchmen had been driven out of mining, abuse and persecution fell on the inoffensive and usually defenseless Chinese. Persecution of the Chinese began in the early 1850's when white laborers found themselves unable to compete with the more industrious Chinese. Newspapers of the time frequently mentioned the murder of a Chinese; seldom was the murderer hanged. Frequently, during the early days of immigration, tax collectors would kill Chinese. In 1862, the Chinese Six Companies reported to the California Senate that eighty-eight Chinese had been murdered in that year, eleven of them by tax collectors. With the increase of demands by laborers and of political campaigns for the restriction of Chinese immigration, attacks on Chinese became more and more serious. In several parts of California the houses of Chinese were destroyed; Chinese were driven away from their places of occupation. The few who took their injuries to court received no redress, even though a case was decided in favor of the plaintiff. Those who employed Chinese occasionally suffered cruel beatings, even death, at the hands of lawless hoodlums.

The largest and perhaps the most spontaneous riot before the restriction act was passed by Congress occurred in Los Angeles on

October 24, 1871, when a feud between two rival Chinese companies resulted in the wounding of two police officers and the killing of one civilian who attempted to intervene. In the course of a few minutes, Chinatown was stormed by a large mob. Houses were burned, movable property was carried away, and at least eighteen persons were killed—all within four hours.[11] Gradually such lawlessness diminished, partly from boycotts or strikes against employers of Chinese, and finally because of the hostile reaction in the East and the middlewestern states toward brutalities. The fact that acts of physical violence might jeopardize the movement for restriction led the Californians to control themselves and to become very cautious, at least until restriction had been achieved.

The Bases of the Anti-Chinese Movement

The general public has virtually acknowledged the distinct service to California performed by the Chinese. They believe that the Chinese contributed largely to the state's prosperity and to the development of its natural resources. Before the late 1870's the Chinese engaged only in such work as white laborers refused to perform. Thus the Chinese not only were noninjurious competitors but in effect were benefactors to the white laborer. In spite, however, of such patent facts, the Chinese, long before 1870, were hated and singled out for attack. A number of causes were responsible for the anti-Chinese movement. The presence of southerners in California, with their principle of a White Man's Country, plus the doctrine of Know-Nothingism, led to the attitude that America is for the Americans and that all foreigners, particularly those of a different color, were interlopers and trespassers. The fact that the majority of the citizens of California were laborers, largely miners, prompted many politicians to conduct anti-Chinese campaigns in order to secure votes. The rise of Kearneyism and the organization of the Workingmen's party in 1877 aggravated the situation. Democrats and Republicans alike, though in somewhat different degree, were anxious to give the working people the impression that they championed the anti-Chinese crusade. All this became particularly noticeable during the presidential campaigns in the last forty years of the nineteenth century. As long as the Chinese, having been denied naturalization, had no vote, politicians might, without much opposition, crusade against them. While prosperity prevailed and demand exceeded supply all was well in the community. But with a depression setting in, with consequent lack of employment, employees thrown out of work blamed their hardship at least partly on the foreigners, whose presence seemed to deprive the native of his job.

Thus, during the business recession of 1854, and of 1862 in California, and during the national panic of 1873, workers bitterly blamed the Chinese, the Negroes, the railways, the corporations, and the banks. Decidedly we see a correlation, in the ups and downs of the anti-Chinese movement, between periods of prosperity in California and periods of depression.

The behavior of the Chinese aroused both curiosity and suspicion. Early Chinese immigrants were men from the laboring and farming classes in China, uneducated, unfamiliar with the customs or culture of their new land. They understood but little English; they wore strange clothes and did their hair in queues; they lived in seclusion and ate strange food. Suspicion therefore pointed at them. Their goal, to get a small competence quickly, made them overlook making friends among the local population.

The early Chinese who came to the United States were migrants by nature, working wherever there was demand for them. During the Chinese New Year or other festivals they flocked for relaxation to Chinatown in San Francisco to meet friends, relatives, and fellow countrymen. Thus the number actually present at one time made a considerable impression. Coincidence led the early Chinese to concentrate in mining areas, where there were great numbers of Spanish-Americans, British, Germans, French, Italians, and Irish, and where antiforeign tension had already risen high. With seven eighths of all Chinese living in mining areas, and in view of the fact that about 38 per cent of the California population in 1860 was foreign born and that the Chinese constituted one fourth of all those born between 1860 and 1880, it was small wonder that the presence of such a large number of Chinese attracted attention and invariably created tension.[12] After all, mining is an unpleasant and roughneck business, and workers engaged in it become unavoidably ill-tempered and even highly emotional. That there should be, between the white and the Chinese mining workers, a tension eventually culminating in bloodshed was more or less inevitable.

Their timidity, unaggressiveness, and lack of protest provoked further attacks, simply because such characteristics were interpreted by westerners as signs of weakness. The Chinese mining workers and other laborers belonged to none of the labor unions. They seldom patronized the rum shops. All these factors prompted the general feeling that the Chinese were weaklings and therefore ripe for a sort of semilegalized robbery perpetrated on them by lawless men and hoodlums.

What made the Chinese unwelcome, especially during the general business recessions in the second half of the nineteenth century, was that they were too industrious and too efficient, and that they took up whatever jobs were most available and profitable. Denying themselves many recreations, they lived so frugally that many Caucasians thought they were men with few wants. The white workers found it difficult to meet the competition of this intense and persistent type of Chinese. Bret Harte pondered:[13]

> Do I sleep; do I dream; do I wander in doubt?
> Are things what they seem or are visions about?
> Is our civilization a failure and is the Caucasian
>   played out?

Inability to speak English was perhaps the main difficulty confronting the Chinese laborers. No doubt many anxiously endeavored to improve their lot by studying English at night schools and in Sunday schools established by missionaries. In fact, the Chinese in the 1870's had already been influenced by their surroundings. Evidence to that effect can be seen by the way they mastered the use of the American concise wording of telegrams.[14]

The Chinese were not unaware of the importance and even the necessity of spreading to as many cities as possible. They knew that it would be better for them to move to the East, where sentiment was at least not against them. This movement, however, was not easily accomplished. Up to the 1860's, practically all Chinese in this country lived in the Far West; by 1870 a little over 100 had moved to the East; and in 1880 about 1,650. In California, the cities where Chinese lived increased from thirty-nine in 1860 to fifty in 1870, and fifty-two in 1880. The number of Chinese and whites in the mining centers fluctuated from decade to decade, indicating the changing fortunes of the mining kingdom. In 1870 about 12,700 Chinese were in Idaho, Montana, Nevada, and Oregon; by 1880 the number had increased to about 20,000, with an additional 4,100 in Washington and Wyoming.

Anti-Chinese Legislation, and Other Actions

The anti-Chinese movement in the West developed consistently for almost half a century. It was a typical example of race conflict and competition with white labor, with other issues secondary.[15] There were various kinds of agitation and attacks against the Chinese: the organized opposition to the Chinese by Dennis Kearney and his Workingmen's party mentioned earlier, sensationally unfavorable newspaper reports on Chinatown's antagonistic political platforms—these contributed greatly to the momentum of the anti-Chinese movement. The extensive efforts of the state of California to deal with the Chinese question were, however, chiefly by constitutional, legislative, or municipal enactment.[16] Even though practically all such laws and ordinances were eventually carried to defeat in the federal court, the agitations continued until they culminated in the final passage of the Exclusion Act.[17]

Though the causes of the anti-Chinese movement were many, in reality organized labor and political parties were the main instruments responsible for the eventual Chinese restriction. The consistent opposition of organized labor to Chinese immigration had been carried on for over fifty years.[18] The fact that employers such as railroads, transportation companies, and landholders all used Chinese workers to their advantage made the antagonism of labor all the more persistent. To labor, the big corporations and Chinese labor were both evil.

On the other hand, the position of political parties in California was unique. Except for a brief period of six years after California joined the Union, the two major parties in the state were more or less of equal strength; and on some occasions even a difference of a thousand votes would affect the outcome of the election. Under such circumstances, the politician had no choice but to follow the wishes of labor in advocating Chinese restriction. United, the parties constituted a strong force. They were actually complementing each other.

One of the first actions taken against the Chinese in California was the Foreign Miners' License Tax Law, passed originally in 1850 to collect taxes from Chileans, Mexicans, and Australians, but repealed the next year. In 1852, however, the California legislature imposed a new tax of three dollars a month on foreign miners, with employers made responsible for the payment of tax. It was increased the next year to four dollars.

Also in 1852 the California legislature passed a bill requiring masters of vessels to pay not less than $5 and not more than $10 for each of their passengers. In that year, the tax paid aggregated $433,654.94, of which the Chinese payment amounted to 45 per cent; in 1869 it was 85 per cent. This law was rendered unconstitutional by the provisions of the Fifteenth Amendment.

Two forms of capitation taxes were passed by the California legislature in 1855 and in 1862—both aimed at the Chinese. The 1855 tax required the owner of a vessel to pay $50 for each passenger who would be ineligible for citizenship. The 1862 tax—called a police tax—required the payment of $2.50 by each Mongolian over eighteen who had not paid the miners' license tax. Both taxes ultimately were declared unconstitutional by the Supreme Court of California.

Another law, passed in 1860, required Chinese engaged in fishing to pay a tax of $4.00 a month. It was repealed in 1864, after a very meager return.

During the 1850's and the 1860's two important decisions on the Chinese were made by the courts. In 1854, the state supreme court held that the laws of California intentionally excluded all people of color from giving evidence in court against white persons. This decision, no doubt, was responsible for many outrages committed against the Chinese. However, the law was practically voided by the Civil Rights Act and the Fourteenth Amendment. Soon after 1867 the federal circuit court rendered a decision declaring the Chinese ineligible for naturalization. This important decision affected the Chinese in the United States as a whole; indeed its consequences were much more serious than those of most state or municipal laws.[19]

Though many burdensome bills were at one time or another proposed and passed by the state legislature, practically all have been declared unconstitutional. Nevertheless a great variety of ordinances, especially in San Francisco, seriously hampered the Chinese in many of their occupations.

For example, the "cubic air" ordinance, passed in 1870 but obstructed by Mayor Alvord, soon became state law. It required a lodging house to provide at least 500 cubic feet of clear atmosphere for each adult person in his or her apartment. At first it was applied generally, but by 1873 it remained in force only in the Chinese quarter. Then when the Chinese landlords and lodgers jointly refused to pay their fines, the prisons soon filled with Chinese. The board of supervisors in retaliation passed three more ordinances, all aimed at the Chinese, among which was the so-called "queue ordinance," which declared that every male imprisoned in the county jail was required to have the hair of his head cut by a clipper to a uniform length of one inch from the scalp. The custom of wearing queues was observed by practically every Chinese, a fact well known.[20] But the ordinance was invalidated by the Circuit Court of the United States in the case of *Ho Ah Kow* v. *Matthew Noonan*.[21]

The "California school laws," reorganized in 1870 into one act, provided for separate schools for the whites and for other races. The law was amended in 1880 to provide segregated education for Chinese children.

An ordinance prohibiting the removal of a body—without a permit from the local health officer—from the country in which it had been buried was in fact one of the few legislative acts which won approval in the federal courts, as this act was considered within the police power of the state.

In later years the prime motive of practically all this legislation was not revenue but exclusion. Only two out of the more than twenty-five bills enacted into law remained permanent. These were acts

prohibiting the importation of prostitutes and criminals and preventing coolie slavery.

The constitutional convention that met September 30, 1878, to
frame the second constitution of California had much influence on
the whole Chinese question. The atmosphere of the entire convention
reeked with anti-Chinese feeling. A memorial was prepared to
be addressed to Congress calling attention to the reasons for opposition to Chinese immigration, citing the serious effects of the continuous influx of Chinese, and asking for federal legislation to prevent the further admittance of Chinese into this country. Article XIX
of the new constitution gave the legislature power to prohibit any
corporation from employing Mongolians; furthermore, Mongolians
were forbidden engagement on public works. Coolie trade was pronounced unlawful; a person attempting to import coolies was liable
to penalty. Chinese were subject to removal by the legislature to
regions beyond the limits of cities and towns. This constitution
eventually received ratification, but by only a small majority.

The Supreme Court of California, on the ground that the passing
of such legislation did not lie within the power of the state, declared
practically all these acts unconstitutional. Presently the California
politicians perceived that the only means of obtaining satisfaction
would be to take this whole matter of legislation to the federal Congress. They foresaw many obstacles but sensed that the political
outlook favored their cause. As a matter of fact, Mayor Bryant of
San Francisco had already made such a statement as early as 1876,
the year that marked a crisis of agitation in California:

I believe that this is the best time to go to Washington. The House is controlled by one party and the Senate by another. We are on the eve of a presidential election, and both parties are looking toward this coast for aid. If
you can get a bill before one House and have it passed, the other will not
be likely to kill it.[22]

In line with this suggestion and in order to present California's
grievances to Congress and to the executive branch in Washington, the state senate appointed a special investigating committee
to inquire into the status of Chinese immigration. Thereupon a memorial was sent to Congress. The committee also published "An
Address to the People of the United States upon the Evils of Chinese Immigration," which is a more detailed statement than that
in the memorial. As a result of the efforts made by the Californians, Congress took its first action by appointing a joint special
committee to find out "the character, extent and effect of Chinese
immigration to this country," and opened its investigation in San
Francisco in October, 1876. Subsequently, the committee presented

to Congress a report rather unfavorable to the Chinese as a whole. Among other things, it stated that the presence of the Chinese contributed to the prosperity of the capitalistic class but was distinctly deleterious to the laboring class. White laborers suffered from competition with cheap Chinese labor. The intelligence of the Chinese the committee considered inferior to that of other races, including the Negro. Coolies, it held, were men of vice; therefore, they were denied naturalization and the suffrage in order to keep republican institutions unimpaired. This report was frequently quoted in the course of the subsequent Congressional debate.

With a sense of frustration at their previous failures to regulate and to check the Chinese immigration, with the full impact of the national panic of 1873, with the strong showing of the Workingmen's party in local elections, with the passage of several anti-Chinese articles in the state's new constitution, both Democrats and Republicans determined to do something strenuous about the anti-Chinese measure. In the Forty-fifth Congress, the westerners introduced a number of bills: absolute prohibition of all contract labor; prohibition of Mongolians on public works; prohibition of Chinese naturalization and suffrage; and many resolutions requesting the federal government to open negotiations for modifying the Burlingame Treaty. At length, Congress enacted the Fifteen Passengers Bill which stated that, if the imperial Chinese government objected to modification of the existing treaty, Congress would undertake to abrogate the obnoxious stipulation of the treaty after January 1, 1880. As the title of the bill implies, it imposed the restriction that no ship should carry more than fifteen Chinese passengers. President Hayes vetoed the bill on the ground that it violated the Burlingame Treaty. He appended that the abrogation of any treaty may be justified by high necessity only, and there was no high necessity involving the existing treaty with China. He said furthermore that the treaty gave many advantages to Americans living in China, and consequently served the interests of most Americans.

The Burlingame Treaty and its Revisions

The treaty signed in 1868 between the United States and China is known as the Burlingame Treaty after Mr. Burlingame, for six years (1861-67) the United States minister to China. After he had resigned that post, he was appointed by the Chinese government as the head of a goodwill mission to the United States and to the principal European nations. The treaty was in fact proposed by the United States. It contains the following significant statement:

The United States of America and the Emperor of China cordially recognize the inherent and inalienable right of man to change his home and allegiance, and also the mutual advantage of the free immigration and emigration of their citizens and subjects, respectively, from one country to the other, for purposes of curiosity, of trade, or as permanent residents.[23]

Thus the treaty recognized among other things the right of voluntary emigration and the guarantee of mutual privileges on the part both of the Chinese and of the Americans, with the exception of naturalization, which was reserved. Mr. Burlingame and his delegation were accorded a very warm welcome everywhere in the United States. The ratification of the treaty was generally hailed as a step that would benefit the United States for many years to come.

In California, however, the labor group raised objections to the treaty. In fact, during the decade following the signing of the treaty, the anti-Chinese forces on the Coast demanded its modification or abrogation. Even after the enactment of the restrictive laws, Anson Burlingame was frequently under attack for his alleged connection with the influx of Chinese.

With the veto in 1879 of the Fifteen Passengers Bill and with the blast of Western protests, especially in California, that followed the veto, the federal government recognized the necessity of negotiating with China for a modification of the Burlingame Treaty in order to secure some discretionary control of Chinese immigration. Accordingly a commission went to China to open negotiations. The Chinese government declared itself willing to permit the United States to "regulate, limit, or suspend" for a limited time the entrance of Chinese laborers, but insisted that the United States should "not absolutely prohibit" Chinese immigration; whereas all classes other than skilled and unskilled laborers should be permitted to come and go in accordance with the most-favored-nation principles of international law. The treaty of 1880, which resulted, left the length of suspension and interpretation in the hands of Congress.

The Chinese Restriction Act of 1882

When the leaders of the anti-Chinese movement realized in 1876 that their hope of restricting the Chinese depended on federal legislation, they made every effort to bring about a national hearing. Political and economic factors were also favorable to obtaining such a hearing. The pattern of politics in California (for a number of years both parties had badly needed the labor vote) existed also on the national scene. The Pacific states held the balance of power between the two parties. This unique situation made the politicians the most effective allies of the anti-Chinese forces. Meanwhile the growing strength of the labor organizations made itself felt not just on the Pacific Coast but in the whole country. Propaganda was now more loudly voiced than formerly. The ups and downs of the economic upheavals during the last quarter of the nineteenth century caused unemployment and strikes that could easily bring labor's complaints to the attention of Congress. In this adverse situation, Chinese immigration had been increasing since 1872. During the years 1873-76, the number of Chinese on the Pacific Coast grew heavily, due to the occurrence of the large continuous influx of immigrants during the preceding twenty years. All these factors accelerated the movement for a federal statute restricting Chinese admittance.

As a consequence of the revision of the treaty of 1880, no fewer than seven exclusion bills were introduced during the first session of the Forty-seventh Congress (1881-82). After some debate and offering of amendments, Congress voted a twenty-year exclusion bill. President Arthur vetoed it as an unreasonable breach of national faith. Congress, in a bill passed April 29, 1882, reduced the period from twenty years to ten. President Arthur signed this bill; it became law on May 6, 1882.[24] Later it was extended in various forms and was effective until repealed in 1943.

The Chinese Six Companies

Since the Chinese are perhaps the most alien of aliens, being in dress, language, and means of subsistence markedly different from other immigrants, it would seem only natural that they should organize themselves in their own interest. Organization has proved comparatively easy, since 99 per cent came from Kwangtung, and these were from only 15 per cent of Kwangtung's 72 districts. Before the Six Companies, the first organization among the early immigrants was the Kong Chow Association, said to represent 10,000 out of the 12,000 Chinese in California in 1851. The Kong Chow region comprises, out of the province of Kwangtung, only six districts. Chinese from other districts soon organized their own association. Sam Yup or the Three District region was formed also in 1851, and at the close of that year a third association was organized by the name of Sze Yap or the Fourth District Association. They were composed of Cantonese from four of the six districts formerly under the control of the Kong Chow. The Chung Shan people tended to migrate to Hawaii, but the few thousands who were in California formed the Yeung Wo Association in 1852. The Kipkat (a name later changed to Yan Wo) is the fifth district association so organized. The most

numerous and the most powerful group is the Ning Yung Association or the sixth district organization, which came into being in
1854, and was derived from the Sze Yap society. Thus by 1854, the
Six-District Association, or Company, as it was generally known,
had been formed. Anti-Chinese sentiment and the enacting of anti-
Chinese laws increased the will to strengthen the Six Companies
and to make every effort toward cooperation.

The Chinese in California were virtually all members of the Six
Companies. Even though for years many withdrew membership from
one company and set up a new association (the Hop Wo district association, formed in 1862), the name of the Six Companies has never
been changed. As late as 1890, two new associations, Shew Hing
and Yin Hoi, were formed, although the latter was dissolved soon
and merged with the former. At present there are in actual existence seven companies or associations. Reverend Gibson on April 1,
1876, presented the following figures concerning the Chinese members of the Six Companies:

Ning Yung Co.	75,000
Hop Wo Co.	34,000
Kong Chow Co.	15,000
Yeung Wo Co.	12,000
Sam Yup Co.	11,000
Yan Wo Co.	4,300
	151,300

From its organization in 1854 until the end of the nineteenth century, the presidency of each of the six companies was managed by a
scholar, who usually was sent for from the various districts in
Kwangtung, since scholars were almost nonexistent among the Chinese immigrants in those days. At the beginning of the present century, however, it was the businessmen or members of the merchant
class who replaced the scholar.

It was well known that the Six Companies performed many useful
functions for their members. This group offered educational, recreational, and medical services, as well as hospitalization, to its
members. It buried the dead, it cared for their tombs, and returned
their bones to their native land; it settled the disputes among the
members; offered help in money or in other ways to those involved
in lawsuits. These were some of the more important functions it
performed. Before the establishment of diplomatic and consular
offices in America, the Six Companies served as spokesman for
the Chinese imperial government. As a board of arbitration, it

handles disputes referred by the district associations. It also, by periodic registration, keeps account of the Chinese in the western parts of the United States.

During the hysteria of the anti-Chinese movement, the Chinese Six Companies even went so far as to employ a dozen policemen to guard Chinese stores and other Chinese property inside China-town. They fought, by means of legal counsel, all anti-Chinese leg-islation pending in cities, states, and the federal government. They lodged protests, made appeals, and presented memorials to various branches of the government. The scattering of the Chinese to other parts of the United States and the existence of many other Chinese organizations may have lessened the activities of the Six Companies; nevertheless, they are still very active and remain the supreme social organization of the California Chinese.

In summary, failure of the state and federal courts to sustain all the efforts made by the anti-Chinese forces in California compelled the Californians to appeal ultimately to the federal government. Congress, at first reluctant to comply, moved nevertheless, though slowly, to meet their wishes. The Californians took full advantage of the disturbed national politics and economics of the time. The decades immediately following the Civil War were economically and politically uncertain. As Professor William A. Dunning states in his *Reconstruction, Political and Economic, 1865-77,* the United States dropped to "the nadir of national disgrace." Corruption, mis-management, speculation, monopoly, strikes, and unemployment, with consequent depression—all these contributed to nationwide frustration. California may have had its full share of these ex-periences. It is clear that the Californians considered the Chinese the chief source of their many evils; therefore any consideration of the merits of the Chinese as a whole seemed to them quite super-fluous.

Now the Chinese were not without their corporate faults, real or imaginary, that fed the fires of opposition. The motives of the oppo-sition, though varied, may be listed as social, economic, and racial. As we have shown elsewhere the Chinese lived more or less isolated from the community. Because of language and customs, and by temperament, they tended to segregate themselves; religiously, they were apart; sociologically, they were strangers in a strange land. There seemed an invisible barrier between them and others at all times and in all places. Their lower standard of living, which enabled them to accept lower wages, their willingness to perform any function, no matter how menial, their unavoidable competition with American workers—these condemned them in the sight of the powerful labor organizations and the people at large. There were also rumors of plans to use the Chinese as strikebreakers in Chicago. In 1869, the suspicions of the federal government were aroused when some unscrupulous Chinese permitted themselves to be shipped to North Adams, Massachusetts, to serve as strikebreakers at shoe factories. Yet the most significant cause of conflict was racial. Patriotic nationalists opposed them because of the seeming impossibility of assimilating them.

Thus the indigenous probity, the indefatigable industry, the underlying culture of the Chinese, together with their potential contributions toward the development of the United States, were completely ignored. The impatience of the moment precluded a sane and constructive program.

4

From Exclusion to Repeal (1882-1943)

The Chinese Restriction Act of 1882–the first exclusive racial immigration law ever passed by the federal government–brought to an end the free immigration of Chinese laborers, skilled or unskilled. A few months later Congress passed the Act of August 3, 1882, the first general immigration law. After that Congress for several decades laid particular emphasis on the subject.

The first hundred years in the history of United States immigration had been, in general, a period free from all restrictions. Seemingly America had become a refuge for the oppressed of all lands. In 1886 Miss Emma Lazarus wrote "Give me your tired, your poor" for the inscription on the Statue of Liberty. Perhaps she expressed the sentiment of the majority of the people in the United States. She probably did not quite realize that Congress, by passing the acts of 1875 and 1882 as well as the Chinese Exclusion Act four years before, had actually closed the Open-Door Policy.

The first immigration Exclusion Act, barring convicts and prostitutes, was passed on March 3, 1875.[1] The more comprehensive law of 1882 excluded other classes of aliens, such as lunatics, idiots, criminals, and persons likely to become public charges. The next restrictive legislation, in 1885, prohibited contract labor. On the petition of organized labor, Congress passed amendments in 1887 and in 1888 to make the contract-labor law much stricter. Meanwhile, because of the all-time high volume of immigration, a series of congressional investigations from 1888 to 1893 revealed that much still needed to be done to overcome the evils of unregulated immigration. Additional legislation was enacted that broadened the classification of inadmissibles.[2]

But the movement to regulate, or rather restrict immigration developed in the 1890's. In addition to the consistently vast influx, the shift since the 1890's of European immigration from northwestern to immigration from southeastern Europe had alarmed many people, including prominent intellectuals. There spread the apprehension that these newcomers from Italy, Russia, and the Austro-Hungarian Empire would unbalance the racial and cultural homogeneity characteristic of native Americans and of the so-called old immigrants. Another cause for apprehension was the bearing of immigration on nationwide depressions. More than half the years between 1870 and 1910 were lean ones. Farmers and industrial workers particularly felt the pinch. Consequently a demand for restriction became inevitable. The disappearance of free land for new settlements in the West and the crowding of immigrants within the industrial cities led many to ponder the question of whether America could absorb such numbers. The rise of organized labor, struggling to maintain and to improve standards of living, forced congressmen to recognize the ever increasing block of labor votes. These and other considerations bore heavily on policy and helped bring about the National Origins Act of 1924.

Soon after World War I, Congress worked out a bill for restricting the immigration of southeastern Europeans. The temper of the legislators dictated that some action must be taken immediately. Widespread reports were being circulated that ten million people, as a result of the postwar chaos, were already waiting to obtain visas.[3] Again the question of racial homogeneity was raised. Most supporters of restriction policies believed racial purity essential to the preservation and perpetuation of the American form of democratic government. Problems of unemployment and lack of housing alarmed the legislators still more. Fear that "alien indigestion" would replace "melting pot" led some to believe that perhaps it would be better to halt immigration altogether for a number of years. To the many restrictionists, immigration policy was purely a domestic issue.

Immigration to the United States was indeed increasing alarmingly. Only 193,418 immigrants arrived in 1864; 313,339 in 1874; in 1884, 518,592; but in 1907, 1,285,349 arrived, with striking shifts in national origins. From 1871 to 1880 the total number of immigrants from northwestern Europe, including Great Britain, Ireland, Germany, and Scandinavia, was 2,070,373 and that from southeastern Europe only 201,889. During the first decade of the twentieth century, however, the number from southeastern Europe rose to 6,225,981, compared to 1,910,035 from northwestern Europe.[4]

Determination to discourage southeastern Europeans led to the hurried enactment of the Quota Act of May 19, 1921. With a few exceptions, this restricted the immigration of any nationality to 3 per cent of those residing in the United States according to the 1910 census of the foreign-born population. Approximately 350,000 aliens were permitted to enter each year, mostly from northern and western Europe. The act expired on June 30, 1922, but was extended until June 30, 1924, to enable Congress to enact a permanent immigration law. This temporary law marked the first drastic change in the American immigration policy, in that a yearly ceiling was set for each racial and national strain.

There was considerable debate in Congress before the passing of the Quota Act of May 26, 1924. The central theme of debate emphasized biological considerations, the so-called "national origins" provision. The restrictionists, although disclaiming racial discrimination, insisted that national welfare necessitated that the Nordic race maintain its dominance in the composition of population. The antirestrictionists, on the other hand, put forth strong arguments that the adoption of the national-origin system would clearly result in discrimination between northwestern and southeastern Europe—that it would disrupt, not foster, national solidarity. The law was finally passed by large majorities: 323 to 71 in the House, 62 to 6 in the Senate, indicating general sentiment in favor of racial purity. The annual quota from any one nation was reduced to 2 per cent, and the basis was changed to that of the 1890 census.[5] Unused portions of quotas in any year could not be pooled for the use of other countries, nor might these quotas become available in subsequent years. Both features were maintained in later immigration laws. So far there is no indication that any departure from these two policies will soon be made, in spite of the fact that for years the quotas from northern and western Europe have seldom been fully utilized.[6]

After the enactment of the Chinese Exclusion Act, Congress supplemented the law by imposing bars on many Asiatic immigrants,[7] and finally, in the Act of 1924, on all Asian peoples including the Japanese. With the gates closed to all Asians and only slightly ajar to the southeastern Europeans, Congress has since the Quota Act of 1921 emphasized the restriction of immigrants, both quantitatively and qualitatively.

Period of Restriction to Absolute Exclusion, 1882-1904

The goal of the anti-Chinese movement was absolute exclusion; the passage of the first Chinese Restriction Act in 1882 did not reduce but merely dampened the heated agitation of the exclusionists. Different interpretations of the federal courts concerning the Restriction Act were bewildering. Permission for Chinese to pass through the United States at times in transit in large numbers made many Californians fear that some Chinese might remain illegally. The general impression on the Pacific Coast was that the act had many loopholes, and that the federal government had not made much effort to render the law effective or inclusive.

Presently antagonists pressed hard on Congress to amend the original legislative act so that it would, in effect, compel Chinese laborers who were already in the United States to undergo further hardships and harassments if, after temporary absence, they should seek readmission. The law was also to be stricter and more specific in relation to the Section Six Certificate. Thus the Act of July 5, 1884, was passed by Congress as an amendment.

Soon after the passage of this amendment, the Chinese empire proposed to the United States government that China establish a system of strict and absolute prohibition (with heavy penalties for violation) against its laborers coming to the United States, but that all other classes be allowed by both countries to come and go without undue molestation. A treaty was concluded in Washington, in March, 1888 by Secretary Bayard and the Chinese minister, and sent to China for ratification.

While that treaty still awaited ratification by the Chinese government the Senate was already debating a bill embodying the main points of the treaty. In addition, the Senate wished to extend the prohibition to include the returning Chinese laborers who had been temporarily absent from the United States but who nevertheless held certificates valid under the existing law. This prohibition was to apply unless they possessed lawful wives, children, or parents in the United States, or held property valued at $1,000.

The flagrant haste and impatience displayed by the Fiftieth Congress in its deliberations on Chinese matters became clear as soon as a press dispatch reported that China had refused to ratify the treaty. Both houses immediately passed a bill known as the Scott Act. President Cleveland, though he delayed for some time, signed the bill October 1, 1888. The Scott Act provided that Chinese laborers who left the United States should not be permitted to return, and that all certificates of identity issued to Chinese laborers in the United States who had left the country for temporary visits abroad– under Sections 4 and 5 of the Act of 1882–should be declared null and void. As a result of this act, at least 20,000 Chinese laborers who had left with such certificates in their possession, and about 600 persons who were already on their way back to the United States, had their permissions to return revoked. Issuance in the future of such re-entry certificates was forbidden.

With the first Chinese Restriction Act about to expire, and with the opposition to the Chinese in this country unabated, Congressman Thomas J. Geary introduced a bill for sterner enforcement than had been provided in the Scott Act. Congress passed the bill with only slight modification, and President Harrison signed it. This Geary Act of May 5, 1892, specified that the suspension of admission of Chinese laborers be extended for a ten-year period. All Chinese laborers in the United States were required to secure certificates of residence within one year; thereafter, those Chinese found without certificates were to be held liable to deportation.

Very naturally, Chinese residents resented and opposed the requirement of registration. Acting on advice from many prominent lawyers who considered the new law unconstitutional, the Chinese raised a large sum of money with which to test the case before the Supreme Court. Pending a decision, the Chinese Six Companies of San Francisco advised their countrymen to refrain from registering. The Supreme Court, however, in the famous case of *Fong Yue Ting* v. *United States* (149 U.S. 698 [1893]), upheld the Geary Act. The court held that Congress had the right to provide for the expulsion of Chinese on the mere orders of executive officers, unless the Chinese in question possessed certificates or were under the permission and sufferance of Congress. Eventually, after the passage of the McGreary Amendment of 1893 had extended the time necessary an additional six months, the Chinese complied and registered.

In 1894 the United States and China signed a treaty to the effect that the immigration of Chinese laborers was to be prohibited for ten years from the date of the exchange of ratifications. Those who had departed from the United States were to be permitted to return, provided they had wives, children, or parents, or property worth $1,000. Registration of Chinese residing in this country was to be continued. The treaty made little practical difference in the grounds already covered by existing legislation except in the repeal of the Scott Act of 1888, which had refused Chinese laborers the right to return. However, because of the biased treatment of Chinese in the United States, the Chinese government gave notice in January, 1904, of the termination of the treaty.

With the United States's annexation of the Hawaiian Islands, further Chinese immigration there was forbidden; Chinese residents were required to register and to obtain certificates of residence within one year, under the Act of July 7, 1898, and under the Act of April 30, 1900. Chinese living in Hawaii were forbidden to travel to the United States. By the same token, the exclusion laws in 1898 applied to the Philippines by military order of Major General Elwell S. Otis.

The years between 1893 and 1902 saw two presidential elections, in 1896 and in 1900; but there was no great mention of the Chinese immigration problem. Not until the expiration of the Act of 1892 became imminent did interest in exclusion of the Chinese revive. In the first session of the Fifty-seventh Congress as many as twenty bills relating to Chinese immigration were introduced. Finally a bill passed in which all laws in force with respect to the Chinese were to be re-enacted. This bill became the Act of April 29, 1902.

On notification that China had abrogated the treaty of 1894, Congress, by the Act of April 27, 1904, extended, re-enacted, and continued all the Chinese exclusion laws and without any further limitation of time the Chinese Exclusion Act became permanent. Not until thirty-nine years afterward did the Act of December 17, 1943, repeal it, fixing the Chinese quota at 105 a year.

The Quota Act of 1924

Between 1904 and 1924 Congress passed several acts dealing with the administrative problems of Chinese immigration. The Act of 1917 created the so-called "barred-zone" provision, which declared natives of the following portions of the globe inadmissible: parts of China, all of India, Burma, Siam, the Malay States, Asian Russia, part of Arabia, part of Afghanistan, most of the Polynesian Islands, and the East Indian Islands.

The Immigration Act of 1924, signed by President Coolidge on May 26, with a special clause barring all aliens ineligible for citizenship, was obviously aimed at Japanese exclusion. Agitation against Japanese had begun as early as 1900; in 1905 the Japanese and Korean Exclusion League was formed. The alarm and resentment on the Pacific Coast arose mainly because of the rapid increase of Japanese immigrants. Though there were only 2,039 in 1890, the decade 1901-10 saw 132,706 Japanese immigrants admitted.[8] When the San Francisco school board took action in segregating children of oriental races in the public schools, the Japanese government protested. President Roosevelt was forced to intervene. A gentlemen's agreement was reached in 1907 between the Japanese and American governments, whereby the Japanese agreed to withhold passports from Japanese laborers. Meanwhile the agitation against the Japanese in California was unabated, and the agitators made continual demands on Congress for exclusion.[9] The Act of 1924, providing for wholesale exclusion, applied to all Asiatics. Although the Chinese had already been excluded, this act subjected them to additional rules and regulations.

The Status of the Chinese under the Exclusion Act

After the successful passage of the various Chinese exclusion acts

culminating in that of 1904, the "Chinese problem" appeared to have
been effectually solved, and Chinese immigration, therefore, seemed
rather an academic issue. Appearances were unhappily misleading.
To be sure, the "yellow tide," as Californians in particular saw it,
had been dammed. Indeed, statistics plotted the numbers of resident
Chinese year by year steadily downward.

Year	Total	Year	Total
1850	None	1900	89,863
1860	34,933	1910	71,531
1870	63,199	1920	61,639
1880	105,465	1930	74,954
1890	107,488	1940	77,504

The increase in 1930 obviously reflects the large number of admissions of children, born abroad, of United States citizens (Chinese-
Americans)—a total of 8,894 between 1921 and 1924. Then, too,
there must have been a considerable trickling of clandestine entries,
by one subterfuge or another. Also there were those entitled to permanent residence: alien wives of Chinese-Americans, ministers,
professors, and immigrants with permits who had been temporarily
absent.

People rather generally in the West, immediately after 1882,
wondered whether the Chinese question had been dealt with properly,
possibly whether it had been dealt with at all.

At the outset, the Chinese government and even American officials
had been baffled by regulations and other administrative details about
those exempted classes, the admission of members of the families of
Chinese-Americans, desertions of Chinese crewmen, and the deportation of aliens. Often the Chinese themselves made administration
difficult; often the Immigration and Naturalization Service was to
blame in its overtechnical rigidity of enforcement. Ignorance, big-
otry, and political ambition undoubtedly sponsored many of the current administrative evils.

The ridiculous illusion of people of all times has been that a fiat-
legislative or dictatorial—would immediately produce full results.
The Act of 1882 said, "Let no more Chinese laborers come into the
United States"—but there were still thousands here. The people of
California and elsewhere simply could not comprehend why they
kept meeting Chinese competition; the law must have been incon-
clusive. Whereupon the populace proceeded to implement the law:
illogical reasoning, but the explanation of the violence that resulted.

As we have shown, long before 1882 the Chinese in the United
States had been roughly handled by the hoodlum mobs and other law-

less elements, and the tax collectors. In fact a massacre took place in Los Angeles in 1871, and riots in Denver, Colorado, in 1880, but the really large-scale violent outbreaks occurred only after 1882. It was the general feeling of the people in the West that the federal government had not done enough to enforce the Exclusion Law. The times were none too prosperous: in fact, the decade of the eighties was a turbulent one. The first great industrial conflict, the strike of 1877, made the American people realize that there was a labor problem. Under such unstable conditions, the Chinese became the scapegoats.

During those dull times lawless elements succeeded in organizing mobs and in expelling the Chinese from a number of towns along the Pacific coast. At Rock Springs, Wyoming, the Chinese were attacked in September, 1885; a score of them were injured or killed. The governor of Wyoming Territory telegraphed to the President of the United States requesting the aid of federal troops.[10] From Tacoma, Seattle,[11] and many smaller towns, Chinese were expelled, considerable property was destroyed or lost, and some of the Chinese quarters were burned. In the early part of 1886 outrages were committed at Oregon City and Albina, Oregon, where Chinese were ordered out of their dwellings and forced to move on. In August, 1886, an outrage was perpetrated on the Chinese at the mines on Douglas Island in the vicinity of Juneau, Alaska Territory. About a hundred Chinese were attacked and driven to the sea, put on a small schooner, and set adrift.

One should not infer that brutality toward the Chinese in the second half of the nineteenth century represented the attitude of the average Westerner. Many private citizens and state officers came to the rescue of the hard-pressed Chinese, amid protests and expressions of disgust from the lawless elements. According to the Reverend Otis Gibson, a Chinese Protective Society was organized in San Francisco by private citizens whose object was to do what the regular police could not or would not do to secure the arrest and punishment of those who assaulted the Chinese. The society operated for about one year.[12] In Oregon City some 1,500 respectable citizens in 1886 dedicated themselves to uphold law and order. Without them there would certainly have been riot and bloodshed. On February 8, 1886, at Seattle, the eighty members of the Home Guards, George Kinnear, captain, defied the mob during the anti-Chinese riots. These guards escorted the Chinese from the dock to the courthouse, pursuant to a writ of habeas corpus issued by Judge Green, and at the conclusion of the court proceedings escorted them back to the dock.[13] Even amid the ill will against Chinese, the majority of the people were probably opposed to any illegal action. The Methodist Episcopal

Ministers' Association of Seattle, on November 12, passed a resolution denouncing the anti-Chinese movement as "cruel, brutal, un-American and un-Christian."[14]

Individual bravery was also witnessed from time to time. Erskine Ross, later to become a federal judge, exhibited superb courage during the anti-Chinese riots in Los Angeles in 1871. His cousin, W. A. Thom, Jr., tells the story.

> The Chinese quarter was burning. A mob of Americans was in possession, destroying and killing, when suddenly Erskine Ross stood alone before them eyes blazing, jaw set, and revolver in hand. I did not see this myself, but those who did tell me it was the most magnificent exhibition of personal courage ever witnessed. There were no more murders or incendiary acts that night. Ross's determination drew kindred spirits to him, and the mob was dispersed.[15]

When eight or ten Chinese girls from the asylum of the Methodist Mission, accompanied by three American women, were rudely assaulted by a large crowd of lawless men within a few blocks of the city hall, they were compelled to seek refuge in the house of an Irishwoman, who not only sheltered them without hesitation, but valiantly went out to try to disperse the mob.[16] The only man who asserted himself in California's second constitutional convention (1878) was C. V. Stuart, a Sonoma County farmer, who boldly defended Chinese immigration against great odds.[17] Many such courageous actions are not to be interpreted as pro-Chinese, or as actions taken in favor of Chinese immigration; they were manifestations of a belief in justice.

Though some clergymen have opposed unrestricted Chinese immigration, several American churches have undertaken missionary work among the Chinese on the coast, and many religious groups have been against the harsh actions taken by the Californians. Concurring with these religious groups have been numerous persons interested in trade with China, as well as those who believed in the ideal of America as a refuge for the oppressed of all nations. On the other hand, the repeated criticisms aimed at the court for permitting the use of the writ of habeas corpus to apply to the landing of Chinese immigrants tend to show that the real issue of Chinese immigration is racial. Thus Senator Oliver P. Morton of Indiana, in issuing his minority report in connection with the joint special committee appointed to visit the coast to determine the "character, extent, and effect of Chinese immigration into this country," stated that if the Chinese in California had been white people, being in all other respects what they are, the complaints and the warfare instituted against them would not to any considerable extent have existed.[18]

The imperial government, to be sure, did protest regularly all acts of injustice and violence committed, but seldom if ever took a strong stand. Diplomats spoke softly about the need of respecting treaty rights, or explained that great injustice had been done to the Chinese immigrants by the massacres or other acts of violence. To ask for indemnity was all the Chinese ministers in Washington cared to do. When their protests met with rebuffs or received evasive replies from the State Department, the matter was usually dropped. Except for the forceful protests made by Minister Wu Ting-fang from time to time, and a Chinese boycott against American goods in 1905 (which made some impression on the American public), the dissatisfaction of the Chinese with the treatment of their immigrants in the United States was not much publicized in China. That the Manchu dynasty was ignorant, weak, inefficient, and lacking in unified national support few will deny. Compared with Japanese tactics of prolonged negotiations with American authorities on all matters pertaining to Japanese in the United States, Chinese diplomacy was certainly a fiasco.

During most of this period, the lives of average Chinese in the United States were difficult and irregular. No matter how well educated they were, in their living quarters they were confined to a crowded Chinatown. In Oregon, Washington, and California, practically all residential districts were restricted to Caucasians. College training in engineering or other technical subjects did not guarantee decent positions to Chinese. If one should go out, dressed casually for a walk, or go to a club, or even to a church, he was liable to be picked up by the immigration officers on suspicion of illegal residence. For many years officials made a practice of picking up persons in the street or in public places on the suspicion that they were aliens illegally in this country. Such arrests were reported to be very common, especially in the late 1920's.[19] It was up to the Chinese to prove that he was not an illegal alien or even an illegal citizen. But proof is sometimes difficult and takes time. Eventually he would solve his difficulty, but only after suffering much trouble and anxiety.

The irregular life encouraged by the scarcity of Chinese women, both before and after the enactment of the Chinese Exclusion Act,[20] was perhaps responsible for opium smoking, gambling, and most of of all the frequenting of houses of prostitution. New York's Chinatown was described by Jacob A. Riis as composed of a bunch of homeless strangers. He suggested that the government should encourage the Chinese to bring in their wives.[21] The racial prejudice left practically no chance of intermarriage between Chinese and whites, though Chinese have frequently intermarried with natives of Hawaii, of Latin America, and of countries in Southeast Asia and in the Far East.

As late as the 1890's, if a Chinese had a family and had reared children, he would have difficulty in sending his children to the grade school of his choice. The Commodore Stockton School was virtually the only school of elementary grade in San Francisco to which Chinese children could go. If he or a member of his family should happen to be sick, he would have trouble in being admitted to the city and county hospital even though, like many other immigrants, he had paid a hospital tax on arrival at the port. The ground for his nonadmittance was simply that there was no bed available.[22] At one time the only place he could count upon for admission was the pesthouse. Outside Chinatown he had to use his discretion as to whether to try to dine in a restaurant and to have a haircut in one of the barber shops; the chances were that he would be rejected. It would be helpful for him to obtain advance information regarding admission to a public tennis court or a beach house.

Yet the Chinese immigrants carried on under such adverse conditions. They were well informed on current events; they sent their children to school if possible. Chinese newspapers existed in San Francisco, New York, and Honolulu because they were in demand. The democratic form of government in the United States must have made a deep impression on the Chinese immigrants, for money to finance and support the revolutionary leader, Dr. Sun Yat-sen, and his activity in overthrowing the Manchu dynasty was pledged enthusiastically by the Chinese in the United States along with those in Canada, Europe, Southeast Asia, and Latin America.

One of the few things that were universally praised by Californians was the high ethical standard of the Chinese in faithfully fulfilling their contracts and in meeting other obligations. Their commercial honor was always acknowledged. The personal word or bond of the Chinese merchants was readily accepted by American bankers, businessmen, lawyers, and even by customs officials. The Chinese had the reputation of promptly paying their taxes, rents, and debts.

The Geary Act of 1892 empowered the Treasury Department to make and interpret regulations; the strictness of interpretation rendered admission of Chinese unduly troublesome and difficult. From both the American and Chinese press came one of the best-known and severest criticisms, occasioned by the harsh treatment of the Chinese exhibitors at the Louisiana Purchase Exposition in 1904. At the invitation of the United States, through special representatives sent to China, the emperor had instructed the viceroys of all provinces to prepare for and to participate in the exposition. As a result of that mandate, unique in those days, many merchants came to the United States with exhibits; but, some of them were detained hopelessly in the shed at San Francisco, perforce returning to China humiliated. The American press thereupon attacked the immigration authorities for flagrant breach of hospitality and for restraint of trade with China; and the Chinese press did not withhold adverse comment.

Since the exclusion laws hastily considered and enacted had been vague, immigration officers acknowledged the difficulty of their enforcement. The inadequate appropriations encouraged officials to be hasty and superficial. Also, the cunning and fraud to which some desperate Chinese resorted tempted immigration officers to be overzealous in dealing with honest Chinese who had entirely legal cases. Criticism of the Treasury Department and of the Department of Immigration was so extensive and severe that the commissioner-general of immigration found he had to defend himself by publishing a "Compilation of Facts Concerning the Enforcement of the Chinese Exclusion Laws in May, 1906." Though much was presented in defense, and blame for blocking the enforcement thrown on other persons, it is evident that from time to time a variety of restrictions had been eliminated. We may mention the abrogation of all distinction between the immigrant and the Chinese inspector. In addition, a uniform method of arresting and deporting those found unlawfully in the United States, whether of the Chinese or of other races, was adopted. All restrictions on the departure and return of registered Chinese laborers were to be removed, so that such persons might leave and return merely upon the establishment of identity. A few years later, the commissioner-general of immigration made remark in his annual report that "the law is unduly harsh at points where rigidity does no good, but much harm."[23]

An unfortunate effect of the Chinese Exclusion Act was the invitation it seemed to extend to smuggling and to illegal entries of all sorts. There were Chinese who claimed citizenship, either by birth in the United States or as a son or daughter born abroad of a citizen father. Seamen might desert their ships or change places with other Chinese who were going home. Chinese laborers might pose as students, or as sons of treaty traders, in order to gain admission. In fact the charge of fraudulent importation and entry of Chinese into the United States was brought forward for Congressional investigation no later than the Forty-ninth Congress, first session (1885-86). Time and again this question was raised. Ways and means were discussed to prevent the smuggling of Chinese. It was reported that Chinese laborers arrived with certificates purchased at Hong Kong from rightful possessors who had decided to remain permanently in China. Others obtained certificates from lawful holders who had died at home. It is no exaggeration to say that the Exclusion Act actually helped thousands of Chinese, Americans, and Europeans to make millions of dollars by taking up smuggling as a regular and profitable business.

Owing largely to the Exclusion Act of 1904, but based also on cumulative grievances, a boycott against American products was inaugurated in China for the first time in its history.[24] Though not as effective as its sponsors had hoped and without influence on American immigration policy, it did focus public attention on immigration. The Chinese benefited somewhat, for the authorities felt forced to correct certain abuses. It has been asserted that Minister Wu Ting-fang, who had done more than anyone else to present China's case forcibly, had been actually the "personality behind the boycott."[25]

Chinese Immigration under the Exclusion Act

The Immigration Service has made it known that between 1883 and 1898, 22,134 immigrants from China were admitted;[26] in the years 1899 to 1910, 22,590; and from 1911 to 1920, 19,263. In the next four years (1921-24) admissions jumped to an average of about 4,300 a year. The strong influx was evidently an anticipation of the passage of the 1924 National Origins Act, following the passage of the temporary act of 1921. During these four years all classes of Chinese seeking admission to the United States increased conspicuously. After the passage of the 1924 Act, there was a general decline; from

TABLE 16

CHINESE IMMGRANTS ADMITTED TO THE UNITED STATES, 1883-1907

Year	Number	Year	Number
1883	8,031	1899	1,638
1884	279	1900	1,250
1885	22		
1886	40	1883-1900	25,022
1887	10		
1888	26	1901	2,452
1889	118	1902	1,631
1890	1,716	1903	2,192
1891	2,836	1904	4,327**
1892	*	1905	1,971
1893	472	1906	1,485
1894	1,170	1907	770
1895	539		
1896	1,441	1901-7	14,828
1897	3,363		
1898	2,071	TOTAL	39,850

*Figures included in all other countries.
**The figure of 4,327 included 306 debarred and returned; therefore the correct number should be 4,021.

TABLE 17

CHINESE IMMIGRANTS ADMITTED AND CHINESE EMIGRANTS DEPARTED
1908-43

Year	Number Admitted	Number Departed	Gain or Loss
1908	1,263	3,898	− 2,635
1909	1,841	3,397	− 1,556
1910	1,770	2,383	− 613
1908-10	4,874	9,678	− 4,804
1911	1,307	2,716	− 1,409
1912	1,608	2,549	− 941
1913	2,022	2,250	− 228
1914	2,354	2,059	+ 295
1915	2,469	1,959	+ 510
1916	2,239	2,148	+ 91
1917	1,843	1,799	+ 44
1918	1,576	2,239	− 663
1919	1,697	2,062	− 365
1920	2,148	2,961	− 813
1911-20	19,263	22,742	− 3,479
1921	4,017	5,253	− 1,236
1922	4,465	6,146	− 1,681
1923	4,074	3,788	+ 286
1924	4,670	3,736	+ 934
1925	1,721	3,263	− 1,542
1926	1,375	2,873	− 1,498
1927	1,051	4,117	− 3,066
1928	931	4,300	− 3,369
1929	1,071	3,496	− 2,425
1930	970	3,404	− 2,434
1921-30	24,345	40,376	− 16,031
1931	748	3,333	− 2,585
1932*	545	3,311	− 2,766
1933	353	†	†
1934	187	2,372	− 2,185
1935	229	2,031	− 1,802
1936	273	1,648	− 1,375
1937	293	1,808	− 1,515
1938	613	672	− 59
1939	642	524	+ 118
1940	106	941	− 835
1931-40	3,989	16,640	− 13,004
1941	73	735	− 662
1942	13	124	− 111
1943	4	4	0
1941-43	90	863	− 773
TOTAL	52,561	90,299	− 38,091

*1932 to 1939, figures on immigration from China only.
†Not available, causing discrepancy in totals.
Source: Annual Report, 1905, 1928, 1929-43.

1925 to 1930 the total admittance was 7,119. The next decade's admittance was even smaller, averaging only 398 a year. Tables 16 and 17 show the number of Chinese immigrants who were admitted to and the number who left the United States between 1883 and 1943.

To completely comprehend the status of the immigration from any country we need similar notice of departure or emigration of those previously admitted. Unfortunately, before 1908 the number of alien departures was not officially recorded; our study of the Chinese who left the United States to return to China, therefore, is limited to 1908-43. The figures reveal that the number of Chinese who left was larger by 37,738 than the number of immigrants admitted. According to the Immigration Service, these thirty-six years of Chinese immigration witnessed the admission of 52,561 compared with 90,299 departing for China. That is, for each fifty-two Chinese admitted to the United States between 1908 and 1943, ninety Chinese departed. The effect of the Exclusion Act is perceptible. In fact, only seven years out of thirty-six showed admissions slightly increasing over departures. Six of these years occurred between 1914 and 1924, and only one, 1939, after that decade.

Several factors were responsible for this trend toward more departures. The Exclusion Act, together with additional restrictions made by the Quota Act of 1924, had definitely discouraged the Chinese from staying permanently. The scarcity of wives among the Chinese-Americans who came each year is partly explained by the fact that Chinese immigrants could no longer make plans for a permanent stay. The ban in the 1924 Act against admitting Chinese wives of American citizens fortified the belief that the United States wished to exclude the Chinese as far as possible, despite the fact that wives of American citizens of European origin had been accorded nonquota status. Moreover, many second- or third-generation Chinese, after having completed their college education in this country, had to return to China to find suitable positions, even though they were deficient in Chinese background. The severe depression that began in 1929 deprived many Chinese of the opportunity to make a decent living in this country. Many of these left the United States permanently.

Fallacies in the Official Statistics on Chinese Immigration
In reviewing the statistics on the immigration from China between 1883 and 1943, we found a total of 103,006.[27] Since Chinese immigration except for permanent residence was virtually stopped during the period, any thoughtful student would wonder how it was possible that so many immigrants from China had nevertheless been admitted.[28] Unfortunately, the Immigration Service has not revealed

how it compiled its records of immigrants. One notices that from 1820 to 1867 the figures on immigrants represent *alien passengers arrived* and from 1868 to 1891 and 1895 to 1897 inclusive, *immigrant aliens arrived*. There is little doubt that those alien passengers arrived can in no sense be considered entirely as immigrants, nor that the immigrant aliens arrived were always aliens admitted. Thus the statistical figures released inaccurately represented the facts. Indeed, separate figures on races and peoples did not begin until 1899. Data for the years prior to 1906 relate to countries of their origin, and thereafter to the countries of their last permanent residence. The lack of official records on emigration until 1908 has undoubtedly caused misrepresentation. To sum it up: without figures on emigration, a student of immigration can only quote the figures for those admitted from a particular country, while he is unable to point out the number of those who have left the United States from time to time.

A misleading factor, furthermore, in the official statistics released was the inclusion of the returning resident aliens and students as immigrants.[29] We have no way of knowing when this practice was adopted, although we do know that the policy has since been changed and the returning resident aliens and students are now counted as nonimmigrants. At any rate, it is important to take that practice into consideration when evaluating the statistics of Chinese immigration during the period of restriction and exclusion.

Owing to the chaotic instability under the Manchu regime during the second half of the nineteenth century, many young Chinese became anxious to study in Japan, Europe, and in the United States. The movement begun then has been continuous and persistent for many years. Chinese students have, in fact, comprised a very important percentage of foreign students enrolled in the institutions of higher learning in this country. From 1925 to 1943 inclusive, out of 31,112 foreign students who studied in the United States, there were 4,659 Chinese or 15 per cent of the total, more students than from any other country.[30] The Immigration Service's inclusion of students as nonquota immigrants, even though for statistical purpose only, is nevertheless deceptive to the general public.[31]

Evidence is plentiful that Chinese immigrants returned to China frequently for home visits or on business. As a matter of fact, out of 22,590 Chinese immigrants admitted from 1899 to 1910, 13,791 or 61 per cent, had been in the United States previously.[32] In other words, almost all of these 13,791 were returning immigrants. It is probably correct to state that the inclusion of returning resident aliens and, to a lesser extent, students as immigrants exaggerated the whole conception of alien immigration to the United States. The exceptionally large number of immigrants from countries of southern and eastern Europe admitted to this country since the 1890's has been frequently quoted and criticized as a great influx. No one can deny that the number quoted is large, but it is certainly greater than the actual number of new immigrants. Take Italy, for example: more than two million immigrants were admitted between 1899 and 1910, and an additional million or more in the following decade.[33] A search of the available statistics from 1899 to 1910 showed that 14 per cent, or 319,246 Italians had been in the United States previously.[34] Between 1908-10, 549,098 Italians were admitted while 308,978 returned to Italy in those years. This supports the conclusion that many Italians left the United States permanently, while others perhaps planned to return there shortly.[35] It would probably be more desirable to quote statistics on immigration on net basis by subtracting the alien emigration instead of referring to the gross number of immigrants admitted.[36] We know that the figures for emigration were not officially recorded until 1908. Unfortunately the decade 1901 to 1910 was *ipso facto* the period of the greatest influx from southern and eastern Europe. For many years the tide of immigration to the United States has been largely composed of persons who had been in this country once or many times before, and whose entrance and departure were conditioned by the demand for laborers here. The Mexicans, or "wetbacks," come and go because of the seasonal demand for labor. To a lesser extent this has been also true of the movement from Canada, Cuba, and the West Indies.

European immigrants usually apply for citizenship as soon as they legally may. Not so the Chinese, since they were denied the right of naturalization. Their need to visit their homeland was more frequent and necessary than that of European immigrants because, as we have noticed, many Chinese failed to bring their wives to this country. As a result, the official statistics on Chinese immigration appeared surprisingly large.

Another misleading factor: the official figure on the admission of immigrants from China relates to nationals born, or having had their last permanent residence, in China, so that some non-Chinese were included. For example, between 1901 and 1910 the figures relating to China were 20,605; whereas the Chinese immigrants actually admitted were only 19,702, a difference of 903 non-Chinese.[37]

A Suggested List of the Number of Chinese
Immigrants Admitted, 1883-1943.

Although the Chinese restriction and exclusion acts stated that all Chinese were inadmissible, exceptions were made of governmental

officials, visitors, students, teachers, ministers, and treaty traders. Chinese wives of United States citizens were also rendered
admissible, except between 1924 and 1930. Since Chinese governmental officials, visitors, and students are, of course, on temporary visas only, it is proper that Chinese immigrants should be
limited to those Chinese who came to the United States for permanent
residence. Before attempting to compile that proposed list, we shall
review briefly each category of Chinese who might be qualified.
Attention must be directed, however, to a special group of "children
of United States citizens," who were entitled to citizen status; the
number of these seeking admission was large and warrants our
separate consideration.

Children of United States Citizens (Chinese-Americans)

The law in effect from February 10, 1855, until May 24, 1934,
inclusive, stipulated that a child born abroad of a father who was
a citizen of the United States when he was born, acquired United
States citizenship at birth, if the father had resided in the United
States prior to the birth. Or, if the child was born after May 24,
1934, ten years prior residence in the United States by the father
was required.[38] In other words, Chinese born in the United States
are citizens, and therefore may confer citizenship on a child born
abroad of an alien Chinese wife. To be sure, the child was required
to arrive in the United States by a stated time in order to claim
citizenship.

The Immigration Service has not been very consistent in its *Annual Report* in the statistics on "Children of United States Citizens."
In 1925, presumably because of the initial administrative confusion
on the interpretation of the 1924 Act, the immigration officials considered alien Chinese minor children of American citizens inadmissible.[39] On the other hand, there were a number of Chinese who
were alleged to be sons or daughters of Chinese-Americans, whose
citizenship was judicially and administratively determined at the
port of entry. The figures released on such children were under
the category of "United States Citizens," which included also those
Chinese-Americans who returned to the United States from a temporary stay abroad.[40]

Wives of United States Citizens

The alien Chinese wife of a United States citizen was admissible
under the Chinese Exclusion Act; the Act of 1924, however, made
her inadmissible because she was an alien ineligible for citizenship.
The surprising and illogical exclusion of Chinese wives of American
citizens was a practice contrary to the many humane provisions set
forth in the Act of 1924, provisions designed to fortify family unity

and to prevent possible family separations.[41] When first enacted, Section 4 (a) of the act rendered admissible as nonquota immigrants alien wives of United States citizens then residing in the United States. By amendment in 1928, in addition it rendered alien husbands eligible to nonquota status, only if the marriage had occurred before June 1, 1928; and by the Act of July 11, 1932, the cutting-off date was extended to July 1, 1932. The cutting-off date of January 1, 1948, was inserted by the Act of May 19, 1948.

These particular provisions, nevertheless, did not include the Chinese, and no provision was made until June, 1930, for Chinese wives. To make the contrast all the more inhumane, there was—in the Act of June 13, 1930—no provision for the admission of Chinese alien wives married on or after May 26, 1924, and no provision at all for Chinese husbands of United States citizens. The number of Chinese wives of United States citizens admitted has never been large; between 1906 and 1924 the average was 150 a year; from 1931 to 1941 it was only about 60 a year. The law allowed no admissions between 1925 and 1930.

Treaty Traders or Merchants

Until the Act of 1924 treaty traders did not need to maintain status; stay in the United States was permissible as long as desired. Between July 1, 1924, and the amendment of the law on July 6, 1932, the treaty trader might maintain his status, even though he conducted domestic business only. The wife and minor children of the merchant were entitled to come to the United States, either accompanying him or coming afterward. This question was definitely settled in 1900 by a decision made by the Supreme Court.[42] In 1925 the Supreme Court again held that the Chinese wives and minor children of Chinese merchants were admissible under the treaty of 1880, whether they had arrived before or after the 1924 Act.[43] The judicial decision has explicitly placed the treaty trader in a better position than that of alien wives of Chinese-American citizens.[44]

The 1924 Act, however, provided that the treaty trader was no longer given permanent residence but might be subject to deportation if he failed to maintain his status. Since then the number admitted has been considerably fewer, averaging about 210 a year between 1929 and 1943.[45] The necessity of maintaining the status of an international trader, requiring a substantial volume of business between the United States and China, had probably discouraged many from seeking admission. However, the number of aliens (including Chinese) who were deported for failing to maintain status as treaty traders was indeed small: the total number of deportations for all countries combined, between 1930 and 1943, was only twenty-five.[46]

Ministers, Teachers, and Their Families

Another group was given preferential treatment under the Chinese Exclusion Act: teachers and ministers were free to abandon their professions and to take up other occupations after their arrival. Under the Act of 1924 they were admitted as nonquota immigrants and permanent residents. The same privilege also applied to such a person's wife and his minor children under eighteen years of age. It must be noted that the Chinese teacher or minister had shown no disposition to take advantage of the privilege accorded to him; there were only 443 teachers (this number includes their families) admitted to the United States between 1906 and 1924. In the decade following the Act of 1924, only eighty-three (including their families) teachers and ministers came. Perhaps because they were few in number, not many complaints were voiced by the Immigration Service.

There were other classes of Chinese seeking admission or readmission to the United States.[47] The returning laborers and those claiming to be American citizens by native-born parents were of constant concern to the immigration officers. A Chinese-American returning to the United States who claimed the status of an American citizen had to bear the burden of proof that he had actually been born in the United States, or was the child of an American citizen. Returning laborers had also to submit evidence to prove that they were bona fide holders of returning certificates.[48]

This review of the status of Chinese immigrants under the Exclusion Act indicates that a more realistic list of the Chinese immigrants admitted between 1883 and 1943 should include only nonquota immigrants admitted for permanent residence, namely, Chinese wives of United States citizens, ministers, teachers, treaty traders (before 1924), and their unmarried children. The official statistics on such nonquota immigrants run consecutively from 1904 to 1940. Between 1941 and 1943 Chinese immigrants admitted numbered only ninety. Our attention, therefore, should be centered on the time from the enactment of the Restriction Act until 1903. It is concerning this period that the Immigration Service is unable to give much information. Between 1883 and 1889 the service listed 8,526 Chinese arrived. Since many of them were nonimmigrants, it seems proper to use the statistics on Chinese immigrants as submitted by the secretary of the treasury to the Congress: only 1,509.[49] We do not seem to be able to get any statistics on Chinese admitted between 1890 and 1896, except those figures supplied by the Immigration Service: 8,174 Chinese. The figures for these six years (1892 not available) are probably much too high, as they include all passengers or immigrant aliens arriving. In the absence of any other figures,

we shall leave the matter as it stands. However, the Immigration
Service was able to offer for the period between 1897 and 1903,
statistics on Chinese immigrants who had been in the United States
previously. The number of such residents each year is deducted
from the number of Chinese immigrants admitted. The proposed
list of Chinese immigrants admitted between 1883 and 1943 is as
shown in Tables 18 and 19.[50]

TABLE 18

A PROPOSED LIST OF CHINESE IMMIGRANTS ARRIVED
IN THE UNITED STATES, 1883-1903

Year	Number	Year	Number
1883	381	1895	539
1884	84	1896	1,441
1885	57	1897	347
1886	8	1898	12
1887	28	1899	209
1888	1	1900	39
1889	950		
1890	1,716	1891-1900	7,065
		1901	213
1883-90	3,225	1902	83
		1903	70
1891	2,836		
1892	*	1901-3	366
1893	472		
1894	1,170	TOTAL	10,656

*Not available.

Compilation shows that Chinese immigrants admitted during the
exclusion period numbered 35,236, or about 38 per cent of the 92,411
recorded. From 1904 to 1943, when the Immigration Service was
able to supply more details on Chinese immigrants accorded the
status of permanent residence, the number of Chinese immigrants
under our estimates would be 24,580, or about 40 per cent of the
official 61,114. On the other hand, the official records from 1890
to 1896 have been considered high; accordingly, if these figures are
deducted, we obtain a ratio of only 32 per cent of Chinese immigrants
admitted: 84,237 (1883-89; 1897-1943), as officially announced. In
other words, only 32 to 40 per cent were new immigrants; the remainder were either returning residents, students, or aliens in
improper categories. The result of our computation seems to agree
more or less with the immigration statistics during the fiscal years
between 1899 and 1910, that of the 22,590 Chinese immigrants admitted, 13,791, or 61 per cent, had been in the United States. It is
true that, statistically speaking, this 61 per cent is by no means a
good sampling of the whole period of sixty-one years, since the
ratio shown was consecutive for twelve years, and hence did not

TABLE 19

A PROPOSED LIST OF CHINESE IMMIGRANTS ADMITTED
TO THE UNITED STATES, 1904-43

Year	Wives of U.S. Citizens	Treaty Traders	Members of Merchants' Families	Teachers	Professors, Ministers, and Their Families	Total
1904	0	0	216	0	0	216
1905	0	279	159	0	0	438
1906	7	121	391	12	0	531
1907	23	112	516	6	0	657
1908	37	216	806	23	0	1,082
1909	98	292	1,242	14	0	1,646
1910	110	228	1,029	24	0	1,391
1904-10	275	1,248	4,359	79	0	5,961
1911	80	199	559	32	0	870
1912	88	170	558	33	0	849
1913	126	105	738	33	0	1,002
1914	122	180	807	17	0	1,126
1915	106	238	746	15	0	1,105
1916	108	242	741	28	0	1,119
1917	110	180	694	19	0	1,003
1918	132	129	390	17	0	668
1919	91	138	305	16	0	550
1920	141	105	644	28	0	918
1911-20	1,104	1,686	6,182	238	0	9,210
1921	290	287	1,316	33	0	1,926
1922	396	649	1,360	26	0	2,431
1923	387	497	1,377	28	0	2,289
1924	396	452	1,096	39	0	1,983
1925	0	0	0	0	2	2
1926	0	0	0	0	18	18
1927	0	0	0	0	3	3
1928	0	0	0	0	8	8
1929	0	0	0	5	9	14
1930	0	0	0	6	6	12
1921-30	1,469	1,885	5,149	137	46	8,686
1931	19	0	0	3	8	30
1932	99	0	0	0	10	109
1933	43	0	0	0	1	44
1934	19	0	0	1	3	23
1935	41	0	0	0	0	41
1936	38	0	0	0	0	38
1937	55	0	0	0	0	55
1938	82	0	0	0	0	82
1939	112	0	0	0	0	112
1940	99	0	0	0	0	99
1931-40	607	0	0	4	22	633
1941						73
1942						13
1943						4
1941-43						90
TOTAL						24,580

represent every decade under review. Nevertheless, our supposition that only 32 to 40 per cent of Chinese were actually admitted as immigrants may not be wide of the mark. [51]

When the Immigration Service counted the returning residents as immigrants, we presume that they figured all departing Chinese as emigrants, regardless of the fact that a number of them would eventually come back as returning residents. There seems to have been scanty information released annually as to how many emigrants were actually armed with legal certificates permitting them to return. All we can say is that the Exclusion Act had definitely stopped many Chinese who would otherwise have come to this country. The net loss of Chinese immigrants has been confirmed by the gradual decline of the Chinese in the United States, especially between 1890 and 1930. [52]

All in all, during the period of free immigration and until nearly the end of the nineteenth century, all official figures on Chinese immigration can at best be considered as those of Chinese immigrant arrivals in the United States, including a small number of non-Chinese born in China. As a matter of fact, as early as 1896 the Immigration Service had already stated: "Some aliens come and go so often that old officials at the Immigration Station recognized them. They are each year listed as new arrivals."[53]

Chinese Debarred and Deported

Congress has enacted laws to debar excludable aliens and to deport those who have gained admittance illegally. The Supreme Court has always upheld the unequivocal authority of Congress to debar, as well as to deport, aliens whenever it so provides by law. With the exception of the exempt classes, all Chinese who entered the United States illegally were subject to exclusion and deportation under the Exclusion Act. The number of Chinese debarred from entry between 1892 and 1925 under the provisions of the Chinese Exclusion Act was 6,327. No other races, however, when the act was first passed, were subject to such treatment. [54] In addition, the Chinese, along with other races, were subject to the provisions of the general immigration laws.

On the other hand, deportations were executed both by the immigration officers and the United States marshal. Statistics on deportation made by the immigration officers were first compiled by the Immigration Service in 1915, and from that year until the repeal of the Exclusion Act, 2,962 Chinese were deported. [55] The number of deportations made by the United States marshal was 9,057 between 1892 and 1928. [56]

As time went on, the number of Chinese debarred from entering the United States declined; for example, in the ten years (1935 to 1944) before the repeal of the Chinese Exclusion Act, only 894 Chinese were refused entry; whereas during the same period 9,867 Frenchmen and 8,525 Englishmen were refused. Between 1942 and 1944 only twenty-four Chinese were debarred.[57]

Aliens who entered the United States without proper documents, or with none at all, invariably represented the largest percentage of exclusion (the Chinese were certainly no exception). Those who remained longer than authorized, plus criminals, mental or physical defectives, and those previously deported or excluded, comprised about 35 per cent of the total deportations (1908-43). After the enactment of the May 26, 1922, Act, violators of narcotic laws were subject to deportation and summarily deported. Mexicans were the leading violators, followed by Chinese and Italians.[58]

From 1924 to 1944, 92,581 Mexicans, or 42.8 per cent of all deportations, left the United States.[59] Canadians deported reached 37,263, or 17 per cent of the total. Those deported to Italy numbered 10,208, or 4.7 per cent, while the number deported to China was 8,388, or about 4 per cent. The number of Chinese deportees, moreover, has been gradually reduced, especially since 1934. (A great number of the Chinese refugees who were deported had entered from Mexico along the Arizona border; 4,953 of these deportations were made between 1932 and 1933).

The Repeal of the Chinese Exclusion Act

Among many factors underlying the movement for the repeal of the Chinese Exclusion Act, the most crucial is, of course, the heroic resistance of the Chinese against the Japanese onslaught in the Sino-Japanese War which began in 1937. Chinese participation in World War II aroused a vast pro-Chinese sentiment in the United States.

In spite of the anti-Chinese feeling that resulted in the Chinese Exclusion Act, the growth in American public opinion of sympathy for and interest in China has been manifest, especially since the beginning of the twentieth century. Academic and cultural interests in Chinese philosophy, history, folklore, art, language, and literature had been growing rapidly. A number of American colleges established Chinese affiliates for the pursuance of the academic study of Chinese subjects. Farsighted missionaries, with strong support, established Christian colleges in various parts of China. Medical schools, nurses' training schools, and high schools were founded. The number of Chinese studying in the United States also increased significantly. Led by Yung Wing, the first Chinese ever to be graduated from an American college (Yale, 1854), more than a hundred students, forming an *ad hoc* group, came to carry on studies in the United States, beginning in 1874. Assisted by the voluntary remission to the Chinese of the Boxer indemnity, Chinese scholarship students, supported by funds from the Chinese government, and private students poured into American institutions of higher learning, forming in many decades one of the largest contingents of foreign students in the United States. A number of American businessmen, travelers, and diplomats have also shown respect for Chinese culture and Chinese potentialities. The traditional friendly policy toward China, strengthened by the Open-Door Policy and by the Stimson Doctrine, led the federal government, after tremendous pressure had been brought to bear on Congress, to support the repeal of the Chinese Exclusion Act.

On the other hand, with the enactment of the permanent Exclusion Act, western and southern states, which had always followed the policy of California toward the Chinese, lost interest in Chinese exclusion as California lost interest. Since 1904 neither the Republican nor the Democratic party has had any Chinese plank in its platform. California has emerged with the second largest population among the states, increasing to such an extent that in 1950 the Chinese were a mere 0.4 per cent of the total. Meanwhile, their changing occupations and gradual dispersal to other regions of the United States have reduced their conspicuity in California, especially as a source of labor. Whatever racial antipathy was left has since shifted toward Japanese, Filipinos, Mexicans, and other peoples.

The visit by Madame Chiang Kai-shek to the United States during 1943 created a very wholesome atmosphere and favorable public opinion toward the Chinese.[60] After Representative Kennedy of New York had introduced a bill for the repeal of the Chinese Exclusion Act, there were nine bills of more or less the same nature introduced into Congress in the same year.[61] The Citizens' Committee was formed by a group of social workers and publicists, and an intensive campaign was started to publicize and advocate the repeal of the Exclusion Act as an important measure in winning World War II. This group was also supported by representatives of religious organizations and by businessmen interested in postwar foreign trade. From the beginning, the Chinese in the United States also lent a hand. Nevertheless, there was opposition from the American Federation of Labor, from some patriotic societies, and from veterans' groups. The West Coast, champion of the enactment of the exclusion acts, showed very little opposition to their being repealed.

The House Immigration Committee began its hearings on the proposed bills in May and June. The main argument for repeal stressed the necessity of bolstering Chinese morale. Thus Congressman

Walter Judd of Minnesota, who had worked very hard for repeal, stated that it would invigorate and galvanize the Chinese into more active effort and resistance, as no amount of pronouncements or Atlantic charters or even planes and guns could do.[62] Hon. Joseph R. Farrington, delegate from Hawaii, explained: "The record of Hawaii is proof that the Chinese can be accepted in the life of this country without injurious or disastrous results, and on the contrary, can become a great asset to us."[63] The opposition was hostile to the idea that immigration policy affected the war effort, since immigration policy, in their minds, concerned domestic policy only. The statement that the yellow race is unfit for citizenship was also made. Others voiced the conviction that a happy, successful, and coherent democracy cannot be maintained in a country whose population is made up of white, brown, yellow, and black. At the end of the hearing in June the House Committee in executive session decided not to report the bill, which would have created a quota of 105.[64] After the summer recess, however, the committee reported favorably for the repeal of the law. On October 11, when the bill was presented to the House for consideration, the federal government also gave strong support to the bill through President Roosevelt's forceful message for repeal.

During the more heated debate in the House in late October and in the Senate in November, the floor leader of the Democratic party in each chamber supported the repeal. Congressman John McCormick worked hard to bring about the result. The Republican minority also gave repeal their approval. Though House members who felt moderate opposition to the bill tried to stress the issue of difficulty in assimilation, not the issue of discrimination, still some members voiced extreme condemnation of the Chinese as a race unable to accept American standards. Congressman White from Idaho, for example, had the following to say:[65]

The Chinese are inveterate opium-smokers most of the day. They brought that hideous opium habit to this country. . . . There is no melting pot in America that can change their habits or change their mentality. . . . If there are any people who have refused to accept our standard and our education, it is the Chinese.

Judging from such remarks, there undoubtedly was some opposition to repeal; but considering the anti-Chinese movement in the second half of the nineteenth century, repeal, when it came, was brought about with a minimum of wrangling. The Senate and the House passed the bill on October 21 and 26, respectively; President Roosevelt, who had done much to facilitate the legislation, signed it on December 17, 1943. Thus, from the passage to the repeal of the Chinese Exclusion Acts, more than sixty years of American history had elapsed.

5

Recent Status of Chinese Immigration

Though the Chinese was the first Asian race ever to be excluded by the United States (1882), the Chinese was the first to become legally eligible for immigration and naturalization (1943). It was expedient to repeal the Chinese Exclusion Act for many reasons. The repeal may have arisen from the necessity of offsetting Japanese propaganda or from the influence of the "Four Freedoms" of the Atlantic Charter. The argument most frequently heard in the course of congressional debates was that the repeal of exclusion would greatly strengthen the morale of the Chinese, thereby making them more active in resisting the Japanese onslaught. There may have been other factors too; but one thing is certain, repeal was made possible because China was an active Asian ally of the United States. Had it not been for the war, it is possible that exclusion might still be in force. The repeal of the Chinese Exclusion Act has helped to pave the way for members of other Asiatic races to become eligible for admission and naturalization: first the East Indians and Filipinos, and later, under the Immigration and Nationality Act of 1952, all persons regardless of race or ancestry. The small racial quotas assigned to the Asian countries, and the fact that the law did not accord equality of treatment to Asian and to European immigrants, allayed restrictionists' fear of an influx of Orientals. In spite of social progress in the United States, it is still early to evaluate moral and idealistic concepts in American immigration policy. Clearly the crux of present policy is restriction. There has been and will be some piecemeal liberalization, but the quota system for Asia will remain a part of immigration policy.

When the Chinese Exclusion Act was repealed, Congress stipulated an annual quota of 105. In other special rules, place of birth determines the status of European and Filipino immigrants, but the admission of Chinese and East Indian races is on the basis of ancestry. Thus a Chinese is classifiable under the Chinese quota regardless of where he was born, whether in Great Britain, for example, or in China itself. Persons who have as much as 50 per cent Chinese blood are considered to be Chinese. Therefore a person whose father was French and whose mother was Chinese would be assigned to the Chinese quota, regardless of whether he had been born in France, Japan, or in China.[1] Similarly women with more than 50 per cent Chinese blood who are married to non-Asian natives of a nonquota country of the Western Hemisphere are unable to obtain nonquota status. The Act of 1952, however, made certain specific alterations, according nonquota status to any child, wife, or husband of an American citizen, irrespective of ancestry or race. In addition to the Chinese racial quota, there is a quota of 100 to be assigned to non-Chinese born in China.

Because practically every Chinese is assigned to the Chinese quota on the basis of over 50 per cent of ancestry, the quota is readily oversubscribed. Even though the Chinese quota admits only 105, the actual number of Chinese immigrants applying each year is far above this figure, thus tying up the quota for many years in the future. Take for instance the fiscal year ending in 1955. The total number of Chinese immigrants admitted was 2,628, among whom 1,066 were quota immigrants and 1,562 nonquota immigrants. Out of the 1,066 immigrants, 1,012 Chinese were already in the United States and had adjusted their status by suspension of deportation, by private bill, by special acts of Congress, or as displaced persons. Thus only fifty-four Chinese were admitted that year from abroad as quota immigrants. The chief classes of nonquota immigrants are wives, husbands, and children of Chinese-American citizens. Ministers and professors and their families were also in this category, although the separate classification "professor" was discontinued under the Immigration Act of 1952; professors are now listed under the first preference quota of skilled immigrants which is hopelessly oversubscribed.

The Postwar American Immigration Policy

In our brief survey of the American immigration policy before World War II, we understood that the formulation of the immigration policy was not confined to one aspect. The economic consideration, the racial issue, the influence of nationalism, and to a lesser extent, the question of foreign policy, all had something to do with it. The importance of economics has not been stressed in the formulation of American immigration policies. With the growth and expansion of the American economy since the Civil War, except perhaps during the depression period following the 1930's, the American absorption of immigrants was by no means difficult. But the adoption of the "national origins" quota system, with the subsequent passing of the 1921 and the 1924 Quota Acts, revealed that America is rather conscious of racial issues. This evidence of racial discrimination has continued to prevail since World War II, and any change in the "national origins" quota system has been consistently opposed in Congress. Closely allied to the racial issue in formulating immigration policy is the question of national and international security for the United States. The adherents of nationalism, who regard the immigrant's loyalty as uncertain, have been a powerful influence on immigration policy since World War I. The American Legion, for example, advocating 100 per cent Americanism, has usually been in favor of restricting the entry of immigrants. Normally, the maintenance of national solidarity in the selection of immigrants is considered extremely important.

With the conclusion of World War II and the United States's consequent assumption of world leadership, the issue of vulnerability becomes complicated by Soviet Russia's challenging this position of leadership. The contest is not to be confined to military, economic, or political measures; the ideology of social justice and freedom for all people has to be reckoned with. Since the objective is to win the respect of all the people of the world, the international implications of foreign policy have assumed importance over and above the mere formulation of immigration legislation. In fact, the repeal of the Chinese Exclusion Act was to a great extent a war effort that had much effect in gaining good will in the West, as well as in China. Since the bill was not solely an immigration measure, we should not conclude that racial concepts have since been forgotten by American legislators.[2]

The McCarran-Walter Act

Within nine years after World War II the United States did a great deal of work on immigration problems. The Displaced Persons Act of 1948, amended in 1950, the bitter debate over the McCarran-Walter Act (which became effective on December 24, 1952), and finally the enactment of the Refugee Relief Act recognized the distress of peoples in other parts of the world, particularly in Europe. The D.P.A. and R.R.A. were two of the legislative acts that marked a significant deviation from the traditional immigration policy. The Displaced Persons Act had less to do with the Chinese in particular, except for those Chinese who were here temporarily and were eligible for adjustment of status under Section 4 of the act. The Refugee Relief Act of 1953 marked the first time in American immigration history that special authorization was given to admit

2,000 Chinese and 3,000 Far Eastern refugees. In addition, several thousand Chinese temporarily living in the United States on or before August 7, 1953, became eligible for adjustment of status to permanent residence.

The McCarran-Walter Act, or the Immigration and Nationality Act (which governs present American immigration policies) brought within one comprehensive statute the many immigration and naturalization laws of the United States.[3] Among other features, the bill retained the national origin principle. The pooling of unused quotas, however, was rejected. The act introduced instead a system of selective immigration, by giving a preferential quota of 50 per cent to skilled aliens whose service was urgently needed in the United States, and the remainder of the quota to relatives of citizens and permanent residents. The bill was vetoed by President Truman, but enacted by Congress over the President's veto, on June 27, 1952.[4]

The repeal of the Chinese Exclusion Act marked the turning point in extending the privilege of naturalization to Orientals. Naturalization eligibility was granted to East Indians under the Act of July 2, 1946, and six days later President Truman established a quota of 100 for Filipinos. The new immigration act made all races eligible for naturalization, including the Japanese, Koreans, Burmese, Indonesians, Maoris, Polynesians, Samoans, and Thailanders.

Representative Walter Judd of Minnesota introduced a bill in 1947 to eliminate racial discrimination from the naturalization laws and from the quota system. This bill passed the House with not one member opposed to granting quotas to all Asian nations. It reached the Senate in 1949, but not until 1950 were the basic principles embodied into the omnibus immigration bill, which eventually became the McCarran-Walter Act. During the joint hearings in 1950 the section of the bill dealing with Asiatic immigration received considerable attention. The American Coalition is the only organization that expressed any opposition to the bill.[5] Most of the witnesses urged the extension of the country-of-birth formula to Asia, thereby reducing discrimination against the Asian peoples and extending equal treatment to all immigrants. Senator McCarran, however, sounded the warning that under a country-of-birth formula some six hundred thousand inhabitants of the Western Hemisphere who are of Asian descent would be eligible for nonquota admission, a possibility that he did not want to become a reality. He stated that the major oriental organizations in the United States considered the proposals for equality of treatment inappropriate.[6]

The elimination of discrimination between the sexes and the granting of nonquota status to alien husbands of American women, as contained in the new immigration law, has had little effect on the

Orientals, even though these changes may have affected a small number of Chinese immigrants. Chinese aliens who marry American-Chinese or other American girls, as well as aliens who marry those who have been naturalized, as husbands of American citizens are entitled to nonquota status irrespective of race or ancestry.

Quota Immigration

The immigration laws of the United States stipulate that quota numbers must be subtracted from the current annual quota or from a future quota, as the case may be. As stated before, anyone, including a Chinese, who has adjusted his resident status under the Displaced Persons Act or by private bill is chargeable to the quota, as also are those who have adjusted their status to that of permanent residence under the suspension of deportation procedure or special legislation except where legislation has specifically provided otherwise. However, P. L. 85-316, enacted September 11, 1957, has terminated all quota mortgages caused by the Displaced Persons Act. Individual private legislation is not included.

Table 20 on the following page reveals several interesting aspects of Asiatic immigration. Throughout the period under review (1946-60), with the exception of 1954, the annual quota for Asia as a whole had not been fully used, although a number of Asiatic countries for several years have fully utilized their quotas. This suggests that the fear of an influx of oriental races into the United States if the quota were enlarged is unrealistic. The "China quota" of 100 for non-Chinese indicates that between 1954 and 1960 the annual quota had not been utilized in full. That European refugees from China had used only about 45 per cent of the visas available until the termination of Refugee Relief Act (December 31, 1956)[7] indicates that this quota may no longer serve its original purpose. "The Chinese racial" quota, on the other hand, had not been fully utilized between 1946 and 1952. From 1954 on, the quota has been many times oversubscribed. The small number of quota immigrants before 1953 resulted from the closing of the United States consulate and later the Communists' taking over of the mainland. As a consequence, a number of applicants could not avail themselves of the opportunity for visas.

The visa division of the State Department announced that between 1946 and 1949 there were 2,957 applications of intending Chinese immigrants received by the consular officers.[8] The immigration quota list has revealed that beginning with the announcement of June 2, 1953, the quota on the Chinese race had been oversubscribed virtually all the time. Meanwhile the "China quota" has been mostly available, with the exception of the fourth preference, reserved for sons and daughters, brothers and sisters, of American citizens.

TABLE 20

ANNUAL QUOTA FOR ASIA AND QUOTA IMMIGRANTS ADMITTED TO THE UNITED STATES,* 1946-60

Quota Area	Annual Quota	1946	1947	1948	1949	1950	1951	1952	1953	1954**	1955**	1956**	1957**	1958†	1959†	1960
Asia	2,990‡	710	999	1,248	1,003	1,173	1,341	1,085	1,560	3,286	2,653	2,042	1,936	2,098	2,195	2,350††
China	100	77	200	377	281	208	518	178	404	63	49	90	60	85	111	103
Chinese	105	89	65	80	36	59	56	51	105	1,348	1,066	470	267	304	371	454
India	100	120	114	130	110	123	69	70	64	120	116	105	139	109	111	99
Asia Pacific Triangle	100	0	0	0	0	0	0	0	0	21	9	37	59	108	87	86
Other Asia	2,585	1,500	620	661	576	783	698	786	937	1,734	1,413	1,340	1,411	1,492	1,515	1,617

*The annual quota was 154,857 in the fiscal year 1959. On June 1, 1959, the total quota was increased to 154,887.
**The 1954, 1955, 1956, and 1957 figures include 1,283; 1,012; 404; and 222, respectively, Chinese quota immigrants who had adjusted their status in or as displaced persons. Annual Report, 1954-57.
†The Annual Quota for Asia in 1958 was 3,090; beginning 1959 it once more was 2,990.
‡The Philippines are included in Asia; before the fiscal year 1952, the Philippines were included in the Pacific, or Oceania.
††Some of the figures for the years 1956 through 1959 were revised in 1960. See Annual Report, 1960, Table 7, p. 23.
Source: Annual Report, 1950-60.

This "China quota" of 100 is strictly for non-Chinese persons born in China. One of British parentage, for example, who merely happens to have been born in China, becomes chargeable to the quota of China, whereas in reality he is 100 per cent British. The fact that the western people in China are mostly Americans and people from northern and western Europe, and that their own annual quotas for several years had not been fully used, suggests that there could be no unfairness in crediting their admittance to the quotas of their various countries.

As has been stated, selected immigrants whose services are urgently needed in the United States are admitted under the first 50 per cent of the quota. College professors, chemists, meteorologists, physicians and surgeons, dentists, nurses, veterinarians, engineers, tool designers, and draftsmen are included in this category. A number of Chinese who are qualified have applied for admission under this quota. Many of the large American companies and institutions that are employing Chinese scholars, scientists, doctors, and other experts have petitioned on behalf of their employees for first-preference classification.

According to the decisions and interpretations made by the Immigration Service, the so-called skilled aliens whose services are urgently needed have not necessarily received higher education. Chinese chefs, who are always in brisk demand by the Chinese restaurants, are said to have been several times so admitted.

Nonquota Immigration

Aliens permitted to enter the United States as permanent residents but not subject to numerical restriction of the quota are nonquota immigrants. The exempt class that may enter as nonquota immigrants includes wives, children, and husbands of American citizens; immigrants from Western Hemisphere countries; clergymen; women and children expatriates; and military expatriates.

The Act of August 9, 1946, exempted all Chinese wives of American citizens from the quota restrictions. Before that the Chinese wives—other than those married before May 26, 1924—were not granted the status of nonquota immigrants. The husbands of American citizens were subject to quota restrictions until the enactment of the Immigration Act of 1952, which eliminated differences of treatment between the sexes with respect to immigration. As long as there are not many intermarriages between Chinese and whites in the United States, and as long as the ratio of Chinese females and males is still considerably in favor of males, marriages between Chinese-Americans and Chinese in Hong Kong, Taiwan, and elsewhere will continue to occur; and consequently, the entry of

Chinese wives to the United States will continue for a number of years. The entry of Chinese husbands of United States citizens, however, will be as numerically negligible as before.

As we have shown the immigration law provided that children born before May 24, 1934, have derivative citizenship, if the citizen parent had been in the United States before the birth of the child. Thereafter the law was changed to require that a citizen parent whose children were born after May 24, 1934, had to have been in the United States ten years before the birth of the child. Such children—who are not entitled to derivative citizenship—can qualify under the McCarran Act as nonquota, but they come in as aliens. This brings the unusual circumstance of members of a family entering the United States as citizens by derivation and other members of the same family entering as nonquota immigrants.

Under the Act of December 17, 1943, the alien children of an American citizen of Chinese descent were specifically chargeable to the quota. The Immigration Act of 1952 removed this discrimination, and they are now eligible to enter as nonquota immigrants. Though the special subcommittee to investigate the immigration and naturalization system (1950) recommended that children and husbands of American citizens of Chinese descent be accorded the nonquota status, the subcommittee condemned the frauds and subterfuges that have been practised in the Chinese derivative citizenship cases, and insisted that adequate measures be taken to deal with the situation.[9]

For many years the American consular offices in Hong Kong have been strict in investigating the children of Chinese-Americans who apply for a visa. An average of only 196 children a year were admitted between 1945 and 1960, including some children not of the Chinese race. Compared with an average of more than a thousand a year before World War II, the present number is small indeed. This is particularly due to the change in law applying to the derivative citizenship of children born after 1934 and the stiffer screening process followed by the consulate.

Chinese professors, teachers, and ministers were admitted to the United States even under the Chinese Exclusion Act; the numbers admitted annually were necessarily small. The Immigration Act of 1952, however, made only ministers admissible as nonquota immigrants.

For the sake of ready reference we append below a list of numbers of both quota and nonquota immigrants born in China from 1944 to 1960. The number of spouses and children, ministers, and professors admitted each year is included.

The number of Chinese immigrants admitted each year remained

TABLE 21

CHINESE IMMIGRANTS ADMITTED TO THE UNITED STATES, BY CLASSES UNDER THE IMMIGRATION LAWS AND COUNTRY OR REGION OF BIRTH, 1944-60*

	1944	1945	1946	1947	1948	1949	1950	1951	1952	1953	1954	1955	1956	1957	1958	1959	1960	Total
Quota	19	91	145	247	452	317	260	880	301	596	1,502	1,195	647	389	448	599	693	8,781
Nonquota	0	0	0	0	0	0	0	0	0	940	1,268	1,510	3,803	5,036	2,765	5,123	2,988	23,433
Wives of U.S. citizens	2	11	159	902	3,192	2,143	1,062	826	959	722	787	909	1,055	904	980	1,345	1,027	16,985
Husbands of U.S. citizens	0	0	3	4	2	7	3	4	5	19	122	125	138	138	142	235	155	1,102
Children of U.S. citizens	0	1	13	149	232	240	16	19	77	118	335	292	360	296	262	419	307	3,136
Spouses, children of natives of western hemisphere countries	0	0	0	0	0	0	0	0	0	11	10	3	12	8	8	10	12	74
Wives and children of natives nonquota countries	0	2	1	2	3	2	3	5	7	0	0	0	0	0	0	0	0	25
Persons who had been U.S. citizens	0	0	0	0	0	2	0	0	1	1	0	0	0	0	0	0	0	4
Ministers, their spouses and children	5	1	5	45	29	13	29	18	27	12	13	8	18	16	10	30	20	299
Professors, their spouses and children	8	3	11	58	74	98	119	69	43	0	0	0	0	0	0	0	0	483
Refugee Relief Act of 1953	0	0	0	0	0	0	0	0	0	0	0	171	2,219	3,669	676	127	0	6,862
Acts of September 11, 1957, Immigrants	0	0	0	0	0	0	0	0	0	0	0	0	0	0	682	2,304	528	3,514
Act of September 2, 1958	0	0	0	0	0	0	0	0	0	0	0	0	0	0	0	0	2	2
Act of September 22, 1956	0	0	0	0	0	0	0	0	0	0	0	0	0	0	0	0	176	176
Other classes	0	0	0	0	3	1	2	0	1	57	1	2	1	5	5	653	761	1,492
TOTAL	34	109	337	1,407	3,987	2,823	1,494	1,821	1,421	1,536	2,770	2,705	4,450	5,425	3,213	5,722	3,681	42,935

*Non-Chinese immigrants born in China totaling 3,204 from 1944 to 1958. The breakdown was 1944, 0; 1945, 0; 1946, 1,054; 1947, 279; 1948, 413; 1949, 333; 1950, 205; 1951, 738; 1952, 269; 1953, 443; 1954, 23; 1955, 77; 1956, 0; 1957, 302; and 1958, 18. Admitted in 1959 were 5,722 immigrants who had been born in China. These numbers might include children of European refugees born in China and others who were not Chinese nationals. On the other hand, 6,031 of Chinese ethnic origin, regardless of country of birth, were listed under Table 10 of the Annual Report, 1959. The difference of 309 represents those of Chinese ethnic origin born other than in China proper and Taiwan. In 1960, there were nine non-Chinese immigrants born in China.

Source: Annual Report, 1944-60.

very small during World War II and immediately afterwards, but increased from 1947 to 1950, largely because of an influx of war brides and adjustments under the so-called "Seven Year Law." From 1951 on, the adjustment of the status under the Displaced Persons Act helped somewhat to increase the number of immigrants. The large number of Chinese admitted under the Refugee Relief Act of 1953 and under the Act of September 11, 1957, was evidently responsible for the considerable increase in admissions. The annual reports announced that 40,031 Chinese immigrants had been admitted between 1944 and 1960, as against 42,935 immigrants born in China, but not necessarily Chinese.

Adjustment of Status and Suspension of Deportation

Under both Displaced Persons Acts of 1948 and 1950, as well as under the Refugee Relief Act of 1953, provisions were made to allow 15,000 displaced persons and 5,000 nonimmigrants, respectively, temporarily in the United States, to adjust their status to that of permanent residents, provided they could meet the legal requirements. Congress, in view of the inevitable hardship in the enforcement of immigration laws, gave the attorney general certain powers to handle such cases. Every case, however, was required to be submitted to Congress. The grant of the suspension of deportation to a worthy applicant was provided in the 1917 Immigration Act and as amended July 1, 1948, and again in the 1952 Immigration Act.

Prerequisites for applying for the suspension of deportation are the applicant's long presence in the United States and a good moral character. He should also be able to show that deportation would result in exceptional and serious economic detriment to the alien or his spouse, parent, or minor child who is a United States citizen or a permanent resident. By Section 244 (a) (1) of the Immigration and Nationality Act of 1952, deportable aliens who had been in the United States before June 26, 1950, were eligible. This section, however, expired December 24, 1957.[10] Many of the deportable aliens may have entered the United States illegally but may have spouses and children who are American citizens. To deport such aliens would certainly entail serious hardship. If the alien has lived in the United States for a long time, the chances are he has acquired American ideas and assimilated the American way of life better than the alien who is on a quota waiting list, but has not yet come to this country. (The possession of good moral character, is, of course, always a prerequisite.)

Section 245 of the Act of 1952, as well as the so-called "Canadian pre-examination" procedure reinstated in 1955 (and terminated in 1959), does provide relief for some persons in adjustment of their status; but the fact that the Chinese quota is oversubscribed most of the time is already a stumbling block, to say nothing of technicalities that must be complied with. Chinese have unknowingly applied for adjustment of their status (under Section 245) from that of nonimmigrants to that of lawful permanent residents. As a result of the denial of their applications, they have been obliged to leave the country, for the reason that no quota was available to them.[11] Improvement came by the temporary reinstatement of pre-examinations, and also by a change of policy of the Immigration Service, permitting qualified first-preference immigrants to remain in the United States while awaiting their quota numbers. Most of these applicants are working in large corporations or at institutions of higher learning. Several temporary measures taken, such as Public Laws 85-316 and 85-700 (described elsewhere in this chapter) have also helped to relieve the situation.

Since 1949 there have been a number of Chinese in the United States who have taken advantage of the immigration acts and have accordingly adjusted their status. Many of them were illegal entrants, others are students, visitors, or merchants who are unable to return to the mainland because of the fear of persecution. Before 1950, when the mainland of China was still under the control of the Nationalist government, there was little need for the average Chinese to ask for a change of status.[12]

The law stipulates that anyone who entered the United States before July 1, 1924, and has resided here continuously may apply for suspension of deportation and adjust his status to that of an alien lawfully admitted for permanent residence, even though he may have been here without proper documents. In the fire that ravaged San Francisco in 1906 destroying all the files of the Immigration Service, and of the city's vital statistics, a number of Chinese records were also destroyed. It is possible that Chinese born in San Francisco or others who entered here lawfully have no records to check on account of that fire. However, very few Chinese have proof of their residence in the United States for each year they have been here, and the evidence necessary to comply with the provision is difficult to obtain. (This provision has been extended to those who made entry before June 28, 1940, by Public Law 85-616.)

As a matter of fact, the change in political conditions in late 1949 caused the displacement of many "new Chinese immigrants" who would otherwise rather have remained in China, or have eventually returned. The "new immigrants," mostly intellectuals and their families, are certainly no *quid pro quo* for the "old immigrants," who came of necessity because of conditions in the home country; nor are they similar, for instance, to the Italians and to the Japanese,

since overpopulation was behind the motives of those two nationalities; nor is the Chinese movement similar to the present trend
from England, where emigration is caused by lack of opportunity
for the younger groups.

The War Brides and Fiancées Act

Because a great number of men and women in the American armed
forces stationed in the various theaters during World War II had
married nationals of foreign countries, Congress passed the War
Brides Act of December 28, 1945, and the G.I. Fiancées Act of
June 29, 1946, to facilitate the entrance of war brides, alien fiancées
and fiancés, war grooms, and children, by waiving certain visa
requirements. Such alien persons and children entered the United
States as nonquota immigrants. The majority of the wives and children of citizens came from those countries where there were great
numbers of United States armed forces, including both military
and civilian personnel. The following table shows the number of
citizens' wives who entered the United States between 1946 and 1953,
with war brides assuming major proportion.

TABLE 22

NUMBER OF WIVES OF CITIZENS ADMITTED TO THE UNITED STATES, 1946-53

Country of Birth	1946	1947	1948	1949	1950	1951	1952	1953
Great Britain, Northern Ireland	27,094	7,160	1,843	914	241	148	208	176
Germany	303	701	3,638	10,130	3,798	2,042	3,768	6,042
Italy	2,419	5,711	6,385	3,081	2,168	1,534	1,799	1,654
China	159	902	3,192	2,143	1,062	826	959	722
Japan	4	14	298	445	9	125	4,220	2,042
Australia, New Zealand	5,375	2,225	852	286	184	159	157	159

Source: Annual Report, 1951-53.

In addition to the admittance under the War Brides Act, the so-
called Fiancées Act of June 29, 1946, admitted thousands of alien
fiancés or fiancées of citizens who had served in the armed forces
during World War II; under this act 8,312 persons entered the United
States between 1947 and 1949. China accounts for a very small number, a total of ninety-one.[13]

The Displaced Persons Act

At the conclusion of World War II, more than 8,000,000 people in
Germany, Austria, and Italy had fled from the Germans or had been
forced to work for the Germans. These displaced persons came from
all areas of Europe, particularly from Poland and from the Baltic
States. Many fled into Germany during the last phase of World War

II, as the Russian army advanced; they despised or were afraid of communism. These millions of European refugees, uprooted as a result of the war, created a very difficult problem for the Allies. The directive of December 22, 1945, issued by President Truman to give the displaced persons a priority in the issuance of visas under the immigration laws, met with little success; fewer than 40,000 persons were admitted between December 22, 1945, and June 30, 1948.

The need for a separate law was soon felt; Congress, after much discussion and debate, finally passed the Displaced Persons Act of June 25, 1948, permitting the admission of up to 205,000 displaced persons for a period of two years, beginning July 1, 1948. The Act of June 16, 1950, which amended the Act of June 25, 1948, may be considered rather liberal.[14] In addition to increasing the number of those admitted to 415,744, several new provisions were added, such as to admit 10,000 refugees from Greece, 18,000 Polish veterans in exile, and 5,000 European orphans. Four thousand European refugees from China were provided for, since many White Russians and German Jews had fled to China as a result of World War II.

Though the Displaced Persons Act aimed at the assistance of European refugees, the Chinese were affected, though only incidentally. Both the Act of 1948 and that of 1950 provided adjustment of the status of 15,000 displaced persons living here temporarily. Before the amendment of June 16, 1950, eligible applicants were required to have entered the United States before April 1, 1948; under the amended act the date was extended to April 30, 1949. The fact that the Communists had occupied the mainland of China before the end of 1949 had made eligible for application a number of Chinese temporarily in the United States.[15] The requirement, among other things, was that the applicant must prove that he was unable to return to his country of birth, residence, or national origin because of fear of persecution on account of race, religion, or political opinion.

The Refugee Relief Act of 1953

The passage of the McCarran-Walter Act aroused a great deal of attention, both approving and disapproving. Many efforts were made and are still being made to change or to supplement its provisions. So far there have been no permanent changes made in this basic immigration law. The first temporary measure made was the passage of the Refugee Relief Act of 1953 (P. L. 83-203).[16] The act was amended August 31, 1954, authorizing the admission of 214,000 immigrants, and using the displaced-person legislation as its model; indeed, it is a continuation of that act. Unlike the Displaced Persons Act, however, which required all approved applicants to be charged to their respective annual quotas, the Refugee Relief Act admits nonquota immigrants. Definite assurances by a responsible citizen or citizens of the United States as to employment and housing of immigrants, and against their becoming public charges, are required. All other requirements under the Immigration Act of 1952 are also applicable, with the exception of those relating to quota and visa fees. As far as the Chinese are concerned, this act has a special provision for a total of 2,000 visas; passports must be endorsed by the Chinese Nationalist government or its authorized representatives. Chinese persons were also included in the category of 3,000 visas to be issued to refugees from the Far East (Asia). Under the provision of adjustment of the status of nonimmigrants in the United States, a Chinese refugee (as well as a refugee of another race) may qualify for application, if it can be established that he lawfully entered the United States before July 1, 1953, as a nonimmigrant and is unable to return to the country of his birth or nationality or last residence, because of fear of persecution on account of race, religion, or political opinion.

This Act of 1953 expired at midnight December 31, 1956. At the termination of the program, 190,327 visas had been authorized.[17] A considerable number of visas that had originally provided for German expellees were unissued under Section 4 (a) (1); the economy and prosperity of West Germany has been responsible for reducing the demand. In addition, only 902 visas were issued to Far East refugees (non-Asian), out of a total of 2,000 allotted.[18] On the other hand, had it been permitted by the law, the number of these unused visas could easily have been used by the Chinese refugees, as well as by the Far East refugees (Asian) as both categories had been oversubscribed. The State Department estimated that the excess of qualified applicants for visas under these two categories was approximately 18,500 persons.

A number of Chinese adjusted their status under Section 6 of the Refugee Relief Act. As a matter of fact, the majority of applicants whose status has been adjusted were Chinese.[19] But, as under the Displaced Persons Act, some of the applicants had been denied their requests on the grounds that they were not unable to return to their country of birth and that there was no apparent persecution due to race, religion, or political opinion. Mostly they were Chinese with Hong Kong or Macao passports; others were persons who did not show sufficient reason to fear persecution if they returned to China. The Immigration Service, however, reversed its stand, and in a ruling, October 31, 1956, authorized a stay of deportation of those originally scheduled to be deported to Yugoslavia (but the ruling was again reversed on April 23, 1958) and China. The commissioner of the Immigration Service conceded that there is meager information available as to the possibility of persecution, and that unless positive proof can be established that the applicant would be welcomed by authorities at home, because of his expressed or implied sympathy with the present regime, the applicants should be given a stay of deportation.

Public Law 85–316

This special law was enacted September 11, 1957, in response to former President Eisenhower's immigration message to Congress at the end of January, 1957. It failed to give a general overhauling to the Immigration Law or to grant permanent status to Hungarian refugees; thus, the former President termed the measure a "disappointment." Mr. Eisenhower's original message had urged the entry of more than double the present allowable annual flow of immigrants into this country. His request was for the quota of 60,000 that had annually expired without having been used; authorization for the entry of 67,000 refugee parolees; and for an increase of about 65,000 under the regular immigration quotas. In other words, he urged the admittance of 190,000 more persons a year, and bigger quotas for southeastern Europeans, since many of the quotas assigned to northwestern Europeans were constantly unfilled. As the law stood at its passage, it fell short of Mr. Eisenhower's request. The law was *ipso facto* an extension of the expired Refugee Relief Act of 1953, in which 18,656 unused numbers were authorized to be issued as visas to German expellees, Dutch refugees, and other persons escaping persecution.[20] Chinese refugees who have not been able to come to the United States because the quota has already been filled are qualified to apply under the amendment.[21] The standard of selection is based upon (1) the degree of professional, technical, or other skill, (2) hardships or persecution, (3) sponsorship in the United States, (4) ability to speak English, and (5) unification of close relatives.[22] Evidently the act emphasizes immigrants with technical skills and aims at reuniting families in the United States. "Hardships or persecution" is a phrase rather vaguely used.

Since the new law calling for the termination July 1, 1957, of the mortgages placed on immigration quotas after World War II under the Displaced Persons Act and other special acts, there is a definite improvement of quota conditions of all countries. Nevertheless, in a few tight quota areas, such as the Chinese quota of 105 and the Japanese quota of 185, the benefits have been negligible.

To aliens both in and outside the United States whose special skills are urgently needed here, the law has given much encouragement.

Under Section 9 of Public Law 85-316, the attorney general is authorized to adjust the status of a limited number of skilled aliens who were here July 1, 1957, and who are beneficiaries of an approved-first-preference petition filed before September 11, 1957. If the spouse and child were also in the United States on July 1, 1957, they may adjust their status with the alien in question. Some 815 Chinese, including spouses and children, were able to adjust their status to that of permanent residents under these provisions (to June 30, 1960).

Section 12 of Public Law 85-316 permits immigration from abroad of such specialists and also those of second and third preference, namely, alien parents of United States citizens and spouses and children of aliens lawfully admitted for permanent residence, as nonquota immigrants, provided they were the beneficiaries of a petition approved by the attorney general before July 1, 1957, and otherwise admissible under the Immigration and Nationality Act.

Another provision that will also benefit some Chinese in the United States relates to one who seeks, has sought, or has obtained visas or other documentation for entry into the United States by fraud or misrepresentation under certain conditions. The attorney general is authorized to waive the deportation requirement provided this person is the spouse, parent, or child of a United States citizen or a person lawfully admitted for permanent residence. A large number of family units are threatened with permanent separation because one of their members entered the United States by fraud or misrepresentation and remained, or, if he left, is now permanently excludable under Section 212 (a) (19). As a matter of fact, a great number of private bills passed by Congress and enacted into law during the last few years were to relieve the hardships of such families. It is only proper that "humanitarian approach should be extended to an entire defined class of aliens rather than to selected individuals."[23]

Public Law 85-700

Among other features, Public Law 85-700, signed by former President Eisenhower August 21, 1958, provided nonquota status for first-preference immigrants in possession of petitions approved by the attorney general before July 1, 1958, and amended Section 12 of the Act of September 11, 1957. The act has thus advanced the date on first preference from July 1, 1957, as fixed by Public Law 85-316. As far as Chinese are concerned, the oversubscribed first-preference classification has not been eliminated by the Congressional action. The October-December quota of 1958 and of 1959 found all Chinese preference quotas again oversubscribed, indicating that, as the situation stood, the Chinese quota of 105 is indeed too small to keep the list from being oversubscribed.

Public Law 86-363

The Eighty-sixth Congress, first session, adopted several measures of useful though limited scope on the immigration issue. All together three bills were enacted into law. The amendments embodied in P. L. 86-129 (August 4, 1959) liberalize the 1952 Act regarding citizenship. One of the important provisions permits American citizens naturalized for fifteen (formerly twenty-five) years to reside abroad permanently without loss of citizenship, provided they do not return to the country of their birth or former nationality.

P. L. 86-253 (September 9, 1959) gives discretionary authority to the attorney general to admit tubercular aliens until June 30, 1961, and to admit through June 30, 1960, certain alien orphans adopted by American citizens. Both features were contained in the Act of September 11, 1957, and were extended under the present act. It is expected that those two provisions will probably be made a part of the permanent immigration law.

It was P. L. 86-363 (September 22, 1959) that amended the 1952 Immigration Act through the reclassification of preference within the immigration quota to give priority to close relatives of American citizens and resident aliens, and thereby to become part of the permanent act. Unmarried sons and daughters—over twenty-one years of age—of United States citizens may now apply under the second preference and resident aliens under the third preference. Since the Chinese quota of the second preference is already oversubscribed to the number of 450,[24] the inclusion of unmarried sons and daughters will make the quota more heavily subscribed. The same situation is true in the case of third preference.

There are two temporary sections of this law aimed at alleviating hardship caused by family separation due to quota difficulty. Section 4 of the new law grants nonquota status to second-, third-, and fourth-preference immigrants and their spouses and children who have been registered for admission with an American consulate prior to December 31, 1953, and whose preference provisions were approved by the attorney general prior to January 1, 1956. Another regulation will aid those immigrants who came to the United States under the Refugee Relief Act of 1953 but left the family behind. Such families, if petitions on their behalf were filed prior to January 1, 1959, are entitled to nonquota status. A relatively small number of Chinese persons are involved.

There have been a number of stopgap measures taken since the passage of the McCarran-Walter Act of 1952. Examples are the Refugee Relief Act of 1953 and some later legislations, enacted from 1957 to 1959, such as P. L.'s 85-316, 85-700, or 86-363, mentioned above. While this kind of measure may provide temporary relief, insofar as alleviating the problem by actually changing and supplementing the provisions of the 1952 Act is concerned, its real effect is indeed negligible.

Exclusion and Deportation

The Supreme Court has since 1889 held that the power of Congress to exclude aliens is an incidence of its sovereignty, that its power to exclude is absolute. Whether aliens who seek admission into the United States are to be admitted or excluded is to be determined under the immigration laws. Generally speaking any alien whose presence would be detrimental to the interests of the United States is to be excluded. A considerable majority of the excludable cases are those of persons who lack the proper documents. From 1940 to 1944 a number of aliens were excluded because they were likely to become public charges. The number of such cases, however, has been considerably reduced since World War II. Many aliens have been excluded because they were stowaways; this figure has been conspicuously smaller since 1952. Criminals, mental or physical defectives, subversives or anarchists, and persons previously excluded or deported have been responsible for a number of cases each year. From 1935 to 1951 the English and French, despite their high quotas, led in the number of excluded aliens, with the Irish and the Scottish closely following; in recent years, Canadians and Mexicans have taken their places.[25]

TABLE 23

CHINESE EXCLUDED, 1944-60

Year	Number	Year	Number
1944	11	1954	11
1945	13	1955	4
1946	15	1956	3
1947	16	1957	1
1948	19	1958	4
1949	19	1959	9
1950	15	1960	3
1951	22		
1952	8		
1953	10	TOTAL	183

Source: Annual Report, 1944-60.

The number of Chinese excluded has not been large for a number of years. Between 1935 and 1951, a period of seventeen years, there were 1,013 cases, or an average of about sixty a year; from 1952 to 1960 the number was even smaller, with only about six a year. Entry without proper documents or attempted illegal entry were the principal causes for Chinese exclusion. Compared with Mexican and Canadian, the number of Chinese exclusions is small indeed. It is also true that many persons are stopped by the Immigration Service and never reach the exclusion proceedings, because they voluntarily refrain from entering. In cases such as these they are possibly more numerous than the formal exclusion proceedings.

For many years Mexico has had the largest proportion of deportees, the so-called wetbacks, followed by Canada and Italy. Chinese deportees used to be many, only slightly fewer than those of Italy. While World War II was in progress, the number of Chinese deportees was considerably reduced, to about twenty-nine annually. Since the repeal of the Chinese Exclusion Act (1944-60) they have averaged about eighty-one each year. This means either that more Chinese are entering the United States legally or that a number of them have obtained relief by acquiring permanent residence through adjustment of status or are under parole supervision. On the other hand, the reluctance to send to the mainland Chinese who fear persecution may account for the small number actually deported.

Contrary to general impression, illegal entry has not been the leading cause of Chinese deportations; instead, those who have overstayed their authorization and those who have entered without proper documents make the largest number. It may be because a number of crewmen, visitors, treaty traders, students, and former government officials have been unable to obtain permission and have "remained longer than authorized" or have not been sufficiently familiar with the law to know how to proceed legally. The number of violators of the narcotic law was slightly over 10 per cent of the total deportations between 1944 and 1960, out of which 110 deportations were made in five years, 1945-49; but only twenty-nine were made since 1950. This coincides with the finding that, as far as Chinese commission of crime in the United States is concerned, drug addiction or dealing in narcotic drugs have been two of the serious offenses.

In connection with the subject of exclusion and deportation, mention must be made of deserting crewmen. The necessity for permitting temporary shore leave to alien crewmen affords an opportunity for them to remain illegally. Of the Chinese crewmen who deserted between 1944 and 1960, about 47 per cent did so during 1944 and 1945, when World War II was still in progress. It is possible that during the war Chinese seamen were having difficulties in getting back to their homes, because the places that most of them had come from

TABLE 24

CHINESE DEPORTED FROM THE UNITED STATES BY CAUSES, 1944-60

	1944	1945	1946	1947	1948	1949	1950	1951	1952	1953	1954	1955	1956	1957	1958	1959	1960	Total
Criminals	0	0	2	5	0	2	0	0	1	0	0	2	5	1	1	1	0	20
Immoral classes	0	0	1	1	2	0	0	0	0	0	0	1	0	0	0	0	0	5
Violators of narcotic laws	0	3	43	35	20	9	0	0	0	1	2	7	8	2	4	5	0	139
Mental or physical defectives	0	0	0	2	1	1	0	0	0	0	0	0	0	1	1	0	0	6
Previously excluded or deported	0	0	1	9	3	1	0	0	1	0	1	0	0	0	2	1	1	20
Remained longer than authorized	21	9	128	115	56	31	17	23	51	9	11	17	0	0	0	0	0	488
Entered without proper documents or without inspection or by false statements	5	0	0	67	0	0	0	0	0	0	0	0	0	0	0	0	0	72
Entered without proper documents	0	1	48	0	24	18	7	2	11	3	15	14	26	15	15	6	1	206
Failed to maintain non-immigrant status	0	0	0	0	0	0	0	0	0	0	1	5	9	0	0	0	0	15
Failed to comply with conditions of status	0	0	0	0	0	0	0	0	0	0	10	21	20	0	0	0	0	51
Failed to maintain or comply with conditions of nonimmigrant status	0	0	0	0	0	0	0	0	0	0	0	0	0	71	51	62	15	199
Abandoned status of admissions	0	0	15	6	16	0	3	8	6	0	0	0	0	0	0	6	0	60
Entered without inspection or by false statements	0	0	2	0	6	5	1	0	0	0	0	1	4	31	11	0	1	62
Likely to become public charges	0	0	0	1	0	0	0	0	0	0	0	0	1	3	0	0	0	5
Subversive or anarchistic	0	0	0	0	0	0	0	0	0	0	1	0	1	1	0	0	0	3
Under Chinese Exclusion Act	1	0	0	0	0	0	0	0	0	0	0	0	0	0	0	0	0	1
Miscellaneous	0	11	11	3	0	0	0	0	0	0	0	0	14	0	0	0	0	28
TOTAL	27	13	251	244	128	67	28	33	70	13	41	68	88	125	85	81	18	1,380

Source: Annual Report, 1944-60.

had been occupied by the Japanese army.[26] Since the war, the rate of desertion has conspicuously decreased. It reached the lowest average of about eighty-five yearly between 1957 and 1959. That may be because fewer ships with Chinese crewmen came to the United States. It may also mean that "as a result of the stricter provisions concerning control, fewer alien crewmen are remaining ashore or on the beach, and fewer have deserted or are being apprehended as over-stays."[27] However, the number suddenly went up to 186 in the year 1960, following a general upward surge of almost three times the total alien crewmen deserting in 1959. In fact the over-all situation needs attention since the 1960 figures reached the all-time high during the period of our review (1944-60).

So far as the 186 Chinese crewmen deserting in 1960 are concerned, the highest number deserting were those on British-flagged carriers: fifty-six, and the next highest number were those on the Netherlands': forty-nine.[28] It is probable that the deportees sent via Hong Kong and the Netherlands, especially the latter, will end up in Red China.

TABLE 25

ALIEN CREWMEN DESERTING AT THE UNITED STATES AIR AND SEAPORTS,
BY NATIONALITY, 1944-60

Year	British Empire	China	Greece	Italy	Nether- lands	Norway	Spain	All others	Total
1944	1,451	1,406	77	0	152	677	117	1,931	5,811
1945	1,519	1,325	55	126	150	911	82	1,409	5,577
1946	1,115	727	85	72	315	485	107	1,459	4,365
1947	894	367	124	364	269	382	279	1,447	4,126
1948	809	221	210	934	220	377	103	1,479	4,353
1949	557	207	131	884	188	308	103	1,220	3,598
1950	367	199	91	496	94	289	101	773	2,410
1951	521	197	186	705	157	361	274	1,190	3,591
1952	450	193	207	468	201	308	182	1,012	3,021
1953	310	186	145	275	130	271	162	838	2,317
1954	209	136	196	295	112	190	233	592	1,963
1955	474	100	491	286	118	187	159	561	2,376
1956	313	130	837	448	99	162	247	732	2,968
1957	251	67	924	454	66	156	303	659	2,880
1958	244	91	871	349	81	178	162	646	2,622
1959	275	96	747	261	79	146	139	482	2,225
1960	675	186	2,090	429	268	643	264	1,877	6,432
TOTAL	10,434	5,834	7,467	6,846	2,699	6,031	3,017	18,307	60,635

Source: Annual Report, 1944-60.

Naturalization

There were 22,329 persons, formerly owing allegiance to the Republic of China, who from 1944 to 1960 obtained United States citizenship through naturalization. The trend has been upward since 1954; in fact, about 63 per cent or 14,133 were naturalized in the seven years, 1954 to 1960. This was partly a result of the inability of many Chinese to return to the mainland of China, but it also shows that many Chinese immigrants wish to settle here permanently.

Notwithstanding that many Orientals were denied naturalization before the 1952 Immigration Act, exceptions were made of aliens, regardless of race, who had served honorably on active duty during the two world wars. Congress has more than once amended existing legislation in order to liberalize naturalization privileges to aliens in the United States armed forces.[29] In June, 1953, Congress allowed naturalization proceedings even outside the United States, thereby to a certain extent expediting the matter. The authority to enlist displaced persons in the United States armed forces was extended to 1959, permitting aliens to become citizens, under certain conditions. Among other reasons, this accounts for the fact that even before the repeal of the Exclusion Act Chinese had been naturalized, though the number was small.

Only 152 Chinese were naturalized between 1939 and 1942, which suggests that of the total number of Chinese naturalized between 1939 and 1944—1,380—the majority were members of the armed forces. Take 1943 as an example. While the war was still going on, 492 Chinese members of the armed forces were granted naturalization certificates, but in the same year only five Chinese civilians. The situation continued into 1944, when 708 Chinese members of the armed forces were naturalized and only twenty-three civilians.[30]

In addition to members of the armed forces, seamen who had served honorably five years on board an American government or private vessel were permitted to apply for naturalization with or without a legal entry, and a limited number of Chinese seamen have done so. The present law, however, is much more stringent, in that legal admission for permanent residence is a prerequisite.

There are three means of acquiring American citizenship: by birth, by naturalization, and by derivation. It was settled as early as 1898, in the famous case of *United States* v. *Wong Kim Ark* (169 U.S. 649), that a Chinese born in the United States—whether the parents are aliens or not—is an American citizen at birth, and consequently subject to none of the restrictions imposed on naturalized persons. By the same token, birth in the territories or possessions of the United States also confers upon one the status of native born.

The date of July 1, 1924, is important. The Chinese who entered the United States before then, whether with records of lawful admission or with no records of entry, were held to be permanent residents and thus eligible for naturalization, provided they were able first to prove their residence and meet all other requirements. This stipulation included students, merchants, ministers, and their wives and children; wives of United States citizens, and wives of those Chinese of the laboring class who were in the United States before July 1, 1924. A few of the Chinese who were admitted after July 1, 1924, but before December 17, 1943, were also eligible for naturalization. The Chinese wives of citizens married before July 1, 1924, and admitted after June 13, 1930, but before December 17, 1943, belong to this group, as do ministers, teachers, and their wives and children.

TABLE 26

CHINESE PERSONS NATURALIZED, BY GENERAL AND SPECIAL NATURALIZATION PROVISIONS, 1944-60

Year	Under General Naturalization Provisions	Married to U.S. Citizen	Children of U.S. Citizen Parents	Military	Civilian	Total
1944	0	0	0	708	23	731
1945	0	0	0	459	280	739
1946	0	0	0	334	265	599
1947	0	0	0	352	479	831
1948	0	0	0	56	707	763
1949	340	195	38	257	97	927
1950	375	235	35	86	172	903
1951	327	248	20	23	96	714
1952	386	490	28	23	6	933
1953	560	437	27	16	16	1,056
1954	1,515	158	56	101	50	1,880
1955	3,059	199	133	111	25	3,527
1956	1,951	177	102	82	18	2,330
1957	1,152	178	99	51	11	1,491
1958	1,095	203	102	130	12	1,542
1959	859	277	140	109	10	1,395
1960	1,160	441	186	174	7	1,968
TOTAL	12,779	3,238	966	3,072	2,274	22,329

Source: Annual Report, 1944-60.

The increase of Chinese naturalizations since 1954 may be attributed to the fact that a number of Chinese, who had been granted the status of permanent residence through the so-called Seven-Year Law or the Displaced Persons Act, had already fulfilled the residence requirement, and thus had become eligible. The Immigration Law of 1952, however, changed the requirements. The seven-year continuous-residence provision was dropped. The five-year-residence requirement was from the time of adjustment and not from the time of original entry in cases where status had been adjusted after entry.[31] Thus a Chinese who was in the United States for any period before submitting his application for adjustment of status under the Refugee Relief Act of 1953 has to wait five years more after his adjustment of status to permanent residence in order to qualify himself for naturalization; so that by the time of his application he has already spent many years in this country. A large number of Chinese war brides who entered the United States between 1946 and 1950 have been naturalized.

The naturalization of parents has also enabled children to obtain citizenship after meeting certain requirements. More recent marriages between Chinese and Chinese-Americans increase the number. Most Chinese who obtained permanent residence under the Refugee Relief Act of 1953 became eligible about 1960, consequently Chinese naturalizations are expected to increase.

In addition to obtaining citizenship by birth in the United States and by naturalization, a limited number of Chinese obtained citizenship by derivation.[32] Under the earlier laws a child born in China of a United States citizen was considered a citizen by derivation. Later the laws were made conditional, and since 1934 have required the parent to have been in the United States for ten years before the birth of the child. This provision was continued in the Act of 1952.

We have discussed the status of Chinese immigration since the repeal of the Chinese Exclusion Act. We understand that since the repeal a number of Chinese have been admitted through quota, non-quota, private legislation, adjustment of status, and the suspension of deportation. The Displaced Persons Act, the Refugee Relief Act, Public Laws 85-316 and 85-700, and later acts have been instrumental in enabling thousands of Chinese in the United States to adjust their status to that of permanent residents. The Refugee Relief Act and later legislation have brought to the United States more than 10,000, most of whom came from Hong Kong, Taiwan, and nearby places. Thus the number of Chinese immigrants admitted between 1944 and 1960 reached a total of 40,031. During the same period 10,116 Chinese emigrants left the United States.[33]

It will be seen that 28 per cent of Chinese immigrants departed after having stayed for some time, while 72 per cent chose to remain more or less permanently. Between 1949 and 1960 there were 20,773 female immigrants admitted and only 1,306 who departed, while 3,328 male emigrants departed and 14,180 came to this country.[34] It is to be noted that, among the departing emigrants (1944-58), 4,406, or 43.5 per cent, left the United States during 1947 and 1948, at a time when the mainland of China was still under the control of the Nationalist government. From 1949 to 1957 the number of emigrants amounted to 4,632, or an average of about 515 a year. Only two Chinese emigrants departed during the fiscal year 1958. This position, which is not paralleled among other Asiatic immigrants in the United States, is mostly due to the unwillingness of the Chinese to return to their country of birth because of Communist occupation.

TABLE 27

CHINESE IMMIGRANTS ADMITTED AND CHINESE EMIGRANTS
DEPARTED TO AND FROM THE UNITED STATES, 1944-60

Year	Admitted	Departed
1944	34	49
1945	109	257
1946	233	770
1947	1,128	2,168
1948	3,574	2,238
1949	2,490	547
1950	1,289	674
1951	1,083	560
1952	1,152	397
1953	1,093	293
1954	2,747	733
1955	2,628	921
1956	4,450	224
1957	5,123	283
1958	3,195	2
1959	6,031	*
1960	3,672	*
TOTAL	40,031	10,116

*Not available.
Source: Annual Report, 1944-60.

After having reviewed those immigration measures, we may conclude that in the American immigration policy the status of some
nationalities is considered superior to that of others. Thus southeastern Europeans seem to be less welcomed in this country than
northwestern Europeans, let alone Asiatics. The necessity of maintaining a balanced composition of racial homogeneity in the American
population is faithfully adhered to, as evidenced by strict observance
of the national origins system adopted in 1924. The reallocation of
an unused quota is not allowed. In this respect the United States
certainly has many close followers in North America, Europe, and
elsewhere. Mackenzie King's much-quoted statement that the immigration law should not produce a fundamental alteration in the character of Canada's population is still meticulously heeded. Under the
circumstances, it is natural that Asiatic immigration to the United
States should be kept at a minimum. The very limited quotas employed for countries of the so-called Asia-Pacific Triangle are
based on race rather than on the country-of-birth formula used for
European quotas; thus they depart from standard practice. These and
other deviations are but the consequences of the restrictive American policy. As long as there is a different treatment for one European
nation than for another, there will be little reason for Asiatic or
African immigrants to expect anything better.

On the other hand, the record is plain that America admitted between 1941 and 1960 more than thirty-five million immigrants, most of them within the past ten years. This number is about 470,000 more than the annual quota set by the existing immigration law. The Displaced Persons Act, the Refugee Relief Act, the War Brides Act, the admission of Hungarian refugees or orphans, skilled technicians, and those who obtained relief through private legislation, are responsible for the increases. In fact at times there have been sensible annual presidential messages to Congress suggesting a generous change in the immigration law. Also a number of Congressional bills to liberalize the existing act have been introduced from time to time. So far, however, there seems to have been no real effort. The best one can expect is some improvement in the status of minorities through piecemeal legislation and by administrative actions. Naturally administrative actions are likely to be changed under the stress of expediency.

We have to admit that Emma Lazarus' immortal "lamp beside the golden door" to permit any number of homeless refugees to come to the United States is no longer possible, nor is it desirable from all standpoints. The day for absorbing an indefinite number of immigrants has gone. But, it is also true that a nation composed of diverse races from all corners of the world is capable of giving fair and equal treatment to all immigrants, regardless of where they have come from. An impartial and objective observation will discover that the many who in the past twenty years have made achievements and who have contributed to the American way of life are certainly not limited to those from northwestern Europe.

Rational rules and regulations that might eliminate injustice and superstition toward all immigrants would certainly benefit the standing of a true democratic country. As a matter of fact, a well-timed and planned immigration policy should produce economic as well as noneconomic benefits to the receiving country, without any regard to the obligation a civilized and wealthy nation is theoretically supposed to adopt.

6

Relief through Private Legislation

At least 182 Chinese nationals who would otherwise have been unable to secure the status of permanent residents in the United States have been accorded that status through private legislation enacted by Congress.[1] Out of those 182, seventy-three had not lived in this country before the bills concerning them were enacted into law. Among the seventy-three, nine adults had visited the United States, but six adults and fifty-eight minors had never been here. Of the remainder who were in the United States when bills on their behalf were introduced, eleven minors were with their families; a twelfth came in 1942 with returning Americans who had been interned in Hong Kong during the early stage of World War II, and was committed to the care of his adoptive father. Altogether the relief of twenty families—fifty-one persons—was obtained by the enactment of twenty private laws. Of the ninety-nine adults already in the United States, nearly two thirds—sixty-one precisely—had had a college education: six had acquired the degree of Ph. D. ; sixteen are physicians; three are dentists; and others are scientists, engineers, bankers, and businessmen. Three of the immigrants who arrived minus all documents also were granted the status of permanent residence: one was a stowaway, another simply hopped across the border, the third jumped ship and disappeared in the throng. Several persons admitted under this private bill possessed considerable wealth, but the average person was of the middle class, with moderate income.

The bills affecting the 182 Chinese nationals were introduced between the second session of the Seventy-eighth Congress and the Eighty-fourth, and were enacted into 133 private laws—forty-eight originating in the Senate and eighty-five in the House. During the same period, approximately 1,016 bills involving Chinese nationals were introduced which were incapable of passage—363 in the Senate and 653 in the House, affecting about 1,423 persons. Those enacted into law represent only 11.53 per cent of all the bills introduced; in terms of numbers of persons, only 12.71 per cent. On the average, for each hundred bills introduced, only twelve or thirteen would be enacted. On the other hand, the number of private immigration and nationality laws enacted affecting nationals of all countries, had never been very large. The percentage has ranged from 3.26 (Seventy-ninth Congress) to 27.43 (Eighty-fourth Congress).[2]

TABLE 28

PRIVATE IMMIGRATION BILLS INTRODUCED AND LAWS
ENACTED FROM 75TH TO 84TH CONGRESS

Congress	Bills Introduced	Laws Enacted	Percentage
75th	293	30	10.24
76th	601	65	10.81
77th	430	22	5.12
78th	163	12	7.36
79th	429	14	3.26
80th	1,141	121	10.60
81st	2,811	505	17.97
82nd	3,660	729	19.87
83rd	4,797	755	15.74
84th	4,474	1,227	27.43

There appear to have been three principal types of private bills handled by Congress: (1) private claim bills, (2) private immigration and naturalization bills, and (3) private land bills providing for the issuance of patents in fee, and so forth.[3] The number of private bills introduced and enacted varied in different Congresses.[4] They usually occupied a third to a half of their total legislation.[5] Perhaps owing to the restrictive nature of the 1952 Immigration Act, however, the number of private immigration bills introduced in Congress in 1953 increased 48 per cent over those in 1952. In 1954 the private immi-

TABLE 29

PRIVATE IMMIGRATION BILLS AFFECTING CHINESE NATIONALS ENACTED
FROM 78TH CONGRESS, 2ND SESSION TO 84TH CONGRESS

Congress	Session	Senate Bill	Senate Persons	House Bill	House Persons
78th	2nd	0	0	1	1
79th	1st	0	0	0	0
79th	2nd	0	0	0	0
80th	1st	0	0	0	0
80th	2nd	2	3	2	5
81st	1st	1	1	4	6
81st	2nd	4	4	15	22
82nd	1st	6	7	3	3
82nd	2nd	16	24	24	32
83rd	1st	4	4	4	5
83rd	2nd	9	13	9	10
84th	1st	1	1	11	14
84th	2nd	5	6	12	21
TOTAL		48	63	85	119

TABLE 30

PRIVATE IMMIGRATION BILLS AFFECTING CHINESE NATIONALS FAILED TO BE
ENACTED FROM 78TH CONGRESS, 2ND SESSION TO 84TH CONGRESS

		Senate		House	
Congress	Session	Bill	Persons	Bill	Persons
78th	2nd	0	0	1	1
79th	1st	0	0	4	5
79th	2nd	0	0	11	11
80th	1st	3	3	26	30
80th	2nd	9	12	19	24
81st	1st	36	49	26	40
81st	2nd	35	53	43	70
82nd	1st	28	41	76	105
82nd	2nd	29	32	58	73
83rd	1st	37	54	81	107
83rd	2nd	21	30	41	53
84th	1st	71	110	165	245
84th	2nd	94	134	102	141
TOTAL		363	518	653	905

gration laws enacted were 575 out of a total of 774 private laws of all
kinds. One may say that since the 1952 Act the majority of private
bills have referred to immigration matters, mostly involving deportation. The largest number were designed to be humanitarian.[6]

Occasionally there is an item in the newspapers to the effect that,
for example, a certain Chinese physician or his family is subject
to deportation, but that Congress has granted the status of permanent
residence. Such information may also be secured from the *Congressional Record*. Unfortunately, there are no separate lists of
immigration bills affecting Chinese or other nationals.

The purpose, therefore, of our study is to determine how many
Chinese have been granted the status of permanent residence through
private laws enacted since the repeal of the Chinese Exclusion Act[7]–
who they are, and what are their characteristics. We also wish to
find the answers to several questions. Had they ever been in the
United States? When had they come? Under what status? Are they
highly skilled specialists? What are they doing now? Is the principle
of keeping families united in operation? Have there been abuses in
these private bills, to escape deportation, for example? The percentage of private bills enacted deserves attention. The period we
are reviewing extends from January 10, 1944 (Seventy-eighth Congress, second session) to July 26, 1956 (adjournment of the Eighty-
fourth Congress). The best source of information is the documentary
history of each application as prepared by the appropriate department, since it is customary for the judiciary subcommittee of either
the Senate or the House to request a report on each case from the
Department of Justice or some other department according to the

requirements of the case. Also very useful is a check through the voluminous Congressional documents, selecting whatever appears to relate to Chinese nationals. In addition, it may be necessary to look into much personal correspondence, not all of it open to the private researcher.

Our study is confined to determining the number of bills relating to Chinese nationals. This becomes possible by examining the *Congressional Record*, referring to the index of all bills introduced and passed in each session. After having sifted those bills enacted and those rejected, we have a basis for analysis. Some bills were introduced but died at the close of the particular Congressional session before having been considered. The next step was to obtain all the information about those bills enacted, by a study of the Senate and House reports. Interviews were conducted with several families and individuals whose bills were passed.

Occasional similarities of Chinese and American names have been somewhat baffling; for example, there are Chinese names spelled Young, King, and Lee, identical with American names. Koreans furnish even closer similarities, so that several bills formerly thought to refer to Chinese have been found to refer to Koreans. Several private laws affecting the Chinese but having nothing to do with immigration had to be discarded. Also, though the judiciary committee of the Senate or of the House published reports as to when, in the opinion of the committee, the bills should be enacted, nevertheless, since they were merely reports, their information is not always serviceable for purposes of comparison. Sometimes information in one report is lacking in others. The margin of error in not including all bills, passed or unpassed, affecting Chinese nationals, is about 10 per cent.[8]

There are also cases in which Congress has passed an act to make a Chinese a citizen instead of a permanent resident, or to legalize the nationalization of a Chinese.[9] The vast majority of immigration bills are for the granting of permanent residence.[10] In such cases, the alien concerned is legally considered a quota immigrant at the time of his last entry into the United States.

After the repeal of the Exclusion Act, when the Chinese were eligible for naturalization, the first Chinese to be made a permanent resident by private law and thus subject to eventual naturalization was a boy of eighteen. He had been born in Singapore, but whether of Chinese or of mixed parentage, he did not know. His foster father, a native American, saw the boy working in the bay at Singapore, and told the person who had custody of the boy that he himself was the father. He took the boy to Hong Kong in 1941 and placed him in school in Kowloon. When the Japanese invaded Hong Kong the same year, the boy was interned from January to June, 1942, and then, with 1,500 American prisoners, brought to the United States. On September 25, the boy was released to his foster father, who then guaranteed that the boy would not become a public charge. He was sent to Los Angeles to study, where he had just been graduated from the junior high school at the time of his application. A private bill on his behalf was passed by the Seventy-eighth Congress, second session.

Of the eight persons successful in being granted private legislative relief during the second session of the Eightieth Congress, four were males and four were females, including two minors. Two entered the United States in 1939, one in 1940, and five between 1944 and 1948, all eight under the status of visitors. The two in 1939, who came for a temporary stay, were the mother and sister of a Chinese-American honorably discharged after World War I. Among the adults were two physicians, two college graduates, and a former Davis Cup contestant.

During the sessions of the Eighty-first Congress, the percentage of bills passed affecting Chinese nationals was 14.63 per cent whereas the total of the private immigration and nationality bills passed by the same Congress was 17.97 per cent of all bills introduced. Of the thirty-three persons admitted, eighteen were minors who had never been in the United States; however, their fathers or foster fathers were American citizens. Two of the minors were eligible for admission under the provisions of Section 4 (a) and Section 9 of the Immigration Act of 1924 as amended. The children were being supported by their fathers or foster fathers. Of the five fathers who reported their occupations, two managed hand laundries, one was a millworker, one a cameraman, and one a physician.

Of these thirty-three persons admitted, eleven declared their birthplace to have been Kwangtung Province and four Hong Kong; except for five who had been born in countries other than China, the remainder had come from other parts of China.

Of the thirteen adults who were in the United States when their bills were introduced in Congress, twelve had come between 1945 and 1949, one in 1936. Four were physicians, one held the degree of Ph. D. in science, and another a Master of Laws degree. Two others were in college and one in high school. Eight came to the United States as visitors and five as students.

It is interesting to note, among several cases of minors and mothers who were in Hong Kong, the case of a mother and her adult son who were there when their bill was introduced. She had six other sons, four of whom were American citizens, one having been naturalized in recognition of his achievements in World War II and decorated August, 1945, for bravery as a representative of the Su-

preme Allied Command in China. Another minor's father served
in the United States Army during World War II and received an hon-
orable discharge. He purchased $4,000 worth of war bonds, in addi-
tion to having $2,000 in the bank. The father of another, honorably
discharged for disability, receives a small pension from the United
States government. One woman's husband, a Chinese consul in Manila, had been executed by the Japanese for his refusal to cooperate
with them when they seized Manila in 1942. She and her two sons
entered the United States September 21, 1945. The husband had
requested that his sons be educated at Yale University. Meanwhile
the Chinese Nationalist government has assumed responsibility
for his widow's maintenance and for the education of her children.

It is always the intention of Congress to admit highly skilled specialists from all countries, and Congress has done this with many
Chinese nationals. A woman scientist, a Ph.D. from Oregon State
University, is with a well-known electric corporation and is doing
confidential work for the army and navy. A husband and wife, both
physicians in the Western State Hospital of Tennessee, caused the
governor to get in touch with Senator Estes Kefauver and Congressman Tom Murray to sponsor their private bill.

Of all Congresses, the Eighty-second enacted the largest number
of private laws affecting Chinese nationals, with a record of the
passage of 20.42 per cent of all bills introduced. Only four bills,
affecting five persons, failed to pass because of adjournment. The
forty-nine bills passed in that Congress affected sixty-six persons, forty males and twenty-six females, of whom thirty-six were
minors and thirty-four had not been in the United States. Of the
seven adults who were in Hong Kong while their applications were
in process, two had not been in this country, as they were fiancées
of Chinese-Americans. The total stay of the five mothers, who had
been here at various times, was 102 years, ranging from 4 to 37,
an average stay of 20 years. From the record, apparently 33 bills,
or 67 per cent, assisted in reuniting families. The fathers of most
of the minors were American citizens; others had citizen children.
Orphans who have been adopted by American citizens have been
treated in the same manner. The family status of the forty-one
people affected by the thirty-three bills is as follows:

Relationship	Citizenship	Relationship	Citizenship
Father	21	Husband	1
Mother	4	Stepfather	1
Children	4	Father, already filed	
Foster father	3	declaration of intention	1
Parent	2	Unknown	2
Fiancée	2	TOTAL	41

Several of the Chinese nationals who were already in the United States when their bills were passed had relatives who were citizens. At least one applicant was the husband of an American citizen, another had a citizen fiancée. The brother of one was an American-Chinese. The mother who had been in the United States the longest was one who had come to Hawaii as early as 1896, before the annexation by the United States, when she was twenty-two years of age. After having lived in Hawaii about forty years, she left with her husband in 1937 to make a short visit to China; there he became ill and died, and she was never able to return. In Hawaii she had given birth to and had reared eleven children. In addition, she was the grandmother of thirty and the great-grandmother of ten, all of them American citizens.

Though some of the minors had parents who were native-born American citizens, others were naturalized only after 1943. One father had been born in Honolulu in 1913 and married in China in 1938; there he had four children, born in 1939, 1942, 1947, and 1948. The family thereafter moved to Honolulu. Three of the children acquired United States citizenship under Section 793 of the Revised Statutes as amended by the Act of May 24, 1934; the child born in 1942 was not considered an American citizen because of the Nationality Act of 1941. In another case, even though the father was native-born, he had failed to complete five years' residence in the United States before he was sixteen; therefore, his child could not acquire citizenship by birth.

Needless to say, all alien minors entering as permanent residents must show proof that they will not become public charges. Aged mothers depend upon their children for support. The following supporters of dependents have stated their various occupations:

Super- and food market employee	4
Restaurant employee	3
Company employee	2
Taxi driver	1
Salesman	1
Radio and appliance worker	1
Laundry employee	1
Manufacturing employee	1
Government employee	1
Dentist	1
TOTAL	16

Of the remaining twenty-five persons who were admitted to become permanent residents by private bills, three came as students, eighteen as visitors, and four as government officials with their families. Though the majority of them arrived after 1946, one had come as early as 1927.

Date of Entry	Number
1927	1
1940	1
1946	1
1947	2
1948	1
1949	12
1950	6
1951	1
TOTAL	25

Fifteen of the adults have had college education, four have finished high school, and thus all are able to support themselves. One, who is in the jewelry business, reported a monthly income of $1,000 to $2,000; the physicians are receiving about $500 a month.

Of the thirty-two persons admitted as permanent residents during the Eighty-third Congress, twenty had had a college education. Two were Ph.D.'s, two held M.A.'s and two A.B.'s; three were physicians, two were dental surgeons. Among the beneficiaries one will find physicians, dentists, aeronautical engineers, college professors, botanists, and successful private bankers. There were two minors and two orphans who had never been in the United States, though their foster fathers were American citizens. The two adults who were in Hong Kong when their applications were made had been in the United States for more than ten years. Six applicants had citizen children in the United States.

There were more males than females, eighteen and fourteen, respectively; twenty-three married, three widowers. Of those who were in the United States, twenty-five came between 1941 and 1952, and one in 1922. Sixteen came as temporary visitors, four as students.

Three interesting cases appeared in both sessions of the Eighty-fourth Congress. One was a stowaway who had entered illegally on September 15, 1934, and who now had a grocery in Arizona, and was considered by the residents of his community a good and worthy citizen. Another seaman jumped ship in January, 1936; he became a cook and baker, self-supporting and law-abiding, and highly recommended by all those who knew him. The third slipped across the border in March, 1949. He had lived in the United States from 1896 to 1946, when he returned to China because of the death of his father. Though he considered America as his own country, he could not come back, for he had no permit to do so; he resorted to smuggling himself into the country as the most convenient means of returning. After his return he became a restaurateur somewhere in Virginia.

Twenty-nine private bills were passed by the Eighty-fourth Congress for twenty-six males and sixteen females, twenty-six of whom were married, one divorced, and one widowed. Six of the minors had never been in the United States; three adults were in Hong Kong and one in Macao while their bills were going through Congress. Twenty-eight adults, excluding the stowaway, the border jumper, and the ship jumper, entered the United States, chiefly from 1944 to 1955. Thirteen entered as students, ten as visitors, and four as transients. Ten beneficiaries had one or more children who were citizens by birth; one applicant's mother was a citizen; there were also one foster father, two brothers, and one husband. Fifteen applicants had had college educations and three had finished high school.

Ph. D.	2
M. D.	2
D. D. S.	1
M. A.	2
A. B. ; B. S.	5
College	3
High school	3
TOTAL	18

From a study of the bills enacted in each Congress, we can summarize information we have gathered. Unfortunately, complete information on every case is unprocurable; particularly lacking are data about income. In regard to physicians attached to hospitals, for example, remuneration consists of a definite salary plus room

Annual Income	Persons
$1,000-1,999	1
2,000-2,999	5
3,000-3,999	3
4,000-4,999	3
5,000-5,999	3
6,000-6,999	2
7,000-7,999	2
8,000-8,999	1
9,000-9,999	1
10,000 and over	3

and board, to which we have assigned the arbitrary figure of $150 per month for the sake of comparison. On the other hand, information is available on several supporters of dependents who are American citizens and have either regular employment or businesses of their own. One of the judiciary subcommittee's primary conditions for considering a case favorable is based on knowing whether the person in question is earning a living or whether he is dependent on others for support. The annual income of twenty-four beneficiaries is shown on the preceding page.

In regard to moral character and security risk, the subcommittee requires absolute certainty. The principle of maintaining family unity, as part of the immigration policy, is illustrated in many of the private bills enacted. The 133 private laws affected 182 persons, seventy-four of whom were members of American citizens' families. Twenty families, involving fifty-one persons, were already in the United States. The family status of United States citizens follows:

Relationship	Number
Father	33
Children	23
Foster father	6
Mother	5
Stepfather	4
Brother	4
Wife	3
Parent	3
Husband	3
Fiancée	2
Father, already filed declaration of intention	1

Sixty-four entered as temporary visitors, four as transients, twenty-six as students, four as government officials with their families, one as a stowaway, one as a seaman, and one as a border jumper. Probably none of these has had much right to remain permanently. Those who were already here had entered during the following periods:

1920-29	3
1930-39	5
1940-49	64
1950-55	35
TOTAL	107

Of the 182 persons under review, 55 per cent were thirty-four or younger.

Age Distribution

Age	Number
Under 15	38
15-24	31
25-34	24
35-44	38
45-54	18
55-64	11
65 and over	9
Unknown	13
TOTAL	182

There were 115 males and sixty-seven females. Seventy were married, ten were widowers, and three divorced. Forty-three had been born in the province of Kwangtung, thirty-two in Hong Kong, forty in other parts of China; twenty had been born in countries other than China, such as England, Belgium, and Southeast Asia. The remaining forty-seven declared that they had been born in China but gave no particulars.

Besides family unity, Congress stresses the qualifications of applicants, for example, whether they would serve the United States by higher education, technical training, specialized experiences, or exceptional ability. Of the seventy-one who specified their educational background, thirty-three reported degrees beyond that of A.B.; among them were sixteen physicians, three dentists, and several scientists, engineers, and professors.

Educational Background

Education	Number
M.D.	16
Ph.D.	6
D.D.S.	3
J.D.	1
M.A.	7
B.A.	10
College	18
High school	10
TOTAL	71

Profession

Occupation	Number
Physician	16
Businessman	6
Scientist	6
Engineer	4
College professor	4
Dentist	3
Banker	3
Others	14
TOTAL	56

The answer to the question of whether the Chinese have resorted to introducing private bills to forestall orders of deportation would seem to be negative. No bill has been introduced in more than two successive Congresses. Out of 1,016 bills from the Seventy-eighth to the Eighty-fourth Congress, only four, tabled without success, had been introduced in two Congresses. Twenty-three bills introduced in the first session died at adjournment and have not been reintroduced. On the other hand, forty-three bills, successful in passage, had to be continued through a second session. The remaining ninety were introduced and passed in a single session.

The number of bills affecting Chinese nationals enacted in proportion to those introduced has been increasing ever since the Eighty-first Congress: the highest is 20.42 per cent in the Eighty-second; and the lowest 6.29 per cent in the Eighty-fourth. During the same period, all private bills introduced and private laws enacted, affecting all nationals, are of higher proportion, ranging from 15.74 per cent in the Eighty-third to 27.43 per cent in the Eighty-fourth. One explanation of the lower percentage for Chinese nationals may be that few cases of naturalization have been brought up, because the Chinese became eligible for naturalization after the repeal of the Exclusion Act in 1943. The effect, however, should be rather slight. When we take into consideration a margin of error of 10 per cent, we find the percentage of private bills enacted affecting Chinese nationals still very low. It may be inferred that Congress is stricter toward Chinese nationals than toward private bills as a whole.

It has been recognized that, no matter how carefully the lawmakers may enact legislation to ameliorate the hardships of immigration and naturalization, there always remain individual cases that deserve special consideration. The executive branch of the government is usually so hampered by rules and regulations that it does not often wish to use its discretionary powers. Therefore, Congress has been more than justified in meeting the exigencies of persons appealing for relief. The small number of bills passed by Congress affecting Chinese nationals is in accord with Congressional policy of treating all bills cautiously. On the other hand, the increasing number of bills introduced from session to session involves much work, time, and expense, both in Congress and in the executive branch. Skepticism has accordingly been aroused as to whether public bills affecting the interests of people in general have thus been jeopardized. The Department of Justice has long assumed the position that the enactment of private immigration bills might encourage disregard for the existing and regular immigration procedures. This is to the great disadvantage of the vast majority of aliens, who have often been subject to deferment to make place for those who had been residing in the United States unlawfully. Concerning a bill before the Eighty-first Congress (eventually passed) involving a Chinese couple, both of them physicians, and their daughter, a minor, the Department of Justice wrote a letter dated July 5, 1950, to Congressman

Emanuel Celler, Chairman of the House Judiciary Committee, reading partly as follows:

The Chinese racial quota to which the three aliens are chargeable is heavily oversubscribed, and immigration visas are not readily available. There are many aliens of the Chinese race abroad whose cases are quite similar to that of the Chens, in that they desire to enter the United States for permanent residence, but are unable to do so because of the oversubscribed condition of the Chinese racial quota. The facts presented in the instant case do not appear to warrant the enactment of special legislation granting them a preference over such other aliens. To enact this bill would encourage those in whose cases immigration visas are not readily obtainable to enter the United States in a temporary status as students or visitors, and remain in this country hoping to be able to adjust their immigration status to that of permanent residents.

Accordingly, the Department of Justice is unable to recommend enactment of this bill.

The objections raised by the Department of Justice seem to emphasize the desirability of applying for the right to remain in the United States in accordance with existing laws and regulations; the objections are reminders rather than protests. Occasionally the department suggested that the facts in the case merit policy decision. In no case of those whose bills have been eventually passed into law did the Department of Justice raise strong objections nor did it insist that an applicant actually in the United States be deported.

The demand for private immigration legislation is chiefly caused by the lack of quota for countries whose quotas are oversubscribed most of the time or to technical difficulties. A certain modification of the national-origin system to permit the transfer of the unused quotas to areas in demand would automatically reduce the need for many private bills.[11] The improvement of the quota conditions as created by Public Laws 85-316 and 85-700 has to a certain extent reduced the need for the private immigration bill. But in the cases of China and Japan the quotas are still too small for the demand.

In spite of the cautious and reluctant attitude taken by Congress toward granting discretionary authority to the administrative branch in immigration matters, Congress has in recent years shown its willingness to expand the scope of administrative discretion. In 1955, the restoration of pre-examination by the Immigration Service broadened the sphere of the Attorney General's discretion to grant relief to aliens in the country.[12] Public Law 85-700, passed August 21, 1958, modified the existing law, permitting the Department of Justice to allow aliens to adjust their legal status without going through the traditional process of going to Canada to obtain a visa. Thus it eliminates the necessity of pre-examination, and has made the adjustment of status even more convenient. The law includes a provision permitting some specially skilled persons to come in outside the quota, where the countries from which they came had oversubscribed their quotas, provided the aliens were designated as eligible for preference before July 1, 1958. Pre-examinations were terminated altogether in 1959.

Public Law 85-316, passed September 11, 1957, also vested discretionary authority in the attorney general. In addition to the skilled aliens of the first preference, those of the second and third preferences were also permitted to adjust their status as nonquota immigrants, if approved by the attorney general before July 1, 1957. The attorney general is also authorized to waive deportation for those who have obtained visas or documentation to enter the United States by fraud or misrepresentation, provided they are the spouse, parent, or child of an American citizen, or of an alien resident. Many private bills have been introduced in recent years because the administrative branch has been without such discretionary authority. Congress has seen fit to extend the benefit to an entire defined class of aliens whose cases may be as deserving as those cases that fortunately reached Congress for special action. Other provisions gave authority to the attorney general to waive, on behalf of spouse, child, or parent of an American citizen or a resident alien, charges of criminal or immoral actions, and certain health charges as grounds for inadmissibility.

Class	Number of Persons	Number of Private Bills
First Preference		
Scientists and engineers	18 (including 6 dependents)	12
Medical doctors and dental surgeons	24 (including 5 dependents; on 2 bills both husband and wife are M.D.'s)	18
Nonquota		
Children of American citizens	39	34
Spouses of American citizens	4	4
Orphans adopted or to be adopted by American citizens	8	7
TOTAL	93	75

The Immigration Service has estimated that nearly half the private bills would have been unnecessary had the attorney general previously been vested with such discretionary authority as is given under Public Law 85-316.[13] The number of private bills will probably further decline as a result of the passing of Public Law 85-700. Among bills affecting Chinese nationals, the need for private legislation will also be lessened in view of the availability of nonquota status immigrants as first preferences under both Public Laws 85-316 and 85-700. Of the bills passed affecting Chinese personnel, it was found that between 55 and 60 per cent would not have had to be introduced had Public Laws 85-316 and 85-700 and the nonquota status of children and spouses of American citizens been in effect under the 1952 Act. On the preceding page are listed private bills affecting Chinese nationals who, if Public Laws 85-316 and 85-700 had been in force, could have obtained administrative relief within the provision of immigration laws and thereby would not have needed to ask Congress for relief.

There appears to be little doubt that the private bills for immigration, claims, patent, or relief from paying taxes will be introduced from time to time.[14] The burden on Congress will undoubtedly become proportionately heavier. The fact that a large percentage of bills has been rejected, session after session, proves that not all bills introduced are considered meritorious or exceptional. It has been recognized, though, that the enactment of private bills may produce inequitable results. Many suffer hardship and need assistance just as critically as those to whom Congress later offers relief. The large number of bills introduced also indicates that there is a clear need of improvement or change in the general statutory provisions under the present immigration laws.

There is no question that the best and only means of relieving Congress of the heavy burden created by private legislation lies in the hands of the congressmen themselves.[15] It is for Congress to decide whether there are more private bills than can be handled. After all, the congressman has the responsibility of deciding whether the problem of the necessity of the great number of private bills should be solved by a modification of existing law or by a revised immigration law. Though the large percentage of failures may have created an impression that not many bills are meritorious, Congress does not seem ready to determine in advance definite criteria for accurate guidance of all its members. Strict adherence to a certain predetermined standard will surely help the situation. Rules, regulations, and governmental principles are necessary, but a humanitarian policy in applying them is essential. The strength of the democratic process lies in the willingness of the government to guard the rights of the most humble, the most unorthodox, and the most despised persons. It is true that the enactment of private legislation may be a "petty business";[16] but, at its best, it is a means of conferring justice on individuals.

7

Litigation, Court Decisions,

and the Problem of Illegal Entry

Elsewhere we have discussed highlights of important decisions, affecting the interests of Chinese immigrants, made by the California State Supreme Court during the early period of agitation against the Chinese. They were denied counsel, except in case of an appeal. They had to produce credible white witnesses to testify that they were legal residents; American nonwhite persons were held as unqualifiable. Such discrimination has been gradually done away with. When the restriction of Chinese laborers took effect in 1882, and when the Quota Acts of 1921 and 1924 had been passed, the number of Chinese immigrants was greatly reduced. Judicial reviews of lawsuits involving Chinese immigration, however, still went on. Here and there court rulings set aside decisions of the Immigration Service, though in many cases the courts refused to accept jurisdiction. Such challenging of the decisions made by the secretary of labor or later by the attorney general usually involved habeas corpus proceedings.

The repeal of the Chinese Exclusion Act in 1943, however, and especially the Communist occupation of mainland China in 1949, prompted the Chinese again to seek entry into the United States. Some came as visitors, others as students though they had long finished their studies. Technically, a number of Chinese were unable to maintain the status under which they had entered the United States, and yet because of the Communist regime in China many Chinese were unwilling to return. Some who had entered as students or visitors were unable to support themselves, and were therefore compelled to seek employment, thereby losing their standing under the immigration law. As a result, because of the immigration requirements and the technical procedures involved, many of these Chinese were in unintentional and continuous difficulties with the Immigration Service. As various relief laws were passed by Congress, a number of Chinese asked suspension of deportation for fear of physical persecution; and though many of the Chinese did qualify under the laws, others did not qualify, mostly for technical reasons, and were refused adjustment of their status. Such technical questions of the suspension of deportation have been major causes for court action.

Meanwhile a great number of children of Chinese-Americans who made application to come to America to join their families had a difficult time convincing the American consulate in Hong Kong of their true identity. Since a number of these applications were found to be fraudulent, it was necessary for the authorities to take extraordinary precautions. Many Chinese appealed to United States courts for judicial relief. Some won, but many lost. Much of this litigation invariably involved the right to enter the United States as children of Chinese-American citizens.

Judicial Review of Immigration Cases

Anyone familiar with immigration laws in the United States is aware of the uncertainty that prevails today in the areas concerned with judicial review. There has been little statutory authorization for judicial study covering this important branch of law, yet there has been remarkable expansion in litigation on immigration cases. It is only through case-by-case development that some controlling principles are evolved, and the lack of stability in the formula of judicial review is understandable. No doubt the law is still in need of change and development. For many years the Department of Justice and its predecessor in charge of Immigration Service, the secretary of labor, had taken the stand that the attorney general had the final say in the matter of deportation or expulsion, and that judicial intervention, except with habeas corpus proceedings, was not warranted. But when the Department of Justice was later affected by the Administrative Procedure Act, more immigration cases were subject to review by the courts.

In challenging a deportation order, an alien may obtain judicial review by an application for a writ of habeas corpus, as well as by an action under Section 10 of the Administrative Procedure Act. The alien in question may also in certain cases file a suit for review and injunctive relief on constitutional questions. An order of deportation can be reviewed either in a writ of habeas corpus proceeding, which if the alien is detained is guaranteed by the United States Constitution, or by declaratory judgment action. Under decisions of the United States Supreme Court the latter recourse is available to aliens not in detention.[1] A number of court actions involved judicial review of the denial of administrative relief, even in cases where deportability was conceded.

It is the duty of the court to take an interest in reviewing the constitutionality of the immigration laws, in examining carefully whether there has been any unfairness in the hearings, a lack of qualification on the part of officers, and noncompliance with the Administrative Procedure Act.[2] The court has frequently taken the stand "the price for greater fairness is not too huge."[3] In the case of deportation Justice William O. Douglas said that deportation is certainly a serious penalty.[4] As early as 1893 Justice Brewer, in his notable dissent in the case of *Fong Yue Ting* v. *United States* (149 U.S. 698), said:

Deportation is punishment. It involves first an arrest, a deprival of liberty; and second, a removal from home, from business, from property. . . . If a banishment of this sort be not a punishment among the severest of punishments, it will be difficult to imagine a doom to which the name can be applied.[5]

It is only proper that the courts should see that the deportation order is made according to due process of law. The court has to recognize that every person, including the alien, is entitled to the protection of the Constitution, and that no punishment should be inflicted without judicial trial.[6] On the other hand, the court is not supposed to interfere with the lawful decisions of the Executive. If the hearing has been fair, and if no error of law has been committed, the ruling of the Department of Justice must stand, and it cannot be altered in judicial proceedings.[7] As a matter of fact, more cases have been dismissed than sustained.

In administrative hearings before the Immigration and Naturalization Service, procedures, as set out in the regulation of the Immigration and Naturalization Service (Title 8, Code of Federal Regulations) and, to some extent in the Administrative Procedure Act, must be observed.[8] Failure to observe the statutory and regulatory procedures would be considered a violation of "due process."

In those situations where administrative discretion is given under the statute to the attorney general in connection with various applications, the courts are most reluctant to review the exercise of such discretion and will grant review only where the alien can show that the administrative discretion was abused or if it can be established that the procedure violated "due process" under the Constitution and statutes of the United States. This is so with regard to applications for suspension of deportation, for adjustment of status by a temporary visitor to permanent residence, and with regard to applications for a stay of deportation because of persecution.[9]

The decisions of the various courts concerning deportation or exclusion cases are naturally watched with interest and concern by the Department of Justice, of which the Immigration Service is part. Frequently the opinions given and the decisions made by the court have helped the Immigration Service to improve its conduct of hearings. After the decision in the Wong Yang-Sun case, in which the Supreme Court held that the administrative hearing must be conducted in conformity with the Administrative Procedure Act, the Immigration Service realized that prosecutive and adjudicative functions have to be separated, so that an officer cannot act as "investigator, prosecutor, and judge" at the same time.[10] In the case of those who apply for stay of deportation on the ground that they fear they may be subject to physical persecution by being deported to the mainland of China, the Immigration Service has eased its stand somewhat, so that since October 31, 1956, there is no need to produce proof for such fear, except by persons whom the Immigration Service believes to be friendly to, or sympathetic with, the Communist regime. The use of confidential information unavailable to the attorneys, which has in the past caused difficulties to Chinese who were seeking to adjust their status, has lately been restricted to certain cases designated by the commissioner of the Immigration and Naturalization Service.[11]

The Department of Justice also has authority to review certain immigration matters on the appeal of the aggrieved party from an administrative decision of the Immigration Service. The Board of Immigration Appeals, a quasi-judicial appellate tribunal with limited jurisdiction, is responsible directly to the attorney general.[12] The decisions made by the board are binding on the Immigration Service and are held to be precedents for similar cases. Many such cases have been decided in favor of the aggrieved party; thus the use of discretionary power has resulted in relief to deportable aliens.

For example, in 1946 a Chinese secured his admission to the United States as a citizen. In 1951, since he admitted alienage, deportation procedure was instituted. He was, however, inducted into the army and served in Japan and Korea from November, 1952, until honorably discharged in March, 1954. The Immigration Service refused his application for the suspension of deportation on the ground that he had failed to meet the requirement of presence in the United States for a continuous period of seven years immediately preceding the date of his application. The Board of Immigration Appeals, in a unanimous decision, ruled that his service in Japan and Korea as a member of the army did not interrupt the physical presence prerequisite for a suspension of deportation. The board made the following bold statement:

We believe it is inconceivable that Congress could have intended that one who risks his life in active combat duty in a foreign country would thereby be barred from suspension of deportation, whereas another alien who preferred no military duty whatsoever and who was thus able to remain in the United States would be entitled to the benefits of Section 244 (a) (1) of the Immigration and Naturalization Act.[13]

In another case, a deportable Chinese seaman had had continuous residence in the United States since 1944. His request for the suspension of deportation was granted after the decision made by the board that the seaman had fulfilled the minimum residence requirement of seven years in the United States; that he had rendered a substantial and meritorious service in the United States Merchant Marine from June 25, 1943, to December 12, 1944; and that he held a citation from the President.[14]

As in all lawsuits, the starting of actions on immigration matters involves a long series of legal maneuvers which may occupy many years before a case finally reaches the Supreme Court. Suits may be instituted in the district in which the alien resides or in the District of Columbia. There has been concentration of litigation in Washington, D.C., partly because only there can the attorney general or the commissioner of the Immigration Service be sued as an indispensable party to a declaratory judgment action.[15] The Immigration Service complained repeatedly in its *Annual Report* on the difficulty and delay in carrying out a deportation order. Mr. Eisenhower, in his immigration message to Congress, January 31, 1957, called to the attention of Congress the need of strengthening the laws in respect to the aliens who resort to repeated judicial reviews and appeals for the sole purpose of delaying their expulsion from this country.[16] Mr. Eisenhower, on the other hand, admitted that any alien has the right to challenge, through judicial process, the government's findings of deportability. He emphasized the necessity for legislation to limit and to define the judicial process in the light of the growing frequency of such cases brought for purposes of delay, particularly those involving aliens found to be criminals, traffickers in narcotics, or subversives.

While there are always some aliens who will take advantage of the existing laws to fight being deported, it is also true that any alien would like to utilize all available means to obtain his right to stay. We need not add that in a number of cases involving deportation, the government turned out to be the loser before the court.

The Problem of Illegal Entry

The Hong Kong American consulate reported half a century ago that the smuggling of Chinese into the United States was a regular business. It has been carried on persistently with few interruptions. In Cuba, Mexico, and Canada, well-organized rings had been set up for the purpose of smuggling in Chinese as well as Mexicans and Europeans. The extent of the smuggling can be seen by the fact that in 1952 a typical case involved smuggling Europeans and Chinese by airplane from Cuba to the United States.[17] The price for smuggling a European or a Chinese has been known to be as high as $2,500. The prevention of illegal entry and the expulsion of undesirables are always considered important functions of the immigration authorities.[18] The detection of those who operate smuggling rackets as a means of making quick profits is being given constant attention. One way to combat smuggling of aliens is to develop an intelligence service to collect, evaluate, and disseminate information concerning smuggling and other methods of illegal entry. Liaison work with officials of neighboring countries has frequently been conducted. In the Border Patrol, the Immigration Service has well-trained inspectors and forces equipped with trucks, jeeps, buses, ships, and airplanes.

The Immigration Service considers that the most flagrant fraudulent practice used to evade the immigration law is in Chinese claiming the right to enter the United States as children of Chinese-American citizens. The *Annual Report* substantially stated:

Something of the extent to which fraud is being perpetrated in Chinese cases may be seen from the result of an investigation made by the San Francisco Immigration Office. During April, May and June, 1925, 256 Chinese men who are American citizens and held certificates as such, and who claimed to be married, returned to the United States through that port, of which 253 claimed wives in China, 19 of them pregnant. The 256 Chinese-Americans claimed a total of 719 children, 670 males and 49 females. The ratio is fantastic . . . foundation laid in the records for future entry. Chinese entered through other ports claiming about all the children they could possibly have in China and most of them denying having any girls.[19]

Under the laws in effect from February 1, 1855, any child born abroad of an American parent is a citizen of the United States, provided the parent in question has resided in this country before the child was born or that certain other conditions existed.[20] After 1934 the law required the citizen-father to have been in the United States for at least ten years before the birth of the children, so that the children might acquire derivative citizenship. Though this change may have reduced the number of applications for entrance as citizens, it left the possibility of coming in on a nonquota basis. Indeed, judging from the rejections made by the American consuls and the investigations made by the State Department and the Immigration Service year by year, there must have been many illegal claims.

While the Chinese-Americans are taking advantage of the existing law, the early exclusion of Chinese immigrants through the enactment of the Chinese Exclusion Act has certainly had a great deal to do with the situation. When the discrimination against the Chinese in the United States reached its climax during the last quarter of the nineteenth century and until well after permanent exclusion took effect in 1904, there was a necessity for the average Chinese to visit his family in China periodically. The situation was slightly improved when Congress passed an act on June 13, 1930, that rendered admissible the Chinese wives of American citizens on the condition that they had been married before May 26, 1924. The act was not helpful to those who had married after the deadline.[21] There is reason to believe that those Chinese who returned to China for periodic visits were moved more by necessity than preference.

The four years before the passage of the 1924 Act saw a large number of children born abroad of native parents admitted to the United States, the number from 1921 to 1924 being about 2,200 a year; from 1933 until 1941 about 1,200 yearly. There were few admissions during World War II. Of immigrant aliens born in China and admitted as children of United States citizens, there were altogether 3,136 children admitted between 1945 and 1960, or an average of 177 a year. Some of them were undoubtedly non-Chinese, though born in China. The number of native-born children admitted as citizens was not included under this category, and no separate figures have been released.

The rush for admittance to the United States was made in 1949 after the fall of Canton to the Communists. The number of applications was so large that the immigration commissioner in his *Annual Report* of 1951 again mentioned the fraudulent practices. It was reported that for that particular fiscal year 1,688 Chinese claiming the right to entry arrived at San Francisco. Only a few cases were approved.

The *Annual Reports* several times have mentioned that Chinese-Americans who visited their families periodically usually reported back that their wives had conceived, or that several children had been born, sometimes twins, invariably boys. If the Chinese man were single, he would report to the authorities that he had married while abroad. For those who wished to utilize the racket, the immigration "slots" were thus created. This "paper father" would make contact with a broker to sell his "paper son," as registered a number of years before, for a consideration, usually from two to three thousand dollars. The buyer of a "slot," as the alleged "son," would then go to the United States consulate claiming derivative citizenship as a child of an American citizen and asking to be admitted to the United States. The "paper son" would of course receive all the parentage affidavits and, with the assistance of the broker, would be armed with detailed information about his alleged family.

The consul and the immigration inquiry officer long ago devised an interrogation system so elaborate and complicated that ordinarily the alleged "son" could not answer all the questions consistently.[22]

The broker accordingly soon devised ways and means of overcoming the difficulty. Sometimes through manipulation with the attorney, and even with the connivance of immigration officers, all pertinent questions and answers were prepared carefully in a "book." The master text is called by the Chinese the "halgoon," or by the immigration officers "that damned Chinese book."

The American consulate in Hong Kong then found a new means of coping with the situation. In 1951 the consulate required blood tests of the father, mother, and children. These tests were reported to be very successful at the start, as the novel device caught the immigration racket by surprise. As a result of this practice, the consulates declared that about 40 per cent of the applicants were proved to be fraudulent. But the racket found means of getting around this new move: steps were taken to match the blood type of the alleged father and family. The service of serologists in the United States was used to type the blood of the alleged father and send it to Hong Kong so that the brokers might sell the slot to those who could match the type of blood. Though the blood test has limited the number of applicants, a complete blockade of the immigration racket has been impossible. Meanwhile a number of cases were brought to United States courts for decision. The plaintiff would claim that the use of a blood test was unconstitutional, since the test was employed only against the Chinese.

According to the report the American consul general made to the State Department in December, 1955, the racketeers had been able to pass whatever obstacles had been thrown in their path. A fantastic system of passport and visa frauds for a time frustrated the efforts of the consulates. The consul general estimated that the brokers would ask $3,000 apiece for faked citizenship documents, with $500 down and the balance payable after the arrival in the United States. There are said to be more than 100 such rackets operating in Hong Kong, with good connections in New York, San Francisco, and elsewhere. In response to the urgent request of the consul general, the State Department has asked Congress for a special appropriation to engage trained investigators; the State Department added 102 employees to its staff at Hong Kong in the second half of 1956 for the sole purpose of investigating and screening immigrants.[23]

The attorney general's office states that there are three important passport rings operating in this country and supposedly reaping a profit of about $3,000,000 a year. The latest move the government has taken is an attempt to wipe out the ingenious passport racket by investigating the slot brokers themselves.[24] In February, 1956, grand juries were impaneled in New York and in San Francisco to investigate charges made by the government. In San Francisco a turmoil arose among the Chinese residents when the grand jury subpoenaed the officers of many Chinese family associations to bring them all the records of their associations, including membership rolls, personal files, and photographs.[25] The government surmised that the Chinese family associations possessed all the membership records with surnames like Wang, Chen, or Lee. When a certain applicant named Chen was found actually to bear the surname Wang, with the records of the Wang family association listing this particular person as a member, he could be identified as one who had entered the United States illegally. The government also wished to know whether the family association had anything to do with helping the "paper sons." This action drew the sharp protest of the family associations, which said the subpoenas were too sweeping and actually constituted illegal search. The Six Companies, representing twenty-four family associations, fought the issue through the court. Federal Judge Oliver J. Carter ruled on March 20, 1956, that the federal government may not subpoena the membership records of a Chinatown ancestral family association, and that a wholesale examination of the records by a federal grand jury would constitute unreasonable search and seizure under the Fourth Amendment. The judge's opinion was that the subpoenas had the effect of being a mass inquisition of the family records of a substantial portion of the Chinese population of San Francisco. The judge told the government attorney that the issuance of a subpoena must be sufficiently specific and must be properly related to the subject of inquiry, as some limitation on subpoenas is one of the burdens the Constitution places on the prosecution.[26] As a result of that decision, the government attorney promised that any new call would be specific and would conform with the judge's ruling.[27] The Chinese also agreed to cooperate.

The result of the investigation of the Hong Kong passport-fraud program is said to have been better than expected, even though this old problem is by no means completely solved. At the request of the Committee on Appropriations of the House of Representatives, the State Department has furnished the following information as to the progress of the whole program:

The investigation in Hong Kong together with the related counterpart activities, you might say, in the United States, from July 1, 1956, to December 31, 1957, resulted in final consideration of 908 civil action cases in the courts. Of these 908 only 51 were lost at trial or conceded by the Government, 49 cases were won and 808 were dismissed at the request of the plaintiff, which is tantamount to winning. In addition to that, we have developed 57 cases during the calendar year 1957 where criminal prosecution seemed to lie.[28]

Many Chinese have conceded that they were in the United States illegally. In an exceptional case, investigators have charged that almost an entire Chinese clan of approximately 225 members had come to this country with false identities. Soon the Chinese clan met and decided that all who faced deportation should volunteer information to the government and plead for leniency. Some thirty or forty of them were war veterans who could become United States citizens; and there were many others who might get temporary stays of deportation on the ground that if returned to their village at that time they would face physical persecution.[29]

With the United States government taking drastic action to stamp out the immigration rackets, there is good reason to suppose that the brokers functioning in Hong Kong have lost much of their business.[30] The indictment of some of the notorious racketeers in this country and their resultant prison sentences will undoubtedly have a good effect. As long as there are claimants there are always problems to be solved. Unfortunately it has to be recognized that mere rigidity in the enforcement of the law will only make the smugglers more persistent. The smuggling of Chinese into the United States has had a history of over half a century. Although the practice of smuggling immigrants has not been confined to the Chinese, lack of a good system of vital statistics in China has made the prevention of illegal Chinese entries especially difficult.

The McCarran-Walter Act of 1952 provided no judicial review of consular discretion and decision, since this jurisdiction belongs to the Department of State, so that all the cases now pending in Hong Kong are under the jurisdiction of the consul general. It remains to be seen how far the American consulate can get the cooperation of the Hong Kong authorities.[31] It is well to remember that the Hong Kong government, too, has had trouble in distinguishing genuine birth certificates from false ones. It will also be recalled that years after the enforcement of the Chinese Exclusion Act, many Chinese claiming to be native-born Americans found their way into Canada, crossed the border into New York or Vermont, and submitted themselves to arrest, to be taken before the United States commissioner for trial. More than half of them were discharged as citizens of this country. It was through the cooperation of the Canadian government that the apprehension of these persons took place.[32]

On the other hand, there seems no better way to solve the situation than to work closely with the Chinese leaders in this country. The Chinese in the United States are known to be cooperative with the authorities. While thoughtful Americans, as well as Chinese, would say that the root of the trouble goes back to the Chinese Exclusion Act and to the small quota of 105 Chinese annually, still the whole problem reflects unfavorably on the Chinese organizations. In fact, the honest Chinese suffered all the more in that their legitimate wives, sons, or daughters were denied admittance because of the difficulty of proof under the rigid standards set by the Hong Kong American consulate to prevent fraud. It is true that the bona fide Chinese can bring cases to court for redress; such action, however, would be very expensive, would take many years to come to trial, and still would require proof to obtain a favorable decision. The problem of smuggling Chinese is indeed an important one that concerns both the Chinese and the American authorities.[33]

The Blood Test

As we have pointed out, the blood test used by the American consulate in Hong Kong in 1951 as a means of determining whether the applicant were the genuine son or daughter of a father who was a citizen of the United States, detected many fraudulent cases until the immigration racket came up with the plan of matching the blood type in advance. At first the consulate requested the father, mother, and other members of the family to be tested for blood type A, B, or O. Since the matching of blood for both "paper sons" and "fathers" by the brokers had been made well in advance, the consulate extended the blood typing to include the M-N and Rh factors. Again the racket retaliated by matching "paper fathers" and "sons" for these factors. The blood test requirement is mostly confined to Chinese applicants, and has seldom until recently—under similar circumstances—been required of other immigrants. In the case of *United States* ex rel. *Lee Kum How, et al.,* the attorney for the plaintiff stated that blood tests were being used only for Chinese, and that this limitation constituted discrimination. The counsel stated further that the following questions had been asked, and requested the Immigration Service for a statistical report:

1. How many persons have been given blood tests for the purpose of disproving paternity since May 8, 1952?
2. How many of these persons have been from the Chinese race and how many from other races?
3. How many of the Chinese persons tested had birth certificates or other documentary evidence of their identity and how many did not?
4. Of the persons of other than the Chinese race, how many of those given blood tests had birth certificates or other documentary evidence of their identity and how many did not?[34]

The court directed the Immigration Service to reopen the hearing for the purpose of (1) the introduction of evidence with respect to the requirement of blood-grouping tests in the cases of persons of the Chinese race and the omission of the requirement of blood-grouping tests under similar circumstances in the cases of persons of other races, and (2) the determination, on such evidence, of the issue of discrimination.

These four questions were not answered by the Service because the special inquiry officer stated during the reopened hearing ". . . that it has no bearing on the decision in this case as to whether it is the policy of the Immigration Service to test all Chinese applicants for admission to the United States." In other words, the Service regarded as immaterial evidence that persons of other races, though they did not produce birth certificates, were not subjected to blood tests.

A writ of habeas corpus was followed by three hearings, and the writ was sustained on the grounds that the imposition by the immigration authorities of blood-grouping tests violated the relators' constitutional rights to be free from discrimination, in view of the omission of the requirement of such tests under similar circumstances in the cases of persons of other races.

The Immigration Service, well aware of the issue of discrimination, immediately began to apply blood-grouping tests to white persons.[35] When the case was appealed to the United States Court of Appeals, the Immigration Service was able to offer an affidavit made by an investigator of the New York Immigration Office on sixty cases, each identified by file number, of white persons whose blood had been tested between January 10 and August 4, 1955, and another list of 124 Chinese-born persons admitted between March 31 and June 2, 1952, of which forty had not been blood tested.

With one judge dissenting, the Court of Appeals reversed the judgment and ordered the writ of habeas corpus dismissed. The court held that there was no evidence that discrimination had been involved in administering blood tests to Chinese, and that under the circumstances the tests were a valid means of establishing the truth of the claims of citizenship.

The case was finally appealed to the Supreme Court. On *certiorari*, the Supreme Court vacated the judgments below and remanded the case to the district court, with directions for the reopening of hearings before the Immigration Service, where the blood tests made were in some respects inaccurate and the reports thereof partly erroneous and conflicting. The opinion of the court was that since ". . . the blood-grouping test requirement here involved is now and has been for some time applied without discrimination in every case, irrespective of race, whenever deemed necessary, and in view of our remand of the case, we need not pass upon the claim of unconstitutional discrimination."[36]

The Immigration Service has taken the position followed by the courts in paternity cases that the blood tests can conclusively show that certain persons cannot be related by blood to other persons,

even though a positive showing is only a possibility. They can prove
negative blood relations reliably, provided the tests are properly
conducted. If negative blood tests are to be recognized at all, they
must be deemed conclusive and not rebuttable; they should not be
weighed against other evidence on the same issue. The courts agree
that the tests are admissible evidence; but there is conflict of opinion
as to the weight to be given in cases other than negative showings.[37]

The application of blood tests to determine parentage, on the other
hand, has been extensively applied in the case of domestic relations.
From the scientific point of view, the blood test has its practical
value; under proper procedure its use can rebut the parentage in
case the blood type is negative. The matching of the blood type
cannot be held positive proof of parentage, since the blood can be
matched even when there is no relationship. Therefore the negative
results are conclusive proof that there is no parental relationship
between an alleged father and son, but the positive test would show
only that another member of an alleged family could be a true son.

In addition to the blood test, other medical tests, such as the use
of X ray on bones and a dental examination to determine the correct-
ness of age as claimed by the applicant, have long been applied.
The Board of Appeal has taken the stand that when there is a discrepancy between the claimed age and the possible age, as determined by the testimony of medical experts, the issue is considered
as one of fact finding for the consideration and determination of the
immigration authorities.

Failure to Maintain Nonimmigrant Status

Of the leading causes of deportation, entering the United States
without proper documents or without inspection or by false statements usually stands at the top of the list. Criminals, subversives,
and those remaining longer than authorized make up the balance. But
persons who fail to maintain their nonimmigrant status or to comply
with the conditions of their status are also subject to deportation.
Thus Section 241 (a) (9) of the 1952 Immigration and Nationality
Act, General Classes of Deportable Aliens, stated:

Any alien in the United States (including an alien crewman) shall, upon the
order of the Attorney General, be deported who was admitted as a nonimmigrant and failed to maintain the non-immigrant status in which he was
admitted or to which he was changed pursuant to Section 248, or to comply
with the conditions of any such status.

Crewmen, visitors for business or pleasure, transit aliens, agricultural laborers, foreign government officials, students, or treaty
traders make up most of the nonimmigrants admitted each year into

the United States. All the nonimmigrants whose status is not maintained are subject to deportation, if they do not depart voluntarily within the times set by the Immigration Service. Each year many persons in this category are deportable. Crewmen who have deserted their ships are subject to deportation when found. A Chinese government officer who is admitted into the United States as such but who subsequently loses his position by remaining in this country is deportable. A visitor on business or pleasure is subject to deportation if he stays longer than the time limit, although request for extension for certain periods is usually granted if sufficient reasons are given. This visitor is deportable once he violates his status by doing something else, such as accepting a job with a company or settling down to start a business of his own. The law insists that the reception of an alien into this country is purely a matter of permission and is in the nature of a conditional grant from Congress; and therefore the alien's right to remain in this country is subject to revocation as soon as he violates the status on which he was admitted. All this does not mean that the alien cannot obtain status as a permanent resident, should there be laws in operation of which he can take advantage. Many Chinese with the status of students, visitors, treaty traders, and others have obtained their legal status as permanent residents by the provisions of the Displaced Persons Act of 1948, the Refugee Act of 1953, by private or public legislation, or by marriage to an American citizen. [38]

The annual desertion of Chinese crewmen deserves analysis. [39] Each year a number of these have entered, and each year a number of them have been deported for failure to maintain their nonimmigrant status. Those who classify as deserters may have jumped from any one of a variety of carriers, including Chinese ships. The Immigration Service considers that any crewman staying on shore for more than twenty-nine days is a deserter, if it is shown that he does not intend to depart in accordance with his conditional landing permit.

The desertion of crewmen of practically all nationalities in the United States is a constant annoyance to the immigration authorities. Because it appears easy for the crewmen to disappear in the throng after obtaining a conditional permit to land, they are strongly tempted to evade the law, hoping that they will not be caught. The number of deserters used to be alarmingly large. From 1907 to 1931 the alien seamen who deserted averaged 12,292 per year, [40] but their number has been drastically reduced since then. Between 1944 and 1960, they have averaged 3,550 each year. A number of Chinese crewmen were among the deserters. Strange as it may seem, the largest single group of alien deserting crewmen was from the British Empire. Though the British have seldom utilized their quotas fully, the British seamen seem to prefer not to wait for the quota but to jump ship instead.[41] Usually the trouble lies in the inability of seamen to find sponsors for their legal entrance into the United States.

There is no way of knowing just how many deserting crewmen have been caught and deported. The number of such deportations has been large. Well-organized search operations by the immigration authorities have apprehended a good many of these crewmen, especially new arrivals. Others have shipped out again or departed voluntarily; some have died. A number who have stayed in this country long enough have become residents by taking advantage of the various regulations under the 1952 Act and other special emergency acts. The actual number of Chinese crewmen still under deportable status is therefore probably much smaller than the figures released by the Immigration Service in its *Annual Report*.[42] Though Chinese crewmen deserters have failed to maintain their nonimmigrant status and therefore have become deportable aliens, many have requested a stay of deportation for fear of physical persecution if deported to the mainland of China.

The Fear of Physical Persecution

Although deportable aliens include those convicted of crime involving moral turpitude and others convicted on subversive or criminal grounds, the records have shown that Chinese failure to maintain nonimmigrant status is also responsible for many cases of deportation. In some instances the Chinese alien's request for change of status has been denied by the Immigration Service for technical or other reasons. In many cases, as we have shown, a Chinese has conceded the legality of the deportation order, but requested stay of deportation because of his fear of physical persecution should he be forced to return to the country of his birth. Such requests were made under the Displaced Persons Act and the Refugee Relief Act; also under the regulation of Section 243 (h) of the Immigration and Nationality Act of 1952. As a result of many denials on the ground that the alien's allegation that he would be subject to physical persecution is not substantiated, a number of cases involving Chinese deportees have emerged in the United States District Court for the District of Columbia.[43] The court refuses to review the exercise of discretion, but will examine whether there has been a failure to exercise it.[44] At times, however, the Immigration Service has been rebuked for lightly dismissing testimony as to physical persecution.[45] There is certainly extreme danger in the lack of safeguards for those for whom deportation might mean persecution.[46] On the other hand, the Immigration Service is having difficulties in securing travel documents for aliens deportable to many of the Iron Curtain countries, including the mainland of China.[47]

A number of Chinese, including students who did not wish to go back to their country of birth, have tried to adjust their immigrant status by requesting a suspension of deportation so that they may satisfy the requirements of Section 244 of the Immigration and Nationality Act in reference to the seven years of continuous residence. Others have sought permanent residence under Section 4 of the Displaced Persons Act and under Section 6 of the Refugee Relief Act of 1953, because their status had long before expired. Many have thus succeeded in having their status adjusted. Some have been less lucky, since their requests have been denied through the technical requirements of these laws, through unfavorable confidential information, gossip, or even hearsay, or because in the opinion of the special inquiry officer the students had made statements indicating sympathy with the Communists at home.[48] They failed to convince the officer that they would be subject to persecution should they return to Communist China. It is true that those who are under technical difficulties may seek relief in a private bill, or by appealing the issue to the central office of the Immigration Service, or by resorting to the court for judicial review. Others, technically ineligible to utilize these established channels, returned disillusioned to the Chinese mainland in the belief that America had not assisted them by preventing such deportation while their country remained in Communist hands.[49]

The question of submitting substantial evidence in support of one's fear of physical persecution if forced to return to the mainland of China is delicate. It is difficult and sometimes almost impossible to ascertain just what is considered as adequate proof. Up to the present, evidence is lacking that Chinese are anxious to return to Communist China. There has been discussed a possible exchange of ten American prisoners in Communist China for thirty-seven Chinese students allegedly imprisoned in the United States. Only a handful of these students have made response to the notices placed in 35,000 post offices offering Chinese the right to return. None of the thirty-seven, of course, were actually in prison. The State Department disclosed in 1956 that it had offered the opportunity to leave the country to the twenty-four Chinese held on common criminal convictions in various state and federal penitentiaries. Two chose to go to Taiwan and only one asked to be returned to Red China; the other twenty-one preferred to stay here in prison.[50] It seems almost sure that when students, crewmen, or Chinese aliens state that their decision to remain here is caused by fear of physical persecution, they are speaking the truth. The Immigration Service has since officially acknowledged that under the control of a totalitarian dictatorship the resort to physical persecution is always possible, and that the necessity of furnishing adequate proof of that fear is not necessary. However, since this is an administrative decision, it is subject to change to suit the situation as evidenced by the change of the ruling against aliens deportable to Yugoslavia.[51] It must be realized that applications for adjustment of immigrant status and requests for suspension of deportation become generally known. The fact that such applications have been made is itself evidence that the applicants might be persecuted if forced to return.

8

The Problems of the Second-Generation Chinese

The lives of the early Chinese immigrants were frequently unhappy and involved definite suffering. With the exception of perhaps their first few years, they were legally and economically discriminated against; they were socially ostracized; often they were subjected to deep humiliation. The increase of discrimination, with consequent passage of the Chinese Exclusion Act in 1882, forced many Chinese to retreat across the Pacific to their fatherland. Those who chose to remain gradually withdrew behind the invisible walls of some Chinatown. It is not surprising that there were those who even sequestered themselves there permanently, not wishing, except in dire necessity, to pass its boundaries.

One should not suppose that discrimination has been leveled only at the Chinese race. The anti-Japanese campaign on the West Coast superimposed itself on the anti-Chinese movement. Filipinos, East Indians, and Koreans—all have been subjected to similar discrimination, though perhaps to a lesser degree. But the Chinese was the first race in the history of the United States to be singled out for absolute exclusion.

Yet the United States itself has been called a nation of immigrants. When the earliest arrivals had become assimilated, they tended to cast scornful glances at later immigrating foreigners who happened to have different customs, speech, and manners. The newer immigrants appeared to them shy, shabbily dressed, unprogressive, even stupid. Then, in turn, these new immigrants would look with disfavor upon any immigrants who arrived still later; those from northeastern and southern Europe were at one time considered unassimilable. Later, Mexican immigrants were said to be unassimilable. Only when economic absorption capacity and economic needs were such that the services of new immigrants were required did the problem of assimilation no longer seem acute. Whenever new immigrants come in greater numbers than can be economically absorbed, a hostile attitude on the part of the dominant population makes assimilation seem difficult. As a consequence comes a popular demand to exclude or at least restrict newcomers.

When the first Chinese entered the United States, their peculiar dress and manners, their long queues, and their fumbling English speech made them seem eccentric. Furthermore, the fact that they were of the laboring class limited their contact with the American middle and upper classes. Since the Chinese displayed marked physical differences, they were targets of ridicule as immigrants. Those earliest Chinese had their fate sealed.

Our present-day problem of assimilation concerns the second, third, and possibly the later generations. Since these persons were born in the United States, they are recognized as American citizens. Our purpose is to determine whether the Chinese in the United States are assimilable. If the answer is yes, then how and to what extent may they become assimilated? Are the Americans disposed to accept the Chinese and their descendants on the basis of personal character and individual achievement, regardless of color, creed, and ancestry?

The Problem of Race Prejudice

Prejudice against races, nations, religions, institutions, and ideas is ageless. Prejudice tends to overlook values, to give special emphasis to unfavorable qualities, to destroy the use of the reason. Race prejudice emphasizes unfavorable traits in order to justify partiality. Cultural differences between western and eastern Europeans seem to be merely natural ones; but the much more striking differences between Occidentals and Orientals seem unnatural. Though physical differences are conspicuous, cultural ones are even more significant.

Yet prejudice is by no means innate. We should like to know what kinds of experience have aroused prejudice. The customary attitude of whites toward blacks or Orientals has not necessarily been determined by contact, but more probably by the influence of theoretical attitudes. Prejudice follows a set pattern and therefore is not easily overcome. Thus racial evaluations are customarily not judicious—often their source is complete ignorance; ignorance and prejudice go hand in hand.

Race prejudice is an acquired behavior; therefore children, especially in preschool years, are free from it. They are too young to fix hostility on any group as a whole. This means that dislike of the unlike is by no means an instinct. Pearl Buck tells an interesting anecdote. Her little daughter informed her that a lady wished to see her. "Is it a Chinese or an American?" Pearl Buck asked. "I don't

know," replied the child, "I didn't ask her." Miss Buck's explanation
is that in social environments in which racial differences mean
nothing, differences simply go unnoticed. L. L. Thurstone undertook
measurement of the effect of antiprejudice movies. His study revealed that when the pro-Chinese film, *Son of the Gods*, was shown
to children, the average attitude shift was in a direction favorable
to the Chinese.[1]

Liking the English and the Canadians but disliking the Turks and
the Hindus is virtually an American tradition. Few Americans have
ever had personal contact with either Turks or Hindus; yet an antipathy against them is prevalent. Preference for one ethnic group as
against another has been revealed through studies of the so-called
social distance. An early research made by Emory S. Bogardus,
based on the "social distance scale" to forty racial, national, and
religious groups, showed preference ranking of the forty groups,
with British, native white Americans, and Canadians at the top;
and near the bottom, Negroes, Japanese, Chinese, East Indians,
and Turks.[2] Studies made about the same time by J. P. Guilford,[3]
and in 1946 by Eugene L. Hartley,[4] gave the same result. This is
not to say that this pattern will remain constant or permanent, but
any change will be very slow. Indeed, there appears to have been
a slightly more favorable disposition toward the Chinese since they
became allies of the United States of America in World War II.[5]

Even though in all countries there is a "pattern of preference,"
group antagonism fluctuates with changes in social and economic
conditions. The question of economic gain has always been a prime
factor in prejudice. For example, the mutual dislike of Chinese
and East Indians prevalent in Southeast Asia is due chiefly to economic causes. Likewise, when the gold rush in California made
plenty of work, the timely arrival of the Chinese laborers was welcomed; they were considered adaptable, thrifty, industrious, orderly,
and law-abiding. But after they had gradually gained some economic
status and had at times become competitors of white workers, they
began to be accused of clannishness, servility, slyness, untrust-
worthiness, deceitfulness, and unscrupulousness. "The Chinese
must go!" was the popular cry; all their former good reputation
was forgotten. In the business recessions of 1854 and 1862 in California, and in the national depression of 1873, white workers bitterly
blamed the Chinese for their own frustration. Frustration often
begets aggression, and the Chinese became the scapegoats.

The sudden rise of a minority to a higher social or economic
status arouses animosity. One of our human weaknesses is to enjoy
looking down on those beneath us. The racial point of view of the
whites in South Africa serves to protect and preserve the dominant

position of the Europeans against any threat from the nonwhites. Privileges are jealously guarded. Similarly, the Chinese came into special disfavor during the last quarter of the nineteenth century, because in certain fields they had become competitors of the white workers. Their competition aggravated an already tense situation.

Since in the nineteenth century very few Chinese were naturalized, they were negligible as a voting bloc. Most had come from the farming and laboring classes in south China, with the motive of earning and saving as much money as possible in order to return to China to live a life of pleasant retirement. Except for economic opportunities, their environment in the United States was unfavorable to permanent residence. Even if they had had the right to vote, few of them would have cared to avail themselves of it. Politicians therefore had no interest in them; yet both parties made Chinese exclusion an issue in their platforms, and the Chinese had no power of reprisal.

The "social visibility" theory of the cause of racial prejudice apparently holds true in regard to the Chinese and other Orientals. In the South there is little prejudice against Orientals, in contrast to strong convictions in regard to Negroes. Indeed, Chinese who have traveled in the South have been delightfully surprised at the traditional southern hospitality given them. The obvious explanation lies in the vast numbers of Negroes and the few Orientals there. The concentration of early Chinese immigrants in California certainly caused much racial feeling; and the spreading of the Chinese into other parts of the United States has had at least something to do with the recession of prejudice in California.

Few persons, no matter how prejudiced they may actually be, will admit that they are prejudiced, though they express their prejudice in words and deeds. Writers doing research on racial problems may appear totally unprejudiced in their monographs; yet, their work completed, they will return to their original bias. When in the early 1930's Richard T. LaPiere traveled about ten thousand miles in the United States with a married Chinese couple, only once in 256 visits to restaurants, tourist camps, and hotels were they refused service. But later when LaPiere sent written questionnaires to the 128 hostelries he had visited, asking them to confirm whether they would accept Chinese as their guests, the replies were about 92 per cent in the negative; and about the same percentage occurred in replies from 128 establishments he had not visited.[6] This lack of correlation between experience and replies may possibly be explained by the supposition that, had the Chinese couple been without LaPiere, the refusal of service might have been as high as 90 per cent. The attitudes and actions of the average person do not always coincide. Those hotelkeepers and restaurateurs who replied may have seen few Chinese, and their prejudice may have been based merely on a traditional dislike of Orientals. When they actually saw the Chinese couple, they probably considered them quite acceptable. On the other hand, it is also possible that refusal of service may have been due more to a fear that the establishment might lose other guests; the refusal of a certain barbershop to serve Orientals was from the apprehension of losing business, not from prejudice. Nowadays in many university towns, hesitation to rent rooms to Chinese students is often caused by ignorance about Chinese. Safety first is the principle: better to refuse than to take a chance.

There are always intellectuals in both camps, the dominating and the dominated; but to a person with racial prejudice "all coons look alike." As E. Franklin Frazier has pointed out, "A person who has race prejudice does not perceive any specific individual of a different race, but rather sees each one in terms of the categoric picture."[7] There are also intramural prejudices within minority groups, though with some variation. An American-born Negro's or Jew's attitude toward Orientals is about the same as that of the native white Christian American.

Curiously, in Hawaii Orientals mingle freely with Haoles, as the whites there are called. The Orientals, especially the Chinese and the Japanese, engage extensively in trades and professions. Only a small portion of the people spoke openly against the Japanese immediately after Pearl Harbor, while newspapers and many organizations, including the military, counseled caution and tolerance. A mere 981 out of about 160,000 Japanese were actually interned. That the varied racial elements have contributed to the economic prosperity of the islands is a well-recognized fact. One reason for the establishment of racial equality in Hawaii is the nature of the earliest contacts between the white and the nonwhite races. The fact that an early white adviser to the court of Hawaii felt honored when the king of the island granted him the distinction of marrying a woman of the court set a precedent of racial equality. Thus absence of racial prejudice was established long ago and, like prejudice, absence of prejudice is extremely difficult to alter.

The Pattern of Discrimination in the United States

When we observed the prejudice against minorities in the United States, we noticed that discrimination is shown not only against the Orientals but against Negroes, Jews, Mexicans, Puerto Ricans, and to a lesser extent, South Americans and eastern Europeans. These have been subjected to prejudice varying in intensity in different regions and, at different times, within the same region. In fact, in the United States there exists a semblance of a caste system that apparently differentiates between the dominated and the dominant. According to an estimate made by Professor MacIver, there are roughly 37,000,000 in the United States who constitute what might be called an allegedly inferior social caste, composed heterogeneously: 13,000,000 Negroes, 2,000,000 Mexicans and other Latin Americans, about 335,000 Orientals, 370,000 American Indians, with various other racial strains in negligible proportions.[8] Distinct from all those, forming as it were the semblance of an upper low-caste stratum, are the 5,000,000 Jews and about 16,000,000 Poles, Czechs, Ruthenians, Hungarians, Greeks, Slavs, and Italians. These are generally subjected to less rigid discrimination, and they often have little difficulty in breaking through social barriers. Yet the stereotype still exists, so that even small racial groups are sometimes unable to avoid the crosscurrents of disparagement. Since there is only a small number of Turks in the United States (and few Americans have ever seen a Turk), it is surprising that prejudice against the Turks has become almost an American tradition. Apparently one of the reasons used to justify such prejudice is that the Turks fought the Crusaders and that Turkey was an ally of Germany in World War I.[9] In the words of Professor MacIver, "Discrimination has become a feature of the national mores." The conflict of interests between the dominated and the dominating peoples has created tensions and embitterments that deeply disturb the solidarity of the nation. Racial prejudice has been one of the most urgent domestic issues.

Simpson and Yinger indicate that many instances of racial prejudice can be found in the history of the United States; for example, the constant conflict between the early settlers and the Indians, who were the natural enemies of the white frontiersmen—the only good Indians were dead Indians.[10] Greed and brutality prompted the whites to rob and murder the Indians or to treat them as slaves. Motives, of course, were economic. As economic gain was achieved, the racial prejudice conspicuously lessened but also there were proportionately fewer Indians.[11]

The American colonists came from the British Isles, Holland, Germany, France, and Scandinavia, but chiefly from England. They were Nordic peoples, with a culture considered superior to that of the much later immigrants from southern and eastern Europe: Austro-Hungarians, Russians, Italians, Greeks, Portuguese, Spaniards, and Syrians. It was the gathering momentum of the "new immigration" (1891-1924) that brought on the great debate about needful restrictions. The principle of selection by nationality and race, instead of by individual qualification, was adopted under the Quota Act of 1924, and has since become the model for all immigration laws.

These "new immigrants" came largely from the lower classes. With almost no exceptions, they lacked training and education for skilled or professional pursuits. They had had virtually no political experience. Nevertheless many of them, by hard work, occasionally by intermarriage, and by their ability to adjust themselves, did attain higher social status. Though these groups may still be subject to some disparagement, they fare much better in the United States than Mexicans, Negroes, and Orientals.

With the passage of the permanent Chinese Exclusion Act in 1904, the problem of Chinese immigration became more or less an academic one; therefore, having settled, as they thought, the Chinese question, the Pacific Coast states turned their attention to the other Orientals in their midst. Although prejudice against the Chinese still continued here and there, the tempo became much slower; for one thing, the retreat of many Chinese into their Chinatowns, with the consequent renunciation of occupations competitive with white laborers, helped considerably to slacken tensions. During World War II, especially after Pearl Harbor, the Chinese enjoyed at least a temporary equality in the eyes of the American public. Soon after the war, however, when several batches of Chinese immigrants came by ship to the West Coast, the pattern of prejudice and discrimination against the Chinese returned. Again, during the early phases of the Korean War, a number of episodes involving dislike of the Chinese as a group occurred in this country. These were due more to the lack of clear understanding of the situation than to the actual revival of discrimination against the Chinese.

Thus, early in 1952, the refusal to sell a house in Southwood, South San Francisco, to a Chinese who had a Chinese-American wife and a small son, attracted nationwide attention. Sing Sheng, a former Chinese intelligence officer and a graduate of Earlham College, Indiana, had made a down payment of $2,950 on a $12,300 house. After strong protests had been made by the prospective neighbors, the owner suggested to Sheng that he withdraw, because if Sheng should move in, children might throw rocks at the window and dump garbage about the house. Sheng thereupon requested the owner to call a meeting of townspeople to decide the controversy, stating that he would abide by the verdict. At the meeting, he was shouted down as he tried, before the vote was taken, to explain his position. The result by secret ballot was refusal—174 to 28. Two days after the meeting, the five members of the City Council of South San Francisco unanimously voted to disavow Sheng's not having been accepted

in the Southwood residential district; and he received many telegrams and telephone calls from all over the country condemning the
outcome of the secret ballot. Many persons in San Francisco offered
Sheng their help in procuring some other house.[12]

On July 4, 1959, Dr. Chiao-min Hsieh and his family were denied
admittance to two Maryland beaches because they were not Caucasians. Dr. Hsieh, an assistant professor of geography at Catholic
University in Washington and a former director of research projects
for the Office of Naval Research at the Massachusetts Institute of
Technology, said that he just did not know what to tell his seven-
year-old, American-born daughter about the incident.[13]

Few of such incidents appear to result in court actions when both
plaintiff and defendant are white Americans. Here is an exception.
Officially the American Legion recognized no color barriers. Nevertheless, its fun-making subsidiary, the famous 40 & 8, admits only
white male members. Recently its chapter in San Jose, California,
admitted Gerald Lee, a Chinese-American, a post and a district
commander in the Legion. The national headquarters of the 40 et 8
told the chapter to drop Gerald Lee, who promptly offered to resign.
When the chapter refused to obey, or to accept the resignation,
headquarters revoked the chapter's charter, and then moved to
establish a new, all-white chapter in San Jose. Whereupon Mr. Lee's
chapter went to court to regain its charter and to keep Mr. Lee.[14]

The rapidly increasing population of minority groups and the tendency to have residential segregation in many of the large American
cities made housing discrimination an important problem to be dealt
with by the federal as well as the state governments. Economic and
educational advancement on the part of Chinese and Japanese may
help to weaken the prejudice against them, but discrimination is
still a real factor affecting and limiting the housing choice of Orientals. There are always restricted areas in which Orientals may
not live.

Some real estate agencies consider it poor practice to sell two or
more adjacent houses to Orientals, but they do not object strongly to
selling a single house. In apartment dwellings, especially when
several buildings are connected, agencies carefully limit to one or
two the number of oriental families in each building, hoping thereby
to avoid complaints of white tenants. The University of California's
recent comprehensive studies of housing discrimination in American cities covered the topic of housing bias as encountered by the
Japanese-American. The conclusion thus reached may well apply to
the Chinese. Their findings read as follows:

The Nisei have adequate housing in terms of space and physical facilities;
their houses are generally old, and often in old neighborhoods, and they

consequently do not have favorable financing; they are more satisfied with the housing than with their neighborhoods, but hope to improve both; they have often experienced discrimination, and expect to find it when they go house or apartment hunting."[15]

We cannot say whether discrimination of group against group is decreasing or increasing. Discrimination is volatile; changes depend on social conditions. The caste treatment of the Chinese certainly is no longer as rigid as it once was. Before World War II their occupational opportunities were limited practically to being laundrymen, waiters, cooks, and restaurateurs. They met insuperable barriers when they attempted to attend institutions of higher learning, or to enter skilled trades or professions; but after World War II they were able to find places.

Except, possibly, for housing difficulties, Japanese immigrants now encounter little discrimination. In Los Angeles, Minneapolis, Chicago, Detroit, and New York, there are few occupations in which Japanese-Americans are not represented. The status of Negroes has also greatly improved, helped by the higher level of prosperity; the increasing participation by Negroes in the politics of northern and border cities has become conspicuous. Furthermore, the historic decision of the Supreme Court in 1954 to end segregation in the public schools has already accomplished much for the Negro race.[16]

That racial questions have since 1947 been uppermost in the minds of most Americans helps us to understand the situation of minority groups.[17] The United States, as a world power, has acknowledged its corresponding responsibility of maintaining good relations with all peoples. The people of Asia, Africa, South America, Europe, and especially the Soviet Union, are watching closely the group prejudices and discrimination that Americans practice. The school integration troubles in Little Rock in 1957 may have done a great deal of damage to the prestige of the United States. Unfortunately, the incidents in Oakland, in Philadelphia, in Houston, and in Nashville, occurring about the same time, gave the impression to the world that race riots have been developing all over the country. Even though many observers abroad believe that what has been happening affects only a limited number in certain areas, and that reports have been exaggerated, still they ponder, with many reservations, just how far-reaching American democracy is.

The United States government has taken considerable action in attempting to eliminate discrimination; at least it has been making an honest effort to set things right. The Supreme Court decision in 1954 was acclaimed almost everywhere in the world; it will rank as one of the major events in contemporary American history. Former President Eisenhower said:

We must find ways of assuring to every American that in his search for employment he will be judged on the basis of his character and his ability, and not on the basis of his race, his religious faith, or the land from which he or his forebears came to America.[18]

Several builders have complied with the law of their state, prohibiting discrimination in private housing since the passage of these laws. Many volunteer and official commissions and committees have been organized at state and municipal levels in order to try to solve race relation problems. Although they have not always been able to cooperate closely, they have taken concrete steps to arouse public opinion. It has been demonstrated that determined governmental actions—legislative, judiciary, or executive—are effective in combating racial injustice.

The Question of Assimilation

The theory that there are "superior" and "inferior" races of mankind is one still held tenaciously by many people. Some agree with the Germanic view of the inherent superiority of Nordic peoples. To be sure there are both national and racial groups, but there is no such mixture of the two as a "French race" or a "German race." Some continue to allege that physiological differences indicate and explain the differences in the intelligence of one race from another.[19] The fact is that any racial or national differences in intelligence which might be evident are due to cultural differences rather than to heredity. Professor Klineberg has stated that cultural differences may be caused by physical environment, by acculturation, by independent invention, by specific needs, or by other phenomena, often found by accident.[20] Therefore, one culture can be described as superior or inferior in relation to another on the basis of a given standard or criterion, but "race" or "nation" or even "culture" are purely descriptive terms.

Nevertheless, the ideology of racial superiority is certainly not limited to North America, Europe, or Australia; it exists in practically all multiracial communities such as South Africa, Southern Rhodesia, and others. The difficulty in forming an acceptable government in these lands lies in European insistence upon the maintenance of white supremacy. In many white-controlled territories, the native Africans have very little political influence. About 50 per cent of the land in Southern Rhodesia belongs to the whites, and there is a white trade-union supported "Dominion Party" advocating apartheid. In Kenya, the Mau Mau terrorism between 1952 and 1956 was precipitated by conflict between the Europeans and the natives over the question of land. In South Africa, after 1948, the Nationalist party passed one law after another to achieve the complete separation of native Africans and whites—they maintained a racial register of the population and defined areas in which each race might live separately. After a demonstration against the law in March, 1960, sixty-nine Africans were massacred and about 18,000 jailed. A never-before-seen crisis arose because of the large-scale boycott.

Since the Belgian Congo's obtaining of independence in June, 1960, internal dissension and chaos have prevailed, leading to the white residents' flight for safety. There also are many involved issues of multiracialism in Tanganyika and Zanzibar; and in Angola and the French Congo, there is unrest and opposition on the part of the natives.

It is significant that fifteen African countries achieved independence in 1960, and the prognosis is that more will do so. In order to achieve world peace it may be important for the West to help these countries to settle their problems, especially the problem of ugly racialism. It is natural and healthy for a culture group to appreciate its own culture and society and to respect them more than alternative ones. In fact, uncritical ethnocentrism (with each group considering itself as a "chosen people") is characteristic of practically all autonomous human societies. Nevertheless, the West must accept the challenge of promoting racial tolerance and harmony and developing opportunities for all races.

The Chinese in their own country have demonstrated that they have succeeded in assimilating diverse elements. They incorporated into Chinese society their tribal neighbors, such as Mongols and Manchus who invaded China and ruled for several hundred years. These groups have maintained separate communities of their own for some time, but due to frequent social intercourse and consequent intermarriage with the Chinese, any barriers of segregation have been merely nominal. No doubt the Chinese culture and way of life contributed to the fact that minorities were willing to become integrated with the dominant society. Also, the fact that their physical characteristics were quite similar favored integration. We may say that the fundamental solution lay in the family system.

On the other hand, the Chinese in Southeast Asia are said to be unassimilable. Instead of being absorbed by the native inhabitants, the Chinese have swamped them. The Chinese are sometimes criticized for considering themselves superior racially: they retain their Chinese customs and maintain their loyalties to China; they send their sons to China for education; they have created and maintained separate Chinese communities within the countries to which they have migrated. No doubt much of this is true. But when one studies the history of the Chinese immigration into Southeast Asia, he soon finds that the life of the Chinese abroad is by no means entirely pleasant. The massacres of early Chinese immigrants in the Dutch East Indies and in the Philippines and elsewhere, together with the political and economic discrimination against them, have compelled them to be nationalistically inclined. The creation of a separate Chinese community is mostly due to the policies of colonial governments. The Dutch had long confined the Chinese to exclusive quarters, and other colonial governments did likewise. Most Chinese preferred to send their youths back to China for advanced education, because there were very few colleges or universities in Southeast Asia. The bulk of the annual remittances to China represents a part of the profit out of the Chinese investment, rather than the salaries or wages earned; part of these remittances are for the support of wives or families left behind. The more bitter the discrimination, the less the Chinese desire assimilation, or seek through it an eventual protection. In spite of prejudice and discrimination, still every year a great number of Chinese are assimilated and pass among the natives largely unnoticed. It is no secret that in Thailand many of the political leaders, past and present, had a Chinese origin. They speak Thai perfectly, they regard themselves as Thai, and they support the nationalistic movement. In fact, as one writer has put it: "It was these sons of China who passed the immigration, educational, and labor laws which operated to the great disadvantage of overseas Chinese."[21] So it was in the Philippines and in other countries of Southeast Asia.

In the United States mainland, the race relations experiences have been quite different from those enjoyed by Chinese in Hawaii. The early Chinese laborers and the native-born Chinese were never able to acquire such a social status as their compatriots did in Hawaii. The fact that the first and only United States senator of Asian parentage comes from Hawaii proves how peoples of different racial and cultural background can live and grow together there. America, although itself probably a melting pot of the majority of European peoples, has always been very sensitive about race relations. The large numbers of Negroes living side by side with the white Americans have aroused social tensions and patterns of racial prejudice that are by no means easy to erase.

Intermarriage is, of course, one method of assimilation, and its frequency is an index to the progress of assimilation. Intermarriages between Chinese and whites have not been frequent, since sentiments among people of both races are unfavorable. The future seems to promise some change in this attitude, although a number of states have laws prohibiting such marriages. Social contacts among

Chinese and Americans have so far been little better than superficial. Although economic opportunities are now plentiful, the Chinese, with the possible exception of the technical and scientific
fields, have not been granted sufficient opportunities.

Naturalization forms another approach toward assimilation. It
is at least a barometer of progress, for it indicates a degree of
interest. The number of naturalized Chinese between 1944 and 1960
was 22,329, about 1,319 a year. This suggests that more have become permanent residents than have remained aliens; progress in
the past seven years (1954-1960) has been far above the average.

Assimilation depends on mutual understanding; there must be at
least a semblance of intellectual equality. In these respects, the
native-born Chinese fulfills his part of the bargain; many a native
Chinese-American speaks English as well as any American; his
thoughts and his behavior have become Westernized. Only in frustration may he go back to his family for temporary relief. The Chinese are anxious that their youngsters acquire a good education; and
in the school real assimilation has its beginnings. Sons and daughters
of Chinese descent are usually serious students; many have been
elected class presidents, valedictorians, or have become captains
of swimming, fencing, and soccer teams. Chinese students appear
on debating teams; they become editors of school or college publications. Indeed, the native-born Chinese, with few exceptions, have
been Americanized in every respect, and many of them firmly believe that their home is America.[22] One often hears from the native-
born such words as these: "I am an American citizen, and I like to
do things as Americans do them."

Many Chinese still enjoy celebrating the Chinese New Year and
participating in other native festivals; but the average Chinese in
America has learned to observe Christmas, Thanksgiving, Easter,
and various American holidays. Chinese join the American Legion,
the Boy Scouts, and the Girl Scouts. Even in Chinatown parents
have little influence over their children in the selection of partners
in marriage; to be Americanized is the rule, not the exception.

All this does not mean that the Chinese in the United States have
been completely assimilated. Complete integration cannot be achieved
until the problem of racial bias has been entirely solved, and that
solution may take several decades or even longer. At the moment,
there is little prospect of an entire solution. Responsibility rests both
with the majority and with the minority; the minority should make
every effort to become useful, to enter as fully as possible into the
life of the whole community, and to contribute to the general welfare.
Through self-awareness of interrelationship and with an attitude
of give and take, the Chinese immigrants will more easily adjust

themselves into the communities in which they must assume full membership. With the possible exception of the older people, many of whom prefer to be isolated in congested Chinatowns, the majority of the Chinese—the second, third, and later generations—have tried hard to adjust themselves in the community. This problem of adjustment and assimilation is universal, but the Chinese immigrants have shown an ability to learn and to continue learning. Current cultural and liberal forces active in this country will certainly be of assistance to the Chinese immigrant who hopes to adjust himself to community living.

9

Occupational Adjustment

No longer do the Chinese in the United States confine their occupations within the ramparts of Chinatown, nor do they limit them to those of restaurateur and laundryman. Today the Chinese functions in a variety of employments. He may become a mortician, an aerophoto inspector, a surgeon on the staff of a hospital, a policeman, a biostatistician, a Nobel prize-winning physicist, or even a United States senator. The fields of specialization followed by Chinese, indeed, are so various that of the 186 American colleges that have Chinese on their faculties (1959-60), there are more than two hundred different specializations pursued by 1,124 Chinese scholars. No doubt they have been encouraged to specialize, and have taken full advantage of their opportunities. For instance, in cancer research, one will find several outstanding Chinese: Dr. Min-Chin Li, of the Sloan-Kettering Institute, has caused "regressions" of cancer with a chemical called "Don," developed by Sloan-Kettering and Parke-Davis and Company; Dr. Shih-man Chang, assistant professor of microbiology at Harvard, has made an important breakthrough in cancer research by achieving the first man-made mutation of a human cell. Many Chinese engineers and scientists are employed by large corporations as directors of research departments, heads of divisions, and vice-presidents. As a further illustration, K. C. Li, an outstanding metallurgical engineer, had built the Wah Chang Corporation; Joe Shoong, who as a young man worked for thirty dollars a month in a shirt factory, was the owner of the National Dollar Stores, a good-sized chain store corporation on the West Coast.[1]

Most of these important positions have been reached by Chinese within the past fifteen years. Before that it was almost impossible to place a Chinese or Japanese, either of the first or of the second generation, in any kind of good position in engineering or business.[2]

The Right of Chinese to Work, before World War II

The motive of the early Chinese laborers in coming to California was to meet the urgent demands for their services, as a result of the rush to the gold field. Beginning with the most menial tasks in mining camps, on farms, and on railroads, they advanced to become domestics, cooks, and launderers; with the passing years, a small number of them became workers in factories in San Francisco, such as those making boots and shoes, cigars, or woolens. The 1870 census reveals that cigar makers were employing 1,727 Chinese, shoe and woolen manufacturers only 649. To be sure, a few Chinese workers were in such manufacturing as fruit canning, in salmon packing in Oregon, in Washington, and even in Alaska.

Only a few years after their arrival the Chinese were being discriminated against, first by labor, and later by other interests. To keep the Chinese out of the mines was the initial effort of the authorities; soon in public works of state, county, and municipality, the Chinese were denied employment as they were ineligible for citizenship. Even corporations doing business with the states were forbidden to employ Chinese. In consequence of such discrimination, the Chinese were forced to seek marginal and noncompetitive occupations, though it was not possible to avoid contact with white workers altogether.

One may say that it took the Chinese several decades of trial and error before they formed a retreat into laundry and restaurant work, the trades least competitive with white neighbors. Furthermore, since Chinese were denied naturalization, and since many states required citizenship to perform a number of jobs, the Chinese were sensible enough to withdraw to those trades in which the right to work would at least not be questioned by the law.

Many states of the Union have enacted laws restraining aliens from participating in certain occupations. Twenty-seven occupations in New York are restricted to citizens or declarants. Other states are less rigid. In the case of attorneys, however, all states (including Alaska, Hawaii, and the District of Columbia) require citizenship. Twenty-one states require physicians to be citizens, and seventeen states are satisfied with first papers.[3] Interestingly enough, the list of restrictions also includes barbers (9 states), guides (9 states), peddlers (5), plumbers (4), and chauffeurs (2).[4] Colorado law prohibits aliens from working as waitress, dishwasher, or janitor in any establishment licensed to sell liquor.

It may make some sense that lawyers should be required to be citizens; even so, there appears to be no cogent reason why thoroughly qualified aliens should not practice law. Likewise with physicians, dentists, architects, and engineers, for the requirements of admission into those callings are so rigid that an incompetent alien could no more practice than could an incompetent citizen. It is important that the American public be well guarded in its more vital services. However, the citizenship of a barber, painter, chauffeur, or the like seems to have little bearing on the quality of his services. Such legislation exists only because of the strength of the pressures within the particular callings.

On the whole, the economic opportunities offered Chinese immigrants and Chinese-Americans, citizens or not, have been very limited.[5] Under the circumstances, the Chinese have had to be content with humble occupations or confine their ambitions to Chinatown. A certain number of professional men returned to China in order to utilize whatever knowledge or technique they had acquired in the United States. Discrimination against oriental races has been at least partly responsible for their not building up large businesses and industries in this country.

Professions and Occupations since World War II

Both the censuses of 1930 and 1940 revealed the paucity of Chinese professional men, particularly physicians, chemists, and college professors; the majority were laundry operatives, laundry owners, restaurant workers and restaurant keepers, and persons in domestic service. In 1930, there were still a few thousand farm laborers; but by 1940 the number had been reduced to fewer than a thousand, mostly in California. World War II quickly changed all that. War industries such as shipyards and aircraft factories which had seldom employed Chinese began to show an interest in engaging Chinese engineers, technicians, workers, and even clerks. That China was an ally of the United States against the Axis, that there was an acute shortage of manpower, that the Japanese had gone off into relocation camps, and that the Chinese were devoted, skilled, and hard working made the employment of the Chinese highly advantageous. Soon other industries followed suit in utilizing the Chinese to ease the personnel shortage.

The Chinese Restaurant

The Chinese in the United States have proved themselves capable of many diverse achievements in business. Though there are many more laundries than there are restaurants, the importance of the restaurant business far surpasses that of the laundry. The restaurants in this country have been estimated at well over six thousand. In 1960 New York City, Newark, and the surrounding country had 600, of which fifty were in the New York Chinatown. San Francisco and its suburbs have more than New York. More and more restaurants have been opened in large cities as Chinese cuisine gains in popularity.

According to a study made in 1938, there were 447 Chinese restaurants within the five boroughs of New York City, but the rate of failures was high. From January, 1928, to September, 1938, of the 447 restaurants established, 140 lasted no more than a year, whereas a mere 5 per cent remained open for ten years or longer, the average time being 2.39 years.[6] This was the period of the great depression, which in 1938 was just beginning to come to an end. Since World War II, the Chinese restaurant business has been fairly brisk, the rate of failures low. The opening of a restaurant is expensive; a desirable location and a tasteful interior are prerequisite to doing good business. The average prospective proprietor frequently requires an initial capital of $30,000 to $50,000. From 1928 to 1938, a small Chinese restaurant needed $20,000 to $25,000; a large one, probably in excess of $75,000. Today, the outlay would have to be doubled or tripled. The newly opened "Four Seas" restaurant in San Francisco, headed by K. L. Woo, a prominent Chinese businessman, is a quarter-million dollar corporation which features Shanghai, Peking, as well as Cantonese cuisine. Accommodating 650 guests in its third-floor dining room, it will be the largest restaurant in that Chinatown.

As in many other types of Chinese business, the majority of restaurants are owned by single persons, partnerships, and proprietorships; only a few have been registered as corporations; for example, in 1938, 57 per cent of the restaurants were owned by partnerships, 33 per cent by individuals, and fewer than 10 per cent had been incorporated. These ratios remain today, except that there are perhaps more partnerships. There are no chain restaurants, though the same person may own a pair of restaurants. More and more restaurateurs have been concerned with the problem of improving the management of the business. The House of Chan, 7th Avenue at 52nd Street, New York City, has provided scholarships at Brooklyn College for two Chinese-Americans majoring in food store management. This same restaurant once brought seven cooks from Hong Kong under the Refugee Relief Act of 1953.

Much Chinese food is now being canned or frozen, in response to an increasing demand since World War II; some American restaurants serve Chinese dishes; and in supermarkets and other groceries Chinese food is often displayed in special sections. The business of freezing food is a very recent one, but the annual volume of canned and frozen products has been estimated to be about $30 million;

chow mein, egg rolls, and other Cantonese dishes are included. The frozen food can be packed in dry ice and then shipped by air express to any part of the United States. Several firms specialize in this business, especially in San Francisco, the Midwest, and New York City. Some of the large plants are owned by Americans.

The Chinese Laundry

Of all Chinese businesses in the United States, the laundry is certainly the oldest and one employing very large numbers. Chinese laundries had been in operation long before the famous case, *Yick Wo* v. *Hopkins* in 1886, when Yick Wo, with 150 others, was arrested for operating his laundry without a license.[7] By 1870 the majority of more than 2,000 laundrymen in San Francisco were Chinese.[8] Quantitatively the laundry business probably surpasses all other Chinese enterprises combined; but qualitatively it is far in the rear. The number of laundries in the United States is approximately 11,000.

According to estimates, 60 per cent are one-man laundries, only 5 per cent with as many as five or six workers; 90 per cent are hand laundries, with a capital investment of from a few hundred to three or four thousand dollars. As an example of the average small-scale laundry may be cited that of "Maine's Mother of the Year" (1952), who, after the death of her husband, operated her little laundry with the help of one of her daughters.

Chinese laundries may be divided into three categories: the hand laundry, one or two persons doing all the work, with over twenty-five hundred of them in New York City alone; the so-called shirt-processing firms, which do no washing, but only processing and ironing, their customers being various Chinese laundries; the wet-washing establishments, with the single function of washing, their customers again various Chinese laundries.

Hand laundries in New York have two associations, the Chinese Hand Laundry Association and the Chinese Hand Laundry Alliance; but only about a quarter of the local laundries are members. The Yee Gai Association represents shirt-processing firms, with a membership of approximately 50 per cent. The capital required for establishing a shirt-processing unit is about $3,000; the smallest firms own one or two units, large firms as many as twenty. The wet-washing establishments require more capital, since much space and machinery are required; the minimum capitalization is about $100,000.[9] There are about thirty-four wet-washing plants in New York City, and four in New Jersey. A Chinese Wet-Washing Association has been organized, with headquarters in Brooklyn.

Because most Chinese laundries have only one or two workers—

often husband and wife—virtually no competition exists with large-scale laundry establishments; but in spite of that, campaigns have been waged against Chinese laundries. Between 1930 and 1933—perhaps on account of the business depression—systematic propaganda was directed against Chinese laundries in the eastern part of the country; and American laundries carried the campaign so far as to exhibit in their windows a cartoon depicting a filthy Chinese laundryman spitting on a white shirt as he worked. These cartoons did much damage. At times competition between rival Chinese laundries is keen and relentless; there have also been price wars among neighboring Chinese laundries, particularly when new laundries have opened near established ones, where business was not sufficient for two.

Retail, Import, and Export
Chinese businesses in the United States are mostly on a small scale—only a small percentage have been incorporated; statistics on actual investment and capital of each business are not available. In the amount of capital, restaurants certainly are in the lead. There are more laundries than restaurants, but there is no comparison between their respective requirements for capital. Next to these two businesses, groceries and gift shops are the most numerous. There are at least three thousand groceries owned and operated by Chinese in the United States, among which a limited number are supermarkets. In the Sacramento area alone, about one third of the 7,000 Chinese residents earn their living through the food business. They own about 150 groceries and supermarkets, doing an annual business of more than $150 million. The retail business appears to the Chinese to be the most suitable for him, because he prefers to give his business his personal attention. In both San Francisco and New York the large Chinatowns are the supply depots to the Chinese living in other parts of these cities and in their suburbs. Grocers are wholesalers, and they ship quantities of Chinese provisions to other cities that have large Chinese populations. Tourist patronage in Chinatowns makes gift shops and restaurants prosperous. In order to be accessible to their clients, the travel bureaus, insurance brokers, bonding house agents, among many others, almost without exception locate their offices in Chinatown.

Business establishments outside Chinatown, with the exception of laundries and restaurants, are largely gift shops, export and import houses, some small and others employing a considerable staff. Importing and exporting, to be successful, require up-to-date knowledge and much practical experience. The Quon Quon Company in Los Angeles, a family venture which has been successful in the

TABLE 31

CHINESE MERCHANTS IN CHINATOWN, NEW YORK CITY, 1960

Kinds of Merchants	Number	
Food and foodstuff		
Farm products	6	
Groceries	84	
Meat, poultry, vegetables	8	
Bakeries, noodle makers	10	
Total food and foodstuffs		108
Apparel and accessories		
Clothing, haberdashery	10	
Chinese sportswear makers	18	
Total apparel and accessories		28
Selected services		
Agencies, insurance, and travel	39	
Amusements, theatres	5	
Beauty shops, barber shops	5	
Contractor, carpenter	2	
Electric repair shops, electricians	3	
Dry cleaners, laundries	8	
Photograph studios	3	
Total selected services		65
Eating and drinking places, restaurants		50
Other retail stores		
Book stores	3	
Druggists	4	
Florists	4	
Gift shops	21	
Jewelry	5	
Liquor stores	5	
Printers	7	
Miscellaneous	48	
Total other retail stores		97
TOTAL		348

Source: Twenty-Seventh Anniversary Issue, Chinese
American Restaurant Association of Greater New York,
Inc., 1960.

TABLE 32

CHINESE MERCHANTS IN NEW YORK, OUTSIDE OF CHINATOWN, 1960

Area	Laundry	Restaurant	Other Merchants
Manhattan	959	196	113
Brooklyn	894	118	12
Long Island	257	143	7
Bronx	524	45	0
Staten Island	12	3	12
TOTAL	2,646	505	144

Source: Twenty-Seventh Anniversary Issue, Chinese American Restaurant Association of Greater New York, Inc., 1960.

import and export business for nearly two generations, has as its president a University of Southern California graduate, Mr. Albert Quon. The three partners of the Summit Industrial Corporation in New York City, established in 1948, are graduate engineers and chemists from Massachusetts Institute of Technology, class of 1943: J. T. Shaw, C. C. Wang, and P. M. Yen. The corporation has maintained branches in Southeast Asia and in the Far East. The China Trade and Industrial Service, established in 1945, is conscientiously managed by its president, C. Tsang. Mr. Tsang is also the author of *China's Post-War Market,* published soon after World War II. Mr. I. C. Sung, vice-president of the company, was graduated from Harvard School of Business. His wife, Yi Ying Sung, was for a number of years an editorial researcher for *Time* magazine. Others might easily be cited. Likewise many Chinese are working in American export and import houses. As a whole, however, the sons of Chinese immigrants are not enthusiastic about carrying on business, even though their fathers may have themselves been businessmen. Thus, in a study of 198 American-born Chinese college graduates from 1920 to 1942, only 16 per cent have engaged in business.[10] The fact that 81.6 per cent of these graduates are professional men shows clearly that Chinese do not necessarily care to follow their forefathers' pursuits.

The Chicken Farm in Lakewood

An experiment which began well but has been something less than successful had its inception when, some three decades ago, a community of farmer-intellectuals chose to settle in Lakewood, New Jersey, about sixty miles from New York City. In the depression year 1930, there had begun a minor exodus from the cities of people of all ranks of life, looking to farms for relief and security. Several European refugees joined the settlement.

Not until 1950 did the Chinese immigrants follow suit, when two Chinese families newly arrived from Europe settled down and began to raise chickens.

A number of Chinese intellectuals chose to settle in Lakewood. They were mostly immigrants, but among these fifteen families at least four Chinese had seen diplomatic service in Europe. Practically all had received college educations. (It is an old Chinese custom for government officials, after retirement, to become gentlemen farmers in their home-town districts.)

However, because of the wide fluctuation of egg prices beginning in 1956, the plight of the chicken farmers became acute, and about twelve of the fifteen Chinese farmers withdrew. At the moment (early 1960) three are still struggling to maintain their investment. It is possible that the Chinese chicken farmer in Lakewood may soon become history.

Shipping Trade

The resumption of foreign trade after the end of World War II gave a number of Chinese in the United States an opportunity to enter the ocean shipping industry. Some of them have, in conjunction or partnership with other Americans, furnished the initiative to start several new successful steamship companies. Since then these companies have grown into sizable firms, well known in American shipping circles as efficiently operated enterprises. Other Chinese in the United States are running their own smaller firms as agencies for foreign steamship companies or as ship material supply firms. Still others have joined well-established steamship companies, shipyards, ship brokerage firms, and marine insurance companies and have become their key staff members, occupying positions as vice-president, partner, technical advisor, engineer, and department chief.

The postwar years have been a period of alternate ups and downs for the shipping industry. The Korean War and the Suez Canal incident were the industry's heydays. At other times, it starved. With the exception of technicians, who had thorough training in naval architecture or marine engineering, those Chinese who plunged into the shipping business were for the most part originally laymen in the field. They were, however, intelligent and diligent and had already completed their college education in some related fields. They learned the trade quickly, advanced themselves during the shipping booms, and were able to avoid setbacks during the slump periods. A number of these Chinese shipping men are now active planners and workers in a group of oil tanker companies, subsidiaries of an American nonprofit foundation having as its aim the advancement of economic and cultural relations between the United States and Free China. They operate a fleet of tankers aggregating more than three hundred thousand tons deadweight. This group of enterprises is shipping oil world-wide for several large American oil companies and for the American and Chinese Nationalist governments. Also, in conjunction with an American shipyard, this group is operating a shipyard in Taiwan, which has recently completed a 36,000 ton supertanker there, and is building another along with some similar ocean vessels.

Another group of Chinese is actively participating in an American shipping enterprise which owns and operates more than 1,500,000 tons of ships, inclusive of those under construction. This fleet of more than eighty vessels is technologically quite a modern one be-

cause it contains supertankers of up to 46,000 tons deadweight, special tankers for liquid chemicals, liquefied gas, and wine; bulk carriers for ore; combination vessels for alternate carriage of ore and
oil; and self-unloading bulk carriers for rice—all representing new
developments in ocean shipping.

The number of Chinese in the shipping industry is estimated to be
fewer than fifty in the East, and fewer than twenty on the West Coast,
where most are working for American shipping lines. The names of
Dr. C. Y. Chen and Morely Cho are known in the industry.

Physicians

The shortage of physicians in the United States is indeed critical. With the rate of the annual growth of the population at about
three million, the present 7,000 medical school graduates a year
simply cannot meet the requirements. In rural districts the scarcity
of physicians is all the more appalling. Many hospitals are unable
to fill their house staffs without recruiting from among foreigners.
In New York, Ohio, and Illinois, the chances are that more than
30 per cent of all house staff physicians are composed of aliens; in
New Jersey it is more than 65 per cent. In fact 25 per cent of all
residents and interns in this country are foreign physicians. The
total number has been increased from about 2,000 in 1951 to about
8,400 in 1960, a number exceeding that of all physicians graduated
from America's eighty-five medical schools in that year.[11] Those
aliens cannot obtain licenses for private practice, being permitted
to serve only as interns and resident physicians, or to do research,
or to teach in colleges. Since October, 1957, they have been deprived of the right to serve on hospital staffs, should they fail to
pass the qualifying test prescribed by the American Medical Association. There are twenty-one states, including Hawaii and Alaska,
that require a physician to be a citizen, and seventeen that are satisfied if he has applied for citizenship (1958).

Among these foreign physicians, many are Chinese who are permanent residents or have been naturalized, and their number is increasing. Though the majority are graduates of medical schools
in this country, some have been trained in China or in Europe, especially in Germany. The medical profession is extremely popular
among Chinese-Americans, because it offers occupational independence and social prestige.

Dr. Margaret J. Chung, one of eleven children, worked her way
through the University of California as a waitress and at the time of
her death in 1959 was one of the best-known surgeons on the West
Coast. She was a famous patroness of American servicemen during

the war. Ninety per cent of her medical clientele was white. A well-known certified surgeon in the East is Dr. David Y. P. Lin, formerly a captain the United States Army Medical Corps, a fellow of the American College of Surgeons. In addition to his surgical work in the Philadelphia Methodist Hospital and his teaching in the Jefferson Medical College, he has a commendable practice. His clientele is primarily Caucasian. There are several Chinese women doctors in New York City. Dr. Tsai Fan-Yu, of the Mt. Sinai Hospital, is considered an authority on gout; other women doctors in general practice are Dr. Y. C. Chu and Dr. K. L. Lee. Dr. Florence C. H. Chu is a certified radiologist.

In addition to being a practicing gynecologist and obstetrician in Jersey City, Dr. Hazel Lin is also a novelist. She is the author of *The Physicians,* published in 1951 and so well received that it was translated into fourteen languages. Her recent work is *The Moon Vow,* depicting the life of a physician in China.

Many Chinese doctors in the United States serve on the resident staffs of hospitals. Next come those who teach and do research work in medical schools.[12] Most Chinese doctors with private practices have their offices in Chinatown. In New York City alone (1958) there are twenty-six physicians and three dentists who are private practitioners, of whom only six do not have their offices in Chinatown. Chinese physicians are also to be found in Los Angeles, Detroit, Chicago, Cleveland, and in many other large cities. In San Francisco and in New York one may find Chinese herbalists practicing side by side with Western-trained doctors. There are few herbalists, however: eleven in New York, including one handling minor surgery work.

Engineers and Scientists

Chinese engineers and scientists have been accorded a high professional status in many well-known corporations, in research institutes, and on the faculties of universities.[13] Many American companies employ a number of Chinese engineers or scientists. Since some companies are handling government contracts, the checking of security risks is an absolute necessity; so that many of the sensitive positions can be filled only by citizens.[14] San Francisco has a Chinese engineering society with more than two hundred members, whereas the Chinese Institute of Engineers, in New York, has five hundred.

Attorneys

An alien attorney is not permitted to practice in the United States.[15]

The number of Chinese-American lawyers actually practicing is very small, the likelihood of their being accepted by law firms being almost negligible, especially since they have little chance of a clientele other than Chinese. It has been estimated that in New York City there are not more than ten Chinese attorneys, some of them partners of American lawyers. Chinese attorneys specialize chiefly in immigration matters, as Chinese prefer to settle most of their civil suits out of court; as a matter of fact, few Chinese study law.[16] There are also a limited number of Chinese certified public accountants with offices in Chinatown, who mostly assist their Chinese clients in filling out income tax returns. A score of Chinese accountants work in department stores, hospitals, and airlines.

Banks, Insurance, and Stockbrokerage

The Chinese-Americans own three banks in America. The pioneer among these, the Liberty Bank of Honolulu, opened for business early in 1922, and has assets well over $35,000,000, as of 1960. The American Surety Bank in Honolulu (incorporated in 1935) has five branches and assets of slightly over $41,000,000. The only Chinese-owned bank on the mainland of the United States, the Bank of Canton, in San Francisco, has total resources of about $19,000,000. A number of American banks in New York and San Francisco employ Chinese on their staffs. With many Chinese-Americans visiting Hong Kong and other places on business, for pleasure, and sometimes with an idea of getting married, the services of travel agencies become essential. Insurance brokers—life, fire, marine, accident—are very active. Chinese-Americans are following the practice of native Americans in acquiring life insurance at a comparatively youthful age. Out of the increasing business, several brokers in New York Chinatown are known to belong to the "one million dollar club" of one company or another, which means that a broker has written in a year at least one million dollars' worth of business.[17] Another type of brokerage that in the past decade has become popular with the Chinese is stock brokerage, in which the registered representatives, known sometimes as "customers' men," sell securities for various brokerage houses on the New York Stock Exchange, the American Stock Exchange, and others in the West or in Canada. They represent also exchanges dealing in cotton, wheat, barley, and other commodities. In addition, Chinese are employed in the research departments of brokerage firms, and in mutual fund investments, or in Canadian securities. Arthur T. Y. Loh of Pressprich and Co., a Ph.D. in economics from the University of Illinois, is one of the experienced security analysts in Wall Street. With a further expansion of the

American economy, the number of such representatives will no doubt increase. A man most eminent in this field, Dr. Ho-ching Yang, has been employed for the past ten years by Dominick and Dominick on Wall Street. Though some "customers' men" may have been active longer, most of them have been in business only during the past decade.

Government Service

Not many Chinese-Americans are in government service. Perhaps, considering themselves as mere sons of the land, they have been content to leave political matters as they are. Possibly their parents taught them to avoid politics and political persons, because of unfortunate experiences in China or in the United States. By tradition and custom, the Chinese are fearful of government; therefore, to become an official would seem almost unthinkable. Nevertheless, federal, state, and city authorities employ some Chinese. Most of the Chinese-Americans working for the government are persons with special technical skills. In Washington, D. C. alone, there are a number of Chinese on the staff of the State Department, the International Cooperation Administration, the Army Map Service, the Voice of America, the Bureau of Standards, the United States Geological Survey, the Library of Congress, and other departments. Some of them hold rather important positions. In addition, a number of Chinese have served as assistant district attorneys. The first American-born Chinese to become a judge in this country was Delbert E. Wong, appointed on January 23, 1959, by Governor Edmund G. Brown, to the municipal bench in Los Angeles. Irving Hui, a well-known civil engineer and a commissioner of water supply in New York City under the late Mayor La Guardia, was a Chinese-American. Chinese born in Hawaii have participated in the politics of the island, for example, becoming such officials as treasurer of the territory, mayor, chief of police, territorial senator, and councilman.

Teaching as a Profession

The United States government has long encouraged foreign scholars to become professors in its universities, but the actual number who have secured positions is by no means impressive. The Chinese Exclusion Act and the Quota Act of 1924 did not debar teachers, notwithstanding that many other classes of immigrants were barred. Not until the McCarran-Walter Act of 1952 were teachers placed in the category of the preferential quota; previously, they might come under the nonquota status. As a matter of fact, between 1915 and 1934 there were only 94 Chinese scholars teaching in American universities or colleges; between 1935 and 1944, however, there were 190, an average increase of 10 a year.[18]

It may be true that some Chinese scholars, after they have found their way to a higher institution of learning, do reach a dead end when they have completed their education; but from the number of Chinese scholars now engaged by American colleges and technical institutions, the teaching profession may soon become a major one for the Chinese in the United States. In American colleges and universities in 1959-60, there were 1,124 Chinese faculty members; whereas between 1945 and 1953 there was an average of about 137 each year. Surprising as it may seem, only 62 out of the 1,124 are professors of oriental culture, history, literature, or language.[19] The remaining 1,062 are teaching science, medicine, engineering, business, social science; are doing research; or are staff members. Five Chinese are teaching English in American colleges! Contrary to popular supposition, most Chinese are in the large institutions.

TABLE 33

AMERICAN COLLEGES AND UNIVERSITIES WITH TWENTY
OR MORE CHINESE FACULTY MEMBERS
1959-60

Institution	Number
University of California	79
University of Illinois	65
Yale University	39
University of Michigan	36
University of Wisconsin	32
Massachusetts Institute of Technology	31
Harvard University	30
University of Iowa	29
University of Maryland	28
University of Washington	23
Columbia University	21
University of Hawaii	20
TOTAL	433

Between 1854 and 1953 large universities engaged most of the Chinese scholars: the University of Minnesota had 109, Harvard came next with 108, Yale 89, New York University 41, Massachusetts Institute of Technology 26, the University of Oregon 20.

For the academic year of 1959-60, 186 American colleges and

universities engaged Chinese scholars; they represented forty-five states and the District of Columbia. The scholars were distributed as follows:

TABLE 34

DISTRIBUTION OF CHINESE FACULTY MEMBERS IN
AMERICAN COLLEGES AND UNIVERSITIES
1959-60

Number of Members	Number of Colleges
1- 4	129
5- 9	23
10-14	13
15-19	6
20-24	5
25-29	3
30-39	5
40-99	2

Of the 1,124, 569 are teaching, 555 are doing research work, are teachers' assistants, or are otherwise engaged. There are 134 professors,[20] 103 associate professors, 150 assistant professors. From 1854 to 1953, the numbers had been only 20, 18, and 53, respectively. Again—of those same 1,124—498 hold the degree of Ph. D., Sc. D., M. D., D. C. S., D. C. L., or the equivalent of one of these; 334 have the M. A. or M. S.; 211 have an A. B. or B. S.; and 81 have other degrees. As to the subjects in which they specialize, the following chart gives details.

Field of Specialization	Total
Physical and Natural Science	344
Engineering	304
Humanities	149
Medical Science	108
Social Science	105
Agriculture	51
Education	34
Business Administration	17
Others	12

The reason for the rapid increase of Chinese scholars in American colleges is not difficult to explain. The traditional respect in China for the teacher and the scholar has made Chinese, even though the income is modest, prefer teaching as a profession. And perhaps there is less prejudice on campuses. The shortage of professors is critical; it is especially true that in some fields men with a Ph. D. less frequently desire to teach. Chinese with higher degrees, however, are plentiful. That Chinese scholars are conscientious and excellent teachers is generally agreed.

The increase of Chinese professional men—architects, engineers, physicians, surgeons, dentists, and nurses—is now a matter of common knowledge. Their professional standards are high; they readily adjust themselves to whatever occupational or professional duties have been assigned. In the field of social science, however, reluctance to employ Chinese still persists.

As far as we can learn, few Chinese in American banks have been able to rise beyond assistant vice-president or manager. One of the exceptions is the recent appointment of H. J. Shen as advisor to the Bank of America. Shen was educated at Dartmouth, receiving graduate training at the Harvard University and New York University business schools. He is considered one of the most outstanding Chinese bankers. He was former deputy governor of the Central Bank of China under the Chinese Nationalist government. There are thousands of well-educated Chinese, no less competent than their brothers, who major in science or in engineering. We often see in corporations the same reluctance to engage Chinese for other than technical work.

As for business pursuits, laundries and restaurants will for many years be predominant. Laundries may show marked decline; today, not many laundrymen's offspring care to continue their fathers' calling. Conversely, the restaurant business is likely to boom, because of the growing popular appreciation of Chinese food. Its allied trades, the canning or freezing of Chinese dishes, will automatically further expand, for they are not limited to chow mein, egg roll, and fried rice; there are many more genuine and delicious combinations.

A very noticeable fact in Chinese businesses in this country is that there are few comparatively large-scale companies. The Wah Chang Corporation in the East and Joe Shoong's National Dollar Stores in the West are obvious exceptions. Though prejudice and discrimination may be partly responsible, the average Chinese seems to prefer his own management or a partnership in a small firm. Evidently there is little interest among the Chinese in the advantages of large corporations. The need of close cooperation among Chinese businessmen is manifest. Every indication, however, suggests that as more enlightened Chinese become interested in commercial pursuits, at least medium-sized establishments will eventually emerge.[21]

Chinese women, following the men, have adjusted themselves to various kinds of occupations. They are with their husbands mostly in laundries and restaurants; or they may work as nurses, teachers, clerks, laboratory technicians, social workers, or factory hands. But there are also Chinese women physicians, chemists, college professors, and researchers in laboratories. One of the world's foremost women physicists is a Chinese-American, Dr. Chien-Shiung Wu. There appears to be no goal, in any field, to which a Chinese woman cannot aspire.

When the Chinese first came to California, they were welcomed because they were needed for work there. Eventually, as they competed with whites for these jobs, many laws (culminating with the Chinese Exclusion Act) were passed, imposing on them employment barriers and residential segregation and forcing them to retreat to Chinatown. Fortunately, the tremendous tourist trade here helped them to be economically self-sufficient and invulnerable to unemployment. Their cohesiveness and interdependence were noticeable, but their position—as a group with a different culture and physical appearance—was not at all secure.

Since World War II, the Chinese have moved from the traditional occupations and are filling gaps in the ranks of engineers, scientists, professors, nurses, and physicians. There is a growing need for doctors because of the expanding population and for professors because of the expanding college campus. The growing American economy has produced a new force in industry—the emphasis on industrial research, which has quadrupled in finance in the last decade and which will probably double in the next. Therefore, Chinese engineers and scientists will be much in demand.

However, where there is less need of assistance, the Chinese have small chance of being accepted for jobs on their merits as individuals. The Chinese working as lawyers, in banks, insurance companies, or brokerage houses are few, and usually have been employed principally to deal with Chinese clients. It is difficult for a Chinese student of the humanities or social sciences to join a college faculty (although students of science can) and most Chinese scientists and engineers are doing research rather than management.

The early Chinese, coming to the United States as penniless immigrants at a low social level, were aliens in dress, customs, and physical characteristics. They struggled for economic advancement. The first basis of conflict with the whites was the latter's ethnocentric dislike of people with a different culture and their feelings of superiority. After the gold rush, there was much competition for the few jobs left, and the intensified conflict naturally led to discriminatory legislation passed by the majority. Only where there was necessity for compromise did the majority act tolerant—for example, during the building of the Central Pacific Railroad, they had to hire Chinese workers or else delay the completion of the railroad.

Even today not all Chinese enterprises are flourishing. The large Chinese laundry trade is losing ground due to competition. But the Chinese restaurants are fortunate in that the food is well liked by many and is reasonably priced. Not only are there more Chinese restaurants open for business, but Chinese food is being frozen. However, the Americans are competing with Chinese in the frozen foods business.

We must ask whether so few Chinese are in business because of economic competition or because they are attracted to other fields. The old traditions hold that the businessman is beneath the scholar, farmer, and laborer, and is dishonest. There is much respect for the scholar, and Chinese businessmen want their children to have more fortunate lives than they have had. Therefore, many of these children attend college and swell the professional class. With the growth of the American economy, with the lessened ethnocentrism of the majority and the minority, and with the success of the Chinese businessman, many will move out of Chinatown and find residence elsewhere.

10

The Chinese Community

That immigrants of all nationalities should tend to live together in their respective communities, holding tenaciously to even the vestiges of their old-world customs, to their native languages, and to their revered traditions, is quite expectable and natural. Strangers in a strange land where they seem handicapped, at least in the beginning, these freshly arrived peoples nostalgically seek refuge and comfort among their already somewhat-established compatriots, where often they develop organizations to meet fundamental communal needs. As prototypes of these later foreign communities, the earliest settlers and pioneers on these shores founded their colonies with a national, social, or religious bias—the English Cavalier and Puritan; the Spanish or French or English Roman Catholics; the Holland Dutch in New Amsterdam; the Swedes in Delaware; the Quakers, under William Penn, in Pennsylvania. Still later arrivals from northern Europe, approximately between 1820 and 1850, settled themselves, not, to be sure, in separate colonies, but homogeneously in certain geographical regions. The Germans, as the "Pennsylvania Dutch," remain a virtual entity today; the Irish consolidated themselves in Boston and New York. Both strongly patriotic toward their "old countries," they were not without ambition to create a German or an Irish independent state. The Scandinavians established ethnically unified farming communities in the Middle West. In more recent times, Italian and Baltic peoples, tempted by high wages for unskilled labor, then Russians and Semitic strains from all lands, flowed into cities and factory towns. They filled the newly created city slums, each in its own section of town. Meanwhile, the Negroes lived apart, both in the South and in the North. New York had its "Little Italy," its Seventh Ward, and its Harlem. Conversely, Americans or British abroad, especially in the East, tend to establish their own racial zones, with little intercourse with the natives, except officially or on business. They have their own schools, churches, clubs, newspapers, and barber shops. This arrangement is

197

both natural and convenient. Another reason, slightly sinister, for these self-segregated foreign communities, is the apprehension of hostility from the dominant population; sometimes this apprehension has become reality.

Chinatown

Chinatown, My Chinatown[1]

Chinatown, my Chinatown,
Where the lights are low;
Hearts that know no other land,
Drifting to and fro.
Dreamy, dreamy Chinatown.
Almond eyes of brown.
Hearts seem light,
And life seems bright,
In dreamy Chinatown.

Chinatowns developed first from the immigration of peoples seeking economic and social betterment. Chinatown, however, differs from zones established by European immigrants, in that it has usually been too small to maintain complete community functions. Moreover, since the Chinese, until 1943, were not permitted naturalization, thorough integration remained a very slow and tedious process, and racial and cultural differences aggravated the difficulty. But it must be emphasized that Chinatowns are by no means synonymous with the entire Chinese community in the United States. As soon as a Chinese has improved his economic status sufficiently or can accept a position superior to any that Chinatown can offer, he usually leaves and settles in a better residential portion of town. Thus, in the early 1880's, 73 per cent of the 5,000 Chinese in Honolulu lived within the district of Chinatown; but, only 40 per cent by 1900, and by 1950 the proportion was reduced to about 10 per cent of the 28,800 in the city.[2] Where did the remaining 90 per cent go? Some moved to a much larger Chinatown, sometimes referred to as the Greater Chinatown. As early as the middle 1920's, a group of Chinese families began to move to Bingham Tract, sometimes called "Chinese Hollywood." As their economic status further improved, the Chinese moved to even more desirable locations. There is at present a concentration of Chinese families on the lower slopes of Tantalus, known as Mandarin Heights.[3] In New York City there is, of course, a Chinatown, but many Chinese live near Columbia University; also in Forest Hills and Rego Park, in Great Neck, in Flushing, and in other parts of Long Island. Nowadays, others besides the Chinese inhabit parts of Chinatown: there are also Japanese, Ko-

reans, Filipinos, and Caucasians filling the gaps left by the departure of the opulent Chinese.

For more than a century Chinatowns in various metropolitan cities, particularly in San Francisco, have been attracting sightseers
in vast numbers, especially those who have never been in the Far
East, who look with wonder and almost with envious interest. Many
go to Chinatown to regale themselves on delectable oriental dishes,
or to purchase oriental works of art. Then, because these sightseers are also looking for some excitement, the guides escort them
to temples, theaters, joss houses. Previously they were also shown
gambling dives, opium dens, and even resorts of vice. Most of
these no longer exist.

Chinatown is a center of social and business activity within a non-
Chinese community.[4] Most Chinatowns are situated near a railway
station (for example, in Boston, Pittsburgh, St. Louis) because
the early Chinese wished to be readily accessible to relatives and
friends. In New York and San Francisco, however, they are situated
near the docks, to be convenient for debarking immigrants. Since
the place has no independent economic structure, the prosperity of
Chinatown depends much on the prosperity of the surrounding city.
The Chinatowns of San Francisco, New York, and a few other cities,
because of their historical, commercial, and picturesque importance, will probably remain for many years to come.[5] But elsewhere Chinatowns are rapidly receding, sometimes because of a
general economic decline in the city, sometimes, as in Butte, Montana, since 1940, because the city has lost its single industry. The
same situation obtains to some extent in Denver, Salt Lake City,
Rock Springs, Wyoming, and Boise, Idaho. In Denver, Chinatown
disintegrated because of a decline in Chinese residents; the complete razing of it in 1910 sealed its fate.[6] Yet not every Chinatown
is receding; some are expanding, with many indications of progress.
Boston is a notable example. Its Chinatown may have been a shabby
low-rent district previously occupied by Irish, Jews, Italians, or
Syrians, but the district was taken over about 1890 by the Chinese;
and for more than sixty years the Chinese residents have maintained
attractive restaurants and art shops. The district is considered
thoroughly respectable and desirable, patronized by both Chinese
and non-Chinese. It is somewhat too congested for residence. The
Chinese, however, while increasing the population from 200 in 1890
to 3,590 in 1960, have at the same time maintained an enviable record for good citizenship.

It must be noted that practically all the Chinatowns in the United
States, judging from the standpoint of residential desirability, are
much below par. Many of the buildings, constructed for shops or

stores, are quite unsuitable for residences; and many are too old to be equipped with modern sanitary facilities. All Chinatowns are overcrowded. The prevalence of tuberculosis is one natural consequence of very congested living quarters. The majority of Chinese merchants are skeptical about rebuilding Chinatowns because they are afraid of losing good business; perhaps they are justified. Yet the children, especially, are entitled to a far better standard of living. Surely a well-planned oriental exhibit, an exotic Chinatown but a healthful one, might attract even more tourist trade. Furthermore, the *esprit de corps* of the Chinese themselves would redound to the welfare and interest of all concerned. Under their existing conditions, many Chinatowns will certainly disintegrate rapidly.

Professor Rose Hum Lee has found that if a city's total Chinese population falls below 360, or if the total population of the city is fewer than 50,000, the city can scarcely support a Chinatown indefinitely.[7] The exception is that a small Chinatown may exist if it is related to a nearby Chinatown or if in the neighboring states there is strong Chinese support. Pittsburgh, for instance, with a Chinese population of only 141 in 1940, has, because of its nearness to the Ohio Valley and parts of West Virginia and Pennsylvania, for years maintained a very small Chinatown. As the Chinese population in the United States increases, many cities will have far more Chinese residents. What then will be the status of Chinatowns, no one can foretell. With less prejudice and discrimination against the Chinese, and with more and more Chinese desirous of being assimilated into American society, those Chinatowns with fewer than 1,000 inhabitants will in the not too distant future go out of existence. As the Chinese gradually disperse among the white population, the usefulness of even the more important Chinatowns is doubtful. The tourist attraction may in fact induce many Chinese shops to get together and keep the name of Chinatown. With the disintegration of Chinatowns, laundries and restaurants and gift shops will remain.

The social changes in Chinatown, meanwhile, have been far-reaching. There is a ban on trade with the Chinese Communist mainland. Chinese-Americans no longer find it necessary to visit China, even though they were permitted to do so, since most of them long ago (before the 1950's) had brought their wives and children to this country. Very soon those Chinese-Americans who have even seen the mainland of China will shrink into a minority. True, the immigrants from Hong Kong or Formosa may cause a continuing demand for Chinese food, but most Chinese families in Chinatown prepare both Chinese and American foods at home, with breakfast and luncheon mostly in the American style. To have a Chinese lunch at a Chinese restaurant on Sundays or on holidays is a practice enjoyed by many. Strange as it may seem, not all children in Chinatown have an appetite for Chinese food. Hot dogs and hamburgers are many times preferred to Chinese won ton or chow mein. Children's and men's clothes are practically all western, whereas women are still accustomed to the Chinese style of dress, both rich in appearance and reasonable in price. In gift shops it is difficult to stock genuine Chinese souvenirs because of shortage of supply; instead, many items come from Japan, countries in Southeastern Asia, or even from Mexico. Indeed, Chinatown is changing speedily toward westernization.

From the census figures, taken every ten years, it is evident that a redistribution of the Chinese population continues throughout the cities and states. Because Chinese usually do not marry within their own clan, or with those of the same surname, and as the clan organization is in fact the backbone of any Chinatown, the moving away of any large number may affect the status of a particular Chinatown, especially the smaller ones organized on the extended kinship structure.

Chinatown in San Francisco is doubtless the oldest and the largest Chinese settlement in the United States, with a history of more than one hundred years. The deadly earthquake and conflagration on April 18, 1906, destroyed three-fourths of the city and obliterated the former unhealthful Chinatown *in toto;* but the rebuilt and well-developed Chinatown has become exceedingly prosperous. Though Los Angeles may boast two newer Chinatowns, constructed in the late 1940's, the one in San Francisco remains the largest, the most picturesque, and the most attractive. In spite of the migratory movement of Chinese from the West Coast shortly before the Chinese Exclusion Act in 1882, San Francisco still has the largest Chinese contingent. The Chinatown of San Francisco derives benefit and support from the fact that California is growing faster than many other states. Many of the new Chinese immigrants who arrived under the Refugee Relief Act of 1953 and later acts settled in California, mainly in San Francisco because it was one of the nearest ports of entry. The Chinatown there will remain for a long time the most important.

Thus like other immigrants who came to the United States during the nineteenth century, the Chinese established, in San Francisco about 1850, a racial quarter, not only for self-protection but also for companionship. Self-protection appeared to be imperative, since, a few years after their arrival, the anti-Chinese movement spread throughout the West Coast; but, in addition, the Chinese found it hardly possible in those days to obtain lodgings outside Chinatown.

As early as 1853, practically all the Chinese in San Francisco managed to live within the crowded two blocks between Kearney and Stockton Streets, and between Sacramento and Jackson Streets. Gradually the quarter expanded, so that by 1906 it occupied fifteen blocks, all below Mason Street and south of Sacramento Street.[8] In those days the streets were wide and well paved, and had sidewalks similar to those in other parts of the city. Most of the two- to three-story buildings used by the Chinese were of brick, with a cellar or a basement; and there were strange signboards inscribed with bright red and gilt lettering, most striking in those dominant colors of Chinatown.[9] Because of the uncertainty of their future in this country, the Chinese tended to invest their money in personal property rather than in land, preferring to take long leases in order to sublet. As the anti-Chinese movement gained momentum, more and more Chinese sought sanctuary in Chinatown, hoping to avoid conflict with the white agitators. The absence of decent living conditions, the horrors of overcrowding, the dangerously unsanitary state of things—landlords were never required to make any repairs—brought about in 1904 threats of the bubonic plague. Then only were the landlords compelled to do some cleaning and repairing; many buildings actually had to be torn down. The earthquake and fire of 1906 automatically made a thoroughgoing sweep of the noisome districts.

The earliest Chinatown was intended for the lodging of single persons and for business, as Chinese women and children in those days were very few.[10] Nearly all were members of the Six Companies, formed for the protection, mutual assistance, and general benefit of their members. Many accusations based on gross distortions of fact were leveled at the Chinatown Chinese in general and at the Six Companies in particular. Newspapers, the police, and especially the politicians maintained an anti-Chinese attitude, so that exaggerations of the vices of Chinatown became the rule; and they singled out the Six Companies as being responsible for all unfortunate acts and for all outrages. To be sure, there were gambling and opium dens, prostitutes, and there were the hatchet men—the Chinese criminals of Chinatown. In fact, the Chinatown special police squad was organized in 1875, when Chinese racketeers were employed by the rival tongs to kill members of other tongs; evidently such lawlessness was provoked by competition for business or for location. Tong wars lasted in San Francisco for a long time, being carried on intermittently. In 1902 a war between rival tongs killed seven men; the last murder attributed to the tongs was committed in 1926. Though atrocities were not as extensive as in New York, they prevented the abolition of the famous police squad. Not until after repeated news editorials asserted that the retention of the squad showed discrimination was it finally abolished in 1956.

Another unique feature of Chinatown that has been done away with in the past ten years was the telephone switches for the use of Chinese subscribers only. Since 1894 the 2,100 subscribers of Chinese descent did not need to ask for telephone numbers but simply gave the name and address of the person with whom they wished to talk. The telephone operators, well versed in five Chinese dialects, had memorized the numbers of all the subscribers. Now, however, Chinese subscribers dial their telephones as do all others.

Chinatown in San Francisco remains the most picturesque quarter for tourists, who, though they may be able to purchase a Chinese idol in some joss house, no longer see anything mysterious or horrible. Grant Avenue, the main street of Chinatown, is one of the busy San Francisco thoroughfares. Even though their opportunities were limited, Chinese residents are trying to expand, since the twenty square blocks are insufficient to house all the Chinese in the city. Though there are now newly built apartments in Chinatown and the Chinese are legally able to own land, and though Chinese have moved out to live among the middle-class whites, pressure in Chinatown has not been much reduced; in fact, Chinese have been living in an area dedicated to shops, restaurants, and institutions. In addition, there are a number of Chinese developments, usually situated not far from Chinatown, which cater to Chinese residents. Restaurants and gift shops form the majority of places in Chinatown; a few are owned and operated by Japanese or Koreans. There are, besides, grocery stores selling American and Chinese foods produced locally or imported from Hong Kong or Formosa. Some of these stores also handle wholesale goods, shipping large consignments to other Chinatowns.

The second largest Chinese settlement in the United States is in New York. Its first Chinese resident is said to have been Pung Hua Wing Ching, who was a servant of John Jacob Astor around 1807, but did not stay in New York very long. Three Chinese, who came at different times in sailing vessels from San Francisco, are said to have been the pioneers of the New York Chinatown. Lee Ah-bow came about 1850 as cook of the *Valencia;* he died at the age of ninety in the State Hospital for the Criminally Insane. In 1858, Ah Ken, a merchant on Mott Street, was another early pioneer. A small group of Chinese came to New York in 1869 from the West Coast.[11]

The real beginning of the New York Chinatown, however, came between 1872 and 1882. Some Chinese settled on Doyers Street, then gradually spread to Pell, Mott, Bayard, and Canal Streets, and to Chatham Square. By 1887 the community had 800 to 1,000 Chinese. Like others in the United States, the early New York China-town was composed chiefly of men. They wore pigtails and their native garb, until, becoming somewhat westernized, they had their queues cut off.

More than thirty years ago the New York Chinatown was the muni-cipal problem community; at that time tong wars raged intermit-tently, and though accounts were often much exaggerated, gambling, narcotic traffic, and other abuses flourished there. The tong con-flicts reached New York about a decade after they had begun in San Francisco. In 1925 there were as many as sixty killings in five states, for tong wars usually broke out simultaneously, as the tongs were seeking mastery everywhere at once. In that year, 1,200 Chi-nese were in the custody of the police and 264 were deported, but the authorities' threatening to raze several Chinese settlements brought the strife to a halt. Not until 1933, when the United States attorney told the tong executives that the federal government was investigating narcotic and immigration violations and that the exec-utives would have to submit their tong books for examination, did the conflicting tongs begin to realize the seriousness of the situation. Accordingly they signed a treaty of peace to end tong wars. The Chinese of today are known to be peaceful and law-abiding. In fact, as we have already seen, Chinatown has less crime and juvenile delinquency than most other foreign quarters in New York City.

The New York Chinatown is not only a mecca for tourists but also a homey community. There on holidays and Sundays Chinese from the city and from the suburbs go to have a good meal, meet friends, visit their relatives, have a few rounds of mah-jongg, and get letters from Hong Kong or Formosa. Chinatown is also a supply depot for many Chinese families.

Part of New York's Chinatown is composed of buildings more than fifty years old; sooner or later some of it will have to be razed and rebuilt.[12] Very few residential structures have been added since a five-story apartment at 37 Mott Street was erected in 1925. The Chinese Merchants' Association Building erected in 1952 was the first multistory commercial project. The $800,000 Chinese Com-munity Center, when completed, will contain an auditorium, a gym-nasium, a Chinese school, and offices; doubtless it will be the best building in the quarter.[13] Most of the real estate is owned by the Chinese, who have a passion for owning land; therefore the turnover of property is very slow.

Usually there is only one Chinatown in a city, but Honolulu has two and Los Angeles three or four. In 1909, a small middle-aged man, Louie Quan, became the leader in starting a Chinese colony in

Los Angeles. The $100,000 he raised as capital for a stock company, at fifty cents a share, was used to build a market with two hundred stores. The death knell of that undertaking was sounded in May, 1931, when the construction of a new union station on that site was approved by a court decision. The Chinese had long sensed the beginning of trouble, when in 1913 a lawsuit involved a large portion of Chinatown. Many were the ambitious plans to build a Chinatown somewhere; among them were plans for a modernistic town, recommended by George L. Eastman. Though these plans had the approval of the Chinese as well as of the city council, they were too expensive. The final compromise was two Chinatowns, one promoted by Mrs. Christine Sterling and the other by Peter Soo Hoo. Mrs. Sterling opened "The China City" on June 6, 1938. Her idea was that the "City" as a nucleus might be developed into a huge Chinatown; it had a movie-set appearance, with much that was picturesque and mysterious. Situated at the corner of Main and Macy Streets, less than a block from Olvera Street, the Mexican center of Los Angeles, the "City" forms an oriental oasis in the heart of downtown districts. Around a central plaza, souvenir shops and restaurants group themselves quaintly; from there a narrow lane winds through another cluster of exotic shops; and a wall surrounds the whole. In 1939 a disastrous fire destroyed the major portion. Six months later, however, the "City" re-emerged, with forty-two of the shops reopening on their original sites.

Peter Soo Hoo, a University of Southern California graduate, succeeded in establishing on Broadway at College Street a new Los Angeles Chinatown. The town's stock is controlled by a corporation composed entirely of Chinese. The corporation owns nearly half the lots; the others are owned by individual stockholders. The total investment is close to a million dollars. As the corporation owns one fourth of the buildings, the Chinese need no longer fear dispossession. This new Chinatown was officially opened June 25, 1938. Like "China City" it is a planned project. The buildings are mostly two-story structures, situated exactly between Broadway and Castalar Street. Oriental flavor naturally exists; but the emphasis has been placed on broad and open streets and on nights brilliant with flashing neon lights.

In addition to those two planned projects in Los Angeles, there is a third Chinese community along North Spring Street, between Ord and Macy Streets. A portion of the old Los Angeles Chinatown remains, composed of Los Angeles Street, the 400's block North, and Ferguson Alley.[14]

No doubt the Los Angeles Chinese communities are expanding; from a population of 2,500 in 1930, they have grown to 8,000 in 1950 and 15,000 today, and they are still growing. Since the whole population of the city of Los Angeles is increasing, the Chinese population will proportionately increase. In fact more than half the 20,000 Chinese in Southern California live in Los Angeles City and County.

Family and Social Life

To understand Chinese family life in America, one should familiarize himself with the characteristics of the traditional family in China. The Chinese family is the social unit, and also the responsible element, in the political life of its locality; as such, the family unit has been considered as the state itself in miniature; consequently Chinese allegiance and loyalty are devoted more to the family than to the state.

The typical and traditional family in China has been, ideally, patriarchal, patrilocal, patrilineal, and endogenous. According to this ideal, the grandparents, their unmarried children, their married sons together with their wives and children, all live in one household.[15] Each member of the family shares the domestic expenses and does his best to support the whole. The headship passes from the father to the eldest son. Filial piety receives great emphasis. The youngsters have no voice in the family councils, but simply obey orders from the head. As a rule, marriages take place within the ethnic group. Women have a somewhat inferior status. The teenager is anxious to please his parent. The love, the awe, the fear of the children for their parents, especially for the father, increases all the more with the respect paid to age. One recognizes at once that the traditional Chinese family is far more complex than the Western family, which usually consists of husband and wife and their children. Every child in a Chinese family is involved in an ordered kinship, so that there are often several kinds of uncles, aunts, cousins, and even grandparents; and each bears a title of relationship unheard of in the West. Despite its complications, the Chinese family is nevertheless fundamentally cooperative to the fullest extent. The parents have the duty of rearing the children; the children have the obligation, if necessary, of supporting their parents. Members are in duty bound to assist one another in case of need.

Filial piety is explained as emphasis on the moral principles of mutual respect among those of equal status and of reverence toward the dominant elder. Service and self-sacrifice characterize ideal Chinese family relations. Should one of the members go wrong, the others, even those of kinship units or clans, feel themselves grievously affected. To persuade the wrongdoer to mend his ways is

the duty of the clan as well as the family. The result is that a constant mutual watch leads generally to the maintenance of a satisfactory moral balance. The small number of crimes committed by the
Chinese in the United States and the paucity of juvenile delinquency
in Chinatown may be properly attributed to their closely knit family
life. Since the Chinese community in town, village, or country consists of families and kinship units, mutual assistance and reverence
for the elders is upheld in the clan as within families. As a person
grows older his role shifts from that of a man of action to that of a
man of counsel. The life of the elder, an integrated member of the
family, remains rich and full of enjoyment as long as he lives. Thus
the common household solves the problem of the aged, for both man
and woman, at the time when they most need companionship and a
serene life.

Another characteristic of the Chinese family system is that marriages are not commonly made among members of the clan; girls
are encouraged to marry into households of other clans. That parents
should choose mates for their children is a convention fast being
relegated to the past. Youngsters today fully realize that their parents have no legal right to enforce their marriage choice.

There are disadvantages. The Chinese family system tends to
foster slothfulness and dependence among the young men. They
tend to lack initiative and enterprise, especially when their parents
are overautocratic. The household composed of many members
holding diverse opinions is likely to become one of grave disunity.
The sharing of income for common expenses, especially when only
a few are breadwinners, may or may not be sufficient for the support
of the entire family. Also, there may be too great emphasis on duty
to the family or clan and not enough on duty to country.

In spite of the persistence of the traditional Chinese family and
kin system (though of late it has changed considerably), China—
politically, educationally, sociologically—has been much altered
since its contact with the West. The family is no exception; the large
family of many married sons with their wives and children, and unmarried daughters as well, living together in one enormous com-
pound, is today the exception rather than the rule; the average family
can no longer afford such luxury, even though there may be a wish
to maintain that common household. If a family has two married
sons, one son usually moves out and lives separately; thus families
are becoming much smaller, no longer figuratively living inside
walled castles. Besides, though the primary duty of a married couple
has always been to produce a son and heir to preserve the family
continuity, even that point of view is gradually losing its authority,
However much the older generation desires to maintain the tradi-

tional family system, the younger generation is willing to meet it
only halfway.

When we now come to view the Chinese family in America, we
must realize that the Chinese, in and out of Chinatown, have for
several decades been living in a man's world. In 1867 there were
in California no more than five hundred Chinese children under
fifteen, but the total Chinese population on the Pacific Coast was
estimated at slightly over fifty thousand. If the average were three
children to a family, there would have been only 150 to 200 Chinese
families in California. In 1900 the number of children had increased
to 4,000, showing that the Chinese had begun to live a conventional
family life. Women and girls were not frequently seen on the streets,
and when seen were regularly accompanied by husband or father.
Since the enactment of the War Brides Act in 1945, many veterans
of Chinese descent brought wives back to this country, and the new
immigrants usually brought their families. Thus the number of
Chinese families greatly increased, bringing down noticeably the
abnormally high ratio of the males. Meanwhile, women had gradually come to be considered as equals; the streets of Chinatown
were thronged with women as well as with men.

Though Chinese family life in the United States still tends to follow
to a certain extent the pattern of the traditional system in China,
nevertheless the application of that pattern differs in degree in various families. Naturally much depends on a parent's education,
birthplace, profession, and place of residence, and, to a great extent, on the length of time that this country has been his home. Of
late there has been considerable adjustment to American family
life, especially by those Chinese families that have moved out of
Chinatown to live among middle-class whites. Many things stand
out sharply as having influenced today's American family. Mass
education, urbanization, increased mass employment of women,
and above all the impact of World War II, have contributed to a
great disintegration of parental control over children. All these
factors tend to have an impact also on the Chinese immigrant family.
There cannot be a rigid traditional Chinese family existence, even
in Chinatown.

As we have shown earlier, among the first and second generations
of the early Chinese immigrants those who wished to maintain a
family usually returned to China to marry, and sent for their wives
a few years later. Others left their wives in China, returning to
visit them once in a great while. Daughters here were married to
middle-aged men, because young Chinese men usually preferred
the native Chinese girls. Parents were apt to be very strict, since
they felt the marriage of sons and daughters to be one of the most

important functions of the family. The early immigrant families usually manifested an old-fashioned way of life, often being more conservative toward the children than families would be in China.[16] The Gong family in Miami,[17] the father of Pardee Lowe, the family of Jade Snow Wong,[18] and many others living in Chinatown belong in this category. To be sure, Gong senior wished Eddie to marry Hoo See back in Hong Kong, whom Eddie had never met.[19] Even though Eddie preferred to marry an American, he went to Hong Kong; for, as a dutiful son and the only son in the family, he felt it behooved him at least to attempt to find a Chinese girl with whom he might fall in love.

In another type of family, the father was born in this country, and married a Chinese girl in China. The father may or may not have had a high school education. The family is usually large, sometimes including even married sons and daughters, and various children-in-law. The family life tends to be more Americanized than that of the first group, because of the father's American background; but obedience by the children is often demanded. Both boys and girls are at least high school graduates. The parents usually pay special attention to their daughters' behavior and daily conduct so that their mothers often serve them as chaperone; otherwise, the daughter must return home at night not later than an assigned hour. Generally speaking, parents supervise less carefully the son's matrimonial plans, unless he shows signs of intending to marry a Caucasian. Parents also supervise their children's playmates and later their friends, believing that their conduct can be interpreted from their choice of companions.

Also in this category, we may include those who left their wives at home and did not send for them until much later. The children may have already come here much earlier than their mothers did. Since this type of family sometimes lives outside Chinatown, especially if the father has a good job and fair income, the impact of American society is considerable. Those pairs who have been separated many years necessarily have gone on living in their respective worlds, which were often glaringly different, and consequently each has been experiencing a different life. There are bound to be family problems that need to be resolved and adjusted. For example, the mother may demand more obedience from the children, but the children's response is usually very negative. Compromise by the parents with the children in order to avoid open conflict is generally the rule.

In the third Chinese category both parents have been born in America. One of them is probably a college graduate, the father usually a professional man, the mother a teacher, nurse, or dietician. Most

of them live not in Chinatown, but near where they work. Many of
the immigrants who arrived after World War II and who adjusted
their residential status or came under the Refugee Relief Act may
also belong in this category. As a matter of fact, the father in most
of these families had previously received college training in the
United States. Some were graduates of institutions of higher learning
in Europe. Since the family has a college tradition, the children are
likely to go to college. Such a family has already become wholly or
largely Americanized. The children have much more freedom, but
their parents, still greatly interested in their welfare, do everything possible to maintain a wholesome home life and preserve discipline. Married children tend to live separately, coming home for
reunions and for other special occasions. Recently some daughters
of this type of family have intermarried with Caucasians; both the
bride and groom are usually college graduates.

Perhaps a special type of war-bride family should be briefly mentioned. In World War II many G. I.'s were stationed in Europe, Australia, and later on in China and Japan. A great number of marriages
took place between G. I.'s and local girls. The strain to which such
marriages are subjected, as well as the question of whether Japanese war brides could make proper cultural and marital adjustment,
provoked discussion for some time. Our concern here is with the
native-born and other Chinese ex-servicemen who married Chinese
girls when the war was over. The number of citizens' wives abroad
admitted between 1946-53 approached ten thousand; Chinese war
brides made up the major proportion. Some G. I.'s stationed in
north, east, or south China married girls from Shanghai and north
China. The majority, however, married girls from Kwangtung,
and especially from their home villages, where relatives and friends
made necessary introductions and possible arrangements.

Most of the G. I.'s and their brides were necessarily young, their
courtships usually of short duration. Even though both the G. I. and
his bride were of Chinese ancestry, their differences in culture
might lead to conflict. The need for special adjustment to overcome
the family problem is great. Marital conflicts have resulted. As the
practice of seeking aid from clinical counselors is still new to many
Chinese families, the exact number of those in discord is unknown.

It would be next to impossible to give any clear-cut definition
of the typical Chinese family in this country, for one may always
observe families tending toward extremes. Certainly the Chinese
are not wholly impervious to radical social changes. Further change
depends, to a great extent, on how fully the Americans wish to accept the Chinese in business and society. Yet it is certain that Chinese children are on the whole brought up with firmer discipline and

with a far greater respect for their elders than are most American children. For instance, to call their parents by their first names, as many American children do, is anathema to the Chinese. Chinese parents encourage their children to marry early in life, but the higher the children's education the later will be their marriages.

Chinese mothers are usually employed, and the number increases yearly. In restaurants, particularly in the smaller ones, mothers and aunts function as waitresses, hostesses, cashiers, or kitchen helpers; after school, children often help them. Most Chinese laundries are family businesses. In Boston nearly all married Chinese women have employment in garment factories, even though the wages are not attractive and the jobs are menial.[20] More and more Chinese families have two breadwinners, husband and wife; whereas children usually work part time, and full time during the summer. Chinese far less than Americans observe a retirement age, especially those Chinese who are self-employed.

Even though the Chinese are constantly becoming better adjusted to American ways, certain peculiarly Chinese attitudes remain. They are disinclined to make last wills and testaments; no matter how well educated a paterfamilias may be, he is extremely reluctant to prepare a will far in advance, and this neglect may cause his family serious trouble. Though the Chinese have improved somewhat in this respect, large sums often go quite unnecessarily into the coffers of the state; thus in San Francisco between January 1 and June 30, 1957, $80,144 which had belonged to ten Chinese was by order of the surrogate court turned over to the state of California.

Another ancient tradition is that of removing bones from the cemetery to be transported for interment to the old home town in China. The children have the responsibility of making certain that their ancestors' remains are all snugly buried together in the proper places. No fewer than 1,300 sets of bones are still being stored after ten years in San Francisco warehouses, awaiting transportation. Two cemeteries in San Francisco have been releasing bones every ten years for shipment to China and to make more space for the newly deceased. The year 1947 was the last one in which bones were released; and since then only 500 out of a total of 1,800 sets have been shipped. The permanent settlement here of Chinese families, with their recurring generations, have made many Chinese decide to inter their bones in this country. Soon, presumably, no bones will be subject to transportation.

The average Chinese works very hard; he has not become accustomed to the American ideas of "get rich quick" and "live easily"; consequently his social life is not extensive outside his own circle. Opportunities for participating in American life are few and limited;

though there has been considerable improvement, a superficiality
of friendship tends to exist. A number of native-born American-
Chinese and new immigrants, however, are probably exceptions.
Yet the average Chinese family is fairly busy socially. It has more
days to celebrate and more occasions for family gatherings than
do families in China: the Chinese Lunar New Year; the May Fifth
Festival; August 15, the Full Moon Festival; and in addition, Easter,
the Fourth of July, Labor Day, Thanksgiving, Christmas, and New
Year's. Besides, there are always wedding parties, birthday parties, newborn-baby parties, and baby-haircut parties; even funeral
services. To the Spring Festival Party, celebrated by family, clan,
or district, guests in addition to members are invited to fill as many
as ten to fifteen tables; the rotating of invitations may last a couple
of months, and the invitations include men, women, and children.
Sometimes the party begins early in the afternoon, with musical
and other entertainment. One announcement is almost obligatory,
that a fixed amount of money is to be contributed to the local Chinese
school. Chinese women have other functions to attend, such as the
annual baby contest during the spring season and the annual Chinatown beauty contest usually held shortly before the Chinese Lunar
New Year.[21] Of all occasions, none is more exciting than the traditional welcome to the Chinese New Year. In Chinatowns in every
large city, the celebration begins early in the afternoon with a parade, with lions dancing to the accompaniment of drums, cymbals,
and firecrackers. As part of the ceremony "God Bless America"
is sung.

Chinatown parades are not confined to the New Year. For a long
time, there has been a parade, led by a drum and bugle corps, to
commemorate the anniversary of the founding of the Republic of
China by Dr. Sun Yat-sen. Boys sometimes carry dragons. Firecrackers and Cantonese music resound. In addition to taking part
in celebrations native to them, Chinese immigrants never fail to
participate in the American Loyalty Day parade which provides
pageantry in a contingent of hundreds of Chinese-Americans representing many societies and clubs. Chinese music of cymbals and
stringed instruments is played, with a dozen or so stilt walkers
dressed in ancient Chinese costumes.

Men have more social life than women. As for children, they
have to attend school, and after school those in Chinatown usually
attend a Chinese school for an hour or two, to study Chinese and
oriental cultural subjects. After that there is homework to be done
and possibly errands to be run. Chinese children are like American
children in their interest in sports, movies, and music. The young
men enjoy club life, and join the Lions Club, the Rotary Club, or

some Chinese social organization. Middle-aged men are usually much engaged in business, spending their leisure as members of a clan or other organization. Chatting or playing mah-jongg often completes their day. The average Chinese belonging to a club is very ambitious to be elected head, or to some lesser position in the society. He has many opportunities to dine out, since there is usually an occasion to join some welcome party in Chinatown to meet friends, leaders from other Chinatowns, or dignitaries from China itself. There may be much speechmaking. Chinese merchants respond willingly to various charitable appeals; often the "welcome party" turns out to be one to solicit contributions.

As a rule there is less problem in respect to the aged, for they are usually retained as members of the organized family, and they are respected; they are certainly not forgotten. But for those aged who are not members of family units—and the number is increasing—there is trouble. Before World War II, most of them were prepared to return to China to spend the remainder of their lives. Many are now living in the clan or district association to which they belong. Their daily life and the future prospects can by no means be considered satisfactory. In New York, a group of Chinese Christian ministers are sponsoring an old people's home to accommodate those with no one to depend upon. Contributions have been forthcoming from a number of sympathetic organizations. The fact that this venture is promoted by ministers is all the more important since old age needs opportunity for religious expression in deepening spiritual growth.

All in all the social life of the average Chinese is by no means cramped; his chances of visiting with friends and relatives are many, because most Chinese belong to district or family associations. The influx of women after World War II of course made life much more wholesome. But the social distance between most of the Chinese and the Americans is still measured in miles. As long as immigrants are not fully accepted on the basis of character and achievement, social gaps will be slow to close.

The Problem of Intermarriage

We have already touched on the problems of marriage that faced the Chinese immigrant. The scarcity of women, especially in the second half of the nineteenth century and until the wives of Chinese-Americans were permitted to come into the United States, made the Chinese bachelor's problem difficult. As long as a bride is available, either in Chinatown or better still somewhere in China, the problem is not serious; but the sex ratio still favors the male. Therefore, a marriage between a Chinese male and a white girl might present an alternative, but the proportion of such marriages has not apparently reached alarming heights.

A biological union or amalgamation of differing races usually results after social and economic contact. The interesting story of the fusion in Hawaii of Europeans with non-Europeans, including the Chinese, is well known; so is the marriage of Chinese men and native women in Southeast Asia. In Latin America Portuguese mixed with Negroes. In the French West Indies racial mixtures reached a high percentage. Well known also are the Eurasians of India, Southeast Asia, and Shanghai. Frequent contact and a dearth of European women have encouraged intermarriage. Hong Kong is now a place where Europeans and Chinese women intermarry almost daily.

Even though the intermarriage of Chinese men and white women in this country is infrequent, it has been going on for almost a century; and occasionally Chinese have taken Negro brides. American women have also married Chinese men students, and, after the latter's education was completed, returned with their husbands to live permanently in China. Dr. Yung Wing married Miss Mary Louise Kellogg in 1876. The first Chinese admitted after the repeal of the Exclusion Act was Mrs. John Lossing Buck, whose husband was a professor at the College of Agriculture of Nanking University. The former president of St. John's University, Shanghai, Dr. F. L. H. Pott, and his son, James Pott, both married Chinese women. Marriages of American women to Chinese students, professors, and engineers have increased since World War II; also Chinese college women have married American college men. Occasionally news of such marriages has appeared in the *New York Times* which noted that an American of Chinese descent from Honolulu, graduated from Beaver College, was married to a white alumnus of the University of Alabama and of the School of Law of New York University; that a Chinese girl graduate of Pembroke College married a white textile engineer of the Philadelphia Textile Institute. In spite of the increasing number of marriages of Chinese women to white Americans, the marriages of white women to Chinese are still more frequent. Since the nullification of the antimiscegenation law in California in 1948, there has been no haste in that state to apply for marriage licenses involving different races.[22]

An early study of mate selection by Chinese males in New York City (1931-38) revealed that of 254 marriages slightly more than 26 per cent were with non-Chinese females.[23] Inasmuch as the sex ratio was eight to one[24] (census of 1930) and there was an absence of legal or social prohibition of intermarriage in a highly urban community, it is surprising that the Chinese had not resorted to many out-of-group marriages.[25] Evidently the average Chinese who wished to marry went back to his native land to do so; those who chose to seek their mates in this country, in a proportion of one to four, married American women.

Apparently many white and Chinese families are still somewhat opposed to interracial marriages. Many Americans believe that miscegenation and mongrelization are synonymous, and that they are harmful to the nation as a whole. Some Chinese assume that differences in culture may in themselves lead to harmful misunderstandings, and therefore to marital unhappiness. Of course, very frequently public and family disapproval and ostracism by friends have made the matrimonial life of the mixed couples difficult; but marriages between whites and Chinese are increasingly frequent, especially on the college level. Elmo Roper found that of the 1,000 college seniors whom he interviewed, 43 per cent preferred that none of their close relatives should marry outside of the racial group.[26]

In addition to the social, there is also the legal aspect to be considered. Mississippi has a criminal statute which stipulates punishment for anyone who publishes or circulates printed matter favoring interracial marriage; Georgia (1927) and Virginia (1930) passed acts requiring every person in those states to give racial data about his forebears; in South Carolina a white man may marry a Chinese woman, but not vice versa; practically all the southern states have antimiscegenation statutes, but their effectiveness is open to question. In California, Filipinos continued to intermarry with whites even before the law prohibiting it was nullified in 1948. Those who wished to disregard the law went to states without discriminatory laws. Except in California, charges that those laws violated the Fourteenth Amendment have never been upheld in an unbroken line of decisions.[27]

The Virginia law was tested by the Supreme Court in a case of a white woman who had married a Chinese: *Ham Say Naim* v. *Ruby Elaine Naim*. The couple had left Virginia to be married in North Carolina (June, 1952) and had immediately returned to cohabit in Norfolk, Virginia. Later the woman brought suit in the Virginia court for an annulment on the grounds that the marriage was void under a Virginia statute in effect at the time of the marriage. The statute provided that if a white person and a colored person went out of state to marry and returned to live as man and wife, they should be punished. The Chinese husband, Ham Say Naim, appealed, and the court of appeals held that the marriage had been invalid. Then, when Naim asked the Supreme Court to remand the case to the state court to decide the constitutionality of the Virginia statute, the Supreme Court denied the motion and held that the constitutional issue was not squarely before it, and said: "The decision of the Virginia court leaves the case devoid of a properly presented Federal question."[28]

Unlike the situation in many states on the United States mainland, intermarriage involving any two races is entirely legal in Hawaii. Though endogamy may be preferred by many families, there is evidently no widespread objection to interracial marriages. The respect for racial equality has become a definite pattern; any attempt to oppose the general practice of interracial marriage would certainly meet little sympathy. During the middle of the nineteenth century, a number of Chinese laborers came to Hawaii to work on the plantations—young men and unmarried. They married Hawaiian women, if they married at all. By 1900 the number of Chinese women had increased, mainly because of the growth to maturity of Hawaii-born girls. Not until 1916, however, did the Chinese notably cease to marry local women, but it must be borne in mind that a marriage between a Chinese man and a Hawaiian woman usually resulted in a happy family. Since 1930, however, there has been again a great increase in the outmarriage ratio of both sexes.[29]

Organizations and Societies

In our discussion of the organization of the Six Companies in San Francisco, we mentioned the *raison d'être* for forming societies among the early immigrants: for mutual protection and mutual assistance; to keep peace and order; for contributions to relief; and to provide places for relaxation, warmth, and fellowship for the members. The Chinese immigrants in the United States (and elsewhere) who had come mostly from the same districts, spoke the same dialects, and bore the same surnames found it to their advantage to form organizations. Invariably they had to have a representative to act and to speak for all of them. Like the Six Companies in San Francisco, the Chinese Consolidated Benevolent Association in New York City was established by the Chinese immigrants. In Honolulu, there emerged the Chinese United Society, which celebrated its seventy-fifth anniversary in 1959. As the immigrants improved in economic status, leaving mining and farming to devote themselves to trade, industry, and various professions, they began to form trade or professional associations. Apparently the activities and influence of such organizations have been reduced in view of the gradual assimilation of Chinese-Americans.

Many Chinese belong to political parties.[30] Kuomintang, the ruling party in Free China, was organized by Dr. Sun Yat-sen and has maintained branches in the United States since the turn of the century. Another party, Chee Kung Tang, of which Dr. Sun was once a member, flourished from 1898 to 1911, and was reorganized in 1945 as the Hung Man Ming Chi party with headquarters in Vancouver. The *Min Chih Journal* (New York), published since 1960, is the party's newspaper. A third, the Chinese Democratic Constitutional party, with headquarters in San Francisco, owns the *Chinese World* (San Francisco) and the *New China Daily News* (Honolulu). It was organized by the followers of Liang Chi-chao, one of the leaders who instituted the "hundred days reform movement" in 1898.

One of the outstanding organizations that existed more than half a century ago and that has been run by Chinese-Americans ever since is the Chinese-American Citizens Alliance (C. A. C. A.), founded at San Francisco in 1895. The original name was "United Parlor of the Native Sons of the Golden State." Its activities were limited to California. The name was changed to "The Native Sons of the Golden West" in 1904. Since 1915, activities so far expanded that it became necessary to establish branches in other states. Consequently, the name of Golden West had to be dropped.

The aim of the C. A. C. A. is to promote fraternal fellowship and to foster mutual interest among the Americans of Chinese ancestry. Its members are necessarily limited to the native born and to those who have been naturalized. A well-organized and well-supported society, having headquarters of its own in San Francisco, the C. A. C. A. is one of the most active organizations in Chinatown. Among other activities has been its vigorous stand on practically all immigration matters that affect the interests of Chinese-Americans. They have taken active interest in the 1924 Quota Act that forbade the admittance of foreign-born wives of Chinese-Americans, the fight for the repeal of the Chinese Exclusion Act, and the endorsement of the 1952 McCarran-Walter Act. The C. A. C. A. urged full support for the 1952 Immigration Act as the fairest and most realistic possible approach to immigration and naturalization problems at that time.[31]

The C. A. C. A. held its twenty-fifth biennial convention in Oakland, California, August 5-8, 1959. The important events on the agenda were the giving of an award to Jackson Hu of San Francisco, tax appraiser, and to Delbert E. Wong, Muncipal Court Judge, Los Angeles Judicial District, for betterment of citizenship and for good community service.

Of all the Chinese organizations in the United States, none is as well known as the Six Companies in San Francisco, which created so much misunderstanding and aroused so many disputes about its real function that it became a subject for debate and a target for attack, especially in the second half of the nineteenth century. There have been other organizations, such as the family and district associations, trade guilds, the Chinese Chamber of Commerce of San

Francisco and that of New York.[32] Any attempt, however, to list all
the Chinese organizations in the United States and to make a study
of their functions and activities would require a separate volume;
therefore, we select New York City as typical.

On September 21, 1954, the *New York Times* printed a full-page
advertisement in which there appeared a declaration by American
citizens of Chinese origin and by Chinese living in the United States
opposing the seating of Red China in the United Nations. The advertisement was unusual in that few if any such advertisements on
so large a scale have been issued by a Chinese group.[33] The sponsors
were one Cuban and seventy-seven American-Chinese organizations,
out of which there were sixteen Consolidated Benevolent Associations, located in San Francisco, Los Angeles, Sacramento, Cleveland, Philadelphia, Boston,and so forth, and sixty-one in New York.
A list of the sixty-one follows, grouped according to their nature
and activities.

1. *Representative*
   The Chinese Consolidated Benevolent Association

2. *Mutual Benefit and Welfare Organizations*
   Chee Yue Community Association
   Chinese Community Club
   Hip Sing Association of U. S. A.
   Lun Yee Association
   Lun Sing Association
   On Leong Chinese Merchants' Association of U. S. A.
   Sze Kong Mutual Benevolent Association

3. *Political Party*
   Kuomintang of U. S. A.
   Min Chih Tang of U. S. A.

4. *Veteran Group*
   American Legion, Chinatown Post

5. *Business and Professional Organizations*
   Chinese-American Restaurants Association
   Chinese Association for the Promotion of Aviation
   Chinese Chamber of Commerce
   Chinese Dramatic and Benevolent Association
   Chinese Hand Laundry Association
   Chinese Musical and Theatrical Association
   Chinese Wet-Wash Laundry Association

National Chinese Seamen's Association
Tai Look Merchants' Association

6. *Culture and Student Associations*
   Chinese Anti-Communist League of New York
   Chinese Catholic Students' Society in America
   Chinese Women's New Life Movement Association
   Sino-American Amity of U.S.A.

7. *Religious Organization*
   First Chinese Presbyterian Church

8. *Clan and Family Associations*
   Chee Tuck Sam Tuck Association
   Chew Lun Association
   Eng Suey Sun Association
   Fong Lun Tong
   Gee How Oak Tin Association
   Gee Poy Kwok Tong
   Goon's Family Association
   Kim Lan Association
   Lee's Family Association
   Leung Chung How Tong
   Lung Kong Tin Yee Association
   Moy's Family Association
   Num Young Association
   Sam Yick Association
   Soo Yuen Tong
   Wong Kong Har Won San Association
   Yee Fong Toy Association

9. *Locality and District Organizations*
   Chung Shan Association
   Dong Som Sing Tong
   Fay Chow Merchant Association
   Fukien Association
   Hok Shan Society
   Hoy Ping Association
   Hoy Sun Ning Yung Association
   Hoy Yin Association
   Kang Jai Association
   Nam Shun Association
   Som Kiang Association
   Sun Wei Association

Tai Pun Association
Tai Pun Yok Ying Club
Tsung Tsin Association
Tung On Social Club
Wah Pei Association
Yan Ping Gong Yee
Yee Shan Benevolent Association

At the top of the list is the Chinese Consolidated Benevolent Association, the Chinese name for which is "Chung Hwa Kung So," meaning simply the "Assembly Hall of Chinese," or the "Chinese Society." Though there may be only a score of Chinese organizations in some of the smaller Chinatowns, a Chinatown will somehow manage to have one Chinese Consolidated Benevolent Association to represent it. There are thirty-four associations of that name in different Chinese communities in the United States, including the one in Honolulu.[34] In San Francisco the forerunner of the present Chinese Consolidated Benevolent Association, organized January 25, 1901, was the Six Companies. The name, however, is still being widely used, since it is familiar to the public.[35] The Chinese name of the Six Companies may be translated as the Seven Companies, because the seventh district, the Shew Hing group, joined in 1876, at a time when the name had become widely known. The Chinese Consolidated Benevolent Association of New York registered with the city government in 1890. The functions of such associations are more or less the same in each Chinatown: to maintain a community school, to keep peace and order, to do charitable work, and to supervise immigration and other important matters affecting the interests of the Chinese residents. At times the association undertakes the role of arbitrator in settling disputes among its constituents. Rules and regulations are announced in advance, and if necessary are enforced. The association may be considered the representative organization of the Chinese community; in fact the chairman is the unofficial mayor of Chinatown. In San Francisco it was agreed beforehand that the president of the largest company, the Ning Yung, should serve as chairman of the Six Companies every other term, or for six months each, because the Ning Yung had a membership of 46 per cent of the Chinese community; the two smallest groups, the Yan Wo and Shew Hing, agreed not to serve. The president of the other four companies would serve for terms of two months each. The Six Companies support five Chinese schools. In New York there are two Chinese schools. It is customary for Chinese children living in Chinatown, after their regular school sessions, to attend Chinese classes, from four to six o'clock or from five to seven, where they learn Chinese history, geography, calligraphy, and the Chinese language, both Cantonese and Mandarin.

The second group of associations is business and professional, including, for instance, the Chamber of Commerce and the restaurant and laundry associations. Some, like the On Leong Merchants' Association and the Hip Sing Association, are national in scope, the former composed of merchants, the latter of workers; but the demarcation is not clear-cut; several decades ago they were rivals and brought on the worst of tong wars.[36] Indeed it was their strife that gave Chinatown the sinister reputation of being full of gangsters. Now both promote the welfare and interests of their members. To illustrate how one association tried to protect its members, the New York branch of the On Leong Merchants' Association, because of the frequency of attacks on Chinese merchants by New York gangsters, advertised a bonus of $1,000 to anyone giving evidence that led to the capture and conviction of an offending gangster. Attacks on Chinese laundries are the most frequent because they are the easiest places to rob. Since both On Leong and Hip Sing are nationwide, for many years each has held an annual convention to elect officers and to discuss matters of mutual interest.[37] One thing on the agenda is certain to be the earmarking of funds to be contributed to worthy causes; a typical example of the contributions made by the Hip Sing Association's thirty-ninth convention, held in Washington, D. C., in September, 1957, will be sufficient to show what other associations do. The amount to be contributed was set at $10,000, to be divided as follows:

1. New York Overseas Christian Old-Age Home $3,000
2. Building Fund for Chinese School of Chicago   3,000
3. Building Fund for Chinese Consolidated Benevolent Association, Sacramento   3,000
4. Chinese Christian School, Washington, D. C.   600
5. Tung Hwa Hospital, San Francisco   200
6. Chinese Central High School, San Francisco   100
7. St. Mary's School, San Francisco   100

$10,000

The Ning Yung Association of New York City represents the districts of Taishan and Ning Yung, where a great many of the Chinese immigrants who settled in New York had originated. The chairmanship and other offices of the New York Consolidated Benevolent Association are served in turn by two of the organizations, the Ning Yung and the Lun Sing, for no other reason than that together they had contributed about 85 per cent of the constituents of the Chung Hwa Kung So.

From the list of the organizations named for places in China, it is clear that the Cantonese can no longer claim a monopoly on Chinatown. The Fukien Province furnished all the members of the Fukien Association; in fact, the Fukienese are the most numerous of the Chinese in Southeast Asia, their numbers far exceeding those of the Cantonese. The Sam Kiang Association, organized in 1929, drew its membership from the eastern part of China, the provinces of Kiangsu, Chekiang, and Kiangsi. Beginning modestly in the early thirties with a couple of hundred members, the association has steadily enlarged, especially since 1949, to its present membership of about six thousand. The northern Chinese, who speak Mandarin, organized the Wah Pei Association, but with a limited membership. Realizing the business prospects in Chinatown, many of the Cantonese owning groceries there have employees speaking Mandarin or Shanghai dialects.

Next come the family associations. There are some sixty families in New York City, most of whom have family associations, some representing only one family, like Lee, Moy, or Goon. Others are jointly organized by several families. The largest single family is probably the Wong family, with a membership in California alone of 5,000, and in the whole United States of 15,000 to 17,500. For years its headquarters have been in San Francisco. It is so large that in 1951 its association was divided into a Western and an Eastern section. Members pay small annual dues. Its chief function is to perform philanthropic deeds within the family of Wong. Strangely enough, though the surname may be used in common, many of the members have no discernible blood relationship; yet they address each other as "cousin" or "uncle," the latter term used especially to an elder. All this makes for a feeling of closer relationship.

Several organizations aim at the promotion of understanding and good will between Chinese and Americans. The oldest is the China Society of America, formed in 1913; one of its eminent original sponsors was V. K. Wellington Koo, formerly Chinese Ambassador to the United States. The newest is the Sino-American Amity, Inc., under the able management of the Most Reverend Archbishop Paul Yu Pin.

Not one of these organizations has had wider support or shown more extensive activity than the China Institute. The meeting point of China and America to discuss cultural, philosophical, and political problems of mutual interest has for many years been in a handsome building on the East Side of New York, the well-known "China House" that was donated to the China Institute in America by the Henry Luce

Foundation. The institute was founded in 1926 by Dr. P. W. Kuo and Dr. Paul Monroe, made possible by the subsidy of the China Foundation for the promotion of education and culture. Dr. Kuo was also its first director, succeeded by the versatile Dr. Chih Meng in 1931, who has served continuously ever since.[38] The president of the institute is Alexander D. Calhoun, a well-known international banker.

Offerings by the institute of lectures on Chinese culture and on various Chinese problems have received enthusiastic response. One is a history course, "Peoples of the World," given in American elementary schools. Since 1935 courses in Chinese civilization have been given, with marked response, to New York schoolteachers, An annual affair for more than a decade is an intensive study course at the New Jersey State Teachers' College. Courses in philosophy and history have been given in the morning, panel discussions in the afternoon, followed in the evening by informal discussions and social gatherings. Similar programs have been offered at the New York State Teachers' College at Cortland. A round-table conference on Sino-American relations was tried at the University of Maryland, first in 1955, and then in 1956; the second was attended by 150 delegates, representing officially or unofficially about 50 organizations. In 1957 the China Club of Seattle and the University of Washington cooperated in holding such a forum on the Pacific Coast; the University of Michigan did likewise for the Middle West. The institute also acts as a liaison office for Chinese graduates and for Chinese students, who utilize its facilities, make it a meeting place, and take advantage of its manifold means of assistance. It has been instrumental in enabling many of them to complete their studies through aid provided by governmental and private funds. Through its placement service, many graduates have secured employment.[39]

In the past, cooperation among the different organizations of the various Chinatowns may have been somewhat loose and superficial. However, a unique and unprecedented conference, attended by representatives of Americans of Chinese descent and by Chinese immigrants, was held in Washington, D. C., March 5-7, 1957. This conference may have paramount significance for the relationship of Chinese and Americans. One hundred twenty-four representatives, elected by Chinese organizations in the United States and Hawaii, including thirty-four Chinese Consolidated Benevolent Associations, attended the meetings. At the conclusion of the three-day conference, an official declaration was issued. Among other things, this statement made known that the conference encouraged closer cooperation of all Chinese-Americans, emphasized Chinese culture and moral philosophy, and stipulated that, above all, loyalty to this country should be preserved. The statement further declared that Chinese-Americans should support the Chinese policy adopted by the United States government. The convention felt that, as a faithful body of good citizens, the Chinese should not be discriminated against by the allotment to the Republic of China of the negligible annual quota, 105. Lastly, the convention resolved that a national Chinese welfare council of Chinese-Americans in the United States should be organized and a convention should be held every two years. The second conference took place in April, 1959.

The Chinese Press

Along with benevolent societies for the immigrants in the United States, the foreign language press plays a helpful role for the millions who otherwise could not be reached until they had learned enough English to read American newspapers. Since the immigrants of any nationality usually congregate in their own communities and speak their native tongue, the publishing of foreign papers is for them educational and inspiring. The 1940 census estimated more than eleven million foreign-born white immigrants; and according to the next census, the number was over ten million. In fact, people who speak languages other than English are not only limited to the foreign born. The Common Council of American Unity, in a survey in October, 1946, reported that there were 1,010 publications printed in whole, or in part, in thirty-nine foreign languages. The number, however, has grown gradually smaller. Foreign language dailies numbered ninety-five in 1946, but early in 1960 there were only sixty-five foreign language daily newspapers, printed in twenty foreign languages.

In 1946 there were fourteen Chinese dailies but now (1960) there are only eleven. New York leads with five, San Francisco is next with three, Honolulu with two, and Chicago with one. The *Chinese World*, which has the honor of being the first Chinese daily published, first appeared in San Francisco in 1891. The *New China Daily News* was second, appearing in Honolulu in 1900. Unlike many of the immigrants from Europe, the Chinese did not establish their newspapers until almost four decades after their arrival more than a century ago. The early immigrants were mostly laborers and farmers, illiterate both in Chinese and in English. It was not until almost the end of the nineteenth century that there were sufficient Chinese merchants and other literates to justify at least one Chinese daily.

The crushing defeat of China by the French in 1885 and by Japan in 1895 drove young patriots like Dr. Sun Yat-sen and his followers to seek reform and national salvation, with the aim of overthrowing the Manchu regime. Another group, meanwhile, led by two renowned scholars, K'ang Yu-wei and Liang Chi-Chao, tried to effect constitutional reform from within. The disintegration of the Hundred Days reform movement in 1898 forced its leaders to flee to Japan. Both Dr. Sun and Mr. Liang had traveled extensively in Hawaii, Canada, and the United States. Mr. K'ang had been in Canada, seeking assistance and attempting to arouse sentiment among the Chinese immigrants. In 1910, Dr. Sun helped to establish the *Young China* at San Francisco; to this day the paper is prospering. Also early in the twentieth century, editorials in the Chinese newspapers in San Francisco and in Honolulu were divided in rallying behind Dr. Sun's revolutionary movement and that of the constitutional reform advocated by K'ang and Liang. In 1912, Dr. Sun Yat-sen became the first president of the newly established Republic of China.

The majority of readers of the Chinese newspapers are the old immigrants from Taiwan and Hong Kong who can read Chinese. It is only natural that the younger generation of Americans of Chinese ancestry should be gradually losing its ability to speak and read the Chinese language. Immigrants from all countries tend to disuse their mother tongues. The Japanese newspapers published in this country have long sensed the need of meeting the changed situation by adding an English section, making the paper bilingual. All the Japanese press is now published in that fashion. The *Chinese World*, the only Chinese bilingual paper, failed in its experiment in New York City in 1958, due to lack of demand.

With the increase of Chinese immigration since 1947, the Chinese press will probably find enough readers to support its papers, at least for the time being. Thus in New York City, the Chinese press holds a steady number of readers, though other foreign language papers are losing ground. Out of the twenty-one foreign language papers in the city, five are Chinese. Ayer's Directory of Newspapers and Periodicals (1961) estimates Chinese papers' total circulation at 110,000, of which ten dailies average 9,000 each; only two circulate over 10,000 copies.

It is interesting that New York City, instead of San Francisco, should lead both in number of dailies and in circulation, since San Francisco has a considerably greater Chinese population. This is another indication that the Chinese in the West are assimilated faster than in the East; therefore less and less support in the West and in Hawaii will be given to the Chinese papers. Subscribers to Chinese newspapers are found also in Canada, South America, Europe, and Africa.

The Chinese press has been operating under handicaps. The limited circulation of many of these papers hardly allows the owners to make both ends meet. One Chinese daily in San Francisco closed early in 1960 because of its financial plight. Chinese newspapers cannot afford to send out reporters. They have to rely on wire services and radio broadcasts to keep them informed of the latest developments. The editor has to be a versatile journalist. Most of the newspapers are conservatively edited. No matter how small the size of the paper, it prints a daily editorial. Most of the editorials are on foreign issues and on immigration matters. The Chinese newspapers have had the reputation of printing all the news about immigration and about the Chinese in the United States. Much of this is necessarily a direct translation from American and Canadian newspapers, a practice followed by all foreign language papers. We may say that with few exceptions the Chinese paper is to be classified more as a journal of opinion than as a journal of information.

In addition to the dailies, San Francisco and Los Angeles each have a Chinese weekly, *Chinese Pacific Weekly* and *Kwong Tai*; New York City has an English monthly, the *Chinese American Times*; and the Chicago Chinese-American Civic Council publishes a monthly English magazine, the *Chinese American Progress*. These last two papers are for the consumption of the native-born Chinese-Americans rather than the immigrants.

We have depicted the life of the Chinese-Americans as it is in Chinese communities. Though today Chinese no longer feel restricted to the area of Chinatown, nevertheless some of them prefer to live within its walls, figuratively speaking. It is possible to remain there indefinitely. Both Chinese and American foods are served in Chinatown; in fact, the Chinatown of San Francisco is known for its excellent cuisine, perhaps even better than that of Hong Kong. Clothing of all sorts can be bought there. In addition to newspapers in English, there are Chinese dailies in New York, San Francisco, Chicago, and Honolulu; one will also find Chinese weeklies and magazines. Chinatown provides Chinese theaters, motion picture houses, and radio stations broadcasting in the mother tongue. Organizations—family, district, professional, and fraternal—afford good company. For those in difficulty or actual trouble, Chinese physicians, dentists, and lawyers make themselves available in the leading Chinatowns. Indeed, one could, if he chose, never cross the boundary into the outside world.

But to lead a wholly isolated life in Chinatown would, of course, be harmful. Just as the Chinese emperor's confining himself all his life in the Forbidden City made him virtually an ignorant captive, a Chinese immigrant's isolation in Chinatown would be undesirable for him and for the country in which he had come to live. The need for contact with the outside world and for broad social life are as vital to the Chinese as they are to Americans. If their goal is integration, the Chinese immigrants have to accept the American way of life. In addition, every member of the community has certain obligations to render to the community in which he lives. Community benefits should be enjoyed as well as paid for by all members concerned. It is true that before the repeal of the Exclusion Act there was little sign of willingness to accept assimilation of the Chinese and other Orientals. That attitude has gradually changed in the host society.

Assimilation is certainly and desirably a two-way process. As long as discrimination continues, even to the lesser extent that it still does in this country, so long will some Chinese immigrants make haste to retreat behind the walls of Chinatown. The heartening sign is that most of them do not. In San Francisco and in New York City Chinese will be found in practically all residential districts. When they are allowed to live wherever they please, to purchase houses and land at their pleasure, to become members of the best clubs, to attend motion picture houses, restaurants, and all public places indiscriminately, and come to feel that in no sense are they considered second-class citizens—then will the walls of Chinatown, like the walls of Jericho, come tumbling down in the spirit of freedom and the spirit of brotherhood.

11

Contributions and Achievements

That immigration has been a potent, even dominating, influence in the development of the United States may be considered to be truly axiomatic. The axiom is amply illustrated in literature, the other arts, and the sciences; in business, industry, agriculture; and in the social sciences. As a result, the United States is a land quite unlike that of the early nineteenth century, and her racial strains quite different. Often the loss to Europe and Asia has been a unique gain to America. Yet few treatises on American cultural history have dealt with the important contribution made by the Chinese immigrants, or by those from any other oriental nation. It is hard to believe, however, that future writers will ignore the significance of the Nobel award of 1957 in physics, won by two young Chinese professors, one at Columbia University and the other at the Institute for Advanced Study in Princeton, or will ignore Hiram L. Fong, who became United States senator from Hawaii in 1959. During the past fifteen years or so, the Chinese, particularly scholars and scientists, have remarkably enriched American life, contributing not a little to American prestige.

To be sure, the early Chinese immigrants were for the most part laborers, farmers, and adventurers who had purely economic aims, with scarcely a scholar or a scientist among them; their cultural impact was negligible; and their economic opportunities were so meager that an Andrew Carnegie in their ranks would have been an utter impossibility. Socially ostracized, politically impotent, a Chinese considered himself fortunate if he had a "job," especially one that did not involve harshly prejudicial treatment. His *modus vivendi* to escape molestation was working, keeping silent, avoiding as far as possible all contact with the world outside, because only a few years after the first arrivals California undertook an anti-Chinese campaign. Even functioning as they did under adverse conditions, the Chinese managed nevertheless to do a great deal of work favorable to the growth of the West; they furnished the much-needed labor for building the Central Pacific Railway; they cleared the swamps, they helped to man the mines; they relieved the white population of all kinds of menial tasks, enabling it to follow more worthy and profitable pursuits. Since women were scarce in those early days of the West, the Chinese filled up gaps in the domestic economy. Furthermore, they were expert farmers; they were adept in learning how to manipulate tools and the simple machines available. Thus they became just as competent as white farmers and white workmen; yet they did not wish to force themselves forward in competition. They considered themselves to have come into the United States as guests; as such, they hesitated to strive competitively with their hosts; even under threats and mistreatment they made no impolite protest. Their good manners were viewed as weakness and pusillanimity. But what might a guest do while living in the home and accepting the hospitality of his host? Strange as this idea may appear to a Westerner, it is nevertheless typical of traditional Chinese thought.

In a survey of Chinese contributions to America, we must take into account that between the enactment of the Chinese Exclusion Act in 1882 and its repeal in 1943, not many Chinese immigrants arrived. After the repeal, however, with the assistance of the Displaced Persons Act, of the Refugee Relief Act (1953), of the later legislation, and in a small way, by quota, nonquota, and by private legislation, many Chinese were permitted to become permanent residents and citizens. Our study will give a panorama of important achievements of contemporary Chinese in the United States, as well as of early Chinese immigrants who forewent personal benefits and sacrificed themselves for the betterment of subsequent generations. We shall also discuss briefly the life of Yung Wing, acclaimed as the father of the Chinese student movement in this country.

The Contribution Made by the Chinese Immigrants

If a law-abiding, hard-working, and thrifty people may be considered to be a valuable addition to a country in which they are living permanently, the Chinese immigrants surely qualify as one of the most desirable of the minority groups. The early immigrants were believers in fate; otherwise they would not have had the stamina to risk life and limb on a perilous migration over thousands of miles, herded on board ship like cattle, to a destination fraught with grave uncertainties. Once safely arrived, they must have behaved in an exemplary manner, for certainly they were welcomed, praised, and regarded as well-nigh indispensable. Governor McDougal of California stated in 1852, "The Chinese are some of the most worthy

of our newly-adopted citizens." Furthermore, he recommended a
system of land grants as an inducement to Chinese immigration.[1]

The construction of the Central Pacific Railway was greatly fa-
cilitated by the employment of Chinese labor.[2] When in 1864 the
working forces nominally consisted of 4,000, only 1,000 white laborers could be mustered, despite enticing offers of high wages and
steady employment; this was explainable partly by the draft to fill
the continuing gaps in the Northern regiments, and partly by unwillingness to abandon the more lucrative mining and farming. At
the completion of the railway in 1869, 90 per cent of the 10,000 laborers were Chinese. Indeed, it is likely that, without the Chinese
force to blast tunnels, construct trestles, smooth the roadbed—and
sometimes to fight off attacks of hostile Indians—this undertaking
vital to the entire nation might not have been finished until many
years later.

Likewise, the Chinese made themselves indispensable by rendering
menial service in or out of town; in 1868 at least 40,000 were employed in mining camps staked out by white men. They willingly performed all the petty drudgery in household service, truck gardening,
fruit raising, fishing, woodcutting, ragpicking, and a score of other
occupations. They were involved in little direct competition with
their neighbors, yet contributed materially to the development of
California's vast resources.[3]

Now observe how the Chinese immigrants conducted themselves.
They were known to be loyal and responsible in their family relationships, always willing to shoulder their obligations, and, if necessary, to make sacrifices. As a matter of course they treated one
another with the utmost kindness. They were fond of good food and
drink, but seldom to excess; they cared little about their clothing;
they were scrupulously clean in their habits. They were extremely
frugal, invariably keeping well within their incomes, especially
since their avowed purpose was to save enough to live on comfort-
ably after retirement. All that being so, the Chinese were little
tempted to commit offenses or to indulge in careers of crime. Prof.
Coolidge wrote, "The Chinese were less liable to insanity, and less
criminal even, proportionately than the English, Scotch, and Welsh,
to say nothing of the Irish, the German, the Spanish-American, and
the Italian."[4] The San Francisco police records (1879-1901) show
that the Chinese were responsible for only 8.8 per cent of all arrests, though they constituted 14 per cent of the adult male population. The honesty of the average Chinese merchants and their employees was generally recognized, even in early California.

In those days there was little opportunity or time for interest in
literature, art, or other intellectual pursuits. Few people thought

of attending cultural centers, including museums, exhibitions, and theaters. Dramatists, by distortion of character, often made the "Chinaman" the villain of the piece. Their compelling predisposition to work almost continuously and—by living with extreme frugality— to put by nearly all the fruits of their labors, perhaps could not be appreciated, or ever understood, by the rank and file of their neighbors.

Chinese contributions to the English language are virtually nil. Those words that have been adopted in this country are, for the most part, such verbs as to *yen* (to desire strongly), to *kowtow* (to treat with obsequious deference), also a noun; the noun and adjective *chow;* the adverb *chop-chop;* the nouns *joss, fantan, mah-jongg, tong;* and familiar derivatives *joss house, chopstick, chop suey,* and *chow mein.* H. L. Mencken lists also *flop, yok-a-mi,* and *tong* war.[5]

Likewise, Chinese influence on American literature has been extremely slight. There has of course been a good deal of anti-Chinese writing, stirred up at times by the so-called "yellow peril" feeling, but a very minute part of it could in any sense be defined as literature. Mark Twain devotes an entire chapter of *Roughing It* to the Chinese in Virginia City. Bret Harte in 1871 wrote that incomparable lyric satire, "Plain Language from Truthful James." Then there were mystery and horror stories such as the *Fu Manchu* movie and the play *The Silent House,* in which the Chinese villains were the villains of villains. Charlie Chan, as detective, though he appeared as a pleasantly quaint and astute being, could scarcely be said to represent the highly intelligent Chinese. There have been, however, several works very favorably inclined toward the Chinese. Robert Louis Stevenson found the San Francisco Chinatown "the most interesting city in the Union and the hugest melting-pot of races of the precious metal." Pearl Buck's deep impression of peasant life in China produced such books as *The Good Earth,* opening a new field of interest to American life and literature.

Though not especially literary, writings by Chinese in this country can be found here and there in American magazines and newspapers. There is also Yung Wing's autobiography, *My Life in China and America* (1909); others are Jade Snow Wong's *Fifth Chinese Daughter* (1950) and Pardee Lowe's *Father and Glorious Descendant* (1943). C. Y. Lee's first novel, *The Flower Drum Song,* depicting life in San Francisco's Chinatown, published in June, 1957, has been chosen by Rodgers and Hammerstein as the basis for a Broadway musical. His second novel, *Lover's Point,* a story full of passion and excitement about people with excitable emotion, was acclaimed by reviewers, and appeared within twelve months after the first. *The Silent Traveler in Boston* (1959), prepared by Chiang Yee, a distinguished Chinese author, artist, and poet, has attracted warm and very enthusiastic responses according to the report of the *New York Times*. Lin Yutang's *Importance of Living* (1937), a volume replete with humor, sophistication, and penetrating philosophy of life, was a best seller.

Whatever has been lacking in Chinese literary authorship in the United States has perhaps been amply compensated for in the lives of many Chinese-Americans. Joe Lin Gong, immigrating in 1885 at the age of twenty-three, set up a laundry in Boston, then moved to Albany, Georgia, and then to Tifton, where he worked seven days a week, occasionally returning to China for a short visit.[6] He died in 1924. His son Joseph has had five children, one boy and four girls. The boy, Eddie Gong, was graduated from Harvard in 1952, and after two years in the United States Air Force entered the Harvard Law School. In 1947, while yet a junior at a high school in Miami, Eddie was named "Boy President of the U. S. A." President Truman welcomed him at an American Legion ceremony in Washington, D. C. Helen Gong, the eldest of the girls, studied at Florida State University, where she became vice-president of the student body and a member of Phi Beta Kappa. Her husband, also a Chinese-American, majoring in agricultural science, was graduated from Rutgers University. Lilian, the next eldest, after majoring in chemistry, was graduated from Wellesley; she engaged in medical research at the school of medicine of New York University. May Jewel Gong went to Purdue on a scholarship, was active in Delta Gamma, and the first girl ever admitted into the University's famous marching band. After her graduation in 1955 she was awarded a Fulbright Fellowship to study at the Phillips University at Marburg, Germany; later she accepted a fellowship to do graduate work at Radcliffe. The youngest, "Junie-bug," was graduated from the University of New Hampshire, by virtue of a scholarship and part-time work in the library.

Ta-Chin Chin of Tonshan, Kwangtung, has been operating a laundry in New York City for the past forty years. His family consists of a Chinese-American wife born in Philadelphia, two sons, and two daughters. The elder son, Tien-ling, a physician, graduated from the Columbia University school of medicine. A veteran of World War II, and formerly connected with the Peking Union Medical College, he is practicing in New York Chinatown and at the city hospital. The other son, a Columbia Ph. D. , is an associate professor of psychology at Boston University. The Chin family might very well have opened a Columbia University alumni club, for in addition to two sons, both daughters were Columbia graduates.

Yet the success of those two families does not seem comparable to that of a tiny widowed Chinese mother who reared her eight children by operating a laundry left to her at the death of her husband in 1940. No wonder that Governor Frederick G. Payne of the state of Maine proclaimed her "Maine's Mother of the Year" in 1952. At that time Mrs. Toy Len Goon was the hard-working proprietress of Woodford's Corner Laundry, and her eldest son became at twenty-nine a physician in Salt Lake City. Richard operates a television and radio shop in Lynn, Massachusetts. Albert studied law at Boston University. Edward was graduated from M. I. T. and became a member of the faculty of the Rensselaer Polytechnic Institute.[7] Arthur served in the United States Navy. Of the three daughters, Josephine, Doris, and Janet, the first is employed in Washington, D. C. , the second is an assistant in Mother Goon's laundry, and the third a student at Deering High School.[8]

Though none of these families had had any college tradition, their children nevertheless went to college, perhaps because of China's ancient tradition of the utmost respect for all intellectual studies and pursuits, though their going required much unselfishness and many sacrifices on the part of the parents. In a single San Francisco Chinatown family, four daughters were educated to become, respectively, a public school teacher, a public school health nurse, a dental hygienist, and a nursery school teacher. While this writer was a student at the North Central College, in Naperville, Illinois, in 1925, a Chinese laundry was just being opened; when he revisited his alma mater twenty-nine years later, he was told that the son of the proprietor of that laundry had already been graduated from the University of Illinois. Truly, future generations of Chinese-Americans are going to be infinitely grateful to their early ancestors.

A worthy son of China, who later became an American citizen, Gim Gong Lue, contributed much to American life in the late nineteenth century. On May 11, 1872, at the age of twelve, Lue arrived in San Francisco. He then settled in North Adams, Massachusetts.

One day, while employed at the Calvin T. Sampson Shoe Factory in North Adams, he chanced to meet Miss Fanny Amelia Burlingame, a cousin of the American minister to China. This chance meeting was a stroke of extremely good fortune for Lue. Miss Fanny, whom Lue called "Mother," sent him to school. While studying, he experimented in the art of flower pollination, which his mother had taught him in China. The results were an apple that would ripen thirty days sooner than any other known variety, and a peach that would ripen at Thanksgiving time, either in a greenhouse or in Florida. His contributions to horticulture became very well known, and the production of his variety of orange won him the Wilder Medal.

Gim Gong Lue was naturalized in North Adams on October 25, 1887, and became known as a model citizen. Mother Fanny died in 1903, leaving him her orchard and some funds, much of which he later lost through the fault of others. His friends urged him to sue for damages. In reply Lue quoted Confucius' remark that there should be no necessity for law suits in an ideal society. Invoking his principles, he refused to sue, on the grounds that good relations among men were more profitable than monetary gain.

Three quarters of a century ago a Chinese immigrant named Dean Lung became responsible for the establishment of a department of Chinese and of a Chinese library at Columbia University. In the days of the gold rush, a certain Dean Lung was being employed as a domestic by Horace W. Carpenter, formerly a general in the French army, then retired and an American citizen. In spite of the old general's irascible disposition, he was immensely grateful for Dean's faithful service. One evening after some heavy drinking, the military man, without provocation, struck Dean Lung over the head. In the cold, gray remorse of the morning after, the general was astounded to see Dean Lung calmly doing his tasks as usual. Whereupon the martial penitent asked him why he remained faithful to his most unworthy employer when he could so easily have properly left him and found much better work.

"It is true," Dean Lung said, in typically Chinese fashion, "that you have bad temper—but inside you are a good man. Confucius says, 'Servant no forsake master, when master need servant.' 'True friend always remain friend.' This is why I am still here."

A few years went by, and one day the general, in a specially affable mood, asked Dean Lung what in the world he could do for Dean to prove his everlasting gratitude.

Butler Dean Lung thereupon replied in solemn tones: "You pay me for my service. I desire for myself nothing more. But United States people know little about Chinese culture and philosophy. Could you do something about that?"

General Carpenter, deeply moved by the unique request, arranged with Columbia University, and then gave an extremely large contribution to establish the Chinese department and library. It is still recognized as one of the best Chinese foundations in the country.[9] What was even more astonishing was the gift of $12,000 from Dean Lung himself, representing his entire savings from many years' labor.

Yung Wing, Pioneer of Chinese Students Studying Abroad

The contribution of earlier Chinese-Americans would not be complete without a look into the distinguished career of probably the first Chinese ever naturalized in the United States. Yung Wing came in 1847, just a few years before the first group of Chinese laborers. After he had studied at Yale for two years, he was baptized a Christian and then naturalized, since at that time he contemplated remaining permanently in the United States. But he returned to China in November, 1854. It was he who made it possible for a number of Chinese students to come to the United States, beginning in 1874, to continue their education. He acquired the distinction of being the father of the Chinese student movement in the United States. Indeed, without his pioneering and his follow-up work, both in this country and in China, there would not be nearly so many Chinese scholars on the faculties of American colleges.

In recognition of Dr. Yung Wing's graduation at Yale, in 1854, and also in commemoration of his achievements in the educational field, and for his contribution to China's industry in introducing Western scientific methods and procedures into that country, the "Yale-in-China" Association, in collaboration with Yale University and the China Institute, arranged for a centennial celebration, June 13, 1954, at Battell Chapel on the Yale campus. The celebration was attended by a distinguished audience; it included an academic procession represented by the Chinese branches of Oberlin, Harvard, Yale, Dublin, and the New Asia College in Hong Kong.

Yung Wing arrived in the United States in 1847 with two fellow-students, Wong Hsing and Wong Foon, under the sponsorship of the Reverend Samuel Robbins Brown, principal of the Morrison School at Macao. The trio enrolled in the Monson Academy in Monson, Massachusetts. Soon after their arrival Wong Hsing was forced to return to China because of ill health; but both Yung Wing and Wong Foon graduated from the academy in 1849. Wong sailed to Scotland to study medical science at the University of Edinburgh, while Yung Wing entered Yale and continued his studies for four years. He returned to China in November, 1854, after graduation. In "My College Years," a chapter in his autobiography, he says:

Before the close of my last year in college, I had already sketched out what I should do. Determined that the rising generation of China should enjoy the same educational advantages that I had enjoyed; that through western education China should be regenerated, become enlightened and powerful. To accomplish that object became the guiding star of my ambition. Toward such a goal I directed all my mental resources and energies. Through thick and thin, and the vicissitudes of a checkered life from 1854 to 1872 I labored and waited and waited for its consummation.

From 1854 until 1863 he served in various minor capacities, as interpreter in the Hong Kong Supreme Court and in the Imperial

Customs' Translating Department in Shanghai, until he was requested
by the viceroy, Tseng Kuo-fan (1811-72), to serve with him.

The biggest moment of Yung's career occurred in 1870, when he
succeeded in convincing both Viceroy Tseng Kuo-fan and Li Hung-
chang (1823-1901), the most influential official next to Tseng, of
the importance and even the necessity of sending groups of Chinese
youths to the schools of Europe and America. His personal contact
in observing the progress of Western civilization, particularly its
rapid technological development, had convinced him that China could
not go forward unless the Chinese could be on an equal footing with
the West, and familiar with Western technology. Tseng and Li Hung-
chang jointly proposed the plan in a memorial which they presented
to the throne in July, 1871. The plan, promptly approved, was to
send to the United States thirty youngsters, from twelve to fifteen
years old, every year for four years. One year of preparation would
be undertaken, while the period of staying abroad was to be fifteen
years and the course of study was to be limited to technological
science. The students were to serve the government on returning
to China. Yung Wing and Chen Lan-pin were to be put in charge of
the Educational Mission.

The actual operation of the mission lasted from 1872 until July,
1881. From 1872 to 1875, 120 students were sent to the United States,
about thirty a year. Dr. William Lyon Phelps, well-known literary
critic and former professor of English at Yale, in his *Autobiography
with Letters,* made the following comment in a special chapter on
"Chinese schoolmates":

> When I entered the West Middle School, I found a considerable number of
> Chinese boys there; it seemed natural to have them for playmates. This may
> have been partly owing to the attractive qualities of these Orientals, and
> their genius for adaptation. . . . Thus the pleasant recollections of my boy-
> hood are full of Chinese memories; and although, by the time I entered Yale,
> these fine fellows had gone home, I vainly hoped they might return. . . .

Students from the third and fourth detachments, who came to the
United States in 1874 and 1875, were about to finish their high school
education; but unfortunately in the summer of 1881 the mission was
ordered to close, and the students were recalled to China.

There were perhaps many reasons for officialdom's taking this
sudden and improper step in recalling the students. The relationship between the Chinese and American governments was not very
friendly in the late seventies. The good will created by the reciprocal
Burlingame Treaty, signed in 1868, was largely dissipated by the
Treaty of 1880, the purpose of which was to limit the coming of Chinese laborers to the United States. During the third quarter of the

nineteenth century the California legislature passed numerous discriminatory acts against the resident Chinese. Many other unfortunate incidents, mostly in immigration matters, made a poor impression on the Manchu throne, as well as on the intelligentsia in China. The refusal of the State Department to allow Chinese students to enroll at West Point and at Annapolis aggravated the situation all the more, since Li Hung-chang was perhaps more interested in military reform than anything else.

Yung Wing's idea of modernizing China was not limited to the sending of Chinese youngsters to study abroad; he had in fact mapped a broad program of modernization for China that unfortunately could not be carried out at the time of its presentation, though later it was realized in one way or another.[10]

Yung Wing also participated in the short-lived reform movement, between June and September, 1898.[11] A price was placed on his head, suggesting that he must have played an important part in the Reform party. In 1899 he was advised to leave Shanghai, went to Hong Kong for a few years, and then returned permanently to the United States in 1902. While he was in the United States he had been in constant correspondence with the leaders of the revolutionary party, which successfully overthrew the Manchu dynasty in 1912. Yung died, April 21, 1912, at the age of eighty-four, survived by his two sons, both of whom were also graduated from Yale. His American wife, Mary Louise Kellogg, had died early in 1886, after she and Yung had been married for only eleven years.

The Intellectual Migration and the Chinese Scholar in America

The authors of the repeal of the Chinese Exclusion Act, in trying to compensate for the wrongs dealt the Chinese through earlier immigration policy, probably were unaware that their actions made possible a large cultural migration of Chinese scholars, scientists, engineers, physicians, social scientists, and artists, thus creating in America a reservoir of material and spiritual wealth beneficial both to the United States and to Free China.

For the first time in history, an American of Chinese descent had become a member of the United States Senate.[12] Hiram L. Fong, elected by the Hawaiians in 1959, is a fifty-two-year-old businessman and lawyer. He is the son of a sugar plantation laborer who came to the islands from China in 1872. Fong worked his way through high school and the University of Hawaii by doing many side jobs. He was graduated with honor from the university in three years. Having borrowed $3,000 to attend Harvard Law School, he returned with only

ten cents in his pocket, plus a law degree. With the Army Air Force
he saw service at famed Hickam Air Force Base in Hawaii during
World War II. Fong served fourteen years in the Territorial House
of Representatives, six as speaker. This election to Congress of a
man of oriental ancestry is definite proof that in Hawaii race problems are no longer formidable. The most outstanding event thus far
in Fong's career in the Senate is the six weeks' trip that he made
as self-appointed ambassador of good will to the Far East. His
example enhanced the prestige of the United States abroad. Tufts
University conferred on him the honorary degree of Doctor of Laws
(June, 1960). Four months later, on October 29, 1960, Lafayette
College also conferred on him the degree of Doctor of Laws. President Bergethon read the citation as follows:

Hiram Leong Fong, from Kwangtung to Hawaii to Washington is a journey
across the borders of two continents, over the divisions of two cultures,
and through the dateline of history which defined your birthplace as a state
and has also determined your present public labors. The drama of your life
strikingly fulfills the dream of America—that vision of opportunity and possibility transformed by individual pursuit of happiness into the reward of
personal freedom. Wiser than most, you have advanced beyond prominence
and prosperity to the ultimate success of service.

Science and Medicine

Noteworthy examples of the reservoir of Chinese intellectuals are
two Chinese physicists who received the Nobel prize in 1957, one a
professor at Columbia University and the other in the Institute for
Advanced Study at Princeton.

Many supposedly fundamental laws of physics have, since the days
of Isaac Newton, been revered by scientists. A newer one, the principle of the conservation of parity, has for the past thirty years
been generally accepted. In January, 1957, however, Columbia
University issued a report to the effect that this fundamental concept
of nuclear physics had been negated. It appears that two Chinese
theoretical physicists, Professors Tsung Dao Lee and Chen-Ning
Yang, had shattered the principle. In a series of three papers, "Is
Parity Conserved in Weak Interactions?" they suggested certain
definite experiments to be made. Dr. Chien-Shiung Wu of Columbia
and a team of specialists at the National Bureau of Standards replied
to the question, after they had performed the suggested experiments,
"Parity is not conserved." A rather complete theoretical structure
had been shattered at its base, and physicists are now uncertain
how the splinters can be put together. When the 1957 Albert Einstein
Award in Science was conferred on Dr. Lee and Dr. Yang, the citation read: "For their theoretical studies and suggestion for experi-

ments that led to the overthrow of the principle of the conservation of parity . . . and for bringing about a development of profound importance in the search for understanding of the elementary particles of which the universe is constituted."[13]

These cowinners acquired their doctorates at the University of Chicago, after having been graduated from the Southwest Associated University in Kunmin, China.[14] Dr. Lee in 1957 was thirty years old, probably the second youngest of all Nobel prize winners; he is also at present the youngest full professor at Columbia. He joined the faculty as assistant professor in 1953, became an associate professor in 1955, and a full professor in 1956. Dr. Yang joined the faculty of the Institute for Advanced Study in 1948 and was made a full professor in 1955.

Dr. Chien-Shiung Wu, who performed the experiments for Lee and Yang, has been recognized as the world's foremost female experimental physicist.[15] Her husband, Dr. Chia-Liu Yuan, a senior physicist of the Brookhaven National Laboratory, was one of the "Big Three" mentioned in Life magazine as handling cosmotron, the multibillion electron volt accelerator, Dr. Yuan came to the United States in 1935; he and his wife obtained their doctorates at the California Institute of Technology.

Perhaps one of the most versatile writers in the field of physics and perhaps the one holding the most patents, is the nuclear physicist Dr. Kuan H. Sun, since 1955 manager of the Westinghouse radiation and nucleonics laboratory. Dr. Sun was the first to use a scintillation counter for the detection of neutrons and the first to use the powder method to make a photographic pattern of neutron diffraction. He has had more than 40 patents to his credit and has published more than 120 technical papers.

Noted for his contribution to algebraic geometry is Dr. Wei-Luang Chou, a professor and chairman of the department of mathematics, Johns Hopkins University. He was elected, among four famous Chinese engineers and scientists now in the United States, Academician to the Academia Sinica in 1959.[16]

Foremost among Chinese scientists, Dr. Cho-Hao Li, a professor of biochemistry and a director of the Hormone Research Laboratory of the University of California, is the protein chemist who has been chiefly responsible for the isolation during the past fifteen years of five of the six major pituitary hormones, including ACTH.[17] The use of ACTH has cured diseases hitherto considered hopeless. A woman patient, after a complete cure from rheumatoid arthritis, donated a large sum to the university, with the request that the money be used for further research under Professor Li. She said, "Dr. Li is surely one of the great men of the world. He has devoted himself to the good of mankind; whereas he wants almost nothing for himself. He certainly has earned the respect of all of us." Dr. Li has published a number of papers in the field of endocrinology.

When Dr. Li isolated pure human and monkey growth hormones, he realized that with only human and monkey glands as possible sources of useful hormone, the supply for medical use would be very limited. He and his colleague, Dr. Harold Papkoff, have now determined that the structure of the newly purified humpback whale hormone is similar to that of man and monkey.[18] If the whale hormone is proved to be active, there would be available for the first time a supply of effective growth hormones for the treatment of dwarfism, cancer, and other metabolic conditions.

A new species of protozoa (unicellular animal) has recently been discovered by a Chinese biologist, Dr. Tse-Tuan Chen. The discovery was so commemorated in the United States that the organism is being named after Chen as *Nyctotherus Cheni*. Such taxonomy and nomenclature are rare top honors in the American academic world, and Dr. Chen has won his reputation as an authority on protozoology.

Joining the University of California at Los Angeles in 1940 as a lecturer in zoology, Dr. Chen assumed a full professorship in biology at the University of Southern California in 1951. He is also a consultant in biology to the Argonne National Laboratory. In addition to his work and contributions on antibiotic productivity, he is also well known for his exploration of cytology, for which he is highly regarded in Europe as well as in America. Chen's monographs with illustrations are considered among the best in the world. His publication on "Chromosomes in *Opalinidae* (Protozoa, Ciliata) with special reference to their behavior, morphology, individuality, diploidy, haploidy, and association with nucleoli" has been adapted in France and Germany as text reference, while more than forty-nine plates by Chen appear in *Protozoologie,* published in Germany in 1956.

The president of the American Society of Human Genetics (1960) is Dr. C. C. Li, a professor of biometry and director of Human Genetics Training Program, at the University of Pittsburgh. A former associate editor of the *American Journal of Human Genetics,* Dr. Li has written a number of books and technical papers in his specialized field. His latest publication is a textbook, entitled *Human Genetics: Principles and Methods.*

One of America's outstanding bacteriologists and parasitologists is Dr. George W. Chu, chairman of the department of microbiology, University of Hawaii. After he had received his Sc. D. at the School of Hygiene and Public Health, Johns Hopkins University, in 1934, he spent eight years in teaching parasitology at Shanghai, China; and since 1944 he has been a member of the faculty of the University of Hawaii. In 1958, he received a $44,000 research grant from the United States Public Health Service to enable him to work on the immunological aspect of avian schistosomiasis. In the course of conducting this research. Dr. Chu discovered the cause of seaweed dermatitis in the Pacific (possible relationship to the problem of fish poisoning in man in the South Pacific and Hawaii).

In medicine, Chinese physicians trained in this country have rendered many valuable services in hospitals, serving as resident doctors, doing research work, acting as anaesthetists or radiologists, practicing independently or on the faculties of schools of medicine. One of the best drugs for the treatment of ulcers was developed by Dr. C. Quotui, who was born in the Philippine Islands and whose father had come from Fukien, China. Dr. Hsien Wu, a codeveloper of the blood analysis known as the Folin-Wu system, was on the faculty of the University of Alabama Medical School from 1949 until his retirement in 1953. After he had obtained a Ph. D. in biochemistry from Harvard Medical School in 1920, he collaborated with the late Dr. Otto Folin to develop the Folin-Wu system of tracing termination of sugar in the blood system. He was head of the biochemistry department of the Peking Union Medical School for twenty years.

Ko-Kwei Chen is well known in pharmacology; he has been research director of the Eli Lilly Company since 1929; he has taught at Indiana University; he was awarded in 1944 the Certificate of Merit by the American Medical Association.

Viadril, a new anaesthetic developed by Pfizer and Company and said to be safer and more efficient than its predecessors, was discovered by three research scientists. One was a Chinese, Dr. S. Y. Pan, and the others were Dr. Gerald Laubach and Dr. Harry W. Rudel. The three doctors had made and tested more than a hundred new steroids.

Engineering

Engineering science has been a favorite subject of the Chinese student for a number of years. In practically all well-known engineering schools, there are Chinese scholars either pursuing studies in their major fields or on the faculty to disseminate their knowledge and specialities among the students. In the research laboratories, in the factories, and to a lesser extent in the administrative levels, one will find distinguished Chinese engineers holding responsible positions. In 1954 it was estimated that the number of Chinese engineers in metropolitan New York alone was about four hundred, while in the entire United States there might have been eight to ten times as many. Today the number must be considerably more. We have been able to find many worth-while topics regarding the contributions of Chinese engineers to the American way of life.

While many Chinese professors have taught at American colleges and not a few have acted as department heads, the first Chinese engineer to be given the appointment of dean is Dr. A. T. Liu, now dean of the college of engineering at Detroit Institute of Technology. Dean Liu received his college education in China and obtained his doctorate from the University of Michigan in 1940. He has resigned as a project director of Giffels and Rossetti, Inc., Detroit, an architectural firm, to accept the deanship.[19]

In August, 1953, the Air Force announced the development of a new electronic tube producing four million watts of radar power. Responsible for the development were Dr. Chao-Chen Wang and his associate, Dr. C. E. Rich of the Sperry Gyroscope Company. Dr. Wang's tube, known as Magawatt Klystron, eight feet in length, controls more precisely the frequency of the power, and opens the way for the large, powerful radar tubes needed for missiles, aircraft, television, communication systems, and for medical and atomic research. Dr. Wang has been, since 1956, head of the engineering department for microwave tube research at Sperry. He was appointed to the Victor Emmanuel Distinguished Professorship at Cornell University, college of engineering, for the spring term 1959-60.

While the American Bosch Arma Corporation may be the brain for the Air Force in developing the initial guidance for Titan and Atlas intercontinental ballistic missiles, the brain at Arma, responsible for the design of the brain—or the digital computer—for the guidance system is Dr. Wen-Tsing Chow, a young Chinese electronic engineer, 1941 graduate of Chiao-tung University, Shanghai, and trained at M. I. T. Chow had not only set the basic concept for Arma's system, but had succeeded in producing the computer in only two square feet. Chow has made an even more startling development—photochemical circuits, which will reduce the computer to a box less than a foot square.[20] The successful miniaturization by Chow has enabled the computer to be cramped with a limited payload into the shell of the ICBM.

Foremost among the Chinese electronics engineers is Dr. L. J. Chu. He is an expert consultant in the office of the Secretary of War and a professor of electrical engineering at M. I. T. Dr. Chu is one of the authorities on the design of microwave aerials.

Two of the outstanding Chinese electronics engineers have been entrusted by their respective companies with the management of the engineering divisions. Jeffrey C. Chu, who played an important part in developing the Univac electronic computer, is the manager of commercial engineering of the Remington Rand Univac Corporation of Philadelphia. He has served also as director of research and as an assistant chief engineer of the company. Dr. Pei Wang, who joined Sylvania Electric Products, Inc. in 1953 as a senior engineer in their semiconductor laboratory, has now been made the engineering manager in device services, a technical development and backing-up operation for Sylvania's production and other engineering functions.

Dr. Y. H. Ku, an authority in the nonlinear systems, is now a professor at the Moore School of Electrical Engineering at the University of Pennsylvania.[21] Mr. T. C. Tsao, a brilliant graduate of Harvard and author of scientific articles, is with the Electronic Research Laboratory, Columbia University.[22] Ernest Kuh, on leave of absence from the Bell Telephone Company's laboratory to accept a professorship at the University of California, is an authority on the network theory.[23]

Other notable electronic engineers are Dr. Eng-Lung Chu, authority on wave guides; Dr. Yuk-Wing Lee, eminent in information theory; Dr. L. P. Yen, experienced in tropospheric scatter system, and Dr. Julius Tou, in control and simulation problems. Dr. Chai Yeh is an authority on electron tubes; Dr. W. Y. Pan, on developing radio broadcast; Dr. Chih-Tang Sah, on traveling wave tubes; Dr. T. C. Chen, on magnetic devices and electronic computing systems; Dr. Kern K. N. Chang, on microwave tubes; Dr. Shelton S. L. Chang, on induction motors; Mr. John H. K. Kao, on electron tube life with Weibull's cumulative distribution function; and Dr. Woo-Foung Chow, on transistor circuitry.[24]

The distinguished Yuan-Chu'en Lee is known to the world by the Navy's successful launching of the *Vanguard* in orbit March 17, 1958. A veteran of the Chinese Air Force during World War II, and a graduate in aeronautical engineering from the California Institute of Technology, Lee joined the Aerojet General Corporation, Azusa, California, in 1949. He has done brilliant research on combustion stability in liquid propellant engines, high-energy propellant combustion, free radical propulsion, and electrical propulsion systems. Lee is now director of corporate research and in charge of the astronautical and other planetary endeavors.

Another brilliant engineering scientist, Dr. Frederick Fu Liu, now an executive vice-president of the Dresser Dynamics, Inc., is the top instrumentation man in jet propulsion and rocket combustion studies. Dr. Liu developed and patented the Fu Liu pickup, an improved device for measuring slight variation of pressure at very high temperatures. This electronic recording system is considered by the Army and Air Force to be the best in the country.[25]

Dr. Shao-Wen Yuan, professor of aeronautical engineering in the Polytechnic Institute of Brooklyn, initiated a special design for a helicopter for the United States Navy. Also eminent in aeronautical engineering is Dr. Chieh-Chien Chang of the University of Minnesota. Another in the field, Dr. S. L. Pai, published three important books: *Fluid Dynamics of Jets, Viscous Flow Theory I– Laminar,* and *Viscous Flow Theory II–Turbulent Flow.* A research professor, he is a specialist in aerodynamics at the University of Maryland.[26]

The newly appointed director of the University of Pennsylvania's Towne School of Civil and Mechanical Engineering is Dr. Hsuen Yeh, who has a doctorate in science from M. I. T. and has been a professor of mechanical engineering since 1956. Dr. Yeh is a specialist in a number of fields, including fluid dynamics, gas turbine design, and aerodynamics design. Equally prominent in mechanical engineering is Professor Yi-yuan Yu, of the Polytechnic Institute of Brooklyn. A Guggenheim fellow in 1959, he has made numerous contributions to technical journals, on engineering mechanics. Dr. S. L. Soo, a professor of mechanical engineering at the University of Illinois, is an authority on thermodynamics. He published his textbook, *Thermodynamics of Engineering Science,* in 1958.

The Philadelphia Inquirer, November 1, 1954, carried a headline, "China Mathematician Solves Firm's Dilemma." The story was that the Bearing Products Company of Philadelphia had received a million-dollar order for a very special type of loom, but vibration had caused the needles of the loom to break. Concerned about filling the order, the company made an appeal to the National Association of Manufacturers, which recommended Dr. Peter Pei-Chi Chow, assistant professor at Drexel Institute, a mathematical specialist adept in mechanical engineering. At once he worked out calculations that completely solved the vibration problem. Later, he and Walter M. Gelaski, president of the company, perfected an insulator. Since then the production has moved swiftly and easily.

In the field of chemical engineering, Chinese scientists hold responsible positions in many companies. A gifted Chinese chemical engineer is Dr. Ju-Chin Chu, a professor at the Polytechnic Institute of Brooklyn. He was director of research and development of the Chemical Construction Company, a division of the Ebasco Corporation. Since 1946 Dr. Chu has been actively engaged in industrial consulting work. His activities cover the fields of process design, plant data correlations, pilot-plant and laboratory data scale-up, economic evaluation, heat transfer, and distillation. He has served as consulting expert of the United States Department of Agriculture and has been consultant to a number of chemical, petroleum, and engineering companies including Sun Oil, American Cyanamid, Pittsburgh Plate Glass, Shell Chemical, Union Carbide, General Electric, Research and Development Corporation of Illinois, and a score of others. He is the author of more than forty-five articles and books, among them *Vapor Liquid Equilibrium Data,* and an article on thermodynamics in Kirk-Othmer's *Encyclopedia of Chemical Technology.*

In an advertisement of the Union Oil Company in the *United States News and World Report* of June 10, 1955, there appeared several pictures and a brief account of how Dr. Norman Ch'in had managed to recover for the company about 120 tons a day of sulphur from hydrogen sulfide (supposed to be a waste product of petroleum refining), thereby conserving part of the natural resources. Dr. Ch'in had been process engineer of the original sulphur recovery unit at the Los Angeles refinery of Union Oil.

Another field in which Chinese have distinguished themselves is hydraulic engineering. Dr. Chia-Ling Sung, a research associate in the Iowa Institute of Hydraulic Research, was the inventor of a flow measurement machine which is being used by the United States Navy. Dr. S. K. Liu, professor of hydraulic engineering at Colorado State College, was commissioned by the National Science Foundation for the task of carrying on research in the analytical study of channel roughness. The first English language book on the subject, *Open Channel Hydraulics,* was prepared by Professor Ven-te Chow, of the University of Illinois. The book is in the McGraw-Hill civil engineering series.

Chinese civil engineers have contributed greatly in the designing of highways and bridges. Dr. Shu-Tien Li, formerly president of a well-known engineering college in north China, is now chief of the technical specification department of Palmer and Baker, Inc., at Mobile, Alabama, one of the largest engineering firms in the South, which makes bridges, tunnels, and highways. Dr. Li had been associated with Rutgers University as visiting professor of civil engineering, and with Erdman and Hosley, Syracuse, New York, as chief structural engineer. The winner of the American Society of Civil Engineers' "James R. Croes Medal" for 1954 was Dr. F. K. Chang, who designed the projected Narrows Bridge between Brooklyn and Staten Island.

An internationally recognized authority on prestressed concrete structures is T. Y. Lin, professor of civil engineering at the University of California. In 1957 he was general chairman of the world

conference on prestressed concrete, held in San Francisco. Lin
had been instrumental in organizing the conference, which drew a
world-wide attendance of more than five hundred. Recently (1958)
he headed a delegation studying Soviet work with prestressed concrete.[27]

Architecture in the United States has had the distinguished contributions of I. M. Pei, connected for a number of years with Webb
and Knapp. The Mile High Center, designed by Pei and built in 1956
at Denver, Colorado, is considered representative of the typical
trends of architecture in this country.[28] Mr. James Y. S. Chen is
the assistant marine manager and naval architect of the United Operators' Shipping Agencies Corporation, well known for his ship
conversion and tanker construction designs. In 1953 he originated
the forced ventilated shaft tunnel design, eliminating cofferdams,
for American liberty tankers carrying grade A petroleum.

In Boston—perhaps because many M. I. T. or Harvard professors
of engineering serve as consultants to industry—several Chinese
scientists have organized their own engineering consulting firms.
Wang's laboratory is well known to many industries and engineers.
Dr. A. Wang had developed the magnetic core memory units for
electronic computers, the patent eventually acquired by the International Business Machines Corporation. Another consulting firm
in Boston is under Professors Y. T. Li and S. Y. Lee; its specialization is instrumentation and associated electrical and mechanical
engineering.

Social Science, Language, and Law

Whereas the list of eminent Chinese men of science might be indefinitely prolonged, a list of eminent Chinese lawyers, economists,
executives, and governmental officials would be disproportionately
brief. We can well perceive the reason. Because of the shortage of
engineers and scientists, applicants for such positions meet a just
appraisal. On the other hand, students of the humanities are plentiful;
thus in this field the Chinese are more inclined to be subject to
public prejudice. Nevertheless, we do find Chinese scholars who
have distinguished themselves in the humanities and in the social
sciences.

Various colleges maintain Far Eastern departments or offer
courses in Chinese subjects, with one or more Chinese scholars in
the department. The China Institute (1954) revealed that of the 481
professors and instructors in Chinese culture, language, and history
in 220 American colleges, 64 are Chinese or Chinese-Americans.
Many instances might be cited of Chinese instructors doing excellent
work in their specialized fields. On May 7, 1955, at the Eleventh

International Festival at Michigan State University, Professor and Mrs. Chao-chang Lee were presented with a scroll that read in part:

In grateful recognition of the devotion and service of Professor and Mrs. Chao-chang Lee to Michigan State University. By establishing our first International Center, and by directing the first International Festival, you have pioneered in better international understanding programs for the campus and for the state. Many foreign and American students have a broader outlook because of your leadership in these activities.

American Men of Science, ninth edition, Volume III, under "The Social and Behavioral Sciences," lists fifty-three Chinese scholars. No doubt that number could be considerably increased if American institutions treated all Chinese intellectuals alike, whether specializing in science or in the humanities. At least, the ability of Chinese graduates in the arts has been questioned, irrespective of the fact that they undergo the same rigorous system of education in the arts as they do in the sciences.

Chinese scholars in social sciences, languages, and law are found on the faculties of many colleges. More Chinese are professors of economics than of any other subject except Far Eastern studies. Dr. Franklin L. Ho, a visiting professor of economics at Columbia, is a Yale Ph. D. , and a disciple of the late professor Irving Fisher. He has recently been invited by the East-West Center at the University of Hawaii as its first senior scholar. Dr. S. C. Tsiang, professor of economics at the University of Rochester, is an authority on money, credit, and banking. Y. C. Kuo, treasurer of the International Monetary Fund, an accomplished economist, contributed to the abolition of the silver standard in China in the early 1930's.

The students of Michigan State University in 1956 voted Dr. Anthony Koo, professor of economics, most distinguished teacher of the year, and a gold watch was presented to him. Dr. Koo, a Harvard Ph. D. , is the author of many articles in the field of international trade.

Dr. Ta-Chung Liu, a Ph. D. of Cornell University, is now a professor of economics at his alma mater. His special contribution is his study, *China's National Income.*

A solid but lucid academic work that will take a basic place in the literature of the subject is Professor Choh-Ming Li's latest publication, *Economic Development of Communist China* (1959). Dr. Li is a professor of economics in the school of business, University of California.

Dr. Richwood Chin, professor of economics at Berea College, was among the five awarded national research professorships in economics by the Brookings Institution, Washington, D. C.[29]

"The world can lead to survival through cooperation," remarked Dr. Loh-Seng Tsai, a well-known psychologist, after repeated experiments showed that cats and rats—so-called natural enemies—can and do cooperate. Dr. Tsai, at Tulane University, proved that a habitually rat-killing cat could be made to live, eat, and play with a hooded rat. His unique experiment may have laid a biological foundation for a theoretical possibility of world peace.[30]

The school of law at Seton Hall University has on the faculty a distinguished Chinese jurist, Dr. John C. H. Wu, who has published a number of books since he obtained his law degree some thirty years ago from the University of Michigan.

An authority on Tibet is Dr. Tieh-Tseng Li, a professor of international relations at the University of Hartford. *Tibet, Today and Yesterday* (1959) is considered an indispensable reference work in the field. Dr. Li was Ambassador to Thailand under the Nationalist Chinese government.

In the field of anthropology, Professor Francis L. K. Hsu of Northwestern University is outstanding. He has done field work in China and has made studies of Chinese in Hawaii and on the mainland of the United States. *American and Chinese: Two Ways of Life,* and the *Aspects of Culture and Personality,* a symposium edited by him, are among his many publications, and considered excellent.

The first American of Chinese ancestry to head a department of sociology, Rose Hum Lee, who joined the faculty of Roosevelt College in 1945, is now a professor and the chairman of the sociological department. Dr. Lee, an authority on the Chinese in the United States, has written extensively on that subject.

Dr. Yuen-Ren Chao, professor of oriental languages at the University of California, is one of the best linguists China has ever produced. His authorship has won him an international reputation. He was elected in 1946 president of the American Association of Asiatic Studies.

One of the well-known Chinese scholars in the West is Professor Theodore Hsi-en Chen, head of the department of Asiatic studies of the University of Southern California. Before joining the faculty of the University of Southern California, he had served as dean, and later as president, of Fukien Christian University in Foochow, China. In 1954, he represented the United Board for Christian Colleges in China to help organize Tunghai University in Taiwan. In addition to being a professor and administrator, he is a public lecturer and the author of five books, among them the *Developing Patterns of the College Curriculum in the United States,* and *Thought Reform of the Chinese Intellectuals*. He has written more than eighty articles and has contributed to a number of encyclopedias, including the *Encyclopaedia Britannica* and the *World Book Encyclopedia.*

Another eminent scholar is Dr. Kung-chuan Hsiao, professor of Far Eastern and Slavic languages and literature in the University of Washington. He is one of the recipients of ten prizes of $10,000 each, awarded by the American Council of Learned Societies on January 20, 1960, in New York City.[31] The citation in honor of Dr. Hsiao may be quoted as follows:

Professor K. C. Hsiao combines the best of two great scholarly traditions, those of China and the West, in a manner virtually unequaled. Thirty years ago as a young man writing on Western political theory he was hailed for his creative insight. In the interim years he has established a record as a historian of Chinese political thought and experience that displays both matchless command of Chinese scholarship and great originality of conceptualization. To all aspects of his life work he has brought the richness of humanistic learning—he is poet, writer, and philosopher, as well as scholar.

The Arts

There have been a few Chinese who have become notable in music and art. The bass-baritone Yi-Kwei Sze is the first Chinese singer to win international fame as an interpreter of leading roles in classical operas and as an artist on the recital stage; he sang Sarastro in the NBC television presentation of Mozart's *Magic Flute,* January 16, 1957; earlier in the same season he sang the leading part in William Walton's *Troilus and Cressida;* he has appeared with the San Francisco Opera Company. His singing, whether in opera, with symphony orchestras, or in recitals has invariably elicited enthusiasm from both audiences and critics. One New Zealand critic wrote, "The magnificent bass-baritone of Yi-Kwei Sze is surely one of the world's great voices."

Wen-Chung Chou is the first Chinese composer to be given a Guggenheim fellowship. Chou is a graduate of the New England Conservatory of Music. Orchestral works by him have been performed by the San Francisco Symphony Orchestra under Leopold Stokowski and by the Louisville Symphony. Chou is notable for his amalgamation of the styles of classical Chinese music with those of the West. In 1957 he composed a piece for chamber orchestra, "In the Mode of Shang," following it with "Suite for Harp and Wood-Wind Quintet." He has received a two-year Rockefeller Foundation grant.

Other Chinese musicians of consequence are the young pianist Tung Kwong-Kwong and her husband, the violinist Ma Si-Hon, who played with the Cleveland Orchestra under George Szell. Ma received the Heifetz award at Tanglewood in 1951.

Watercolor painting and the name of Dong Kingman, a Chinese-American, are synonymous in the art world today. He has won virtually every award granted in the watercolor medium. His brilliant paintings are often seen on the covers of such magazines as *Fortune* and *Holiday*. *Life* has printed five leading articles on his work.[32]

The Chinese movie actors and actresses for the most part play merely supporting roles. Anna May Wong, however, who has been making a strong comeback from the days when she was notable upon the silent screen, has appeared in television. Arabella Hong, a graduate of the Juilliard School of Music, made her Broadway debut in *Flower Drum Song;* she has won several major awards for her performances in concert and in opera. France Nuyen, the leading lady in the *World of Suzie Wong,* on Broadway, was born in Marseilles, of a Chinese father and a French mother. She appeared first in *South Pacific.* Nancy Kwan, daughter of a Scottish fashion model and a Chinese architect, played the movie role of Suzie Wong, succeeding France Nuyen.[33] She has recently been assigned the top feminine role in the screen version of *Flower Drum Song* (1961). James Wong Howe won an Oscar in 1957 for his photography in *Rose Tattoo.*[34]

Business

The Chinese are known to possess considerable business acumen, a quality amply demonstrated in Southeast Asia, where they have for many years taken commanding positions in business, especially in both retail and wholesale trade; but this is not true in the United States. Here discrimination compelled Chinese immigrants to retire behind the walls of Chinatown, a small part of them to scatter in a thin line throughout the nation. They felt forced to restrict their endeavors to businesses not in competition with their white neighbors. Not that the Chinese have any special skill in managing restaurants or laundries, but until World War II their opportunities seemed restricted to those two enterprises. Nevertheless, the various Chinese enterprises that did develop have interesting histories.

An outstanding example of those companies is the National Dollar Stores, Ltd., a chain of fifty-four retail stores (featuring men's and women's wear) spreading throughout California, north to Seattle, Washington, east to Salt Lake City, Utah, south to Arizona, west to Hawaii. The president of the chain is a Chinese-American. The business began in San Francisco in 1907, the year after the great earthquake and fire, under the proprietorship of Joe Shoong, at 929 Market Street, and in 1921 became known as the China-Toggery-Shoong Company. In 1928 the name was changed to the National Dollar Stores, Inc. From 1921 to 1947 Joe Shoong remained the president of the corporation; then he became chairman of the board. The Shoong family own the entire outstanding capital stock of the National Dollar Stores. All the principal officers of the company are Chinese, including eight directors; the ninth is an American attorney. The stores have an annual volume of sales of over $10,000,000, based on a capital stock of $1,000,000. There are approximately 600 employees. During the past two decades the growth of the company has been notable; its net worth increased from $1,600,000 in 1941 to $7,000,000 in 1959.[35]

In contrast to this retail business in the West, a company specializing in tungsten operation and manufacturing in the East deserves attention. Starting with trading and processing operations of tungsten, the company in recent years has extended its field into zirconium and tin smelting. Incorporated according to New York law in 1916 as the Wah Chang Trading Corporation, the name Wah Chang (meaning "great development") was adopted in 1949 by charter amendment. It opened the world's largest tungsten refinery in 1953. Then in May, 1956, the company took over the operation of a zirconium purification plant in Albany, Oregon, previously operated by the Bureau of Mines. Nine months later, Wah Chang purchased a tin smelter plant in Texas City from the United States government for $1,350,000; thus the company now is in the fields of tin metal, tin alloys, and zirconium. It mines and refines tungsten; it also manufactures tungsten rods, heavy tungsten wire, and tungsten powder for carbide tools and bits used in steel, electronics, and the automobile industry.

Like Joe Shoong of the National Dollar Stores, Mr. K. C. Li is responsible for building the Wah Chang Corporation up to its present secure position. Its net worth has expanded from 1950 to 1958 by $4,500,000, reaching a present figure of $7,600,000. Mr. Li, educated in London and the Royal School of Mines as a mining and metallurgical engineer, came to the United States in 1916 and organized the Wah Chang. He helped invent the Li process for tungsten carbide manufacture and was the author of the book *Tungsten,* published in 1947. He died in March, 1961, and is succeeded by his son, K. C. Li, Jr., as chairman of the board. The president of the corporation is now Steve Yeh, an accomplished electrical engineer.[36]

To disparage the significance of the contributions and achievements of the Chinese-Americans would decidedly be an error; on the contrary, it is much more likely that they have been somewhat underrated, especially for their services during and since World War II. We gave a number of Distinguished Service Crosses and Presidential Citations to Chinese seamen in the Merchant Marine;

furthermore, in all the fields of their contributions they have been
individual rather than collective. Beyond this, it is evident that
the Chinese have met the challenge and taken advantage of their
opportunities here, and thus have become more beneficially influential. As Adam Dan, a Danish immigrant poet, wrote:

> We came not empty-handed here,
> But brought a rich inheritance.

12

Conclusions

When we view in retrospect the history of Chinese immigration in the United States, we perceive that it has been one of sad struggle against apparently relentless obstacles. The early immigrants were in fact ambitious workers willing to labor tirelessly at any trade in order to make a living. Their sacrifices were heavy; their sufferings were great. Prejudice against them was widespread; discrimination against them came not only from American laborers, politicians, and a host of others but from the very law of the land, for the Chinese was the first race to be singled out for exclusion, and therefore not eligible for naturalization. To be sure, Chinese born in this country were technically citizens; yet they did not receive treatment equal to that of citizens from southern or eastern Europe, not to mention the favored Nordic strain. For a number of years they could not obtain permission to bring their wives to this country; they always had trouble in bringing their children. The exclusion of the Chinese and the unequal status of Chinese-Americans inevitably produced an impact on the immigration policies of the Philippine Islands, Canada, Australia, and, to a lesser extent, Latin America. Few persons are clearly informed of the conditions to which Chinese immigrants have been subjected. Their lack of occupational adjustment before World War II may be laid to the caste treatment of the Chinese: little economic opportunity was afforded them, except as launderers, waiters, cooks, domestics, and restaurateurs. Indeed, the Chinese were hardly considered members of the community, and as a result they restricted themselves to the squalid isolation of an overcrowded Chinatown.

Finally, in the midst of World War II, the Chinese Exclusion Act was repealed. Urging the repeal, President Roosevelt sent a message to Congress: "By the repeal of the Chinese exclusion laws, we can correct a historic mistake and silence the distorted Japanese propaganda." Long before that message, authorities on immigration problems, such as Professors Maurice R. Davie and Henry P. Fairchild, had stressed that the history of the treatment of the Chinese in the United States was something of which Americans could not be proud. That chapter of exclusion is now closed; a new era in the history of the Chinese in the United States has opened.

The Chinese as Contributors

After the repeal of the Exclusion Act, thousands of immigrants were admitted; more than 60 per cent were naturalized. Hundreds of Chinese scientists, engineers, and other professional men now work side by side with their American colleagues. It may or may not be coincidental that Chinese immigrants filled the gaps at times when the United States most needed their assistance, during the third quarter of the nineteenth century and the period since World War II. When America moved westward there was a great dearth of laborers, and the Chinese helped to meet that situation. They served as laborers and as domestic servants, so that the whites could pursue more remunerative occupations. The Chinese built the railways and cleared the swamps; they appeared to be ready to assist in emergencies. But soon, with the depression in the mid-seventies, with the gradual influx of cheap immigrant labor from Europe, with the apparently overwhelming competition of Chinese labor, and with the use of some California Chinese as strike-breakers in Massachusetts—with all these and other irritants, the Chinese became the principal victims of American prejudices. The result was the enactment of the Chinese Exclusion Act. Life was dull and the future to most of the Chinese, was very dark.

To a marked degree World War II altered the situation, for then both government agencies and private corporations desperately needed technically skilled men. The Chinese responded; employers found them capable of handling mechanical and other specialized jobs; more and more Chinese were engaged. At the conclusion of the war and with the subsequent expansion of the economy, there was a shortage of engineers and scientists in American industry. Recruits had to be secured from schools of engineering and from the undergraduate and graduate bodies of universities. Again the Chinese answered the call, and large corporations such as General Electric, Westinghouse, and International Business Machines Corporation have engaged not five or ten Chinese but forty, fifty, or even more. Since many Chinese consider engineering and science their favorite fields, American industry can count on them as a rich source of potential supply. Furthermore, American colleges have experienced difficulty in obtaining qualified instructors, because many graduates with Ph. D. degrees prefer industry to teaching, in which they acquire less pay and prestige. But Chinese scholars have begun to fill a number of the vacancies in the universities. Because respect for intelligence is an ancient Chinese tradition, the teaching profession may become a Chinese specialty.

Likewise, the growth of the population in the United States, in contrast to the somewhat limited graduation of physicians each year, may cause an acute shortage of medical personnel, particularly resident doctors and nurses in hospitals. Chinese physicians and surgeons have joined hospital staffs; others conduct research in the laboratories. Chinese women with scientific interests, of whom there is a skilled supply, are often eager to become nurses and laboratory technicians. Many other fields of specialization are competently served by Chinese-Americans; only in the fields of social science, business, and the arts is the employment of Chinese very limited.

Surprising as it may seem, facts support the assertion that sons and grandsons of Chinese laundrymen and restaurateurs are unwilling to follow their fathers and grandfathers into these businesses. A number of them have become professional men. Though the forefather may himself be a son of the soil, he will slave and save to procure a decent education for his children. This is a Chinese tradition. For centuries many of the *literati* and government officials in China came from forebears of humble origin. By following the teaching of scholars, however, and by hard work, many a poor Chinese became a learned man and famous in his chosen field.

With the possible exception of those who gambled or violated the narcotic laws, the Chinese immigrants have been excellent citizens, committing very few crimes. Since the close of the tong wars, some three decades ago, Chinese communities have been considered peaceful spots in almost any city. The paucity of juvenile delinquency among the Chinese, widely acknowledged, may well induce sociologists to investigate the Chinese home and the Chinese community as desirable territory for further research.

The American as Benefactor

Professor Chen-Nien Yang, co-winner in 1957 of the Nobel Prize in Physics, stated in his acceptance speech in Sweden that the West provides better facilities for conducting research than does the East. The scholar-scientist needs proper environment and adequate facilities. Therefore the Chinese, who are able to participate freely in the life of this country, may make significant contributions as well as receive substantial benefits.

The Christian missionaries in China accomplished a great deal toward the education of the Chinese. Hospitals they established provided certain phases of technological instruction; missionary high schools and colleges were also of immense benefit. Graduates from these schools who came to America for advanced study have returned to China to serve in diverse capacities. American missionary activities also, to a certain extent, have given many worthy Chinese students assistance, financial or otherwise, toward securing their education in the United States. It should be a satisfaction to those missionaries that a number of their students are now in institutions of higher learning or are working in other fields, and that thus they help to ease shortages in various occupations in this country.

Because of free public secondary education, and provisions for scholarships and employment for the needy in private institutions, American schools and colleges afford the Chinese in the United States excellent facilities for study, for research, and for enjoying a high standard of living. Even the old immigrants to the United States were heavy beneficiaries, for had they remained in China, or migrated elsewhere—to Southeast Asia or Latin America—most of them would not have been in a position to give their children an adequate education. A laundryman or a restaurateur would have had much less opportunity elsewhere to make the amount of money and to lead the kind of life he could in the United States.

The present generation is living in what has been termed the machine age, with a business society civilization. With the development of technical "know-how," the exploitation of natural resources, and the innovation of automation, the average American's income is rising much higher every year, higher than was ever possible in the past. The Chinese are among those sharing the new benefits. Though many of the old immigrants may still regard thrift as a virtue, the present generation has followed the mass trend toward comforts and luxuries.

No doubt the Chinese immigrants have enjoyed all the freedom possible under a democratic form of government. Nearly all the privileges accorded to citizens are enjoyed equally by residents not yet naturalized. True, some occupations and "sensitive" positions are not open to aliens; nevertheless, the opportunities that are open offer a stimulating challenge even to those with outstanding ability.

The American judiciary has in recent times shown itself to be fair and upright, in keeping with the steady progress of society. It is now merely a matter of past history and the early Chinese immigrants were not permitted to be witnesses in court. Even though court procedure has often been costly and time-consuming, many

Chinese have been able to receive full redress for their grievances. From Congress the Chinese, through the enactment of private bills, through the Displaced Persons Act, through the Refugee Relief Act of 1953 and recent legislation, have been given the opportunity to come to the United States; or if they were already here, have been given the right to remain permanently. The executive branch in many respects has taken a humanitarian point of view in interpreting and administering existing laws. A number of Chinese who have for years lived illegally in this country have obtained either an adjustment of their status or a suspension of deportation. From time to time the American sense of fair play has come to the aid of a vast number of worthy Chinese immigrants. We need not mention the enormous amount of help that Chinese students have received from the American government, from colleges, and from missionaries.

The West Meets the East

The future of the Chinese in the United States depends much on how well they are received as they adjust themselves to the American community. When the Chinese sing "God Bless America," as they often do at celebrations of special events, they mean that they are unreservedly casting their lot with the United States. America has a great deal to offer the Chinese. Conversely, there is a great deal she may learn from the East, particularly in cultural, moral, and spiritual values. Though America has her own mores, her ethical codes, and religious beliefs, a certain materialistic pragmatism nonetheless pervades: material prosperity is healthful to a nation only if it be considered a concomitant of greatness, not greatness itself.

The philosophies of the West at times appear to preach one doctrine but to practice quite another. For instance, churches profess the brotherhood of man, but many in their congregations have belied that tenet in their approach to racial questions. A few wealthy men in the United States, though loudly championing the poor, part with not even a small portion of their wealth in behalf of the needy. To the Western mind that sort of paradoxical thinking may not be seriously inconsistent; but to the oriental mind it is contrary to all philosophical sense. Such homiletics secure few converts.

The Chinese have a tale that comes down from the sixth century, when Buddhism was at its height. A poor girl went to a certain temple and timidly inquired whether she might offer a small gift. The chief monk immediately summoned all his disciples, to the number of five hundred, to engage in a most impressive ceremony attendant on the girl's offering of a piece of silver, her entire savings. Five years later she became queen of the land. Then she sent many rich gifts to the temple; but when she arrived with her retinue, the monks accorded her only a restrainedly courteous reception. Much surprised, she asked the chief monk for an explanation. "It is not the amount of the gift, or the richness thereof, that signifies its worth," he replied. This explains the widow's mite in China.

Truly, if there should ever exist a Chinese Hall of Fame, the butler Dean Lung ought to have his name emblazoned therein.[1] For it was he, as we have pointed out, who gave all his accumulated savings to Columbia University, in addition to relinquishing a very large sum of money that might easily have been his. Dean Lung practiced what he preached. It would be unthinkable for a Chinese who had espoused Buddhistic detachment not to lead a life of detachment.

Two tendencies today in America are quick earning and easy living. Inflation is in the saddle; deficit spending, both personal and public, is the way of the land; thrift is an old-fashioned bugaboo. A hard-working, moderately paid man of simple integrity receives slight recognition. Prosperity has made Americans complacent and easy going. There are no short cuts through hard work; hard work is discipline. Distinguished Americans such as Benjamin Franklin and Thomas Edison worked extremely hard all their lives, and certainly they contributed greatly to the culture of the nation. As Longfellow sings in "The Ladder of Saint Augustine":

> The heights by great men reached and kept,
> Were not attained by sudden flight,
> But they, while their companions slept,
> Were toiling upward in the night.

The machine age, in exerting its profound influence upon American culture, has undermined traditional American individualism. The scholar and the artist have been ignored. Compare the relative prestige and income of notable professors in the great universities with those of chief executives in the large corporations, of opulent politicians, of expensive Hollywood stars. The abysmal disparity at least partly accounts for the shortage of professors. Scholars and educators are truly the forgotten men. Conversely, in China the status of teacher is equivalent to that of parent: to the student, once a teacher always a teacher, and always revered. Learned men seek the field of education and are welcomed. Their second choice may be in government officialdom; even though he should prove a complete failure in his official work, the scholar's prestige would remain high.

The admirable paucity of juvenile delinquency among the Chinese-Americans owes much to the family regimen, as well as to the quality of the youngsters themselves. Far too frequently among Western families there are woeful lapses in the ancient ideal of honor to one's father and mother, an ideal nobly maintained among the Chinese. In American families, the independence of the members often leads to a lack of filial respect that induces family disintegration. At the same time, the emotional security provided by family ties is often sacrificed—there is no longer the fear of God, the beginning of domestic wisdom. Again and again, parents have become so selfishly engrossed in their own interests and pleasures that they no longer show sincere interest in their children. William Faulkner expressed his belief that the false values of parents and schools are endangering American education. He deplored the fact that the successful teacher rarely receives equal recognition with the professional athlete.[2] Increase in juvenile delinquency results partly from the youngsters' freedom after school hours. Oriental parents willingly sacrifice the added time and devotedly make every effort to maintain family ties.

To the Chinese, old age is not a problem as it is to many Americans. The Chinese aged are seldom neglected; they retain the respect of their families; their counsel is eagerly sought. This is extremely important because since 1900, with a doubling of the total population in the United States, the number of persons over sixty-five had more than quadrupled—from 3,000,000 to 14,000,000. The deplorable fact is that parental neglect of children is often later translated into a lack of responsibility on the part of the children towards their elders.

Views on the fundamentals of life also differ between East and West. The philosophical attitude of the Chinese presents a contrast to his more pragmatically minded American counterpart. According to the Chinese viewpoint, to make money is good, but to make no money is not bad. They know it is important to work and struggle hard in order to compete and to advance; but they also realize that life has to be accepted as it comes. They do not readily become emotional, they do not suddenly become depressed. Even though there have been a number of suicides there are fewer Chinese with mental diseases, compared to the thousands of Americans who are confined in psychiatric hospitals or under the care of psychiatrists. Hysteria will mend no crisis, not even that caused by Russian missiles. Oriental calm might prove an efficacious base for sober surveying and sober planning.

The world stands in dire need of more statesmen and fewer politicians. Statesmen are concerned with principles, politicians with expedience. To maintain principles is often unpopular. To attain and maintain leadership, a nation cannot content itself with military, economic, or even scientific leadership; it must assume and maintain moral and cultural leadership.

The Chinese Look to the Future

Except in regard to problems and difficulties of immigration and to a lesser extent in regard to the question of racial discrimination, the Chinese in the United States are on the whole satisfied with their present status. To some a problem of immigration may be merely a nuisance, but to others it may be almost a matter of life and death. They do not understand why blood tests have to be applied almost exclusively to them. They do not so much doubt whether the blood test is sound for determining the true relationship of parent to child as they object to the seeming discrimination. They cannot see why a central board may not be established, so as to allow rejected applicants an opportunity to plead their causes. There must be genuine cases, to be sure, of children of Chinese-Americans who are entitled to be admitted, but who are now still waiting in Hong Kong. All those problems, and others, distress the Chinese.

The Chinese consider that their annual quota of 105 is unfairly small. Accordingly, since the standard country-of-birth formula prescribed for quotas of Europeans has not been applied to the Chinese, they are at a manifest disadvantage. This special rule for Chinese persons has made their quota even smaller, because a quarter of it has been reserved for Chinese born throughout all parts of the world. It has been stated that this regulation is designed to forestall an influx of Chinese born in Hong Kong, or in countries in the Western Hemisphere—surely not all Chinese abroad are citizens of their countries. Since the Chinese who are well settled in Southeast Asia or in Latin America are prosperous, it does not appear likely that they would all want to come to the United States. Strange as it may be, the quotas assigned to Asiatic peoples as a whole, except in 1954, have not been fully utilized. From 1948 to 1960 the actual quota used was only 23,979 or 61.5 per cent of that assigned, which is—yearly—2,990, or a total of 38,970.[3] Thus for those thirteen years about fifteen thousand of the quota remained unused.

Further difference between the Europeans and the Asiatics in regard to the immigration law is the ceiling of 2,000 on quotas within the so-called Asiatic Pacific triangle. This area ceiling is in fact a quota of the quota. Perhaps a little more justice will help the lawmakers to think that such restriction might be removed with profit. It is unnecessary to state that the quota system based on the census of 1920 is somewhat outdated, since in 1920 the United States had a population of slightly over 105,000,000, whereas in 1960 the total figure came close to 180,000,000.

Since 1924 the immigration policy of the United States has been re-

strictive. The desire to create a homogeneous America, with its persistence in retaining the national origin quota in favor of the Nordic
race; the opposition to pooling on a global basis the regularly unused
quotas; the increasing emphasis on the needs and interests of the
United States in determining who shall be welcome; the lack of enthusiasm of the lawmakers for the handful of immigration bills introduced since the Refugee Bill of 1953; and the lack of both academic
and popular interest in the problems of immigration—all these factors indicate that the United States is at present not ready to become a utopian haven for refugees en masse and for all the oppressed. Until Americans realize that immigration is good, if selective, we may expect few fundamental changes. It should be pointed
out, however, that the extension of the country-of-birth formula to
Asia has nothing to do with the modification of national-origin principles; instead, it was expected that the formula would clash with
the national quota system now being enforced.

On the other hand, as we have pointed out in Chapter 5, the "China
quota," which covers also the non-Chinese born in China, has not
been fully used between 1954 and 1958. The fact that the western
people in China are mostly Americans and people from northern
and western Europe, and that their own annual quotas for several
years had not been fully utilized, suggests that there could be no
unfairness in crediting their admittance to the quotas of their various
countries. Now this "China quota" of 100 is another special provision
that confuses the public; it is strictly for non-Chinese persons born
in China. One of British parentage, for example, who happens to
have been born in China, becomes chargeable to the quota of China,
whereas in reality he is 100 per cent British. The "China quota," if
merged with the regular Chinese quota, would have no effect on the
present quota limit.

Another vexation concerns those many applicants in Hong Kong
who claim to be children of Chinese-American parents; on that
ground they insist on their right to be admitted into the United States.
That there are immigration rackets in Hong Kong and elsewhere,
sources of huge profits by providing "paper sons" with all necessary
credentials, no one can deny; yet there are also many legitimate
cases among those applicants. Thoughtful Chinese realize that fraudulent practices bring dishonor upon the Chinese communities in
America and jeopardize honest applicants. A sincere and close cooperation between responsible Chinese organizations and the American authorities is necessary in the best interest of all concerned.

The Chinese do not wish to argue with American policies; all they
ask is equal treatment. Their feeling that they are not regarded as
first-class citizens is a response to injustice. As indicated by their

hearty support of the free world, they believe in freedom and democracy. They are no less loyal to America than are the immigrants
from other lands. They fully realize that they must adjust themselves
so that they may become fully integrated members of the American
community. With increasing numbers being born and being naturalized, with their potential political power rapidly enlarging, the
Chinese have gradually come to understand the true significance of
their right to vote. Nevertheless, they do not think they should forsake their great and hereditary culture; they are certain that in
aesthetics, philosophy, and in the art of living they have much to
offer. Accordingly they want their children to learn the Chinese
language and to appreciate the noble history of China. They take
the position that East and West, in many respects, should complement each other.

The Chinese in the United States seldom have been fairly appraised
of their merits—in the present generation or in the past. While much
toleration may lately have been shown, nevertheless how to prevent
more oriental immigrants from entering the country is still the
thought of many legislators. Difference of treatment, such as the
nonapplication of the country-of-birth formula under the immigration
law, is an example. Apparently it is too soon to expect any considerable change, certainly not while the race problems remain
dominating issues.

Few will challenge the statement that the Chinese as a whole, ever
since they began to arrive in large numbers more than a hundred
years ago, have been of great value to the United States and in no
sense a liability. The "old immigrants" utilized their physical powers to assist in developing California and its neighboring states.
Many of the "new immigrants" as well as those of the third or later
generations are scholars and scientists, who have directly or indirectly contributed to American progress and welfare. The Chinese-
Americans have indeed added significantly to the culture of this
country, which they may properly call their land of adoption. Though
they still encounter some prejudice, it is clear that their difficulties
are a part of the over-all racial problem in this country, which in
the future is bound to be resolved satisfactorily. They perceive also
that time alone will not settle everything. In order to live together
both the majority and the minority require the exertion of honest,
courageous self-criticism and of every effort by the government in
all branches. Indeed, world opinion has gradually been aroused to
the extent that to ignore the seriousness of this problem would be
to court disaster, and eventually to lose world leadership. *E plu-
ribus unum,* the motto of those who formed the American govern-

ment, probably will remain the motto of those who will endeavor to solve the enigma imposed by the fundamental strife of divergent races.

Appendix

TABLE I

ESTIMATE OF ETHNIC CHINESE IN SOUTHEAST ASIA

1.	Burma	(1958)	300,000
2.	Laos	(1959)	40,000
3.	Cambodia	(1958)	250,000
4.	Vietnam	(1957)	825,000
5.	Thailand	(1955)	3,000,000
6.	Federation of Malaya	(1957)	2,332,936
7.	Singapore	(1959)	1,190,100
8.	Sarawak	(1957)	197,723
9.	North Borneo	(1957)	97,248
10.	Brunei	(1947)	8,300
11.	Indonesia	(1955)	2,500,000
12.	Philippines	(1958)	250,000
	TOTAL		10,991,307

Burma   According to Josef Silverstein, no census figures exist, but it is usually estimated that there are approximately 300,000 Chinese. See his "Burma," in George McTurnan Kabin (ed.), *Government and Politics of Southeast Asia* (Ithaca, New York: Cornell University Press, 1959), p. 93.

Laos   Dr. S. H. Steinberg, editor of the *Statesman's Year Book*, explains the number of Chinese residents in Laos as follows: "The difference of the numbers given in the *Statesman's Year Book* 1958 (12,000) and 1959 (40,000) is entirely due to a more careful estimate on the part of the Laotian authorities. They now (1960) assess the number of Chinese living in Vientiane at about 18,000, and those in Laos at large at between 40,000 and 50,000. Personally, I now believe that the previous estimate of 12,000 referred only to the number of Chinese in Vientiane, and that the name of the country was mistakenly inserted instead of the capital."

Cambodia   The Chinese comprise about 10 per cent of the population of the kingdom of Cambodia, which in 1955 was estimated at about 4,400,000. See Clement Johnston, *Southeast Asia*, Report of U.S. Foreign Assistance Program, Survey No. 7,

85th Congress, 1st session (Washington, D.C., 1957), p. 24.

Vietnam	The number of Chinese in South and Central Vietnam in 1955 was 703,120, according to the *Annuaire Statistique*. The latest investigation made by C. T. Tran gives the estimate at about 825,000. Tsung-to Way, "Overseas Chinese in Vietnam," *The Far Eastern Economic Review* (Hong Kong: January 2, 1958), p. 21.
Thailand	See *Southeast Asia, op. cit.*, p. 23.
Federation of Malaya	June, 1957, census. The census listed Chinese males as 1,211,087, females 1,121,849.
Singapore	An estimate made in June, 1959. See the *Statesman's Year Book*, 1960-61, p. 246.
Sarawak	The estimate is made in December, 1957. See United Nations, *Progress of the Non-Self-Governing Territories under the Charter, Volume V, Territorial Surveys* (New York, 1960), p. 323.
North Borneo	The estimate is made in December, 1957. *Ibid.*, p. 315.
Brunei	*Sarawak and Brunei: A Report on the 1947 Population Census* (London: Crown Agents for the Colonies, 1950), Table 7, p. 93 and Table 35, p. 149.
Indonesia	U.S. Department of Commerce, *Investment in Indonesia* (Washington, D.C., February, 1956), p. 17.
Philippines	In 1948, the Philippines Immigration Bureau gave the total number of Chinese as 101,000; in 1956, as 145,595. Opinion is that these figures are low. Like the Chinese in Southeast Asia, the Chinese in the Philippines marry freely with native women, resulting in a great infusion of Chinese blood. The estimate is that more than a million Filipinos are partly Chinese. See J. E. Spencer, *Land and People in the Philippines* (Berkeley and Los Angeles: University of California, 1952), p. 21. David Wurfel stated that the Chinese are the largest alien group in the Philippines and now number over a quarter of a million. See his "The Philippines," in *Government and Politics of Southeast Asia*, p. 451.

TABLE II

CHINESE IN CANADA, BY PROVINCE, 1931-51

Province	1931			1941			1951		
	Total	Male	Female	Total	Male	Female	Total	Male	Female
British Columbia	27,139	24,900	2,239	18,619	16,220	2,399	15,933	12,347	3,586
Ontario	6,919	6,448	471	6,143	5,497	646	6,997	5,529	1,468
Alberta	3,875	3,607	268	3,122	2,817	305	3,451	2,754	697
Saskatchewan	3,501	3,365	136	2,545	2,392	153	2,144	1,786	358
Quebec	2,750	2,549	201	2,378	2,140	238	1,904	1,524	380
Manitoba	1,732	1,636	96	1,248	1,147	101	1,175	1,002	173
Nova Scotia	340	304	36	372	322	50	516	394	122
Newfoundland	0	0	0	0	0	0	386	354	32
New Brunswick	231	214	17	152	134	18	146	112	34
Yukon	1	1	0	0	0	0	37	35	2
Prince Edward Island	31	27	4	45	41	4	35	28	7
Northwest Territories	0	0	0	3	3	0	4	4	0
TOTAL	46,519	43,051	3,468	34,627	30,713	3,914	32,728	25,869	6,859

Source: 7th, 8th, and 9th Censuses of Canada.

TABLE III

CHINESE IMMIGRANTS ADMITTED TO CANADA, BY ETHNIC ORIGIN
FISCAL YEARS 1900-7, CALENDAR YEARS 1908-59

Year	Number	Year	Number	Year	Number
1900-1	7	1920	1,329	1940	0
1901-2	2	1921	2,732	1941	0
1902-3	0	1922	810	1942	0
1903-4	0	1923	811	1943	0
1904-5	0	1924	7	1944	0
1905-6	18	1925	0	1945	0
1900-6	27	1916-25	11,622	1936-45	1
1906-7	92	1926	0	1946	8
1907-8	1,884	1927	2	1947	20
1908	2,163	1928	1	1948	74
1909	1,883	1929	1	1949	797
1910	4,657	1930	0	1950	1,741
1911	6,644	1931	0	1951	2,697
1912	6,992	1932	1	1952	2,313
1913	6,298	1933	1	1953	1,929
1914	1,600	1934	1	1954	1,950
1915	82	1935	0	1955	2,575
				1956	2,093
1906-15	32,295	1926-35	7	1957	1,662
1916	313	1936	0	1958	2,615
1917	547	1937	1	1959	2,561
1918	2,988	1938	0		
1919	2,085	1939	0	1946-59	23,035

Source: Statistical Section, Department of Citizenship and Immigrants, Canada.

The figures in this table represent the most accurate compilation to date and are based on arrivals whose ethnic origin was Chinese but who had not all been born in China. However, some of the figures do not correspond exactly with those recorded in the Canada Year Book (Ottawa: Dominion Bureau of Statistics, 1948-49, 1950-59 editions). It may be said that this reflects a later and more accurate interpretation of returns. The statement in the *Canada Year Book*, 1948-49 (p. 183), that the year 1906 is the earliest in which information on Chinese immigration became available, is perhaps somewhat misleading. The meaning was that it was the earliest year in which information on Chinese immigration was available on a calendar year basis. The statistics on Chinese immigration as released by the Dominion Bureau of Statistics have to be read with caution. For example, in 1954, there were discrepancies in figures that appeared in the *Canada Year Book*, 1956 edition, relating to Chinese immigration (pp. 184-85). The 2,029 persons entering Canada in 1954 (Table 5), whose birthplace was given as China, were not necessarily all of the Chinese race; some may have been of European origin or of other Asiatic origin; seventy-one were not ethnic Chinese. In any case, as Table 6 shows, 1,930 of them were citizens of China. On the other hand, the 1,958 arrivals (Table 7) whose ethnic origin was Chinese had not all been born in China. Assuming that the 1,930 citizens of China entering Canada were all of Chinese racial origin—which they might not have been—then twenty-eight persons of the Chinese race came from other countries. In other words, Table 5 shows birthplaces of immigrant arrivals, regardless of racial origin; Table 6 shows the citizenship of immigrant arrivals, also regardless of origin; but Table 7 shows the ethnic origin of immigrants regardless of their birthplace or nationality.

TABLE IV

CHINESE BY SEX FOR THE STATES OF NEW YORK AND CALIFORNIA, 1880-1960

Year	New York			California		
	Male	Female	Males per 100 Females	Male	Female	Males per 100 Females
1880	897	12	0.0	71,244	3,888	1,832.4
1890	2,902	33	0.0	69,382	3,090	2,245.4
1900	7,028	142	4,949.3	42,297	3,456	1,223.9
1910	5,065	201	2,519.9	33,003	3,245	1,017.0
1920	5,240	553	947.6	24,230	4,582	528.8
1930	8,649	1,016	851.3	27,988	9,373	298.6
1940	11,777	1,954	602.7	27,331	12,225	223.0
1950	14,875	5,296	280.9	36,051	22,273	161.9
1960	23,406	14,167	165.2	53,627	41,973	127.8

Source: United States Census, 1880-1960.

TABLE V

THE CHINESE POPULATION IN THE UNITED STATES, BY SEX AND AGE, 1940 AND 1950

Age	Both Sexes		Male		Female	
	1940	1950	1940	1950	1940	1950
0- 5	4,375	13,628	2,193	7,090	2,182	6,538
5- 9	5,464	6,543	2,869	3,523	2,595	3,020
10-14	6,569	7,128	3,694	4,090	2,875	3,038
15-19	7,318	8,377	4,777	4,885	2,541	3,492
20-24	5,309	12,362	3,545	6,446	1,764	5,916
25-29	6,097	12,718	4,560	7,907	1,537	4,811
30-34	6,373	9,203	5,021	5,746	1,352	3,457
35-39	7,633	9,241	6,180	6,457	1,453	2,784
40-44	7,752	8,339	6,513	6,230	1,239	2,109
45-49	6,421	8,035	5,466	6,379	955	1,656
50-54	4,746	7,181	4,126	5,869	620	1,312
55-59	3,206	5,260	2,814	4,365	392	895
60-64	2,665	3,747	2,370	3,152	295	595
65-69	2,561	2,491	2,310	2,099	251	392
70-74		1,561		1,342		219
75 and over	1,015	1,326	951	1,145	64	181
TOTAL	77,504	117,140	57,389	76,725	20,115	40,415

Source: United States Census, 1940-50.

TABLE VI

CHINESE IMMIGRANT ALIENS ADMITTED TO THE UNITED STATES, BY SEX AND AGE, 1950-60

Sex and Age	1950	1951	1952	1953	1954	1955	1956	1957	1958	1959	1960
Male	110	126	118	203	1,511	1,261	2,007	2,487	1,396	2,846	1,873
0- 5	6	23	30	32	87	54	123	114	48	190	109
5- 9	14	17	4	19	88	116	242	217	105	314	101
10-19	19	29	29	43	102	85	277	272	114	458	272
20-29	7	16	7	32	144	129	360	414	310	392	177
30-39	37	21	26	45	413	392	482	700	399	531	272
40-49	19	11	16	20	338	249	297	390	166	345	266
50-59	6	7	3	10	266	185	174	288	178	326	320
60-69	2	2	3	2	61	43	43	81	65	244	291
70-79	0	0	0	0	8	5	6	8	10	41	60
80 and over	0	0	0	0	3	1	1	2	0	5	4
Age not known	0	0	0	0	1	2	2	1	1	0	1
Female	1,179	957	1,034	890	1,236	1,367	2,443	2,636	1,799	3,185	1,799
0- 5	8	8	24	36	63	42	110	103	43	188	119
5- 9	17	6	8	23	61	107	225	228	86	268	94
10-19	135	77	57	42	106	133	333	339	155	436	248
20-29	450	381	464	346	450	598	734	858	646	923	590
30-39	337	261	233	190	284	253	501	560	358	602	290
40-49	175	156	164	154	156	147	276	317	231	402	225
50-59	46	58	74	80	93	61	154	142	158	248	164
60-69	9	9	9	17	17	21	84	68	80	98	57
70-79	2	1	1	2	5	5	23	15	34	15	10
80 and over	0	0	0	0	0	0	3	5	8	5	1
Age not known	0	0	0	0	1	0	0	1	0	0	1
TOTAL	1,289	1,083	1,152	1,093	2,747	2,628	4,450	5,123	3,195	6,031	3,672

Source: Annual Report, 1950-60.

TABLE VII

CHINESE EMIGRANT ALIENS DEPARTED FROM THE UNITED STATES, BY SEX AND AGE, 1950-58

Sex and Age	1950	1951	1952	1953	1954	1955	1956	1957	1958
Male	523	378	245	202	513	696	158	177	1
0- 5	3	5	6	4	11	7	1	1	0
5- 9	7	8	3	4	8	5	1	2	0
10-19	12	10	10	9	26	22	10	7	0
20-29	149	103	43	55	138	135	62	61	0
30-39	225	148	87	41	158	265	44	66	1
40-49	57	52	34	35	90	136	19	20	0
50-59	20	16	26	24	43	80	15	12	1
60-69	10	9	12	13	26	33	2	5	0
70-79	8	6	4	1	7	7	2	1	0
80 and over	3	0	0	1	1	0	0	1	0
Age not known	29	21	20	15	5	6	2	1	0
Female	151	182	152	91	220	225	66	106	1
0- 5	4	3	4	2	1	3	0	3	0
5- 9	2	7	2	5	5	7	0	0	0
10-19	15	6	13	8	19	15	4	12	0
20-29	58	63	49	27	96	75	37	41	0
30-39	44	64	40	28	56	68	14	28	1
40-49	19	25	10	7	27	39	4	11	0
50-59	3	4	6	7	10	11	4	5	0
60-69	0	2	1	2	3	3	2	1	0
70-79	0	0	1	0	0	0	0	1	0
80 and over	0	0	0	0	0	0	0	2	0
Age not known	6	8	26	5	3	4	1	2	0
TOTAL	674	560	397	293		921	224	283	2

Source: Annual Report, 1950-58.

TABLE VIII

REGISTERED LIVE BIRTHS AND DEATHS FOR THE CHINESE
IN THE UNITED STATES, 1933-59*

Year	Births			Deaths		
	Total	Male	Female	Total	Male	Female
1933	1,190	617	573	1,198	1,086	112
1934	1,064	533	531	1,134	1,015	119
1935	970	492	478	1,129	1,034	95
1936	1,007	513	494	1,080	968	112
1937	988	**	**	1,227	1,090	137
1938	1,021	**	**	1,119	1,009	110
1939	1,034	**	**	1,128	1,022	106
1940	1,098	**	**	1,184	1,049	135
1941	1,183	**	**	1,230	1,099	131
1942	1,220	**	**	1,206	1,096	110
1943	1,364	**	**	1,336	1,187	149
1944	1,291	**	**	1,324	1,204	120
1945	1,382	**	**	1,317	1,195	122
1946	1,534	796	738	1,279	1,139	140
1947	2,170	1,093	1,077	1,123	977	146
1948	4,210	2,218	1,992	1,162	1,004	158
1949	5,062	2,581	2,481	1,162	978	184
1950	5,029	2,562	2,467	1,077	888	189
1951	4,870	2,560	2,310	1,188	1,046	142
1952	4,742	2,504	2,238	1,206	1,038	168
1953	4,592	2,408	2,184	1,195	1,031	164
1954	4,396	2,256	2,140	1,293	1,102	191
1955	4,429	2,252	2,177	1,165	989	176
1956	4,690	2,364	2,326	1,283	1,088	195
1957	4,666	2,364	2,302	1,356	1,150	206
1958	4,706	2,424	2,282	1,335	1,114	221
1959	5,024	2,614	2,410	1,343	1,134	209
TOTAL	74,932	33,151	31,200	32,779	28,732	4,047

*Dr. Halbert L. Dunn, Chief, National Office of Vital Statistics of
the Department of Health, Education, and Welfare, furnished the following information regarding birth and death data for those of Chinese
ancestry in this country.
    Registered live birth and death statistics for the United
States have included data for all States only since 1933. The
numbers of births shown for 1937-39 are from unpublished tabulations. Other figures are published in the annual reports of the
National Bureau of Vital Statistics, which until 1946 was part of
the Bureau of the Census, U.S. Department of Commerce. Births for
the years 1940-58 and deaths for the years 1937-59 were published
in Vital Statistics of the United States. Births for the years
1933-36 are from the reports entitled Births, Stillbirths, and
Infant Mortality Statistics. Deaths from the same years are from
the annual reports entitled Mortality Statistics.
    Prior to 1933—beginning with 1900 for deaths and 1915 for
births—data were available only for those states included in
the birth or death registration areas. The figures are published
in following annual reports:

        Mortality Statistics, 1900-32
        Birth Statistics, 1915-21
        Birth, Stillbirth, and Infant Mortality Statistics, 1922-32

    The States included in the registration areas are listed in
    the report each year.
  **Not available; therefore, grand total in this section does not
correspond to column totals, because of omissions.

TABLE IX

REGISTERED LIVE BIRTHS AND DEATHS FOR THE CHINESE IN HAWAII, 1933-59

Year	Births			Deaths		
	Total	Male	Female	Total	Male	Female
1933*	533	269	264	306	241	65
1934	495	251	244	248	193	55
1935	524	261	263	269	217	52
1936	472	255	217	279	229	50
1937	474	230	244	252	202	50
1938	488	228	260	251	214	37
1939	430	218	212	291	231	60
1940	522	281	241	284	215	69
1941	503	256	247	267	197	70
1942	548	284	264	265	217	48
1943	725	387	338	256	208	48
1944	830	417	413	301	240	61
1945	769	410	359	259	199	60
1946	846	421	425	271	207	64
1947*	898	465	433	291	222	69
1948*	736	379	357	259	195	64
1949**	860	449	411	273	187	86
1950**	836	426	410	260	178	82
1951	830	416	414	252	175	77
1952	858	448	410	229	157	72
1953	884	450	434	236	172	64
1954	844	428	416	247	182	65
1955	814	425	389	252	188	64
1956	818	386	432	244	174	70
1957	848	464	384	231	159	72
1958	774	398	376	224	152	72
1959	780	396	384	223	162	61
TOTAL	18,939	9,698	9,241	7,020	5,313	1,707

*The data on Chinese live births by sex, by place of occurrence in Hawaii for the calendar years 1933-41, are furnished by George H. Tokuyama, Assistant Chief, Office of Health Statistics, Department of Health, state of Hawaii. These figures differ slightly from some of the totals reported from those supplied by the National Office of Vital Statistics (NOVS). The difference appears due to the fact that NOVS tabulations included events according to the month and year in which they were reported, whereas the Hawaiian department of health based its tabulations on month and year in which the events occurred. The NOVS supplies no information on Chinese live births by sex for the years 1933-41 or on the number of deaths by sex for 1947-48. The figures given by NOVS were: 1933, 543; 1934, 491; 1935, 521; 1936, 469; 1937, 468; 1938, 483; 1939, 441; 1940, 515; and 1941, 502. The deaths in 1947 were 280, and in 1948, 260.

**The 1949 and 1950 data were also furnished by Mr. Tokuyama. In those two years the NOVS published births and deaths in Hawaii only by Hawaiian and part-Hawaiian, Caucasians, Japanese, and all other races. The "all other" group contains Chinese, Korean, Filipino, Puerto Rican, and minor racial groups.

Source: Birth, Stillbirth, and Infant Mortality Statistics, 1933-36; Mortality Statistics, 1933-36; and Vital Statistics of the United States, 1937-59.

TABLE X

DEATHS AND DEATH RATE OF THE CHINESE POPULATION IN THE UNITED STATES, BY SELECTED CAUSE OF DEATH, 1950-58

Death Rate per 100,000 Persons

Cause of Death	1950	1951	1952	1953	1954	1955	1956	1957	1958
Diseases of heart	197.7	244.3	242.8	247.8	256.5	229.0	222.0	243.0	223.2
Malignant neoplasms	102.1	117.7	123.1	138.0	135.0	114.5	150.0	133.0	146.6
Vascular lesions affecting central nervous system	57.5	81.5	69.7	63.1	74.2	76.1	72.0	66.5	56.4
Accidents	35.2	41.1	37.9	37.5	43.5	40.2	43.8	36.7	31.2
Suicide	28.0	23.3	22.3	29.6	18.6	19.8	24.6	21.2	25.7
Influenza and pneumonia	30.9	34.1	35.2	32.2	32.0	23.5	28.8	42.4	33.4
Diabetes melitus	12.2	10.4	18.3	13.1	14.1	11.1	13.2	22.9	18.6
TB, all types	81.2	72.4	57.5	46.7	42.9	28.4	28.2	32.7	24.6

Number of Deaths

Cause of Death	1950	1951	1952	1953	1954	1955	1956	1957	1958
Diseases of heart	275	351	359	377	401	370	370	424	408
Malignant neoplasms	142	169	182	210	211	185	250	232	268
Vascular lesions affecting central nervous system	80	117	103	96	116	123	120	116	103
Accidents	49	59	56	57	68	65	73	64	57
Suicide	39	33	33	45	29	32	41	37	47
Influenza and pneumonia	43	49	52	49	50	38	48	74	61
Diabetes melitus	17	15	27	20	22	18	22	40	34
TB, all types	113	104	85	71	67	46	47	57	45

Source: Vital Statistics of the United States, 1950-58. See also Table 12 (p. 45), Estimate of Chinese Population in the United States, 1951-59.

TABLE XI

RANK OF TEN STATES ACCORDING TO THE CHINESE POPULATION IN THE UNITED STATES, 1880-1960

Rank	1880	1890	1900	1910	1920	1930	1940	1950	1960*
1	California 75,132	California 72,472	California 45,753	California 36,248	California 28,812	California 37,361	California 39,556	California 58,324	California 95,600
2	Oregon 9,510	Oregon 9,540	Oregon 10,397	Oregon 7,363	New York 5,793	New York 9,665	New York 13,731	New York 20,171	New York 37,573
3	Nevada 5,416	Washington 3,260	New York 7,170	New York 5,266	Oregon 3,090	Illinois 3,192	Massachusetts 2,513	Illinois 4,207	Illinois 7,047
4	Idaho 3,379	New York 2,935	Washington 3,629	Washington 2,709	Illinois 2,776	Massachusetts 2,973	Illinois 2,456	Massachusetts 3,627	Massachusetts 6,745
5	Washington 3,186	Nevada 2,833	Massachusetts 2,968	Massachusetts 2,582	Massachusetts 2,544	Pennsylvania 2,557	Washington 2,345	Washington 3,408	Washington 5,491
6	Montana 1,765	Montana 2,532	Pennsylvania 1,927	Illinois 2,103	Washington 2,363	Washington 2,195	Oregon 2,086	Texas 2,435	Texas 4,172
7	Arizona 1,630	Idaho 2,007	Montana 1,739	Pennsylvania 1,784	Pennsylvania 1,829	Oregon 2,075	Pennsylvania 1,477	Pennsylvania 2,258	New Jersey 3,813
8	Wyoming 914	Colorado 1,398	Illinois 1,503	Arizona 1,305	New Jersey 1,190	New Jersey 1,783	Arizona 1,449	Oregon 2,102	Pennsylvania 3,741
9	New York 909	Arizona 1,170	Idaho 1,467	Montana 1,285	Arizona 1,137	Ohio 1,425	New Jersey 1,200	Arizona 1,951	Michigan 3,234
10	Colorado 612	Pennsylvania 1,146	Arizona 1,419	New Jersey 1,139	Ohio 941	Arizona 1,110	Texas 1,031	District of Columbia 1,825	Oregon 2,995

*Hawaii with 38,197 (1960) should rank second.
Source: United States Census, 1880-1960.

TABLE XII

ARRESTS OF CHINESE IN THE UNITED STATES, CRIME AGAINST
PERSONS AND PROPERTY, 1934-60*

Year	Criminal Homicide Murder and Nonnegligent Manslaughter	Manslaughter by Negligence	Robbery	Assault	Burglary	Larceny Theft	Auto Theft	Rape	Total
1934	10	0	8	33	14	24	4	13	106
1935	7	0	13	31	12	15	3	5	86
1936	12	0	5	32	14	17	2	12	94
1937	5	0	9	19	9	20	1	9	72
1938	8	0	8	23	12	37	3	16	107
1939	2	0	3	31	21	21	5	9	92
1940	7	0	11	44	9	26	3	15	115
1941	5	0	20	28	16	26	2	2	99
1942	2	0	6	41	16	20	6	6	97
1943	7	0	10	21	7	11	2	17	75
1944	3	0	1	32	14	16	5	9	80
1945	3	0	2	35	10	14	4	7	75
1946	5	0	16	19	11	16	1	5	73
1947	4	0	15	24	14	18	7	7	89
1948	2	0	13	37	22	41	10	9	134
1949	7	0	13	22	17	40	5	8	112
1950	2	0	14	41	21	49	6	3	136
1951	7	0	3	39	16	22	8	8	103
1952	0	0	2	2	5	7	6	1	23
1953	0	1	3	7	13	22	4	2	52
1954	1	1	2	1	3	21	7	0	36
1955	2	0	0	6	0	9	4	0	21
1956	4	0	1	2	2	8	3	0	20
1957	1	0	1	2	4	24	2	1	35
1958	2	2	7	5	27	57	31	0	131
1959	2	1	5	38	24	112	35	3	220
1960	4	1	9	17	56	177	37	3	304
TOTAL	114	6	200	632	389	870	206	170	2,587

*Prior to 1952, manslaughter by negligence and aggravated assault were not separately listed. Beginning in 1958, rape was limited to forcible offenses. Statutory rape, previously included as rape, was included among other sex offenses. Larcenies under $50 will also be excluded from reports of major crimes. The data relating to 1958 (and subsequent years) will not be comparable to the earlier figures published. The Federal Bureau of Investigation has cautioned readers not to use the published figures for purposes of comparison; see Uniform Crime Reports, 1958, pp. 3-4. See also the text, pp. 45-46.

Source: Uniform Crime Reports (Federal Bureau of Investigation, U.S. Department of Justice, Washington, D.C.), quarterly, semiannual, and annual bulletins, 1934-60.

TABLE XIII

ARRESTS OF CHINESE IN THE UNITED STATES, OTHER OFFENSES, 1934-60*

Year	Other Sex Offenses	Narcotic Drug Laws	Weapons Offenses	Disorderly Conduct	Drunkenness	Vagrancy	Gambling	Suspicion	All Other Offenses	Total
1934	9	621	27	13	9	49	76	67	63	934
1935	12	581	37	4	7	48	60	18	118	885
1936	4	698	21	11	12	82	108	31	46	1,013
1937	21	609	8	7	14	48	207	52	82	1,048
1938	8	444	13	18	9	36	103	33	66	730
1939	13	457	11	4	10	45	208	34	68	850
1940	16	527	8	10	15	46	187	28	80	917
1941	15	267	7	14	20	39	169	21	124	676
1942	22	165	6	25	17	16	221	28	134	634
1943	10	169	14	13	15	25	85	16	77	424
1944	8	186	5	14	8	22	134	18	79	474
1945	19	130	5	12	19	22	136	21	105	469
1946	11	96	10	11	25	15	92	13	86	359
1947	8	62	18	9	33	31	67	21	85	334
1948	13	107	17	21	48	32	110	13	158	519
1949	22	135	10	19	36	34	198	15	162	631
1950	14	175	12	20	33	57	172	26	197	706
1951	17	227	8	18	35	62	195	10	187	759
1952	3	7	4	11	66	9	28	7	65	200
1953	9	27	2	19	117	9	38	11	123	355
1954	8	25	5	22	107	25	10	12	113	327
1955	4	22	3	37	59	18	5	6	81	235
1956	8	7	6	20	45	14	18	4	94	216
1957	10	13	4	29	42	9	46	6	73	232
1958	14	34	13	33	297	97	341	42	200	1,121
1959	28	52	20	95	343	72	380	29	247	1,266
1960	43	54	25	58	351	87	723	43	368	1,762
TOTAL	369	5,897	319	627	1,792	1,049	4,117	625	3,281	18,076

*Beginning in 1958, statutory rape, previously included as rape, was included among other sex offenses. The Federal Bureau of Investigation has cautioned readers not to use the published figures for purpose of comparsion. See Uniform Crime Reports, 1958, pp. 3-4. See also the text, pp. 45-46.

Source: Uniform Crime Reports (Federal Bureau of Investigation, U.S. Department of Justice, Washington, D.C.), quarterly, semiannual, and annual bulletins, 1934-60.

TABLE XIV

LIST OF PRIVATE LAWS ENACTED AFFECTING CHINESE NATIONALS, 1944-56

78th Congress, 2nd Session:

380

80th Congress, 2nd Session:

316	318	334	336

81st Congress, 1st Session:

3	147	166	266	HR	6386*

81st Congress, 2nd Session:

667	1067	529	1081	708	1039	1028
375	786	572	587	982	766	
658	602	801	593	757	935	

82nd Congress, 1st Session:

150	155	200	282	34	169	131
92	354					

82nd Congress, 2nd Session:

455	642	647	863	587	942	527
427	461	500	926	599	702	946
494	628	445	510	483	485	979
429	449	918	745	940	601	980
993	432	560	681	526	953	
459	832	561	682	941	958	

83rd Congress, 1st Session:

256	131	171	110	165	103	186
81						

83rd Congress, 2nd Session:

256	685	343	735	352	876	382
663	969	479	736	327	862	783
341	672	658	517			

84th Congress, 1st Session:

373	14	176	53	199	434
167	171	90	333	200	460

84th Congress, 2nd Session:

620	855	542	533	553	557	694
535	793	513	587	497	580	849
613	541	508				

*This is a case involving the legalization of the entry of a certain Amos Chen and therefore no separate number of private laws has been assigned.

TABLE XV

CHINESE ENVOYS TO THE UNITED STATES, 1878-1958

Chen Lan-Pin	Minister	
Yung Wing	Assistant Minister	1878-81
Cheng Tsao-Yu	Minister	1881-86
Chang Yin-Hoon	Minister	1886-89
Tsui Kuo-Yin	Minister	1889-92
Yang Yu	Minister	1892-97
Wu Ting-fang	Minister	1897-1902
Chentung Liang Cheng	Minister	1903-7
Wu Ting-fang	Minister	1908-9
Chang Yin-Tang	Minister	1909-13
Kai-Fu Shah	Minister	1914-15
Vi-Kyuin Wellington Koo	Minister	1915-21
Sao-Ke Alfred Sze	Minister	1921-29
Chao-Chu Wu	Minister	1929-31
William Weiching Yen	Minister	1931-32
Sao-Ke Alfred Sze	Minister	1933-35
Sao-Ke Alfred Sze	Ambassador	1935-37
Chengting Ti Wang	Ambassador	1937-38
Hu Shih	Ambassador	1938-42
Wei Tao-Ming	Ambassador	1942-46
Vi-Kyuin Wellington Koo	Ambassador	1946-56
Hollington K. Tong	Ambassador	1956-58
George K. C. Yeh	Ambassador	1958-

Notes

Chapter 1

1. Thomas E. La Fargue, *China's First Hundred* (Pullman: State College of Washington, 1942), pp. 20-22.

2. Eduard I. Hambro, *The Problem of Chinese Refugees in Hong Kong* (Leyden: A. W. Sijthoff, 1955), p. 128.

3. Harley Farnsworth MacNair (ed.), *China* (Berkeley and Los Angeles: University of California Press, 1946), p. 84. This is the reason that Chinese are considered as Tangjon, and China has been called Tang. In fact, "China Town" in the Chinese language is the street of the Tang people.

4. See Batavia Massacre, text, p. 14.

5. The first Chinese embassy in the United States was established in 1878.

6. C. F. Remer, *The Foreign Trade of China* (Shanghai: The Commercial Press, 1926), pp. 228-29.

7. *Ibid.*, pp. 219-20:

Estimates of the Number of Chinese Abroad

F. Ratzell (1876)	2,300,000
F. W. Williams (1899)	4,000,000
J. Edkins (1900)	3,000,000
H. B. Morse (1903)	7,300,000
H. Gottwaldt (1903)	7,600,000
L. Richard (1908)	9,000,000
H. F. MacNair (1921)	8,600,000

8. For reasons for undercount of Chinese on Thai census returns, see G. William Skinner, *Chinese Society in Thailand* (Ithaca, New York: Cornell University Press, 1957), pp. 184-88.

9. Su-ching Chen, *China and Southeastern Asia* (Chungking, China: Institute of Pacific Relations, 1945), pp. 12-13.

10. Victor Purcell, *The Chinese in Southeast Asia* (London and New York: Oxford University Press, 1951), p. 2.

11. See Appendix, Table 1, *Estimate of Ethnic Chinese in Southeast Asia.*

12. Purcell, *The Chinese in Southeast Asia,* p. 133.

13. Holt S. Hallett, *A Thousand Miles on an Elephant in the Shan States* (Edinburgh and London: William Blackwood and Sons, 1890), p. 461.

14. Hans Mosolff, *Die Chinesische Auswanderung* (Rostock: Carl Hinstorffs, 1932), p. 333.

15. G. William Skinner, *Chinese Society in Thailand* (Ithaca, New York: Cornell University Press, 1957), pp. 181-90. The present review of the estimates of Chinese population in Thailand is based on his studies, unless otherwise stated.

16. Purcell, *The Chinese in Southeast Asia,* pp. 2-3.

17. Between 1919 and 1947 the Thai government undertook four nationwide censuses, with results quoted as of April 1, 1919; July 15, 1929; May 23, 1937; and May 23, 1947.

18. Kenneth P. Landon, *The Chinese in Thailand* (London and New York: Oxford University Press, 1941), p. 23.

19. See Clement Johnston, *Southeast Asia* (Report on United States Foreign Assistance Programs, Survey No. 7, Eighty-fifth Congress, 1st session [Washington, D. C.: U. S. Government Printing Office, 1957]).

20. Dr. Eduard I. Hambro, in his report submitted to the United Nations High Commissioner for Refugees, estimated the number of overseas Chinese as 13,674,300 in June, 1953, against the figures of 13,330,192 as released by the Chinese government, marking a difference of 344,108 during the same period. He surmised that as some of the Chinese government's figures seemed to refer to earlier periods than 1953, he had therefore used whenever possible the latest official figures or estimated those for the year 1953; hence his higher estimate. His calculation on ethnic Chinese in Southeast Asia was 10,954,000 in June, 1953. See his *The Problem of Chinese Refugees in Hong Kong,* pp. 190-91.

21. Thus the mixed blood between Chinese and natives of the Dutch East Indies are called *Peranakans,* in Indo-China *Ming-huongs,* in the Philippine Islands *Mestizo,* in British Malaya *Babas,* and in Thailand *Lukchin.*

22. Su-ching Chen, *China and Southeastern Asia,* p. 36.

23. For a study of anti-Chinese prejudice in the Philippines, see Margaret Wyant Horsely, Sangley: The Formation of Anti-Chinese Feeling in the Philippines. A Cultural Study of the Stereotype of Prejudices (unpublished Ph. D. dissertation, Columbia University, 1950).

24. C. R. Boxer, "Notes on the Chinese Abroad in the Late Ming and Early Manchu Periods Compiled from Contemporary European Sources (1500-1750)," *Tien Hsia Monthly,* No. 9. (August-December, 1939), p. 457.

25. Bernard H. M. Vlekke, *The Story of the Dutch East Indies* (Cambridge: Harvard University Press, 1945), pp. 111-12.

26. Purcell, *The Chinese in Southeast Asia,* p. 223.

27. *Ibid.,* p. 314.

28. *Ibid.,* pp. 427-28.

29. *Ibid.,* p. 369.

30. *Ibid.,* pp. 555-56. David Wehl relates the following about the sufferings of the Chinese since the collapse of the Dutch rule: "The poor Indonesians turned with the anger of jealousy upon the more prosperous Chinese, and the full storm of sudden freedom and revenge fell upon the helpless minority. . . . After the Japanese surrender, now, the position of the Chinese became slowly worse again. They were completely unprotected. In the free and easy time that followed the collapse of all controlling power the Chinese were an easy prey. Their shops were looted, their houses were fired, their people were kidnapped and murdered. In the fighting at Soerabaya, or Bandoeng, or Samarang, they lost lives and property." See his *The Birth of Indonesia* (London: George Allen and Unwin, Ltd., 1948), pp. 18-19.

31. Harley Farnsworth MacNair, *The Chinese Abroad* (Shanghai: The Commercial Press, 1924), p. 210.

32. Watt Stewart, *Chinese Bondage in Peru* (Durham, N. C.: Duke University Press, 1951), pp. 61-63, 65-68.

33. Except for the few who came willingly, the coolies were secured by the following means: (1) Prisoners taken in tong wars were sold by their captors to Chinese or Portuguese man-buyers. (2) Villagers or fishermen along the coast were kidnaped. (3) Prowling agents would tempt workmen in Macao to gamble. They would be tricked into losing heavily. Then they would be forcibly seized in payment of the debt. See MacNair, *The Chinese Abroad,* pp. 210-11.

34. Chen was codirector of the Chinese Educational Mission to the United States and a colleague of Dr. Yung Wing. Chen and Yung were appointed as Chinese minister and assistant minister to the United States, Peru, and Spain, in 1875.

35. *Chinese Immigration: Report of the Commission sent by China to Ascertain the Condition of Chinese Coolies in Cuba* (Shanghai: Kelly and Walsh, 1874), p. 4.

36. About 17,000 Chinese coolies were brought to Canada during the building period to work on the new railroad across the Rockies.

See Foon Sien, "Peoples of Chinese Origin," *Encyclopedia Canadi- ana,* II (Ottawa: The Canadiana Co. , 1957), 355.

37. Census reports on the Chinese in the United States began much earlier than they did in Canada; thus, in 1881 there were only 4,383 Chinese reported in Canada, 9,129 in 1891, 17,312 in 1901, 27,831 in 1911, 39,587 in 1921, and 46,519 in 1931. After the peak of 1931, owing to the effects of the Exclusion Acts, the Chinese population of Canada shrank considerably: 34,627 in 1941, 32,528 in 1951. The Exclusion Act, of course, is mainly responsible for the further decrease of Chinese immigration; another cause may be found in the relatively few Chinese women in the country. The ratio in 1931 was actually little less than 7.5 per cent, to 26.7 per cent in 1951. This abnormally low ratio of Chinese women accounts for the fact that in the census of 1931 there were only 1,045 of them that may be classified in the childbearing-age group (20-44), in 1951 only 2,816. For an account of history of Chinese immigration into Canada, see Stanislaw Andracki, The Immigration of Orientals into Canada with Special Reference to Chinese (unpublished Ph. D. dissertation, McGill University, Montreal, Canada, 1958).

38. Since 1952 the Dominion Bureau of Statistics has released separate figures on persons granted citizenship certificates by the countries of former allegiance. From 1952 to 1959 a total of 16,061 certificates were given to persons who had formerly been citizens of China, whereas the number of certificates given to persons by the country of birth was 16,656, a difference of 595 for a period of eight years. Among them there may have been some who owed allegiance to another country, possibly to the United States, although they were of Chinese origin.

39. Duvon Clough Corbitt, "Felipe, Oriental Friend," *The Inter- American,* V, No. 3 (March, 1946), 20-22, 39.

40. The Bank of China, Havana Branch, has estimated from a 1958 survey that there are a total of about 3,500 commercial enter- prises operated and owned by Chinese in Cuba. See Jerome T. W. Ha, "A Review and Outlook of Overseas Chinese Economy in Cuba," *Bi-Monthly Economic Review,* LXIV (Taipei, Taiwan: July-August, 1958).

41. The Peruvian government took an official census in 1940, and listed the Chinese at 10,915. The small number shown is due to the fact that the children of these Chinese are counted as of Peruvian nationality. There are only about 5 per cent females, and 90 per cent of the Chinese population is between forty and sixty. For ob- vious reasons, intermarriages between Chinese males and Peruvian females have been frequent. See Alice Jo Kwong, "The Chinese in Peru," in *Colloquium on Overseas Chinese* (New York: Institute of

Pacific Relations, 1958), pp. 41-48.

42. Stanley Spector, "The Chinese in Singapore," in *Colloquium on Overseas Chinese*, p. 20.

43. The Cantonese are estimated at about 7 per cent of the total Chinese population in Thailand.

44. G. William Skinner, *Chinese Society in Thailand*, p. 356.

45. Five U.S. cents per baht.

46. A decree that all aliens be banned from engaging in retail trade in rural areas throughout Indonesia went into effect, beginning January, 1960. No doubt this trade ban was aimed at breaking the Chinese stranglehold on Indonesia's rural economy for the Chinese are the most numerous and most successful merchants within Indonesia. It is estimated that about three hundred thousand Chinese will be affected. Another regulation called for the evacuation of all aliens from West Java's rural areas to nearby towns and cities.

47. The mission organized by the World Bank to make a thorough analysis of Thailand's economy has stated that Thailand has been very successful in the past in the assimilation of Chinese into the Thai community. International Bank for Reconstruction and Development, *A Public Development Program for Thailand* (Baltimore: Johns Hopkins Press, 1959), p. 96.

48. The capital, surplus, and reserves of the four Chinese banks in the Philippines, for instance, amounted in 1959 to 63,000,000 pesos, while their total resources were well over 375,000,000 pesos. Two of these four banks have been established only since 1950. See *International Bankers Directory* (1st 1960 ed.; Chicago: Rand-McNally and Co., 1960).

49. The Chinese moneylender usually buys farm products in the interior. There is need for his financing before the reaping of the harvest. The return of the principal and payment of interest are usually in kind. Some risk is entailed in such transactions.

50. In 1926, among the hundred highest income-tax payers in the Dutch East Indies, there were about ten Chinese. Among the thousand highest, 150 were Chinese and only about ten were Javanese. See Amry Vandenbosch, *The Dutch East Indies: Its Government, Problems and Politics* (Berkeley and Los Angeles: University of California Press, 1941), p. 20. In French Indo-China the Chinese are often large property holders. One of the richest Chinese there was said to own half of the real estate in Saigon. Charles Robequain, *The Economic Development of French Indo-China* (London and New York: Oxford University Press, 1944), p. 37.

51. But there are also the losers and the failures. The world-wide depression of the 1930's caught the Chinese in Southeast Asia unprepared. The immigrants, disheartened and sometimes penniless, returning to China, began to outnumber the new arrivals.

52. C. F. Remer, *Foreign Investment in China* (New York: Macmillan Co., 1933), pp. 223-26.

53. Helmut G. Callis, *Foreign Capital in Southeast Asia* (New York: Institute of Pacific Relations, 1942).

54. The United States Department of Commerce stated in 1955 that the resident Chinese in the Philippines accounted for the largest proportion of total foreign investment. See *Investment in the Philippines* (Publication of the United States Department of Commerce [Washington, D. C.: U. S. Government Printing Office, 1955]). p. 7. Estimates of Chinese investments are usually unreliable because of the number of small enterprises involved. It must be noticed, however, that since the war the Chinese have embarked upon many industrial projects in addition to banking and marketing.

The Department of Commerce also suggested that Chinese business capital in Indonesia immediately preceding World War II may have been 300 million guilders or more, an amount similar to that estimated by Callis. Unfortunately, the resident Chinese investment was not listed separately but was included in the Dutch investment. One conclusion, however, is almost certain: after Dutch and British capital, the Chinese is third, followed by the American. See *Investment in Indonesia* (Publication of the United States Department of Commerce [Washington, D. C.: U. S. Government Printing Office, 1956]), p. 12. One guilder is equivalent to fifty-five cents, United States currency.

55. The total civilian population of the colony at the end of 1960 was estimated at 3,014,000, of whom more than 99 per cent were Chinese. The Census Department, established in 1959, has made two sample surveys of the population and has estimated that the over-all population in October, 1960 was 3,190,000. A complete population census was held in March, 1961, and the preliminary figure released was 3,120,414. The last census in Hong Kong took place in 1931. See *Hong Kong Report for the Year 1960* (Hong Kong: Government Press, 1961), pp. 37-38.

56. MacNair, *The Chinese Abroad,* p. 269.

Chapter 2

1. From time to time we shall quote a survey made by the Rho Psi fraternity, New York (a Chinese student organization founded in 1906), conducted in 1956, covering 146 Chinese college graduates and twelve undergraduates showing a median age of thirty. This survey is all the more interesting because it will serve as a model for future characteristics of Chinese in this country, as more and more Chinese-Americans desire a college education. Out of those 158, twenty were born in America, thirty-one are naturalized citi-

zens, and twenty-six have acquired the status of permanent residents. Their median for American residence is nine years. Cantonese are 22 per cent of the total; the remaining 78 per cent came from other parts of China.

2. The first official enumeration of the population of the territory of Alaska was made in 1880 and consisted of a canvass of all accessible settlements, supplemented by estimates based mainly upon records and personal knowledge of missionary priests for those regions which could not be visited. No separate figures are available for the Chinese for that year. The 1890 census report shows 2,288 "Mongolians." It may be assumed that these were mainly Chinese, with a few Japanese. In the 1910 census the number of Chinese in Alaska lists as 1,209, and in 1920 only fifty-six; 1930, twenty-six; and 1940, fifty-six. There were no tabulations for Chinese in Alaska in the 1950 census. This information is based on a letter from Dr. Howard G. Brunsman, Chief, Population Division of the Bureau of Census, dated November 12, 1959.

3. United States Bureau of the Census, *1960 Census of Population: General Population Characteristics* (Advance Reports) (Washington, D. C.: U. S. Government Printing Office).

4. The Immigration Service no longer collected statistics on emigration after the fiscal year 1958.

5. In 1940, women 20-29 years of age comprised only 4.3 per cent of all Chinese in the United States; by 1950 this group had increased to 9.2 per cent.

6. See Appendix, Table VIII, Registered Live Births and Deaths for the Chinese in the United States, 1933-59.

7. Suicide comes next; see p. 53. See also Appendix, Table X, Death Rate Per 100,000 Chinese Population in the United States for the causes of deaths, 1950-58. From the study made by Dr. Ancel Keys, physiologist, of the University of Minnesota, the cause-and-effect relationship between cholesterol and heart disease seems to have positive correlation. Among other researches, the eating habits and coronary death rates of middle-aged Japanese in Japan, Hawaii, and Los Angeles are included in Dr. Keys's studies. His conclusion is that for every heart attack in Japan the Hawaiian Japanese has four, the Los Angeles Nisei, ten. This is because the native Japanese has an average cholesterol count of 120, eating a high-carbohydrate diet of rice, fish, and vegetables. The Hawaiian Japanese has an average of 183, his diet being the same as the native Japanese, but with meat, eggs, and dairy products added. The Los Angeles Nisei's diet being typically American, the average was 213. It is interesting that Dr. Keys lists Chinese food as one of the recommended diets. See "The Fat of the Land," *Time* magazine LXXVII, No. 3, (Jan-

uary 13, 1961), 48-52.

8. The census of 1950 reported native-born Chinese as 62,090, while the number of Chinese with American citizenship was 84,904; therefore, there should be 22,814 Chinese who acquired their citizenships through naturalization. A number are Chinese children who came in as citizens by derivation. In addition, 4,590 Chinese were naturalized between 1944 and 1949 under military and civilian status.

9. See Appendix, Table XI, Rank of Ten States According to Chinese Population in the United States (1880-1960).

10. It is to be noticed that the total United States population increase projected is 209,500,000 for 1970.

11. *The Immigration and Naturalization Systems of the United States, Report Number 1515*, (Eighty-first Congress, 2nd Session, 1950) (hereafter referred to as *Senate Report 1515*), p. 193.

12. *Ibid.*, p. 142.

13. Walter G. Beach, *Oriental Crime in California* (Stanford: Stanford University Press, 1932), p. 93.

14. *Ibid.*

15. Released through the *Uniform Crime Reports for the United States,* by the Federal Bureau of Investigation, U.S. Department of Justice, Washington, D.C. In the first three quarterly bulletins in 1934, the name Division of Investigation was used.

16. The crime index figures for 1957 and 1958, however, have been converted into crime rates (the number of crimes per 100,000 inhabitants) by using population estimates for those two years.

17. Mr. J. Edgar Hoover, director of the Federal Bureau of Investigation, in a letter of April, 1960, stated that reports from the San Francisco police department did not arrive at the headquarters in time for publication (1955-57) but the data from San Francisco appeared in the 1958 *Uniform Crime Reports for the United States*. Mr. Hoover further stated that there is no national program of court or judicial statistics which will show crimes committed on the part of the Chinese race in this country.

18. Information furnished by H. J. Anslinger, commissioner of narcotics, on April 2, 1959. Mr. Anslinger also expressed gratification at the decrease.

19. These articles were incorporated in the appendix of the *Congressional Record.*(August 2, 1955), pp. A5668-72.

20. These 225 cases were supplied by the Juvenile Court of San Francisco. See Rose Hum Lee, "Delinquent, Neglected and Dependent Chinese Boys and Girls of the San Francisco Bay Region," *Journal of Social Psychology*, LIV, 1st half (1952), pp. 15-34.

21. *Senate Report 1515*, p. 200. From a survey made by Harry H. Laughlin in 1939 the following result was obtained regarding

Chinese mentally ill confined to state and federal hospitals and state and federal penal institutions: in 168 state and federal hospitals for the mentally ill, 257 Chinese, of whom sixty-one were native born, 181 foreign born, and fifteen not indicated; in 228 state and eleven federal penal institutions, seventy-nine Chinese, of whom forty were natives, thirty-seven foreign born, and two not indicated. See Harry H. Laughlin, *Immigration and Conquest* (New York: Chamber of Commerce of the State of New York, 1939), pp. 161-214.

22. See Horace R. Cayton and Anne O. Lively, *The Chinese in the United States and the Chinese Christian Churches* (New York: National Council of the Churches of Christ in the United States of America, April, 1955), pp. 55-57; Margaret Ecclesine, "The Church in Chinatown, U.S.A.," *Catholic Digest* (August, 1960), pp. 57-62; Harley H. Zeigler, "Hawaii, Progress in Paradise," in *Concerns of a Continent*, James W. Hoffman, ed. (New York: Friendship Press, 1958), p. 106. The number of Chinese Christians abroad, in fact, varies in different parts of the world. For instance, the Chinese in the Caribbean are not only almost entirely Christian, but also a large number of them have entered the clergy and have assumed important positions in their churches. In North Borneo, the 1951 census listed about 20 per cent of the Chinese as Christians. According to C. William Skinner, the number of Chinese in Java who have become Christians is great, with fewer Catholics than Protestants. There are many Chinese churches throughout Java offering services in different languages. See *Colloquium on Overseas Chinese* (New York: Institute of Pacific Relations, 1958), pp. 5, 14, 55.

23. In 1940, of the 48,469 Chinese of twenty-five and over, 11,289 or 23.3 per cent had no schooling at all. In 1950, of 68,945, 12,610 or 18.3 per cent had no schooling.

24. According to 1920 and 1930 censuses, there were only seventy-nine and eighty-five physicians and surgeons, nineteen and twenty dentists, thirty-four and forty-seven engineers, and ten and thirty-four trained nurses. The number of college professors and lawyers was very limited.

25. The Japanese professional, technical, and kindred workers increased from 3.2 per cent in 1940 to 6.7 per cent in 1950; Filipinos from 1.6 per cent to 2.3 per cent.

26. Katherine Coman, *The History of Contract Labor in the Hawaiian Islands* (Publication of the American Economic Association, third series, IV, No. 3 [New York: Macmillan Co., August, 1903]), 11, 25.

27. *Ibid.*, p. 35.

28. It is suggested that the physiological adaptation of Chinese

to environment in Hawaii may be completed.

29. It has to be remembered that in 1950 the Caucasians constituted 23 per cent of Hawaii's total population, the Chinese only 6.5 per cent. Therefore, in 1951 both ratios were about the same, but since then the Caucasian ratio has advanced steadily, while the Chinese remains unchanged.

30. At the same time, the Caucasian average ratio was 765, or slightly lower than that of the Chinese.

Chapter 3

1. Maurice R. Davie, *World Immigration* (New York: Macmillan Co., 1936), p. 308. Professor Davie's figures are probably based on the report published by the United States Immigration Commission, 1911.

2. Harley Farnsworth McNair, *The Chinese Abroad* (Shanghai: The Commercial Press, 1924), p. 79.

3. Mary Roberts Coolidge, *Chinese Immigration* (New York: Henry Holt and Co., 1909), pp. 498-501.

4. Hubert Howe Bancroft, *History of California,* VI, 1848-1859 (San Francisco: The History Co., 1888), 124 (Vol. XXIII of *The Works of Hubert Howe Bancroft).*

5. Elmer Clarence Sandmeyer, *The Anti-Chinese Movement in California* (Urbana: University of Illinois Press, 1939), p. 16.

6. M. R. Coolidge, *Chinese Immigration,* p. 498.

7. The Chinese name was changed to "Old Golden Mountains" soon after the 1851 discovery of gold in Australia, which was named "New Golden Mountains."

8. The attitude of the Chinese government toward emigration has always been obstructionistic. As early as 1718, the imperial government prohibited emigration; as a matter of fact, it commanded that all Chinese residing abroad be forthwith repatriated. Those choosing to remain abroad in spite of the edict were held to be in banishment; those returning after the year specified were considered to have committed a capital crime. Not until one year after the treaty signed by China and Britain in 1858 did the traditional prohibition of Chinese emigration cease.

9. See section on "Chinese Six Companies," pp. 76-79.

10. Warren S. Thompson, *Growth and Changes in California's Population* (Los Angeles: The Haynes Foundation, 1955), p. 71.

11. Chester P. Dorland, "The Chinese Massacre at Los Angeles in 1871," *Annual Publications, Historical Society of Southern California,* III, Part 2 (Los Angeles, 1894), 22-26.

12. Sandmeyer, *The Anti-Chinese Movement in California,* p. 17.

13. Quoted by Eliot Grinnell Mears, *Resident Orientals on the American Pacific Coast* (Chicago: University of Chicago Press, 1928), p. 195.

14. Albert Dressler collected a number of telegrams sent by one Chinese to another during 1874, in which most of the sentences were terse. Even though not in conventional English, the telegrams formed an important sidelight on Chinese early life in the West. See his *California Chinese Chatter* (San Francisco: A. Dressler, 1927).

15. Mildred Wellborn, "The Events Leading to the Chinese Exclusion Acts," *Annual Publications, Historical Society of Southern California,* IX, (Los Angeles, 1914), 58.

16. Sandmeyer, "California Anti-Chinese Legislation and the Federal Courts: A Study in Federal Relations," *The Pacific Historical Review,* V, No. 3 (September, 1936), 211.

17. In essence, four interpretations were made against the actions of the state of California: (1) the state actions ran counter to the commerce clause; (2) they ran against the Fourteenth Amendment, with its "due process" and "equal protection of law"; (3) they made a breach of the Burlingame Treaty of 1868, with its recognition of the right of free immigration; (4) they ran counter to the Civil Rights Act of 1870, which prohibited discrimination against any person and imposing immigration taxes on a particular group of nonresidents. In fact, the Supreme Court, though it would not define limits of state legislation affecting the entry of immigrants, did suggest that Congress alone was empowered to enact legislation for the admission of aliens. See *Chy Lung* v. *Freeman,* 92 U.S. 275 (1875). More recently Justice Frankfurter of the Supreme Court has reasserted this power of Congress in *Haris-iades* v. *United States,* 342 U.S. 580 (1952).

18. Lucile Eaves, *A History of Californian Labor Legislation* (Berkeley and Los Angeles: University of California Press, 1910), p. 6.

19. Sandmeyer, *The Anti-Chinese Movement in California,* pp. 34, 45-47, 81-82.

20. The practice of wearing a queue was observed in China until 1912 when the Republic of China was established.

21. *The Invalidity of the "Queue Ordinance" of the City and County of San Francisco* (San Francisco: J. L. Rice and Co., 1879).

22. Quoted by Sandmeyer, *The Anti-Chinese Movement in California,* p. 59.

23. Frederick Wells Williams, *Anson Burlingame and the First Chinese Mission to Foreign Powers* (New York: Charles Scribner's Sons, 1912), p. 278.

24. The following is a summary of its provisions: (1) The immigration of Chinese laborers, skilled and unskilled, would be suspended for ten years. (2) Chinese laborers who were in the United States on November 17, 1880, would be permitted to obtain certificates from the collector of customs entitling them to return to the United States after a temporary absence. (3) Chinese persons, other than laborers, might be admitted to the United States on presentation of a certificate, to be known as the Section Six Certificate, from the Chinese government certifying that the bearer had the right to enter under the terms of the treaty. (4) Chinese persons entering the United States illegally after the passage of the act would be subject to deportation. (5) Chinese persons would be thereafter denied naturalization. (6) The entering of teachers, ministers, students, merchants, or those proceeding to the United States for curiosity was not prohibited.

Chapter 4

1. In fact, individual states had, since the Civil War, passed local immigration laws. Those state laws, however, were declared unconstitutional by the Supreme Court.

2. All this federal legislation, however, was negative, in that no provisions were made to select those immigrants who would be valuable to the country.

3. The report proved to be much exaggerated.

4. On the subject of the exaggeration of the official statistics on alien immigration into the United States, see pp. 94-96.

5. The 1952 Immigration and Nationality Act provided the annual quota of any area to be 0.166 per cent of the number from that area in the mainland United States in 1920.

6. Between 1949 and 1958, the average of the quota used yearly for northwestern Europe was 66,982 against the annual quota of 125,165. On the other hand, the average number of quota immigrants admitted from southeastern Europe was 51,469 yearly against an annual quota of 24,502.

7. The Immigration Act of 1917 laid down further restrictions on the immigration of Asian persons, by creating the so-called barred zone, natives of which were declared inadmissible to the United States.

8. The figure was disputed by Professor Yamato Ichihashi as misleading. He asserted that of the 132,706 Japanese immigrants admitted between 1901-1910, only 54,839 were admitted to the mainland United States, whereas 90 reached Alaska and 77,777 were admitted to Hawaii. See his *Japanese in the United States* (Stanford: Stanford University Press, 1932), pp. 56-64.

9. Attempts to pass bills to drive Asiatics from the land were made in the California legislature as early as 1907. Finally a bill was passed in 1913, providing that aliens ineligible for citizenship could hold land only to the extent and in the manner stipulated in the treaties. In fact, the constitution of the state prohibited owner- ship of land by aliens. Thus Chinese, Japanese, and other Asiatics could not own land in California, since they were ineligible for nat- uralization. Ten additional states had since imposed their similar restrictions or prohibitions. The federal Supreme Court's decision against the California alien land law was rendered in 1947. How- ever, during the November 4, 1960, election, voters of the state of Washington failed to pass Senate Joint Resolution 4 which would have repealed land ownership restrictions for aliens.

10. Isaac Hill Bromley, *The Chinese Massacre at Rock Springs, Wyoming Territory, September 2, 1885* (Boston: Franklin Press; Rand, Avery and Co., 1886), p. 91.

11. B. P. Wilcox, "Anti-Chinese Riots in Washington," *The Wash- ington Historical Quarterly,* XX, No. 3 (July, 1929), 207-11.

12. Otis Gibson, *The Chinese in America* (Cincinnati: Hitchcock and Walden, 1877), pp. 51-52.

13. George Kinnear, *Anti-Chinese Riots in Seattle, 1885-1886* (Seattle: Geo. Kinnear, 1911), pp. 2-9.

14. Jules Alexander Karlin, "The Anti-Chinese Outbreaks in Seattle," *The Pacific Northwest Quarterly,* XXXIX, No. 2, (April, 1948), 115.

15. Claude T. Reno, *The Manual of the Alpha Tau Omega Fra- ternity* (4th ed.; Champaign: 1946), pp. 155-56.

16. Gibson, *The Chinese in America,* p. 298.

17. Elmer Clarence Sandmeyer, *The Anti-Chinese Movement in California* (Urbana: University of Illinois Press, 1939), p. 70.

18. *Senate Miscellaneous Documents,* No. 20, Forty-fifth Con- gress, 2nd session, pp. 4, 9.

19. Edith Lowenstein, *The Alien and the Immigration Law* (New York: Oceana Publications, 1958), p. 170. Such investigative search without prior clue is practiced by the Immigration Service even today.

20. For instance, in 1880 males per 100 females for the state of California numbered 1832.4; in 1890, 2245.4; and in 1900, 1223.9.

21. Jacob A. Riis was a Danish emigrant who enjoyed the confi- dence of Police Commissioner Theodore Roosevelt and led a crusade against the worst of the tenements in New York City. See his *How the Other Half Lives* (New York: Charles Scribner's Sons, 1890), p. 102.

22. The Chinese established their own hospital in San Francisco, under the name of "Tung Hwa," in 1924.

23. United States Immigration and Naturalization Service, *Annual Report, 1909,* p. 128.

24. C. F. Remer, *A Study of Chinese Boycotts, with Special Reference to Their Economic Effectiveness* (Baltimore: Johns Hopkins Press, 1933), pp. 29-39. See also Howard K. Beale, *Theodore Roosevelt and the Rise of America to World Power* (Baltimore: Johns Hopkins Press, 1956), pp. 215-52.

25. Remer, *A Study of Chinese Boycotts,* p. 31.

26. The fiscal year of the *Annual Report* ends on June 30. Therefore, the year 1883 covers the period from July 1, 1882, to June 30, 1883.

27. Official figures as released by the Immigration Service cited immigration from China by decades, 1883 to 1943:

1883-1890	10,242	1921-1930	29,907
1891-1900	14,799	1931-1940	4,928
1901-1910	20,605	1941-1943	1,247
1911-1920	21,278		
		1883-1943	103,006

Official figures as released by the Immigration Service on Chinese immigrants admitted:

1883-1890	10,242	1921-1930	24,345
1891-1900	14,780	1931-1940	3,989
1901-1910	19,702	1941-1943	90
1911-1920	19,263		
		1883-1943	92,411

The figures from 1883 until 1898 relate to immigration from China; from 1932 to 1939, inclusive, the Immigration Service gave no separate figures on Chinese immigrants admitted.

28. In Canada, Chinese immigrants were virtually excluded after the passage of the Chinese Immigration Act in 1923. Only a handful, forty-four persons, was admitted between 1924 and 1947, when the act was finally repealed. Dominion Bureau of Statistics, *Canada Year Book, 1948-1949* (Ottawa: Queen's Printer and Controller of Stationery, 1950), p. 183.

29. Section 4 (b) of the Immigration Act of 1924 provides nonquota status for an immigrant previously lawfully admitted to the United States who is returning from a temporary visit abroad. Section 4 (e) of the act provides that a student is eligible for admission as a nonquota immigrant if certain regulations are met.

30. *Senate Report 1515,* Table 14, p. 896.

31. Prior to the passage of the Act of 1924, Chinese students

and merchants after legal admission were permitted to remain permanently in this country, but actually very few Chinese students before World War II took advantage of the offer. The lack of proper employment openings in the United States for Chinese college graduates is one reason, and the good opportunities in China awaiting the returned students is another. In other words, there was so much that he could do in his homeland that there was very little temptation for a student to stay in any other country. This situation has, of course, changed under the present circumstances.

32. "Statistical Review of Immigration, 1820-1910," III, *Report of the United States Immigration Commission* (Washington, D. C.: U.S. Government Printing Office, 1911), 358-59. The Commission gave the percentage as sixty-four, which is obviously a typographical error; Sidney L. Gulick, *American Democracy and Asiatic Citizenship* (New York: Charles Scribner's Sons, 1918), pp. 140-41.

33. The official number was 2,284,601 between 1899 and 1910 and 1,109,524 between 1911 and 1920.

34. "Statistical Review of Immigration, 1820-1910," III, 359. It is known that for a considerable period the emigration of aliens has been approximately one-third as great as the immigration movement to the United States. See *Abstract of the Report of the Immigration Commission*, Vol. I (Washington, D. C.: U.S. Government Printing Office, 1911), 112. Chinese going to China and applying for returning permit were numerous in the latter part of the nineteenth century. When the Scott Act of 1888 was passed there were at least 20,000 certificates of re-entry outstanding.

35. Between 1908 and 1947, 1,248,895 Italians returned to Italy. This was equal to 26.3 per cent of the total number of Italian immigrants admitted from 1820 to 1947. See *Senate Report 1515*, p. 112.

36. The Chinese head the list with the highest percentage—61 per cent of immigrants admitted to the United States, 1899 to 1910, who had been in this country. The average was 12.4 per cent for all countries.

37. With the exception of the period between 1932 and 1939, the Immigration Service has released from 1899 until the present time separate figures for Chinese along with immigrants from China.

38. 10 Stat. 604 (1855), Rev. Stat., Sec. 1993 (1878); 48 Stat. 797 (1934).

39. *Annual Report, 1925* (USINS), p. 22. Under the Immigration Act of 1952, children born outside the United States of one alien and one citizen parent will automatically acquire citizenship in the United States if the citizen parent has resided and been in the United States for ten years before the birth of the child, and the child arrived in the United States in this prescribed time to claim the citizenship;

or, if the citizen parent has not acquired such a period of residence, then if the alien parent is naturalized before the child is sixteen years of age and the child has been admitted to the United States before reaching the age of sixteen, the child will acquire citizenship automatically. Under the varied provisions of the law as it stands today, it is possible for a United States citizen of Chinese descent to have one child come in as a citizen of the United States, while another of his children is admitted with nonquota immigrant status. In the latter case, the residence requirement of five years would have been met before he applied for naturalization.

40. Between 1926 and 1940, 41,722 were admitted as citizens or returning citizens. The majority were Chinese-Americans returning from trips abroad. The remainder were mostly children admitted as citizens. The 1932 *Annual Report* (USINS) specifically mentioned that of 3,252 persons admitted, 2,384 were returning citizens.

41. *Senate Report 1515*, p. 464.

42. *United States* v. *Mrs. Cue Lim*, 176 U.S. 459 (1900). The Supreme Court held that the wife and minor children of a Chinese merchant who is himself entitled under the treaty to come to the United States are entitled to come with him or after him.

43. *Cheuno Sumchee* v. *Nagle*, 268 U.S. 336 (1925).

44. The Chinese treaty traders admitted between 1905 and 1924 averaged about 240 a year. The members of their families were about three times as many. When compared with the admission of Chinese wives and children of Chinese-Americans, an average of about 150 and 1,000, respectively, during the same period, the number of admissions of merchants' families must be considered large. No wonder the Immigration Service cast a watchful eye on the minor children in this particular class, suspecting that many of them were fraudulent. Each year a number of such applications were denied.

45. Figures include treaty traders, their wives, and unmarried minor children. It is possible that some of them were born in China, but were not necessarily Chinese.

46. *Senate Report 1515*, p. 905.

47. The immigration officers surmised that permitting Chinese crewmen to land for even a short while would encourage desertion. The ruling established by the attorney general in 1903 permitting Chinese seamen to land if they worked on an American vessel and were sworn before a United States commissioner, was considered improper by the immigration commissioner.

48. After the passage of the Act of 1924, the Immigration Service maintained that a Chinese laborer cannot apply in good faith for a return certificate for the reason that it would be of no value to him, because the Chinese Exclusion Act of 1892 specifies that he must have obtained a return certificate as a laborer at that time.

49. The yearly figures from 1883 to 1889 were submitted by the Treasury Department to the Committee on Immigration and Naturalization, House of Representatives, on Chinese immigrants, the year ending December 31. The difference between 8,031 in the year 1883 as reported by the commissioner of immigration and only 381 by the Treasury Department is that the former used the fiscal year ending June 30. The "Restriction Act" against Chinese did not pass until August 4, 1882. Very probably a great number of Chinese arrived between July 1 and August 4, before the act was put into operation. Coincidentally, in 1889 the Treasury Department's figure is 950 against only 118 as released by the Immigration Service. It is possible that more immigrants arrived during the second six months of 1889.

50. So far as the official statistics are concerned, the deduction of returning residents does not necessarily mean that the balance represents all immigrants from China. In some of the years, like 1907, 1908, and 1909, both figures are very close as a result of the deduction; but in other years, the official statistics still show a much higher number than seem to be warranted, indicating that the Immigration Service must have included other aliens admitted under the category of immigrant.

51. After 1908 and until 1943 the official records of Chinese emigrants showed that more Chinese left the United States than the number actually admitted, and that consequently there was actually a net loss. The *Senate Executive Documents* No. 97, Fifty-first Congress, 1st session (1889-1890) stated that during the fiscal years June 30, 1883 to 1889, 88,561 Chinese departed against 78,510 admitted, or a net loss of 10,051. Among the arrivals, 52,698, or 67 per cent, were armed with legal certificates to return. See also *Enumeration of the Chinese Population,* The Committee on the Census, U.S. Senate, March 27, 1890, p. 1. The figure of Chinese departures was given as 68,974 against 51,261 arrivals at San Francisco from August 2, 1882, to October 1, 1888, with and without certificates.

52. Another way to test the official statistics between 1882 and 1943 is to check them against the census data. One should also take into consideration the number of births and deaths, the number of immigrants admitted and departed. But with the available statistics since 1933 showing that the natural increase netted an actual loss of 827 between 1933 and 1940 (see Appendix, Table VIII), we shall limit our calculation to the number of immigrants admitted and those departed. Since the Immigration Service did not until 1908 offer figures on emigrants, our comparison had to limit the period from 1910 to 1940. The result is as follows:

1920	68,052	(1910 census 71,531, adding 19,263 im-
		migrants and subtracting 22,742 emi-
		grants between 1910 and 1920)
1930	52,021	
1940	39,370	

With the exception of the figures of 1920, which are only about 10 per cent higher than those of the census, the years 1930 and 1940 are very unsatisfactory. In other words, whereas the census gave us 74,954 in 1930, the figure we calculated from the immigration statistics is only 52,021, and in 1940 the difference is even more startling, 77,504 against 39,370. We may say that the official statistics are unable to withstand one more test. Yet if we check our proposed list with the census data, and if the Chinese emigrants were estimated as 36 per cent, we obtain the following: 1920, 72,554 (1910 census, 71,531, adding Chinese immigrants admitted between 1910 and 1920, amounts to 9,210 according to our proposed list. Then we subtract 36 per cent of the emigrants officially recorded during the same period); 1930, 66,694; 1940, 61,037. These figures are no confirmation that our proposed list is consonant with the census data; all we can say is that they are more reasonable. One possible explanation of the discrepancies is that the census may have counted the children of American-Chinese, whereas the official figure on admittance and departure and our proposed list have been limited to immigrants and emigrants only. Another trouble spot is the possibility of a number of Chinese having entered the United States illegally; the census enumerator may have included some of these in his list.

53. *Annual Report, 1896* (USINS), p. 12.

54. Six years after the Chinese Exclusion Act, in 1888, Congress provided for the deportation of aliens entering illegally.

55. *Senate Report 1515,* Table 5, pp. 873-74.

56. *Annual Report, 1928* (USINS), Table 104, p. 228.

57. *Senate Report 1515,* Table 4, p. 872. During the first three decades of the twentieth century there were always more excludable aliens than were deported; since 1930, the reverse has been true. For aliens excluded and deported 1901 to 1959, see *Statistical Abstract of the United States, 1957,* Table 107, p. 92, and *1960,* Table 113, p. 93.

58. Between 1939 and 1944, of the 423 violators of narcotic laws, 224 were Mexicans, 93 Chinese, and 28 Italians. There were, however, no deportations made to Italy between 1941 and 1944, owing to World War II. See *Senate Report 1515,* Table 7, pp. 877-78.

59. The large influx of Mexican immigrants beginning in 1924

had not escaped the attention of the restrictionists. Bills proposing the setting of quotas for the Western Hemisphere and particularly the Mexicans were introduced in Congress between 1926 and 1930. The strong opposition from the economic interests of the Southwest, which needed the services of Mexican labor, plus the strong stand taken by the State Department in preserving the principle of Pan-Americanism, however, had prevented the bills from becoming laws. For an account of the debate, and failure of Congressional efforts to limit Mexican immigration to the United States, see Robert A. Divine, *American Immigration Policy, 1924-1952*, (New Haven: Yale University Press, 1957), pp. 52-68.

60. Fred W. Riggs, *Pressures on Congress* (New York: King's Crown Press, 1950), p. 52.

61. The suggestion of the repeal of the Exclusion Act was first made in 1924 by the Immigration Service itself. W. W. Husband, commissioner general of immigration, declared that the 1924 Act reduplicated the Exclusion Act. See *Annual Report, 1924* (USINS), pp. 29-30. In 1930, the campaign for the repeal of the Oriental exclusion acts by a number of business and religious groups proved abortive. A bill to extend quotas to the Asian countries, introduced by Representative Charles Kramer of California in 1934, was not enacted. See Robert A. Divine, *American Immigration Policy*, p. 147.

62. "Repeal of the Chinese Exclusion Act," *Hearings before the House Committee on Immigration and Naturalization*, Seventy-eighth Congress, 1st session (Washington, D. C.: U. S. Government Printing Office, 1943), pp. 142-67.

63. *Ibid.*, p. 206.

64. The action of the House Committee prompted the *New York Times* editorial on June 13, 1943, urging the Committee to reconsider the decision. The editorial expressed the fear that a majority of the Committee seemed to be standing where Congress had stood sixty-one years before. "They may not believe that the Chinese are an inferior race, but they act as though they did."

65. *Congressional Record* (October 21, 1943), p. 8626.

Chapter 5

1. Frank L. Auerbach, *Immigration Laws of the United States* (Indianapolis: Bobbs-Merrill Co., 1955), pp. 60-64.

2. Robert A. Divine, *American Immigration Policy, 1924-1952* (New Haven: Yale University Press, 1957), p. 152. Mr. Divine quoted Representative Ed Gosset of Texas as stating that the bill was a war measure, not an immigration one.

3. The McCarran-Walter Bill was introduced in 1950, based on a study of the then existing immigration policy and the Com-

mittee recommendation, and submitted on the judiciary's recommendation to the Senate on April 20, 1950, in Report 1515 entitled "The Immigration and Naturalization Systems of the United States."

4. It is beyond our scope to discuss the pros and cons of the act. For factual data as to the law's actual impact on the individual alien and on his family, the reader is referred to an interesting study made by the Council for American Unity under the direction of Miss Edith Lowenstein. See her *The Alien and the Immigration Law: A Study of 1446 Cases Arising under the Immigration and Naturalization Laws of the United States* (New York: Oceana Publications, 1958).

5. The American Coalition is a combination of various groups with about twenty more kindred societies.

6. *Congressional Record* (May 21, 1952), pp. 5623-24; (June 27, 1952), p. 8254.

7. See p. 119.

8. The exact numbers are: 295 for 1946, 685 for 1947, 548 for 1948, and 1,429 for 1949. *Senate Report 1515,* Table 9, p. 892.

9. *Ibid.,* p. 469.

10. Sections 244 (a) (2)—(a) (5) are still available under specified conditions.

11. The filing of an application for adjustment of status under Section 245 automatically terminated the alien's nonimmigrant status. The ruling that caused loss of status was repealed by Public Law 85-700 (1958).

12. The Immigration Service revealed that fifty-two Chinese obtained the status of permanent residents through the application of the suspension of deportation in 1949, thirty-seven in 1950, fifty-two in 1951, fifty-eight in 1952, and forty-nine in 1953. Between 1954 and 1958, 2,650 persons born in China, including Taiwan, adjusted their status under Section 6 of the Refugee Relief Act of 1953. In 1959, 1,319 in addition adjusted their status, among whom 127 were under the Refugee Relief Act.

13. The exact number is twenty-two in 1947, twenty-five in 1948, and forty-four in 1949.

14. The Act of June 16, 1950, extended the expiration period to June 30, 1951, and its application to war orphans and German expellees and refugees to July 1, 1952. The Act of June 28, 1951, again amended the Act by extending its operation to December 31, 1951.

15. The number of approvals under the country of China was 10 by 1949; it became 35 by 1950, 748 by 1951, 881 by 1952, 882 by 1953, and 909 by 1954. Most of the Chinese applicants who had their status adjusted as permanent residents had been admitted as stu-

dents, visitors, or seamen. The Immigration Service has not released specific information on those Chinese whose applications
were denied, except that, based on the statistics released, out of
the 11,610 applications of displaced persons in the United States
filed before June 16, 1952, 2,481 applications were denied, among
which 864 cases were "not unable to return to country of birth, residence, or nationality; no apparent persecution due to race, religion,
or political opinion"; and 830 cases were "not a lawful entry under
Section 3 or Section 4 (e) of the Immigration Act of 1924." United
States Immigration and Naturalization Service, *Annual Report, 1954,*
pp. 27-28.

16. The Displaced Persons Act of 1948, together with its liberal
amendment in 1950, has been instrumental in solving at least part
of the problem of the resettlement of European displaced persons.
But with the continuous stream of refugees and escapees from the
Communist nations and the overpopulation difficulty created in West
Germany and Italy, the whole problem evidently could not be solved
alone through the Immigration Act of 1952. President Truman, as
early as March 24, 1950, asked Congress to admit 300,000 people
from western Europe as nonquota immigrants. Congress did not
act until President Eisenhower had sponsored a similar program
in 1953. In the course of deliberation, the Senate passed an amendment submitted by Senator McCarran to allot not more than 2,000
visas to refugees of Chinese ethnic origin, but the measure had
trouble in the House Judiciary Committee. When the bill was presented to the Committee, it included among the 240,000 prospective
immigrants small quotas of 2,000 Arabs, 1,000 Japanese, and 2,000
Chinese from Hong Kong. Representative Emanuel Celler, Democrat
of New York, objected to the admission of these Orientals. He maintained that this emergency bill was originally fashioned to take care
of European refugees, and that the inclusion of Arabs would offend
the Israel Republic. On Representative Walter Judd's amendment
to include European refugees who were in Hong Kong temporarily,
Celler withdrew his objection. The bill as passed by the House provided 2,000 visas for nationals of Japan, Arab refugees, Chinese
and European refugees in Hong Kong. The bill as finally agreed to
by the conferees dropped the Japanese and added Far Eastern (Asian)
refugees. It also permitted 5,000 refugee aliens in the United States
to adjust their status. See *Congressional Record* (July 28, 1953),
pp. 10108-109, 10724-725.

17. "Seventh Semi-Annual Report of the Administrator of The
Refugee Relief Act of 1953 as Amended," *Interpreter Releases,*
XXXIV, No. 9 (Feb. 27, 1957), 40-44. A total of 188,917 refugees
were admitted. See also *Annual Report, 1958-59* (USINS).

18. The actual number admitted by June 30, 1957 (1955-57), was

888. *Annual Report, 1957* (USINS), p. 22.

19. Of the 3,608 immigrant aliens who were admitted under the Refugee Relief Act of 1953 and who adjusted their status while in the United States, 2,777 were persons who came from China, including some born in China but not necessarily Chinese. *Annual Report, 1958-59* (USINS).

20. The exact number is for (a) German expellees, 2,500; (b) Dutch refugees, 1,600; (c) other persons escaping persecution, 14,556.

21. The act has been interpreted to include those refugees who have already come to the United States, but not many have been able to qualify because of the condition laid down.

22. A total of 2,986 immigrants from China, including Taiwan, were admitted under P. L. 85-316 (to June 30, 1959). This number includes 395 who adjusted their status while in the United States. *Annual Report, 1958-59* (USINS).

23. "The Act of September 11, 1957 to Amend the Immigration and Nationality Act and For Other Purposes," *Interpreter Releases,* XXXIV, No. 37, 38 (September 17, 23, 1957), 250-64.

24. As reported to the Department of State on May 1, 1959. See "Congress Enacts Bill Benefiting Certain Relatives of United States Citizens and Lawful Resident Aliens," *Interpreter Releases,* XXXVI, No. 32 (September 21, 1959), 240.

25. Between 1953 and 1959 out of 14,989 cases of alien exclusions, the Mexicans had about 46.3 per cent, whereas the Canadians had 24.1 per cent.

26. A majority of the seamen came from Canton and Ningpo, the latter being a port of the Chekiang province, which had been occupied by the Japanese early in the war.

27. *Annual Report, 1953* (USINS), p. 13.

28. *Ibid., 1960,* Table 28, p. 62.

29. Act of June 30, 1950, amended under the McCarran-Walter Act, Section 402.

30. After the repeal of the Chinese Exclusion Act, the first Chinese was naturalized on January 18, 1944, and 500 applications were sent in at the end of March, 1944.

31. A person of good moral character who has resided lawfully for five years in the United States may apply for naturalization. He must be able to sign his name, be attached to the principles of the Constitution, be able to answer questions about the history and the government. Most persons must also speak, read, and write at least simple English. Anyone, however, who was over fifty on December 24, 1952, and had lived in this country at least twenty years does not have to read, write, or speak the language.

32. The Immigration Service has revealed that between 1954 and 1959, 1,027 certificates of derivative citizenship were granted to persons born in China. *Annual Report, 1958-59* (USINS).

33. The Immigration Service no longer collected statistics on emigration after the fiscal year 1958. The period under review is, therefore, between 1944 and 1958.

34. The number of emigrants is for the period between 1949 and 1958 only.

Chapter 6

1. A private bill is a bill for the relief of one or several speci-fied persons, corporations, institutions, etc. It differs from a public bill, which relates to public matters and deals with individuals only by classes. See Clarence A. Berdahl, "The President's Veto of Private Bills," *Political Science Quarterly*, LII, No. 4 (December, 1937), 507. The practice in the British Parliament, however, is that the private bills deal with the powers and problems of local government. Local authorities may seek specific Parliamentary au-thority by promoting a private bill in Parliament. This private act will apply only to the local authority to which it refers and not to all authorities alike. In considering the merits of a private bill, which is promoted from outside, the Parliament is in a way per-forming a judicial function, and acts as a sort of referee before whom the promoters and the opponents of the bill in question are presenting the case. See Sidney D. Bailey, *British Parliamentary Democracy* (Boston: Houghton Mifflin Co., 1958), pp. 105-6, 248.

2. United States Immigration and Naturalization Service, *Annual Report, 1956,* Table 50, p. 118. The close of each Congress usually finds about 50 per cent (some 2,000) of the introduced bills still pending. Approximately two-thirds of such bills have been reintro-duced in the following Congress. *Annual Report, 1958* (USINS), p. 6.

3. George B. Galloway, "Reform of Private Bill Procedure," *Congressional Record* (Appendix, May 12, 1949), p. A2901.

4. The first private bill to be enacted was signed by President George Washington, September 24, 1789, to enable Baron de Glar-beck to collect his salary as captain in the Revolutionary Army from March 9, 1781, to August 24, 1782. Since then a great many claim bills have been introduced, but a very small percentage of them were enacted. Examples are varied; some are rather odd. One authorized a comptroller-general to relieve a certain postmaster of the necessity of refunding to the United States the sum of $400; a lieutenant in the army was granted his claim against the govern-ment for the loss of his household goods by fire while he was on duty; Mrs. Lim Shee-Chang received damages for injuries as a

result of having been struck in Honolulu by an army truck; private law No. 90 authorized the waiver of the statute of limitations, so that the Compensation Commission might have the power to consider Margaret J. Pow's claim on account of the death of her husband.

5. The Fifty-ninth Congress (1905-07) reached the high mark, enacting 6,248 private laws, or 90 per cent of the total legislative output of that particular Congress. From the Seventy-sixth Congress to the Seventy-ninth the proportion of private laws to total laws enacted rose from 39 per cent to 55 per cent. As a result of the partial ban on the introduction of four categories of private legislation by the Legislative Reorganization Act of 1946, the load of private bills introduced in both houses was reduced from 55 per cent in the Seventy-ninth Congress to 34 per cent in the Eightieth. The claim bill used to take most of the time of the Congressmen. Thus, of private legislation introduced in the Eightieth Congress, private claim bills occupied over half of the load, immigration bills about a third, and land bills a little less than 10 per cent; military and naval and private pensions accounted for the rest. Galloway, "Reform of Private Bill Procedure," *Congressional Record* (Appendix, May 12, 1949), pp. A 2901-2.

6. There is no definite rule by which Congress will accord relief to a certain individual or individuals by the enactment of a private immigration bill. Those who are already in the United States stand a better chance to obtain relief than those prospective immigrants who are still in a foreign country. There are several classes of cases, on which Congress has often agreed to waive obstacles of the existing legislation to enable a private bill to be enacted. The largest of these classes concerns aliens whose services are urgently needed and who will benefit the United States. Scientists and engineers are good examples. The second major class involves the preservation of family ties. The ideal of maintaining family unity to avoid permanent separation and hardship has been amply evidenced by a great number of private immigration bills enacted. Another class involves aliens whose deportation may invoke extreme hardship because of old age or illness. For those aliens seeking to enter the United States as immigrants, Congress is usually willing to give special consideration to cases involving adopted children and fiancées, and to waive bars to entry on grounds of health and of crimes involving moral turpitude, a vague term. Private immigration bills also restore rights to persons deprived of citizenship for voting in a foreign country, or they give relief to former naturalized citizens who stayed abroad. See "Private Bills and Immigration Law," *Harvard Law Review*, LXIX, No. 6 (April, 1956), 1083-91.

7. Upon checking the Congressional Record of the Eighty-fifth

Congress, it was found that during its first session, twenty-three private laws involving thirty-five Chinese persons were passed through the Senate, whereas only one private bill concerning one person passed the House. During the second session, the House again enacted only one private law affecting one person, and the Senate passed fifteen bills involving seventeen persons. The *Annual Report, 1960* (USINS), began to release the number of beneficiaries of private laws enacted during the Eighty-sixth Congress, by country or region of birth. A total of fifty-two Chinese persons obtained relief from these laws. Among these fifty-two, forty-five were granted permanent resident status and five were conferred with citizenship benefits. The *Annual Report* did not mention the number of private laws involved. We may say that beginning with the Seventy-eighth Congress, about 288 Chinese persons were permitted to stay in the United States permanently, due to the enactment of approximately 214 private bills by Congress; among those, ten Chinese persons may have been granted citizenship benefits.

8. To facilitate further research, the 133 private laws enacted in each Congress are listed in the Appendix, Table XIV.

9. For instance, a private bill was signed by former President Eisenhower on August 28, 1954, enabling Dr. Liang Nun Wang, resident physician at Shore Memorial Hospital, Shore Point, to become a United States citizen. The bill provided the waiving of the regulation requiring that Dr. Wang return to China and apply for re-entry to this country under the immigration quota. It also lifted the quota to allow entry into the United States of Mrs. Wang and a minor daughter.

10. An alien seeking relief from the Immigration Act may request a member of Congress directly, or indirectly through relatives or friends, to introduce an act. Usually, if the case is considered sufficiently meritorious and beyond the application of the present immigration laws or of other administrative relief, a member of Congress will introduce the bill. It is then referred to the Judiciary Committee of the Senate or of the House. The subcommittee of both houses dealing exclusively with immigration matters bears the brunt of the work and its approval or denial seals the fate of the bill. The passage of a private bill requires a total of twenty-eight steps. For a study of how an individual bill is introduced and the procedure involved, see S. K. Bailey and H. D. Samuel, *Congress at Work* (New York: Henry Holt and Co., 1952), pp. 155-65.

When a bill seeking relief from deportation is introduced in Congress, the Congressman sponsoring the private bill may request from the Immigration Service a postponement of deportation pending the action by Congress. It was the customary practice of the Immi-

gration Service to withhold admininistrative action pending the legislative disposal of the bill, once a request for such action had been
received from the Judiciary Committee of one or both houses. This
policy has been subject to frequent abuse, for a deportable alien
will try to have a bill introduced into Congress after Congress, so
that he may stay in this country indefinitely, since even though a
bill "dies" at adjournment, there is no definite rule preventing its
reintroduction in successive Congresses. We find instances covering
ten years. Ordinarily a bill would protect an alien from one to two
years, or two sessions of Congress. See *Senate Report 1515*, p.
608. The subcommittee to tighten the rules on private immigration
bills has amended rules of procedure adopted in January, 1954,by the
House Subcommittee of Immigration and Nationality. See Frank L.
Auerbach, *Immigration Laws of the United States* (Indianapolis:
Bobbs-Merrill Co., Inc., 1955), pp. 283-85. Supplement, 1958,
pp. 138-40.

11. "Private Laws and Immigration," *Harvard Law Review*, p.
1092.

12. The Immigration Service has this to say regarding the effect
of the renewal of the pre-examination procedure on private bills:
"In fiscal year 1956 there were 1,474 private immigration bills
introduced in Congress. During this period, 573 bills were enacted
into private laws, and 725 bills were adversely acted upon by the
House and Senate Judiciary Committee. The reinstitution of the
pre-examination made such adverse action possible in more than
500 of these cases, and obviated the necessity for countless future
bills." *Annual Report, 1956* (USINS), p. 24.

13. According to the House Judiciary Committee, Public Law 85-
316 has cut the number of private alien relief bills by 40 per cent.
See "Burden of Private Bills Studied," *Congressional Quarterly,
Weekly Report*, XVII, No. 27 (July 3, 1959), 899.

14. Resort to private bill is sometimes rather costly; for example, a Washington lawyer sought a $5,000 fee from a Long Island
woman to push through Congress a private immigration bill for her
husband to be admitted to the United States, despite an old conviction
in Italy for armed robbery. Chairman Francis E. Walter of the
House Immigration Subcommittee requested the Department of Justice to determine whether the lawyer had violated the law by failing
to register as a lobbyist. The Department cleared him, however.
The lawyer had received $2,500 as a retainer, and would receive the
additional $2,500, since Congress authorized the Department of
Justice to adjust such cases administratively. See "Lawyer for
Alien Cleared by United States," *New York Journal-American* (October 19, 1957).

15. Public Law 85-316 and recent legislation will relieve the President and Congress of some of the burden caused by private bills; but unless further discretionary power is vested in the attorney general, no marked decrease can be anticipated. *Annual Report, 1958* (USINS), p. 1.

16. Robert Luce, "Petty Business in Congress," *American Political Science Review*, CXII, No. 5 (October, 1932), 815-27.

Chapter 7

1. *Shaughnessy* v. *Pedreiro*, 349 U.S. 48, 75 S. Ct. 591, 99 L. Ed. 868 (1955); *Brownell* v. *Shung*, 352 U.S. 180, 77 Sup. Ct. 252, 1 L. Ed. 2d 225 (1956). United States Constitution, Article 1, Section 9, Clause 2; *Mao* v. *Brownell*, 207 F.2d 142 (C.A.D.C. 1953).

2. In the case of aliens ordered to be excluded from the United States, the Supreme Court in a unanimous decision against the government made December 17, 1956, held that the "alien must weigh for himself his choice of the form of action he wishes to use in challenging his habeas corpus proceedings as well as by an action under Administrative Procedure Act." *New York Times* (December 18, 1956).

3. Charles Gordon and Harry N. Rosenfield, *Immigration Law and Procedure* (Albany, New York: Banks and Company, 1959), pp. 531-34.

4. Milton R. Konvitz, *The Alien and the Asiatic in American Law* (Ithaca, New York: Cornell University Press, 1946), p. 77.

5. *Ibid.*, p. 51.

6. *Ibid.*

7. According to Professor Milton R. Konvitz, "The Supreme Court has since 1911, in the various decisions affecting Chinese claiming citizenship, stated that the executive hearing on the question of the claim of American citizenship must be a fair hearing; that the administrative decision will be conclusive unless it appears that the claimant was denied an opportunity to establish his citizenship at a fair hearing, or that the officers acted in an unlawful or improper way, or that they had abused their discretion." Cases involved are *Quon Quon Poy* v. *Johnson*, 273 U.S. 352 (1926); *Kwock Jan Fat* v. *White*, 253 U.S. 454 (1920); *Tang Tun* v. *Edsell*, 223 U.S. 673 (1911); *ibid.*, p. 43.

8. *Yep Suey Ning* v. *Berkshire*, 73 F.2d 745 (C.C.A. Cal. 1934).

9. Under the Immigration Act of 1952, there are five categories of aliens that are eligible for suspension of deportation; and if the attorney general finds that the alien meets the requirements he may use his discretion and submit the case to Congress for approval.

See Frank L. Auerbach, *Immigration Law of the United States*, pp. 253-56.

10. United States Immigration and Naturalization Service, *Annual Report, 1950,* p. 7; *New York Times* (February 22, 1950).

11. The Immigration Service has for some years handled more and more immigration cases from a humanitarian point of view. Such changes in procedure, and the decision to abandon Ellis Island, for years considered by aliens as a black place of detention, regardless of whether persons entered legally or illegally, are worth mentioning. The greater care in issuing documentation and the extended use of the parole system have to a greater degree made detention unnecessary.

12. The board also acquires jurisdiction by certification to the board of a decision at the request of the Immigration Service or the board itself.

13. Decision made January 31, 1956. *Interpreter Releases,* XXXIII, No. 39 (September 28, 1956), 324.

14. Decision made by the board on August 25, 1955, and by the attorney general on October 18, 1955. *Ibid.,* pp. 324-25.

15. A Supreme Court decision allowing a district director of the Immigration Service to be named as defendant in any suits by which aliens may challenge the validity of a deportation order, may alleviate the concentration of suits in the District of Columbia, as suits may be brought at the place where the district director's office is located. *Annual Report, 1955* (USINS), p. 21.

16. For full text of former President Eisenhower's immigration message, see *New York Times* (February 1, 1957).

17. *Annual Report, 1952* (USINS), p. 41. In April, 1948, a Miami flight instructor was arrested for making five flights from Cuba to Chicago, Philadelphia, and New York, bringing in nineteen Chinese and four Europeans, from whom he received from $600 to $1,500 each. Twelve Chinese were arrested. See *New York Times* (April 16, 17, 1948).

18. Both before and since the repeal of the Chinese Exclusion Act, the Immigration Service has been concerned about those who claim to be native born, and consequently have rights as citizens of the United States. The Service has worried about the possible desertion of Chinese crewmen, ever since the attorney general ruled that Chinese seamen may be lawfully landed in the United States when they are seamen from United States vessels; they are not sure whether minor children of the merchant class were really the true sons or daughters of the exempt class, or whether those claiming student status were possibly laborers in disguise.

19. *Annual Report, 1925* (USINS), pp. 22-23.

20. Timothy J. Molloy, "A Century of Chinese Immigration: A Brief Review," *Monthly Review, U. S. Immigration and Naturalization Service*, V, No. 6 (December, 1947), 73.

21. As the result of the War Brides Act, passed December 28, 1945, facilitating the entry of alien wives, husbands, and children of citizen members of the armed forces, 9,965 alien wives of Chinese-Americans, mostly war brides, entered the United States between 1946 and 1953.

22. The Immigration Service has for a number of years compiled sizable records of all Chinese who claimed derivative citizenship. These records have the use of cross-reference, since one applicant's statement may be checked with another many years later.

23. *New York Times* (April 8, 1957).

24. In 1954 a Chinese civic leader and former president of the chamber of commerce in San Francisco was sentenced for obtaining false visas for thirty-five Chinese in 1950. *New York Times* (February 16, 1954).

25. Subpoenas served required twenty-four family organizations, seven district societies, and nine other Chinatown groups to turn in all their records. See "Application of Certain Chinese Family B. & D. Associations," 19 F. R. D. 97; *San Francisco Chronicle* (March 3, 1956).

26. *Ibid*. (March 21, 22, 1956).

27. The *San Francisco Chronicle*, in its editorial March 23, 1956, entitled "Chinatown Wins Victory For All," stated that the Chinese Six Companies, representing the twenty-four family associations of Chinatown, have fought this issue through to a victory that is a vindication of the rights of all Americans. "The only thing any American believing in the Bill of Rights is opposed to is the attempted exercise of arbitrary, sweeping powers of subpoena in such a way as to lay the whole Chinese-American community under suspicion of guilt and to violate the privacy of family records having every warrant to remain private." The editorial concluded with the statement that in enforcing the law the government must stay within the law.

28. "Department of State Appropriations For 1959," *Hearings Before the Subcommittee of the Committee on Appropriations, House of Representatives, Eighly-fifth Congress, Second Session* (Washington, D. C.: Government Printing Office, 1958), p. 176. In 1949, the State Department became aware that bribery was being practiced at the American consul general's office in Hong Kong. The investigation resulted in the indictment of a foreign service officer by a grand jury and a sentence of six years in a federal penitentiary. The officer in question received bribes totaling over

$10,000, and some seventy fraudulent visas were issued. *Ibid.*, pp. 179-80.

29. *Annual Report, 1958* (USINS), p. 16.

30. On the drive to overcome the Chinese fraud problem, the Immigration Service in 1957 said:

"Through the medium of publicity reaching Chinese they have been made aware that, even though they are here illegally, they may have, through military service or the establishment of other equities, become eligible for naturalization or discretionary relief from deportation. In many cases Chinese persons illegally in the United States who have long feared deportation or prosecution now make full disclosures knowing the Service will assist them to adjust their status if at all possible under the law. These disclosures have enabled the Service to close many fraudulent slots." *Annual Report, 1957* (USINS), p. 13.

The Immigration Service seems to be well satisfied with the operation of the so-called "Chinese confession program" and its success in thwarting the illegal entry of Chinese aliens into the United States. Under the "confession program," 2,433 Chinese have admitted being in this country illegally, resulting in the closing of 2,077 slots. The result of this program is significant in that the roots of the "paper" family trees bearing possible untold numbers of future generations of fictitious American citizens, at least to that number, will be closed off once and for all. See *Department of Justice Press Release* dated December 27, 1959, covering the year-end report to the attorney general by the commissioner of the Immigration and Naturalization Service, Washington, D. C.

31. "Sniping by West Vexes Hong Kong," *New York Times* (April 1, 1956).

32. Timothy J. Molloy, "A Century of Chinese Immigration: A Brief Review," *Monthly Review, U. S. Immigration and Naturalization Service*, V, No. 6 (December, 1947), 74.

33. About Chinese fraudulent practices the *Monthly Review, U. S. Immigration and Naturalization Service* has the following to say:

"In all fairness to the Chinese, it should be stressed that cases involving fraud are confined almost wholly to a relatively small group of foreign-born Chinese claimants to United States citizenship. As high-minded Chinese persons, through organization of veterans, civic associations, and otherwise, continue to direct their attention to solving the problem presented by those cases, irregular practice eventually may be reduced to a minimum. The great majority of Chinese persons in their dealings with the Immigration and Naturalization Service have conducted themselves in a manner that bears out the excellent reputation for truthfulness and probity enjoyed by the Chinese people in the United States." *Ibid.*, p. 75.

34. U. S. District Court, Southern District, New York, August 31, 1954, (123 F. Supp. 674). See *Race Relations Law Reporter*, I, No. 1 (February, 1956), 225-27.

35. It is probable that the blood test was applied only to the Chinese race before 1955, regardless of the fact that other documents were available.

36. *United States* ex rel. *Lee Kum Hoy, Lee Kum Cherk, and Lee Moon Wah, Petitioners*, v. *John L. Murff*, district director of the Immigration and Naturalization Service, 355 U. S. –, 2 L Ed. 2d 177, 78 Sup. Ct. – (No. 32), decided December 9, 1957.

37. *United States* ex rel. *Lee Kum Hoy et al.* v. *Shaughnessy*, U. S. Court of Appeals, Second Circuit, September 25, 1956 (237 F.2d 307).

38. In a unanimous decision that rejected the federal government's practice of deporting anyone without the prior consent of a foreign government, the Court of Appeals in Washington, D. C. held December 30, 1958, that the United States might not deport Chinese to the mainland of China, since this country does not recognize the Communist regime. Unless reversed by the Supreme Court, all deportations to Communist China will be suspended. The case involved Alfred Dodge Lu, who came to this country in 1948 and failed to maintain his student status. *Rogers* v. *Lu*, 262 F.2d 471 (1958). See also *New York Times* (December 31, 1958).

39. In 1903 the attorney general ruled that Chinese seamen who work in a United States vessel and are sworn before a United States shipping commissioner may lawfully land in the United States under specific conditions. See *Annual Report, 1903* (USINS), p. 105.

40. *Annual Report, 1931* (USINS), p. 31.

41. For years the annual quota assigned to Great Britain and Northern Ireland has been 65,361, whereas the actual immigrants admitted are considerably fewer every year. Thus between 1951 and 1958, immigrants admitted from Great Britain were averaging only about 22,650 yearly. *Annual Report, 1955-58* (USINS), Table 7.

42. See Chap. 5, pp. 124, 126.

43. *Annual Report, 1954* (USINS), p. 8.

44. In December, 1956, lawyers representing ten Chinese urged Mr. Herbert Brownell, the attorney general, to aid these Chinese by paroling those whom the lawyers admitted to be excludable because of false claims of United States citizenship or other illegal entry, as he had paroled the Hungarians. The lawyers further asserted that the attorney general's failure to act on their applications for a stay of deportation to Communist China was tantamount to ignoring a federal court decision. The Federal Court of Appeals

for the District of Columbia in a 1954 decision ruled that if an alien found to be excludable was not deported at once, the attorney general must act on a request for a stay of deportation on the ground that the deportee would be mistreated or liable to persecution if forced to return to his homeland. *Lim Fong* v. F *rownell*, 215 F.2d 683 (1954). See also *New York Times* (December 28, 1956). The Federal Court of Appeals ruled June 27, 1957, that the attorney general possessed the necessary discretionary power to withhold the deportation of paroled aliens, if sending them back to another country would subject them to physical persecution. The case involved five Chinese who sued to compel the attorney general to grant them the right to stay instead of sending them to Hong Kong, as they insisted that deportation to Hong Kong was in fact deporting them to Communist China. *Quan* v. *Brownell*, 248 F.2d 89 (1957). See also *New York Times* (June 28, 1957). There have been many rulings since 1957 on the question of deportation to such countries as Nationalist and Red China; see Charles Gordon and Harry N. Rosenfield, *Immigration Law and Procedure* (Albany, New York: Banks and Company, 1959), pp. 604-6.

45. *United States* ex. rel. *Chen Ping Zee* v. *Shaughnessy*, 107 F. Supp. 607, 608 S. D. N. Y. (1952).

46. In the fiscal year of 1955, of the 503 applications under Section 243 (h) received by the Service, only 48 were granted, while 240 were denied. *Annual Report, 1955* (USINS), p. 18.

47. As many as 10,967 cases were pending as unexecuted orders of deportation at the end of the fiscal year of 1955. *Ibid.*, p. 20.

48. The District Court for the Southern District of New York held that the confidential information could not be used as a basis for denial of the application for change of status under the 1953 Refugee Relief Act *(Chao* v. *Shaughnessy*, September 30, 1955); but in another case involving a voluntary member of the Communist party for several years, the Supreme Court ruled that the use of confidential information in considering application for suspension of deportation be sustained *(Jay* v. *Boyd.*, U. S. L. Week, 4335 opinion, 503).

49. "Chinese Students in the United States, 1948-55," *Committee on Educational Interchange Policy* (New York, March, 1956), p. 14. The result of losing status was repeated by P. L. 85-700.

50. *New York Times* (December 23, 1956).

51. See "Staying Deportation to Yugoslavia Because of Physical Persecution," *Interpreter Releases*, XXXV, No. 22 (June 18, 1958) 161-64.

Although the attorney general may withhold deportation when "in his opinion" an alien would be subject to physical persecution if he were deported, six Chinese in this country on parole lost their deportation fight. The Chinese said they feared physical persecution if sent back to Communist China. The attorney general contended that an excluded alien admitted on parole was not an alien "within the United States" and that Section 243 (h) of the 1952 Immigration and Nationality Act applied only to aliens ordered expelled and not to exclusions. In the Supreme Court this decision was sustained by a 5-4 vote in deciding two cases involving the same issue. The majority held that the attorney general may not defer the deportation of six Chinese aliens, who came to this country from 1949 to 1954, having been temporarily admitted on parole awaiting exclusion proceedings. *Rogers* v. *Quan*, 78 Sup. Ct. 1076 (1958).

Chapter 8

1. L. L. Thurstone, "The Measurement of Change in Social Attitude," *The Journal of Social Psychology,* II, No. 2 (May, 1931), 230-35.

2. Emory S. Bogardus, *Immigration and Race Attitudes* (Boston: D. C. Heath and Co., 1928), pp. 13-28.

3. J. P. Guilford, "Racial Preferences of a Thousand American University Students," *Journal of Social Psychology,* II, No. 2 (May, 1931), 204.

4. Eugene L. Hartley, *Problems in Prejudice* (New York: King's Crown Press, 1946), pp. 4-18, 24.

5. As a matter of fact, in a revised Bogardus "scale of social distance" made in 1953 the ranking of Greeks, Turks, Chinese, and Hindus was higher, while the ranking of Russians, Japanese, and Negroes was much lower. See E. Terry Prothro and Otha King Miles, "Social Distance in the Deep South as Measured by a Revised Bogardus Scale," *Journal of Social Psychology,* XXXVII, 2nd half (May, 1953), 171-74.

6. Richard T. LaPiere, "Attitudes vs. Actions," *Social Forces,* XIII, No. 2 (December, 1934), 230-37.

7. E. Franklin Frazier, *Race and Culture Contacts in the Modern World* (New York: Alfred A. Knopf, 1957), p. 276.

8. Robert M. MacIver, *The More Perfect Union* (New York: Macmillan Co., 1948), pp. 25-26. According to Dr. Davis McEntire, research director to the Commission on Race and Housing, some 27 million Americans still suffer to some extent from housing discrimination, including 19 million Negroes, Japanese, Chinese, and Filipinos, 2.5 million Mexican-Americans, one million Puerto Ricans, and five million Jews. See Davis McEntire, *Residence and Race* (Berkeley and Los Angeles: University of California Press, 1960), p. 2.

9. Perhaps another reason for America's dislike of the Turks was that the Turks at the turn of the century and for many years after persecuted the Armenians, who were Christians; therefore Christian America sympathized with Christian Armenia.

10. George Eaton Simpson and J. Milton Yinger, *Racial and Cultural Minorities* (New York: Harper and Brothers, 1953), pp. 184-86.

11. Yet in 1955 an Iowa cemetery refused to allow an American Indian to be buried in a lot previously purchased, on the ground that the wording of the contract permitted burial only of members of the Caucasian race. See *Race Relations Law Reporter*, I, No. 1 (February, 1956), 15-20.

12. *New York Times* (February 17, 19, 1952).

13. *Ibid.*, (July 9, 1959).

14. The American Legion and the 40 et 8 Society have been arguing for years over the latter's rule limiting membership to white persons. Finally the Legion cut its public ties with the society on December 4, 1959. See "Legion Ousts 40 et 8 Over Racial Stand," *New York Times* (December 5, 1959).

15. Nathan Glazer and Davis McEntire (eds.), *Studies in Housing and Minority Groups* (Berkeley and Los Angeles: University of California Press, 1960), p. 195.

16. Prior to 1954 the Supreme Court had on many occasions tested the legality of the separate-but-equal doctrine of public education involving Negroes. One case, however, in Mississippi involved a Chinese girl, Martha Lum, born in the United States. She had sought admission to a white school, but the authorities in the high school district in which she lived directed her to attend a Negro high school. Her father at once made application for a writ of mandamus against the school trustees and the state superintendent of education to have his daughter admitted to a school limited to white children. The Supreme Court of Mississippi reversed the judgment and awarded the writ, but the Supreme Court of the United States in a unanimous decision affirmed it on a writ of error. Chief Justice Taft held that the complaint lacked evidence and that there was no Negro high school in the district that the child could attend. Since the law of Mississippi required a separation of students into white and all other races, and since the Chinese can be classified as colored, there is not a denial of equal protection. The court, therefore, stated that school segregation by race is at the discretion of the state, and in no way conflicts with the Fourteenth Amendment. See *Gung Lum* v. *Rice,* 275 U. S. 78 (1927).

17. 1947 is the year when the President's Committee on Civil Rights published its famous report and made recommendations for

change. Liston Pope, *The Kingdom Beyond Caste* (New York: Friendship Press, 1957), p. 16.

18. *New York Times* (Oct. 23, 1955).

19. In January, 1957, Dr. Frank C. J. McGurk, associate professor of psychology at Villanova University, stated flatly that, as measured by psychological test performance, Negroes as a group do not possess as much capacity for education as do whites. See "Experts Dispute White Supremacy," *New York Times* (January 20, 1957).

20. Otto Klineberg, *Race and Psychology* (UNESCO Publication No. 842) (Paris, 1951), pp. 37-38.

21. Lin Yu, "Twin Loyalties in Siam," *Pacific Affairs,* IX, No. 2 (June, 1936), 191-200.

22. As to how an active and successful Chinese-American should best integrate in the American community, one group declares rather determinedly that those born in this country should think of themselves as Americans. In order to achieve this goal one must first remove the psychological barrier of thinking oneself Chinese. Thus by this argument one may eliminate the fight against prejudice and gain legal, economic, and social equality as a fully accepted citizen. The other group is also in favor of full participation in American community life, while arguing that it would be foolish to overthrow the Chinese tradition and thereby forego the benefits of a double tradition. There is no means of determining which method of assimilation is followed in the Chinese communities of this country. However, it has been generally acknowledged that the Chinese in Hawaii and on the West Coast have a better record of assimilation than do the Chinese in the eastern United States.

Chapter 9

1. See Chap. 11, pp. 250-51.

2. "Stanford University Report," as quoted by Yamato Ichihashi, *Japanese in the United States* (Stanford: Stanford University Press, 1932), p. 357.

3. The information on requiring citizenship as a qualification for admission to the bar was furnished by the American Bar Association. In the case of physicians, the reader is referred to the data (pertinent as of 1958) published by the Council on Medical Education and Hospitals, state board of the *Journal of the American Medical Association,* CLXX, No. 5 (May 30, 1959), 593.

4. For a list of occupations restricted by states see Milton B. Konvitz, *The Alien and the Asiatic in American Law* (Ithaca, New York: Cornell University Press, 1946), pp. 190-211.

5. Until after World War II, organized labor did not accept Chi-

nese as members of labor unions. This alone accounts for the retardation of the progress of skilled and semiskilled Chinese labor in American industry. See Rose Hum Lee, "The Hua-Ch'iao in the United States of America," in *Colloquium on Overseas Chinese* (New York: Institute of Pacific Relations, 1958), p. 37.

6. Louis H. Chu, The Chinese Restaurant in New York City (unpublished master's thesis, New York University, 1939).

7. The Board of Supervisors issued eighty licenses, and all but one were to whites; 200 Chinese were denied licenses. Yick Wo operated his laundry without a license; he and 150 other Chinese were arrested on the ground of violation of the ordinance. The court declared unconstitutional the city ordinance whereby the San Francisco Board of Supervisors refused to grant permits to Chinese, since only buildings constructed of brick or stone might be used for laundries. Justice Matthews went on to say: "Though the law itself be fair on its face and impartial in appearance, yet if it is applied and administered by public authority with an evil eye and an unequal hand, so as practically to make unjust and illegal discriminations between persons in similar circumstances, material to their rights, the denial of equal justice is still within the prohibition."

8. *U. S. Census 1870,* Vol. I, listed Chinese and Japanese launderers and laundresses in the United States as 3,653; in California, 2,899. Only fifty-three Japanese were reported by the 1870 census.

9. The annual volume of business of some of the biggest wet-wash establishments is about half a million dollars.

10. Beulah Ong Kwoh, "The Occupational Status of American-born Chinese Male College Graduates," *American Journal of Sociology,* LIII, No. 3 (November, 1947), 192-93.

11. Howard A. Rusk, "Foreign Physicians," *New York Times* (July 22, 1956); *ibid.* (June 8, 1960).

12. According to the available statistics, there are sixty-four Chinese on the faculties of twenty-one medical schools, of whom forty-two are professors or instructors, and thirteen do research work or act as residents in college hospitals. In addition, there are five doctors of dental surgery, and ten teachers in pharmacology. See *Directory of Chinese Faculty Members of American Colleges and Universities, 1959-1960* (Publication of the Embassy of the Republic of China [Washington, D. C., 1960]).

13. *Ibid.* A total of 304 engineers are on the engineering faculties: forty-six in civil engineering; ninety-two in electrical engineering; seventy-two in mechanical engineering; and ninety-four in other branches of engineering. Of the 344 scientists on the faculties of American colleges, 107 are chemists, sixty-one are math-

ematicians, and seventy-two physicists, including two Nobel prize winners.

14. The scarcity of engineers prompted the General Electric Company to advertise in 1956 for recruitment of noncitizen engineers.

15. "Alien Attorney Faces Curbs Here," *New York Times* (March 13, 1957).

16. Out of 20,926 Chinese students in American colleges between 1854 and 1953, only 266, or 1.3 per cent, took law. Of the nine Chinese with law degrees who are teaching in American colleges, only four are actually teaching legal subjects; one has something to do with a legislative reference bureau; the remaining four are teaching subjects other than law.

17. Pon Gordon Gee of San Francisco, general agent for the Western Life Insurance Company for eighteen years, is included in the 1958 *Who's Who in the West.* He has more than $20,000,000 worth of insurance on his books.

18. *A Survey of Chinese Students in American Universities and Colleges in the Past One Hundred Years* (Joint Publication of National Tsing Hua University Research Fund and China Institute in America [New York, 1954]), p. 58.

19. Of those sixty-two teachers in the Chinese language and cultural subjects, thirteen are well-known scholars who had full professorships in eleven American colleges and universities. The University of Washington and the University of California have on their faculties two each. They are Dr. Fang-Kuei Li, professor of Chinese linguistics and of anthropology; Dr. Vincent Yu-Chung Shih, professor of Chinese literature; Dr. Kenneth K. S. Chen, professor of Far Eastern languages and Buddhism; and Dr. Shih-Hsiang Chew, professor of Chinese literature. The other colleges have one professor of Chinese each: Dr. Shau-Wing Chan of Stanford, Dr. Wing-Tsit Chan of Dartmouth, Dr. Shou Yi Chen of Pomona, Dr. You-Kuang Chu of Skidmore, Dr. George Kennedy of Yale, Dr. Yi Pao Mei of Iowa State, Dr. P. K. Mok of Occidental, Dr. Chi-Chen Wang of Columbia, and Dr. Lien-Sheng Yang of Harvard. Dr. Paul K. T. Sih, director of the newly established Institute of Asian Studies at St. John's University, former director of the Far Eastern Institute at Seton Hall University, is a scholar and a devout Catholic, the author of the recent outstanding work, *Decision for China: Communism vs. Christianity* (1959). Dr. Wu-chi Liu is director of the Chinese Language and Area Center at the University of Pittsburgh, one of thirteen such centers throughout this country established by the Office of Education of the United States federal government.

Mr. C. S. K'wei, a well-known journalist and a scholar in the Chinese language, has developed a phototypesetter for Chinese, making the typesetting of Chinese characters comparatively easy. In addition, there is the renowned lecturer on Chinese culture and civilization, Dr. P. W. Kuo, formerly president of Southeastern University, Nanking, China.

20. Including twenty as chairmen of the department or as directors.

21. As a matter of fact, during the 1950's the Chinese in America began to show an interest in participating in industry, often cooperating with American businessmen. All the companies were necessarily small. The Lantex Industries, Inc., of Farmingdale, New York, was established in 1955; its products consist of plastic tubing and plastic molding. The net worth amounted to $142,000, as of April, 1959. Founded in 1959, the Foilcraft Printing Corporation, West Hempstead, New York, manufacturer of foil printing, label, and box wrapping for special orders, had a net worth of over $350,000 at the end of 1958. Another recent concern, the Tang Industries, Inc., a Massachusetts corporation organized in May, 1959, with an initial capital of about $100,000, aims to engage in the business of developing, manufacturing, processing, and distributing semiconductor materials, semiconductor devices, and other electronic and electrical products. The president of the company is Hsuing Yuan Tang, formerly an industrialist of Shanghai, China. Though not yet engaged in commercial production as of December, 1959, having made only sample orders, the company had arranged with a New York brokerage house to underwrite the offering of 110,000 shares of common stock to the public at three dollars each. The stock is being traded through the over-the-counter securities.

One of the interesting developments in the investment field is the organization of General Business Investment Corporation in Washington, D.C., by a group of American and Chinese businessmen. Its capitalization is $300,000, half of which will be supplied by the Small Business Administration, which is following the Congressional policy of pumping financial aid into small businesses. The principal Chinese officer is T. L. Tsui, acting as president, and Tuh-yueh Lee, vice chairman, formerly counselor of the Chinese embassy and the manager of the Bank of China, New York, respectively.

Chapter 10

1. The song, composed by Jean Schwartz, is considered one of the old-time favorites. Gertrude Lawrence sang it in *Andre Charlot's Review*, in which Beatrice Lillie was also starred.

2. Andrew W. Lind, *Hawaii's People* (Honolulu: University of Hawaii Press, 1955), p. 54.

3. *Ibid.*, pp. 57-59.

4. Each of these places has a Chinatown: Arizona—Tucson; California—Fresno, Los Angeles, Oakland, Sacramento, San Francisco; District of Columbia; Hawaii—Honolulu; Illinois—Chicago; Maryland—Baltimore; Massachusetts—Boston; Michigan—Detroit; New York—New York City; Ohio—Cleveland; Pennsylvania—Philadelphia, Pittsburgh; Oregon—Portland; Texas—San Antonio; Washington—Seattle.

5. The New York Chinatown appears destined to be permanent, since a part of Chatham Square—the spot where Doyers, Mott, and Worth Streets meet East Broadway, Park Row, and the Bowery—was renamed officially by the New York City government as Kimlau Square, on June 7, 1959, in honor of a Chinese-American pilot killed in World War II. Lieutenant Benjamin Ralph Kimlau was born in Concord, Massachusetts, in 1918, but was reared and educated in the New York Chinatown. He was shot down over New Guinea in an air battle on March 5, 1944. *New York Times* (June 8, 1959).

6. In the Denver riot, October 31, 1880, Chinatown was totally destroyed. The Chinese rebuilt Hop Alley, as it was called, and in 1890, of the 1,447 Chinese in Colorado, 600 lived in Hop Alley. Then the tong war started. By 1910 the residents were only 227; in 1920, 212; in 1930, 154; in 1940, 110. In 1950 they increased to 242; but the number is insufficient to warrant the renewal of another Chinatown in Denver. See Patrick K. Ourada, "The Chinese in Colorado," *Colorado Magazine*, XXIX, No. 4 (October, 1952), 273-84.

7. Rose Hum Lee, "The Decline of Chinatowns in the United States," *American Journal of Sociology*, LIV, No. 5 (March, 1949), 424.

8. Mary Roberts Coolidge, *Chinese Immigration* (New York: Henry Holt and Co., 1909), p. 441.

9. Otis Gibson, *The Chinese in America* (Cincinnati: Hitchcock and Walden, 1877), pp. 63, 92.

10. In 1885 San Francisco established the first and only school for Chinese. See Coolidge, *Chinese Immigration*, p. 78.

11. Mike Berger, "New York Chinatown," *Fiftieth Anniversary* (New York: Chinese Chamber of Commerce, 1957), pp. 28-34.

12. *New York Times* (June 15, 1950).

13. One of the latest buildings completed in Chicago's Chinatown is that of the Chinese Benevolent Association; it dedicated its new $300,000 center on October 8, 1958. The structure is air-conditioned and its auditorium seats 500.

14. Edwin R. Bingham, The Saga of the Los Angeles Chinese (unpublished master's thesis, Occidental College, 1942), p. 129.

15. The family sometimes includes distant relatives who are too young or too old to support themselves, who have no one else to support them.

16. See discussion led by Professor L. K. Hsu in *Colloquium on Overseas Chinese* (New York: Institute of Pacific Relations, 1958), p. 67.

17. See Chapter 11, p. 232.

18. Pardee Lowe is the author of the book, *Father and Glorious Descendant,* while Jade Snow Wong has written *Fifth Chinese Daughter*.

19. See Chapter 11, p. 232. Eddie's father wishes his son to marry a Chinese girl in Hong Kong.

20. Rhoads Murphey, "Boston's Chinatown," *Economic Geography,* XXVIII, No. 3 (July, 1952), 252. There are more than 1,000 women workers in eighteen Chinese sportswear and garment factories in New York City's Chinatown.

21. For years there had been annual Chinatown beauty contests to choose a Miss Chinatown for San Francisco, for New York, and for other cities; but 1958 was the first year in which a "Miss Chinatown, U.S.A." was selected. Sponsored by the Chinese Chamber of Commerce and other organizations of San Francisco, the contest took place immediately before the week-long Chinese Lunar New Year celebrations. A Chinese-American girl, June Gong, a senior at the University of New Hampshire, won the title. The coronation was held in San Francisco on the evening of February 21, 1958. Among her many other gifts was a scholarship for the study of culture in the Far East, from the Jee Tuck Sam Tuck Association in San Francisco, a family society to which the Gong family belongs. See "Co-ed Chosen First Miss Chinatown U.S.A.," *The Asian Student* (March 4, 1958).

22. John H. Burma, "Research Note on the Measurement of Interracial Marriage," *American Journal of Sociology,* LVII, No. 6 (May, 1952), 587-89. Mr. Burma made a study of 1,000 marriage licenses issued to mixed couples of white and nonwhite races between November 1, 1948 and April 30, 1951, in Los Angeles County. He found some 7.6 per cent involving Chinese males, 3.9 per cent females, tabulated thus:

Chinese-Anglo: 54
Anglo-Chinese: 34
Chinese-Mexican: 22
Mexican-Chinese: 5

As a matter of fact, out of the 78,266 licenses issued during the same period, 445, or 56 per 10,000 marriages, were for white and non-white–just a little over 0.5 per cent. From 1924 to 1933 there were only ninety-seven Chinese marriages in Los Angeles, seventy-four of which were not interracial. One Chinese woman married a Filipino, fourteen Chinese married Japanese women; five married Negro women; one married a white woman; two married brown women. Nearly 2,000 Chinese, however, between the ages of fifteen and forty-four, lived in Los Angeles in 1930. This low rate of intermarriage may be partly accounted for by the Chinese preference for returning to China to be married. At that time Chinese wives of American-born Chinese were not allowed admission to the United States (1924-33). See Constantine Panunzio, "Intermarriage in Los Angeles, 1924-33," *American Journal of Sociology*, XLVII, No. 5 (March, 1942), 697-98.

23. Shepard Schwartz, "Mate-Selection Among New York City's Chinese Males, 1931-38," *American Journal of Sociology*, LVI, No. 6 (May, 1951), 564. Of the 254 marriages, there were none between Chinese females and non-Chinese males.

24. The number of Chinese males per 100 females in New York were in 1900, 4949.3; in 1910, 2,519.9; in 1920, 947.6; in 1930, 851.3; in 1940, 602.7; and in 1950, 280.9.

25. Of these 254 marriages, Chinese grooms with white brides numbered fifty-three; Chinese grooms with Negro brides numbered fifteen. Of the white brides, twenty-one married restaurant workers, eight married laundry owners or workers, eighteen married merchants, and two married men not gainfully employed; of the Negro brides, eight married restaurant workers, five married laundry workers. See Shepard Schwartz, "Mate-Selection Among . . . Chinese Males," p. 567. About 60 per cent of the married Chinese in Great Britain are married to Englishwomen, many of whom are themselves the offspring of Anglo-Chinese unions, a situation which causes few family objections. See Maurice Broady, "The Chinese in Great Britain," in *Colloquium on Overseas Chinese* (New York: Institute of Pacific Relations, 1958), p. 33.

26. George Eaton Simpson and J. Milton Yinger, *Racial and Cultural Minorities* (New York: Harper and Brothers, 1953), p. 586.

27. *Race Relations Law Reporter*, I, No. 1 (February, 1956), 221.

28. *Ibid.*, p. 42.

29. Professor Lind has compiled the percentage of Chinese out-marriages between 1912 and 1953 as follows:

	1912-16	1920-30	1930-40	1940-50	1950-53
Grooms	41.7	24.8	28.0	31.2	41.0
Brides	5.7	15.7	28.5	38.0	42.5

See Lind, *Hawaii's People*, pp. 103-4.

30. With the overthrow of the Ming dynasty (1368-1644) by the Manchus in 1644, a number of Chinese fled to Southeast Asia. Secret societies were soon formed, with the avowed purpose of overthrowing the Manchus and restoring the Ming emperor; but as time passed and as undesirables penetrated, the quality of these societies deteriorated. Activities turned against the existing colonial governments. Resisting the attacks of law-enforcement police and assisting members to escape justice were the chief functions of the society in Penang, Singapore, and in many places in the Netherlands East Indies. In 1817 the British became aware of conditions; in 1825 a paper was read before the Royal Asiatic Society entitled "Some Account of a Secret Society, the Triad." Both the British and the Dutch colonial governments passed strenuous laws against such societies. At the end of the Taiping Rebellion many rebels fled abroad, and those societies flourished in consequence. In 1912, on the eve of the overthrow of the Manchus, many of those societies had been reorganized and had become mutual aid societies. Meanwhile, they contributed heavily in money and in men to the ultimate downfall of the Manchu dynasty.

31. In addition to the Chinese-American Citizens Alliance, other oriental organizations, such as the Japanese-American Citizens League, the Filipino Federation of America, and the Korean National Association, have endorsed the principle of racial quotas and have rejected the proposals for complete equality of treatment as ill-advised, impractical, and not in the best interests of persons of Asian ancestry. They are afraid that opening wide to oriental immigration would threaten to revive the now dead anti-orientalism of the West Coast. See *Congressional Record* (April 23, 1952), p. 4316; (May 21, 1952), p. 5624.

32. In San Francisco, the Six Companies, or the Chinese Consolidated Benevolent Association, acts as the representative of all Chinese associations. In addition there are forty-seven family associations, forty-four major district associations, twenty-two school or alumni associations, nineteen churches and temples, twenty-one recreational groups, thirteen trade guilds, ten fraternal organizations, five political organizations, and the Chinese Chamber of Commerce. The Chinese community has also a hospital and three cemeteries.

33. Eight of the largest Chinese Consolidated Benevolent Associa-

tions, namely, San Francisco, New York, Los Angeles, the New England States (Boston), Chicago, Seattle, Washington, D.C., and Philadelphia, advertised in a quarter page in the *New York Times* on December 16, 1956, "A Declaration by Chinese Communities in the United States of America concerning Nehru." A similar quarter-page advertisement was inserted also in the *New York Times* on September 17, 1959, entitled "Joint Declaration of Americans of Chinese Descent and Chinese Residents in the United States in Regard to Khruschev's Visit." Twelve Chinese Consolidated Benevolent Associations in the United States and the National Chinese Welfare Council were the sponsors.

34. According to a study made by Tin-Yuke Char, there are thirty-seven immigrant Chinese societies in Hawaii, excluding political and miscellaneous ones, which may be listed as follows:

1. Representative		
	United Chinese Society	1
2. Regional		
	Hsien or district	14
3. Dialectal		
	See Yup Society	1
	Yi Yee Tong	1
	Tsung Tsin Society	1
4. Family clan		6
5. Trade or occupational		10
6. Fraternal		3

The worth of properties belonging to Chinese societies is estimated at about two million dollars. Mr. Char's observation is that "the younger generation challenges the negative attitude of a segregational community. The immigrant societies should rightfully belong to a colorful past, having served their true needs." See his "Immigrant Chinese Societies in Hawaii," *Sixty-first Annual Report of the Hawaiian Historical Society* (Honolulu: Advertiser Publishing Co., 1953), pp. 29-32.

35. To the Chinese, the Chinese Consolidated Benevolent Association and the Chinese Six Companies are exactly the same organization. In fact, the term Six Companies was bestowed on the organization by Americans probably because of its convenience in reading or remembering. In reality the proper name should be the Seven Companies.

36. The names that appeared then were On Leong Tong and Hip Sing Tong.

37. On Leong held its fifty-sixth convention in 1960, and Hip Sing its forty-second.

38. Dr. Chi-Pao Cheng, who for many years served as Director, Special Cultural Projects, has helped to enable the Institute to go ahead in the cultural field.

39. In addition, the Institute administers the C. T. Loo Chinese Educational Fund Fellowships, which are awarded annually to Chinese students specializing in the studies of medicine, public health, or engineering in the United States. The 1959-60 awards went to ten Chinese students, eight men and two women. Among the recipients, two are to study medicine and the remainder engineering subjects. For a while the Institute published a monthly magazine in both Chinese and English, and a Chinese Student Directory of Chinese professors in American colleges, but reduced resources compelled the Institute to discontinue those publications. A timely and valuable publication of the Institute, in cooperation with Tsing Hua College, is entitled *One Hundred Years of Chinese Students in America* (New York, 1954). The Institute also has a branch in Taiwan.

Chapter 11.

1. Quoted by Mary Roberts Coolidge, *Chinese Immigration* (New York: Henry Holt and Co., 1909), p. 22.

2. The same situation was true in the construction of the Canadian Pacific during the early 1880's. See Charles J. Woodsworth, *Canada and the Orient* (Toronto: Macmillan Co. of Canada, 1941), pp. 26-36.

3. Carey McWilliams has stated, "Few ethnic groups have made a more important contribution to the culture of California than the Chinese; yet today one can see no visible evidence of this contribution, with the exception of Chinatown itself." See his *Brothers Under the Skin* (Boston: Little Brown and Co., 1951), p. 112.

4. Coolidge, *Chinese Immigration*, p. 449.

5. H. L. Mencken, *The American Language* (4th ed. ; New York: Alfred A. Knopf, 1946), p. 162.

6. Eddie Gong, "I Want to Marry an American Girl," *The American Magazine*, CLX, No. 3 (September, 1955), 15-17.

7. Edward Goon was a research assistant in the Department of Metallurgical Engineering (1951-53), and received his Ph.D. in chemistry in 1954.

8. *New York Herald-Tribune* (April 8, 1952).

9. "China and the Chinese" were lectures delivered by Herbert A. Giles, LL.D., in March, 1902, at Columbia University, to inaugurate the foundation by General Carpenter of the Dean Lung

Chair of Chinese. General Carpenter had contributed altogether
$200,000.

10. The program consisted of (a) the suppression of the opium
plantations in China; (b) the establishment of a national banking
system; (c) the building of a railroad between Tientsin and Chinkiang
(150 miles up the Yangtze from Shanghai), a total distance of about
500 miles.

11. The reform leaders had succeeded in bringing the young Emperor Kwangsu under their influence, and the result was a rapid
succession of reform edicts in June, 1898; but these lasted only about
one hundred days on account of the opposition generated by the conservative parties throughout the country, among them being the
Empress Dowager, who placed the Emperor under house arrest and
resumed the reins of government by *coup d'état* in September, 1898.

12. In addition to Mr. Fong's being elected as senator, Daniel
K. Inouye was elected to the House of Representatives, the first
person of Japanese ancestry to hold such an office. He was re-
elected in 1960. The first congressman of Asian origin was Representative D. S. Saund of Westmorland, California, elected to the
House in 1956 and again in 1958 and in 1960. Mr. Saund was born
in Ramistar, India. In Canada, the first Canadian-born Chinese to
be elected as a member of Parliament was Douglas Jung, who won
the election in 1957 and was elected again in 1958. The only other
Chinese-American ever elected to a state legislature was Wing F.
Ong, a state senator in Arizona.

13. Dr. Chen-Ning Yang voiced the common view of Chinese scientists in America when he accepted the Nobel Prize in Physics:
"I am proud of my Chinese heritage and background, as I am devoted
to modern science—a part of human civilization of Western origin
to which I have dedicated and shall continue to dedicate my work."

14. A wartime emergency institution composed of Tsing Hua College, Nankai University, and Peking University, during the Sino-
Japanese War.

15. Dr. Wu became the first woman to receive Princeton University's honorary degree of Doctor of Science, June 17, 1958. She
is a professor of physics at Columbia.

16. The Academia Sinica is a research institute established by the
Nationalist Government of China. Dr. Hu Shih, the well-known Chinese philosopher, has been its president since April, 1958. The
other three Chinese elected were Dr. Y. H. Ku (see p. 243), Dr.
Chia-Liu Yuan (p. 239), and Dr. Hsu-Chiun Fan, a professor of
physics at Purdue University.

17. The mysterious pineal gland philosophers once thought to be
"the seat of the soul," is another research area in which the iso-

lation of hormones was made by a team of five researchers from Yale University School of Medicine, including one Chinese doctor, Teh H. Lee. See "Isolation of Melatonin, the Pineal Gland Factor that Lightens Melanocytes," *Journal of the American Chemical Society*, LXXX, No. 10 (May 20, 1958), 2587.

18. Each whale gland yields about 100 milligrams of hormone, fifty times as much as a human gland yields. Even larger quantities of hormone would come from the blue whale, which might yield glands weighing up to fifty times that of the humpback whale.

In 1959 Dr. Li was granted $38,964 by the American Cancer Society for the third year of a five-year study of pituitary growth hormones.

19. *The Asian Student* (October 29, 1959).

20. "Charles Perelle's Spacemanship," *Fortune* magazine, LIX, No. 1 (January, 1959), 114, 122.

21. Professor Ku is the author of *Analysis and Control of Nonlinear Systems* (1958) and *Electric Energy Conversion* (1959), both published by Ronald Press Company.

22. His latest publication is *Electron Tube Life Factors*, ed. Craig Walsh and T. C. Tsao (Elizabeth, N. J.: Engineering Publishers, by special arrangement with McGraw-Hill Book Co., 1960).

23. Dr. Kuh's textbook on network theory, entitled *Principles of Circuit Synthesis*, was published by McGraw-Hill Book Company in 1959.

24. He is coauthor of a book entitled *Transistor Circuit Engineering* (1957), the first book in the field to supply quantitative design information.

25. *Princeton Alumni Weekly*, LV, No. 23 (New Jersey, April 22, 1955), 18.

26. Nationally known for his research and for his technological writings in aeroelasticity; aircraft structures, plates, and shells; and compressible flow, was Dr. Chi-teh Wang, who received his doctorate in science from M.I.T. in 1944. The author of a textbook, *Theory of Aeroelasticity*, he died in 1955 at the age of thirty-seven while he was professor of aeronautical engineering in New York University and carrying on research for the Air Force into the problems of aerodynamic "flutter," one of the possible causes of jet engine failure.

27. *Scientific American*, CLXL, No. 1 (July, 1958), 25-32.

28. Frederick Gutheim, *One Hundred Years of Architecture in America, 1857-1957: Celebrating of Centennial of the American Institute of Architecture* (New York: Reinhold Publishing Co., 1957), p. 93. Mr. Pei studied at the Massachusetts Institute of Technology and then at the Harvard Graduate School of Design, where in 1946

he received his master's degree in architecture. The American Institute of Architects awarded him its First Honor Award in 1959 for the Zeckendorf Plaza development in Denver and its Award of Merit for the Mile High Center, also in Denver.

29. The award was made on March 15, 1957. Professor Chin's research project was entitled "International Competition in Cotton Textiles."

30. Dr. Tsai received in 1959 a research grant of $59,626 for three years, from the National Institutes of Health, to seek comparative studies on the increase of the applicability of laboratory animals in the testing of drugs.

31. The American Council of Learned Societies is a private nonprofit federation of thirty professional societies in the humanities and social sciences. Through these constituent societies the A. C. L. S. represents approximately 75,000 scholars.

32. Aside from private acquisitions, Dong Kingman's work is said to be owned by galleries or colleges in thirty-three American cities and by the State Department in Washington. See Alan D. Gruskin, *The Water Colors of Dong Kingman* (New York: Thomas Y. Crowell Co., 1958).

33. Anna May Wong died of a heart attack on February 3, 1961. she was eulogized as one of the most unforgettable figures of Hollywood's great days—the nineteen-twenties and thirties. Her last movie, *Portrait in Black,* was with Lana Turner and Anthony Quinn.

34. "Watch especially for those photographed by that amazing Chinese genius, James Wong Howe. He has made motion picture photography a great art." See Aaron Sussman, *The Amateur Photographer's Handbook* (5th ed. ; New York: Thomas Y. Crowell Co., 1958), p. 203.

35. Joe Shoong, one of the wealthiest Chinese in the United States, was a philanthropist who helped deserving individuals and institutions alike. He contributed generously to hospitals and organizations, such as the Chinese Hospital in San Francisco and the Oakland Chinese Community Center; to education, such as the Chung Hwa School in San Francisco, the Joe Shoong School in Lodi; to say nothing of all his other works not made known. A Joe Shoong Fellowship has been set up at the University of California, yielding $1,400, and is open to American-born students of Chinese descent. There is also a Joe Shoong Foundation of scholarships for worthy students. Believing in the good works of Christianity, he helped Chinese Christian churches. However, not wishing publicity, much of his philanthropy was unheralded, even after his death on April 13, 1961. *The Chinese American Times,* VII, No. 5, May, 1961.

36. The Li Foundation was incorporated by Mr. K. C. Li in 1944.

The purpose of the foundation has been to provide a limited number of fellowships to promising young students desirous of working in the United States for advanced degrees. The fellowships, not limited to Chinese students, are valued at $5,000, plus transportation to and from the United States.

Chapter 12
1. See chap. 11, p. 234.
2. "Faulkner Chides U. S. on Education," *New York Times* (March 8, 1958).
3. The annual quota assigned for Asia was 2,990 between 1948 and 1960, except for the year 1958, which was 3,090. Because of the increasing quota assignment to a number of Asiatic countries since the passage of the 1952 Act, the demand for admittance was somewhat higher. Altogether 3,286 quota numbers were used for the year 1954, or 296 more than was allotted. However, between 1955 and 1960 the quota numbers actually used were again fewer than assigned, ranging from 2,042 (1956) to 2,653 (1955) or averaging 2,214 a year.

Bibliography

Source Material, United States Government Publications

Bureau of Narcotics
Traffic in Opium and Other Dangerous Drugs. Annual, 1941-59.
Bureau of Prisons
Federal Prisons. Annual, 1930-60.
Bureau of the Census
Census of Population, 1860 (eighth census) to 1950 (seventeenth census).
Census of Population, 1960, Advance Reports, General Population Characteristics.
Characteristics of the Nonwhite Population by Race, 1940.
Chinese and Japanese in the United States, 1910.
Nonwhite Population by Race, 1950.
Statistical Abstract of the United States, Annual, 1950-60.
Federal Bureau of Investigation
Uniform Crime Reports for the United States. Quarterly, semiannual, and annual bulletins, 1934-60.
Immigration and Naturalization Service
Annual Report:
Commissioner General of Immigration, 1897-1932.
Commissioner of Immigration to the Secretary of Labor, 1933-40.
Special Assistant in Charge of the Immigration and Naturalization Service to the Attorney General, 1941-42.
Commissioner of Immigration and Naturalization to the Attorney General, 1943-60.
I and N Reporter (formerly Monthly Review, 1943-52). Quarterly.
Report of the Immigration Commission (in forty-one volumes with first two volumes as abstract), 1911.
Public Health Service, National Office of Vital Statistics
Vital Statistics of the United States. Annual, 1937-58.
Congressional Record, Hearings, Documents, and Reports*

---

*Beginning in 1853, Congress has taken an interest in various aspects of Chinese immigration problems. The *Congressional Record, Congressional*

36th Congress, 1st session, 1859-60:
House Executive Document 88, "Correspondence on Chinese Coolie Trade."
37th Congress, 2nd session, 1861-62:
House Executive Document 16, "Correspondence on Asiatic Coolie Trade."
42nd Congress, 2nd session, 1871-72:
House Miscellaneous Document 120, "Resolutions of California Legislature on Burlingame Treaty."
42nd Congress, 3rd session, 1872-73:
House Miscellaneous Document 81, "Pennsylvania Petition against Chinese Laborers."
43rd Congress, 1st session, 1873-74:
House Miscellaneous Document 204, "Resolutions of California Legislature on Chinese Immigration."
44th Congress, 2nd session, 1876-77:
Senate Report 689, "Joint Special Committee on Chinese."
45th Congress, 1st session, 1877:
House Miscellaneous Document 9, "Address of California Senate."
45th Congress, 2nd session, 1877-78:
House Report 240, "Chinese Immigration."
45th Congress, 3rd session, 1878-79:
House Executive Document 102, "Veto of Chinese Immigration Bill."
House Report 62, "Chinese Immigration."
House Report 111, "Chinese Immigration."
46th Congress, 2nd session, 1879-80:
House Executive Document 70, "Diplomatic Correspondence on Chinese Immigration."
House Miscellaneous Document 5, "Depression in Business and Chinese Immigration."
47th Congress, 1st session, 1881-82:
Senate Executive Document 175, "Instruction to United States Minister in China."
House Report 67, "Chinese Immigration."
House Report 1017, "Chinese Immigration."
49th Congress, 1st session, 1885-86:
Senate Executive Document 103, "Fraudulent Importation of Chinese."
Senate Miscellaneous Document 107, "Memorial of California Anti-Chinese Convention, 1886."
House Report 2043, "In Relation to Chinese Restriction."
50th Congress, 1st session, 1887-88:
Senate Miscellaneous Document 90, "Statistics of Arrivals and Departures, San Francisco."

Globe, and *Congressional Documents* had published a great number of hearings and reports up to the 59th Congress, 1st session, when the Permanent Chinese Exclusion Act had already been enforced for about two years. After 1906, Congress showed less interest in the Chinese in the United States until the bills for repealing the Chinese Exclusion Act were introduced, while the world war was still going on.

51st Congress, 1st session, 1889-90:
    Senate Executive Document 41, "Execution of Exclusion Laws."
    Senate Executive Document 97, "Arrivals of Chinese."
    Senate Executive Document 106, "Chinese in Transit."
    House Report 486, "Enumeration of Chinese."
    House Report 2915, "Restriction of Chinese Immigration."
52nd Congress, 1st session, 1891-92:
    House Executive Document 244, "Execution of Exclusion Laws."
    House Report 255, "Need of New Exclusion Legislation."
    House Report 407, "Exclusion of Chinese." Minority Report.
53rd Congress, 1st session, 1893:
    Senate Executive Document 13, "Cost of Enforcing Chinese Exclusion
    Law."
    House Executive Documents 9 and 10, "Enforcement of Geary Law, 1893."
    House Report 70, "Need of Amending Chinese Exclusion Law."
53rd Congress, 2nd session, 1893-94:
    Senate Executive Document 111, "Appropriation for Enforcement of Ex-
    clusion Law."
    House Executive Document 152, "Chinese Registration."
54th Congress, 1st session 1895-96:
    House Document 372, "Amendment of Exclusion Law."
55th Congress, 1st session, 1897:
    Senate Document 120, "Alleged Illegal Entry of Chinese."
    House Document 68, "Chinese for Omaha Exposition."
55th Congress, 3rd session, 1898-99:
    Senate Report 1654, "Extension of Immigration Laws to Hawaiian Islands."
56th Congress, 2nd session, 1900-01:
    House Documents 471 and 472, "To Strengthen Exclusion Laws."
    House Report 2503, "To Prevent Smuggling of Chinese."
57th Congress, 1st session, 1901-02:
    Senate Document 106, "Arguments against Exclusion."
    Senate Document 137, "Some Reasons for Chinese Exclusion."
    Senate Documents 162 and 164, "Wu Ting-fang on Chinese Exclusion."
    Senate Document 191, "For the Re-enactment of the Chinese Exclusion
    Law; California Memorial."
    Senate Document 254, "Chinese on American Vessels."
    Senate Document 281, "Chinese on American Vessels."
    Senate Document 291, "Laws, etc., Relating to Chinese Exclusion."
    Senate Document 292, "Petition for Exclusion of Japanese and Chinese."
    Senate Document 300, "Regulations Relating to Chinese Exclusion."

The record of Congressional transactions, and particularly the *Congressional Record,* with its complete account of all speeches and votes by the legislators, is probably the most important source for the study of immigration policy, including that in regard to the Chinese. The *Hearings* and *Reports* are also significant sources; the former reveal the interests that show pros and cons of each measure, while the latter explain the nature and objective of the proposed bills.

Senate Document 304, "Exclusion of Chinese Laborers."
Senate Document 776, "Chinese Exclusion: Hearings before Committee on Immigration."
House Report 1231, "Chinese Exclusion."
59th Congress, 1st session, 1905-06:
House Document 847, "Enforcement of Chinese Exclusion Laws."
65th Congress, 2nd session, 1918:
Hearing before House Committee on Immigration and Naturalization, January 17, 1918, "Relative to Chinese Immigration into Hawaii."
67th Congress, 1st session, 1921-22:
Hearing before House Committee on Immigration and Naturalization, November 8, 1921, "Registration of Chinese Refugees."
Hearing before House Subcommittee on Immigration and Naturalization, January 24, 1922, "Inquiry into Activities of Charles F. Hille with Relation to Certain Chinese Refugees."
68th Congress, 1st session, 1924:
House Report 350, "Restriction of Immigration."
70th Congress, 1st session, 1928:
Hearing before House Committee on Immigration and Naturalization, February 7, 1928, "Wives of American Citizens of Oriental Race."
71st Congress, 2nd session. 1929-30:
House Report 1565, "To Admit to United States Chinese Wives of Certain American Citizens."
74th Congress, 1st session, 1935:
House Report 7170, "To Permit Certain Resident Oriental Veterans in Armed Forces of United States during the World War to Apply for Citizenship."
78th Congress, 1st session, 1943:
Hearings before the House Committee on Immigration and Naturalization, May 19, 20, 26, 27, June 2, 3, "Repeal of the Chinese Exclusion Acts."
House Report 732, "Repealing the Chinese Exclusion Laws."
81st Congress, 1st session, 1949:
House Report 65, "To Make Immigration Quotas Available to Asian and Pacific Peoples."
81st Congress, 2nd session, 1950:
Senate Report 1515, "The Immigration and Naturalization Systems of the United States."
House Report 1507, "Displaced Persons in Europe and Their Resettlement in the United States."
House Report 2187, "Amending Displaced Persons Act of 1948."
82nd Congress, 2nd session, 1952:
House Report 1365, "Revising the Laws Relating to Immigration, Naturalization and Nationality."
Senate Report 1137, "Revision of Immigration and Nationality Laws."
83rd Congress, 1st session, 1953:
House Report 1069, "Refugee Relief Bill of 1953."
83rd Congress, 2nd session, 1954:
House Report 1323, "Amending the Refugee Relief Act."
Senate Report 2045, "Amending the Refugee Relief Act of 1953."

85th Congress, 1st session, 1957:
Senate Report 1057, "Public Law 316, Certain Revisions of Immigration and Naturalization Laws."
85th Congress, 2nd session, 1958:
House Report 13451, "To Amend Section 245 of Immigration and Nationality Act, Relating to the Admission of Aliens."
86th Congress, 1st session, 1959:
Senate Report 475, "Amending Section 4 and Section 6 of the Act of September 11, 1957."
House Report 398, "Amending Sections 353 and 354 of the Immigration and Nationality Act."
House Report 291, "Amending Section 6 of the Act of September 11, 1957."
House Report 582, "Providing for the Entry of Certain Relatives of U. S. Citizens and Lawfully Resident Aliens."

Books, Articles, and Miscellaneous

ABBOTT, EDITH. *Historical Aspects of the Immigration Problem: Select Documents*. Chicago: University of Chicago Press, 1926.

"The Act of September 11, 1957 to Amend the Immigration and Nationality Act, and for Other Purposes," *Interpreter Releases*, XXXIV, No. 37, 38 (September 17, 23, 1957), 250-64.

ADAMS, ROMANZO. *The Peoples of Hawaii*. New York: Institute of Pacific Relations, 1933.

ALLEN, G. C., and AUDREY G. DONNITHORNE. *Western Enterprise in Indonesia and Malaya*. New York: The Macmillan Co., 1957.

ANDRACKI, STANISLAW. The Immigration of Orientals into Canada, with Special Reference to Chinese. Unpublished Ph. D. dissertation, McGill University, 1958.

AUERBACH, FRANK L. *Immigration Laws of the United States*. Indianapolis: The Bobbs-Merrill Company, Inc., 1955, and *Supplement*, 1958.

BAILEY, S. K., and H. D. SAMUEL. *Congress at Work*. New York: Henry Holt and Co., Inc., 1952.

BAILEY, SYDNEY D. *British Parliamentary Democracy*. Boston: Houghton Mifflin Co., 1958.

BANCROFT, HUBERT HOWE. *History of California. (The Works of Hubert Howe Bancroft*, Vols. XVIII-XXIV.) 7 vols. San Francisco: The History Co., and A. L. Bancroft Co., 1883-90.

BARNETT, MILTON L. Alcohol and Culture: A Study of Drinking in a Chinese American Community. Unpublished Ph. D. dissertation, Cornell University, 1952.

BEACH, WALTER G. *Oriental Crime in California*. Stanford: Stanford University Press, 1932.

BEALE, HOWARD K. *Theodore Roosevelt and the Rise of America to World Power*. Baltimore: The Johns Hopkins Press, 1956.

BERDAHL, CLARENCE A. "The President's Veto of Private Bills," *Political Science Quarterly*, LII, No. 4 (December, 1937), 505-31.

BERGER, MIKE. "New York Chinatown," *Fiftieth Anniversary*. New York: Chinese Chamber of Commerce, 1957.

BERNARD, WILLIAM S. (ed.). *American Immigration Policy: A Reappraisal*. New York: Harper & Brothers, 1950.

BINGHAM, EDWIN R. The Saga of the Los Angeles Chinese. Unpublished master's thesis, Occidental College, 1942.

BOEKE, J. H. *The Evolution of the Netherlands Indies Economy*. New York: Institute of Pacific Relations, 1946.

BOGARDUS, E. S. *Immigration and Race Attitudes*. Boston: D. C. Heath & Company, 1928.

BOWERS, D. F. (ed.). *Foreign Influences in American Life*. Princeton: Princeton University Press, 1944.

BOXER, C. R. "Notes on the Chinese Abroad in the Late Ming and Early Manchu Periods Compiled From Contemporary European Sources (1500-1750)," *Tien Hsia Monthly*, IX, No. 5 (August-December, 1939), 447-68.

BRISCOE, EDWARD EUGENE. "Pershing's Chinese Refugees in Texas." *The Southwestern Historical Quarterly*, LXII, No. 4 (April, 1959), 467-88.

BROMLEY, ISAAC HILL. *The Chinese Massacre at Rock Springs, Wyoming Territory, September 2, 1885*. Boston: Franklin Press; Rand, Avery and Co., 1886.

BROWN, F. J. and J. S. ROUCEK (eds.). *One America: The History, Contributions, and Present Problems of Our Racial and National Minorities*. 3rd ed. Englewood Cliffs, N. J.: Prentice-Hall, Inc., 1952.

"Burden of Private Bills Studies," *Congressional Quarterly Weekly Report*, XVII, No. 27, 899.

BURMA, JOHN H. "Research Note on the Measurement of Inter-Racial Marriage," *American Journal of Sociology*, XLVII, No. 6 (March, 1952), 587-89.

BURROWS, EDWIN G. *Hawaiian Americans*. New Haven: Yale University Press, 1940.

CALLIS, HELMUT G. *Foreign Capital in Southeast Asia*. New York: Institute of Pacific Relations, 1942.

CAMPBELL, PERSIA CRAWFORD. *Chinese Coolie Emigration to Countries Within the British Empire*. London: P. S. King and Son, 1923.

CARTER, HUGH (ed.). "Reappraising Our Immigration Policy," *The Annals of the American Academy of Political and Social Science*, CCLXII (March, 1949), 1-192.

CAYTON, HORACE R. and ANNE O. LIVELY. *The Chinese in the United States and the Chinese Christian Churches*. New York: National Council of the Churches of Christ in the United States of America, 1955.

CHAR, TIN-YUKE. "Immigrant Chinese Societies in Hawaii," *Sixty-first Annual Report of the Hawaiian Historical Society*. Honolulu: Advertiser Publishing Co., 1953, pp. 29-32.

"Charles Perelle's Spacemanship," *Fortune*, LIX, No. 1 (January, 1959), 112-15, 122, 124.

CHEN, LEE-TAI. *Chung Kuo Hai Hwai Yee Ming Sze* ("History of Chinese Immigration"). Shanghai: Chung Hwa Press, 1946.

CHEN, SU-CHING. *China and Southeastern Asia*. Chungking: China Institute of Pacific Relations, 1945.

CHEN, TA. *Chinese Migrations with Special Reference to Labor Conditions*. (Bulletin of the United States Bureau of Labor Statistics, No. 340). Washington, D. C.: U. S. Government Printing Office, 1923.

————. *Emigrant Communities in South China*. New York: Institute of Pacific Relations, 1940.

CHENG, T. F. *Oriental Immigration in Canada*. Shanghai: The Commercial Press, 1931.

CHENG, TE-CHAO. Acculturation of the Chinese in the United States: A Philadelphia Study. Unpublished Ph. D. dissertation, University of Pennsylvania, 1948.

China Yearbook Editorial Board. *China Yearbook*. Taipei, Taiwan: China Publishing Co., 1958.

Chinese-American Restaurant Association of Greater New York, Inc. *Twenty-seventh Anniversary*. New York, 1960.

Chinese Chamber of Commerce. *San Francisco Chinatown on Parade in Picture and Story*. San Francisco, 1961.

Chinese Chamber of Commerce of New York, Inc. *Fiftieth Anniversary*. New York, 1957.

Chinese Immigration. (Report of the Commission Sent by China to Ascertain the Condition of Chinese Coolies in Cuba.) Shanghai: Kelly and Walsh, 1874.

Chinese Ministry of Information (ed.). *China Handbook 1937-1945*. New York: The Macmillan Co., 1947.

Chinese Students in the United States, 1948-1955. New York: Committee on Educational Interchange Policy, 1956.

CHRISTIAN, JOHN LEROY. *Modern Burma: A Survey of its Political and Economic Development*. New York: Institute of Pacific Relations, 1942.

CHU, LOUIS H. The Chinese Restaurant in New York City. Unpublished master's thesis, New York University, 1939.

CLARK, J. P. *Deportation of Aliens from the United States*. New York: Columbia University Press, 1931.

COLE, FAY-COOPER. *The Peoples of Malaysia*. New York: D. Van Nostrand Co., Inc., 1945.

COMAN, KATHERINE. *The History of Contract Labor in the Hawaiian Islands*. (Publication of the American Economic Association, 3rd series, Vol. IV, No. 3.) New York: The Macmillan Co., August, 1903.

COMMAGER, HENRY STEELE. *Documents of American History*. New York: F. S. Crofts and Co., 1940.

COMMONS, JOHN R. *Races and Immigrants in America*. New York: The Macmillan Co., 1924.

"Congress Enacts Bill Benefiting Certain Relatives of United States Citizens and Lawful Resident Aliens," *Interpreter Releases*, XXXVI, No. 32 (September 21, 1959), 235-43.

COOLIDGE, MARY ROBERTS. *Chinese Immigration*. New York: Henry Holt & Co., Inc., 1909.

CORBITT, DUVON CLOUGH. "Felipe, Oriental Friend," *The Inter-American*, V, No. 3 (March, 1946), 20-22, 39.

DAVIE, MAURICE R. *World Immigration: With Special Reference to the United States*. New York: The Macmillan Co., 1936.

————, et al. *Refugees in America*. New York: Harper & Brothers, 1947.

DENNETT, TYLER. "Seward's Far Eastern Policy," *American Historical Review*, XXVIII, No. 1 (October, 1922), 45-62.

Department of State Hearings before the Subcommittee of the Committee on

Appropriations, House of Representatives, Eighty-fifth Congress, Second Session. Washington, D. C.: U. S. Government Printing Office, 1958.

"Deportation Proceedings Decided by the Board August 2, 1955," *Interpreter Releases*, XXXIII, No. 38 (September 28, 1956), 324-25.

Directory of Chinese Members of American College and University Faculties, 1956-57. New York: Chinese Advisory Committee on Cultural Relations in America, 1957.

Directory of Chinese Members of American College and University Faculties, 1959-60. Washington, D. C.: Embassy of the Republic of China, Office of the Cultural Counselor, 1960.

DIVINE, ROBERT A. *American Immigration Policy, 1924-1952*. New Haven: Yale University Press, 1957.

Dominion Bureau of Statistics. *Canada Year Book, 1948-59*. Ottawa, Canada: Queen's Printer and Controller of Stationery, 1949 and 1960.

DORLAND, C. P. "Chinese Massacre at Los Angeles in 1871," *Annual Publications, Historical Society of Southern California*, III, Part II (1894), 22-26.

DRESSLER, ALBERT (ed.). *California Chinese Chatter*. San Francisco: A. Dressler, 1927.

DUNCAN, H. G. *Immigration and Assimilation*. Boston: D. C. Heath & Company, 1933.

DUNNING, WILLIAM. *Reconstruction, Political and Economic, 1865-1877*. New York: Harper & Brothers, 1907.

EATON, A. H. *Immigrant Gifts to American Life*. New York: Russell Sage Foundation, 1932.

EAVES, LUCILE. *A History of California Labor Legislation*. Berkeley: University of California Press, 1910.

ELEGANT, ROBERT S. *The Dragon's Seed*. New York: St. Martin's Press, Inc., 1959.

ENNIS, EDWARD J. "Some Current Problems in the Administration of Immigration Laws," *Interpreter Releases*, XXXII, No. 49 (December 12, 1955), 379-85.

FAIRBANK, JOHN KING. *The United States and China* (rev. ed.). Cambridge: Harvard University Press, 1958.

FAIRCHILD, HENRY PRATT. *The Melting-Pot Mistake*. Boston: Little, Brown & Co., 1926.

————. *Immigration, A World Movement and Its American Significance* (rev. ed.). New York: The Macmillan Co., 1933.

————. *Race and Nationality as Factors in American Life*. New York: The Ronald Press Company, 1947.

FISCHER, LOUIS. *The Story of Indonesia*. New York: Harper & Brothers, 1959.

FORBES, W. CAMERON. *The Philippine Islands*. Cambridge: Harvard University Press, 1945.

FOSTER, JOHN W. *American Diplomacy in the Orient*. Boston: Houghton Mifflin Co., 1903.

FRASER, CHARLES F. *Control of Aliens in the British Commonwealth of Nations*. London: Hogarth Press, 1940.

FRAZIER, E. FRANKLIN. *Race and Culture Contacts in the Modern World*. New York: Afred A. Knopf, Inc., 1957.

FRIED, MORTON H. (ed.). *Colloquium on Overseas Chinese.* New York: Institute of Pacific Relations, 1958.

GALLOWAY, GEORGE B. "Reform of Private Bill Procedure," *Congressional Record* (Appendix, May 12, 1949), pp. A2901-2.

GARIS, ROY L. *Immigration Restriction.* New York: The Macmillan Co., 1928.

GIBSON, OTIS. *The Chinese in America.* Cincinnati: Hitchcock and Walden, 1877.

GIBSON, WILLIAM M. *Aliens and the Law.* Chapel Hill: University of North Carolina Press, 1940.

GLAZER, NATHAN and DAVIS McENTIRE (eds.). *Housing and Minority Groups.* Berkeley and Los Angeles: University of California Press, 1960.

GLICK, CLARENCE. "Transition From Familism to Nationalism Among Chinese in Hawaii," *American Journal of Sociology,* XLIII, No. 5 (March, 1938), 734-43.

————. "The Relation Between Position and Status in the Assimilation of Chinese in Hawaii," *American Journal of Sociology,* XLVII, No. 5 (March, 1942), 667-79.

GONG, EDDIE. "I Want to Marry an American Girl," *The American Magazine,* CLX, No. 3 (September, 1955), 15-17, 82-85.

GORDON, CHARLES, and HARRY N. ROSENFIELD. *Immigration Law and Procedure.* Albany: Banks and Co., 1959.

GOTTWALDT, H. *Die Überseeische Auswanderung der Chinesen, und ihre Einwirkung auf die gelbe und weisse Rasse.* Bremen: Nossler, 1903.

GRAHAM, VIRGINIA TAYLOR. "The Intelligence of Chinese Children in San Francisco," *Journal of Comparative Psychology,* VI, No. 1 (February, 1926), 43-71.

GRISWOLD, A. WHITNEY. *The Far Eastern Policy of the United States.* New York: Harcourt, Brace & Co., 1938.

GRUSKIN, ALAN D. *The Water Colors of Dong Kingman.* New York: Thomas Y. Crowell Co., 1958.

GUILFORD, J. P. "Racial Preferences of a Thousand American University Students," *Journal of Social Psychology,* II, No. 2 (May, 1931), 179-204.

GULICK, SIDNEY L. *American Democracy and Asiatic Citizenship.* New York: Charles Scribner's Sons, 1918.

GUTHEIM, FREDERICK A. *One Hundred Years of Architecture in America, 1857-1957: Celebrating the Centennial of the American Institute of Architects.* New York: Reinhold Publishing Corp., 1957.

HALLETT, HOLT S. *A Thousand Miles on an Elephant in the Shan States.* Edinburgh and London: William Blackwood and Sons, 1890.

HAMBRO, EDUARD I. *The Problems of Chinese Refugees in Hong Kong.* Leyden: A. W. Sijthoff, 1955.

HANDLIN, OSCAR. *This Was America.* Cambridge: Harvard University Press, 1949.

————. *Uprooted: The Epic Story of the Great Migrations That Made the American People.* Boston: Little, Brown & Co., 1951.

HANKINS, FRANK. *The Racial Basis of Civilization.* New York and London: Alfred A. Knopf, Inc., 1926.

HANNAN, JOHN A. *Korea, Japan, Taiwan (Formosa), and the Philippines.* (Report on United States Foreign Assistance Program, Survey No. 5,

Eighty-fifth Congress, 1st session.) Washington, D. C.: U. S. Government Printing Office, 1957.

HANSEN, MARCUS LEE. *The Atlantic Migration, 1607-1860.* Cambridge: Harvard University Press, 1940.

————. *The Immigrant in American History.* Cambridge: Harvard University Press, 1940.

HARTENDORP, A. V. H. *History of Industry and Trade of the Philippines.* Manila: American Chamber of Commerce of the Philippines, 1958.

HARTLEY, EUGENE L. *Problems in Prejudice.* New York: King's Crown Press (div. of Columbia University Press), 1946.

HEYER, VIRGINIA. Patterns of Social Organization in New York City's Chinatown. Unpublished Ph. D. dissertation, Columbia University, 1953.

HIGHAM, JOHN. *Strangers in the Land: Patterns of American Nativism, 1860-1925.* New Brunswick: Rutgers University Press, 1955.

HO, PING-YIN. *The Foreign Trade of China.* Shanghai: The Commercial Press, 1935.

HOFFMAN, JAMES W. (ed.). *Concerns of a Continent.* New York: Friendship Press, 1958.

Hong Kong Report on the Year 1960. Hong Kong: Government Press, 1961.

HORSELY, MARGARET WYANT. Sangley: The Formation of Anti-Chinese Feeling in the Philippines. A Cultural Study of the Stereotype of Prejudices. Unpublished Ph. D. dissertation, Columbia University, 1950.

HOY, WILLIAM. *The Chinese Six Companies.* San Francisco: The Chinese Consolidated Benevolent Association, 1942.

HUANG, FOO-LUAN. *Hua-Chiao Yu Chung Kuo Ke Ming* ("The Overseas Chinese and Chinese Revolution"). Hong Kong: Asia Publishing Co. , 1954.

HUANG, TSEN-MING. *The Legal Status of the Chinese Abroad.* Taipei: China Cultural Service, 1954.

HUNT, ROCKWELL D. (ed.). *California and Californians.* Chicago: The G. W. Lewis Publishing Co. , 1926.

HUNTER, EDWARD. *In Many Voices: Our Fabulous Foreign Language Press.* Norman Park, Georgia: Norman College, 1960.

ICHIHASHI, YAMATO. *Japanese in the United States.* Stanford: Stanford University Press, 1932.

INGRAM, JAMES C. *Economic Change in Thailand Since 1850.* Stanford: Stanford University Press, 1955.

International Bankers Directory, 1st 1960 ed. Chicago: Rand McNally & Co. , 1960.

International Bank for Reconstruction and Development. *The Economic Development of Malaya.* Baltimore: The Johns Hopkins Press, 1955.

————. *A Public Development Program for Thailand.* Baltimore: The Johns Hopkins Press, 1959.

The Invalidity of the "Queue Ordinance" of the City and County of San Francisco. San Francisco: J. L. Rice and Co. , 1879.

Investment in Indonesia. (Publication of the United States Department of Commerce.) Washington, D. C.: U. S. Government Printing Office, 1956.

Investment in the Philippines. (Publication of the United States Department of Commerce.) Washington, D. C.: U. S. Government Printing Office, 1955.

ISAAC, JULIUS. *Economics of Migration.* London: Kegan Paul, Trench, Trubner & Co. , Ltd. , 1947.

JENKINS, SHIRLEY. *American Economic Policy toward the Philippines.* Stanford: Stanford University Press, 1954.

JENKS, JEREMIAH W., and W. JETT LAUCK. *The Immigration Problem; A Study of American Immigration Conditions and Needs.* 6th ed. New York: Funk & Wagnalls Co., 1926.

JENSEN, KHIN KHIN MYINT. The Chinese in the Philippines During the American Regime, 1898-1946. Unpublished Ph.D. dissertation, University of Wisconsin, 1956.

JOHNSON, EMORY R. "Chinese and Japanese in America," *The Annals of the American Academy of Political and Social Science,* XXXIV, No. 2 (September, 1909), 1-203.

JOHNSTON, CLEMENT. *South East Asia.* (Report on United States Foreign Assistance Program, Survey No. 7, Eighty-fifth Congress, 1st session.) Washington, D.C.: U.S. Government Printing Office, 1957.

JONES, L. W. *British North Borneo: A Report on the Census of Population Held on 4th June, 1951.* London: Crown Agents for the Colonies, 1953.

KAHIN, GEORGE McTURNAN (ed.). *Government and Politics of Southeast Asia.* Ithaca, New York: Cornell University Press, 1959.

KARLIN, JULES ALEXANDER. "The Anti-Chinese Outbreaks in Seattle, 1885-1886," *The Pacific Northwest Quarterly,* XXXIX, No. 2 (April, 1948), 103-30.

KINNEAR, GEORGE. *Anti-Chinese Riots in Seattle, February 8, 1886.* Seattle: George Kinnear, 1911.

KLINEBERG, OTTO. *Race and Psychology.* (UNESCO Publication, No. 842.) Paris, 1951.

KOHLER, MAX J. *Immigration and Aliens in the United States.* New York: Bloch Publishing Co., Inc., 1936.

KONVITZ, MILTON R. *The Alien and the Asiatic in American Law.* Ithaca, New York: Cornell University Press, 1946.

————. *Civil Rights in Immigration.* Ithaca, New York: Cornell University Press, 1953.

KUZNETS, SIMON, and ERNEST RUBIN. *Immigration and the Foreign Born.* (Occasional Paper, No. 46.) New York: National Bureau of Economic Research, 1954.

KWOH, BEULAH ONG. "The Occupational Status of American-Born Chinese Male College Graduates," *American Journal of Sociology,* LIII, No. 3 (November, 1947), 192-200.

LA FARGUE, THOMAS E. *China's First Hundred.* Pullman: State College of Washington, 1942.

LANDON, KENNETH PERRY. *The Chinese in Thailand.* London and New York: Oxford University Press, Inc., 1941.

LANG, OLGA. *Chinese Family and Society.* New Haven: Yale University Press, 1946.

LaPIERE, RICHARD T. "Attitudes vs. Actions," *Social Forces,* XIII, No. 2 (December, 1934), 230-37.

LAUGHLIN, H. H. *Immigration and Conquest.* New York: Chamber of Commerce of the State of New York, 1939.

LEE, ROSE HUM. *The Chinese in the United States of America.* Hong Kong: Hong Kong University Press, 1960.

————. "The Decline of Chinatowns in the United States," *American Journal of Sociology*, LIV, No. 5 (March, 1949), 422-32.

————. "Delinquent, Neglected and Dependent Chinese Boys and Girls of the San Francisco Bay Region," *Journal of Social Psychology*, XXXVI, 1st half (August, 1952), 15-34.

LEE, SAMUEL D. *San Francisco's Chinatown*. San Francisco: National Youth Administration, 1940.

LEE, TEH H., *et al*. "Isolation of Melatinin, the Pineal Gland Factor that Lightens the Melanocytes," *Journal of the American Chemical Society*, LXXX, No. 10 (May 20, 1958), 2587.

LEVENSON, JOSEPH R. *Liang Chi-Ch'ao and the Mind of Modern China*. Cambridge: Harvard University Press, 1953.

LI, TIEN-LU. Congressional Policy of Chinese Immigration; or Legislation Relating to Chinese Immigration to the United States. Unpublished Ph. D. dissertation, Vanderbilt University, 1916.

LIN, YUTANG. *Chinatown Family*. New York: The John Day Company, 1948.

LIND, ANDRED W. *An Island Community: Ecological Succession in Hawaii*. Chicago: University of Chicago Press, 1938.

————. *Hawaii's People*. Honolulu: University of Hawaii Press, 1955.

LING, PYAU. "Causes of Chinese Emigration," *The Annals of the American Academy of Political and Social Science*, XXXIX (January, 1912). 74-82.

LORDEN, DORIS M. "The Chinese Hawaiian Family," *American Journal of Sociology*, XL, No. 4 (January, 1935), 453-63.

LOWE, PARDEE. *Father and Glorious Descendant*. Boston: Little, Brown & Co., 1943.

LOWENSTEIN, EDITH. *The Alien and the Immigration Law*. New York: Oceana Publications, Inc., 1958.

LUCE, ROBERT. "Petty Business in Congress," *American Political Science Review*, XXVI, No. 5 (October, 1932), 815-27.

LUI, GARDING. *Inside Los Angeles Chinatown*. Los Angeles: Garding Lui, 1948.

McENTIRE, DAVIS. *Residence and Race*. Berkeley and Los Angeles: University of California Press, 1960.

MacIVER, ROBERT M. *The More Perfect Union*. New York: The Macmillan Co., 1948.

MACKENZIE, NORMAN ARCHIBALD MACRAE (ed.). *The Legal Status of Aliens in Pacific Countries; An International Survey of Law and Practice Concerning Immigration, Naturalization and Deportation of Aliens, and Their Legal Rights and Disabilities*. London and New York: Oxford University Press, Inc., 1937.

McKENZIE, R. D. *Oriental Exclusion*. Chicago: University of Chicago Press, 1928.

MacNAIR, HARLEY FARNSWORTH. *The Chinese Abroad; Their Position and Protection, A Study in International Law and Relations*. Shanghai: The Commercial Press, 1924.

———— (ed.). *China*. Berkeley and Los Angeles: University of California Press, 1946.

McWILLIAMS, CAREY. *Brothers Under the Skin*. Boston: Little, Brown & Co., 1951.

MANEY, E. S. "New Trends in American Immigration," *United States Department of State Bulletin*, XXX, No. 773 (April 19, 1954), 599-602.

MEARS, ELIOT GRINNELL. *Resident Orientals on the American Pacific Coast: Their Legal and Economic Status*. Chicago: University of Chicago Press, 1928.

MENCKEN, H. L. *The American Language*. 4th ed. New York: Alfred A. Knopf, Inc., 1946.

MOLLOY, TIMOTHY J. "A Century of Chinese Immigration: A Brief Review," *Monthly Review* (United States Immigration and Naturalization Service), V, No. 6 (December, 1947), 69-74.

MOSOLFF, HANS. *Die Chinesische Auswanderung*. Rostock: Carl Hinstorffs, 1932.

MURPHEY, RHOADS. "Boston's Chinatown," *Economic Geography*, XXVIII, No. 3 (July, 1952), 245-55.

Orientals and Their Cultural Adjustment. (Social Science Institute.) Nashville: Fisk University, 1946.

OUARADO, PATRICK K. "The Chinese in Colorado," *Colorado Magazine*, XXIX, No. 4 (October, 1952), 273-84.

Overseas Chinese Year Book, 1958. Taipei, Taiwan: Overseas Chinese Affairs Commission, 1959.

PALMER, ALBERT W. *Orientals in American Life*. New York: Friendship Press, 1934.

PANUNZIO, CONSTANTINE. "Intermarriage in Los Angeles, 1924-33," *American Journal of Sociology*, XLVII, No. 5 (March, 1942), 690-701.

"Peoples of Chinese Origin," *Encyclopedia Canadiana* (1st ed.), Vol. II. Ottawa: The Canadiana Co., Ltd. (div. of Grolier Society, Inc.), 1957.

PETERS, C. A. *Immigration Problem*. (Reference Shelf, Vol. XIX, No. 7.) New York: H. W. Wilson Co., 1948.

PHELPS, HAROLD A., and DAVID HENDERSON. *Population in Its Human Aspect*. New York: Appleton-Century-Crofts, Inc., 1958.

PHELPS, WILLIAM LYON. *Autobiography with Letters*. New York and London: Oxford University Press, Inc., 1939.

POPE, LISTON. *The Kingdom Beyond Caste*. New York: Friendship Press, 1957.

"Private Bills and Immigration," *Harvard Law Review*, LXIX, No. 6 (April, 1956), 1083-96.

PROTHRO, E. TERRY, and OTHA KING MILES. "Social Distance in the Deep South as Measured by a Revised Bogardus Scale," *Journal of Social Psychology*, XXXVII, 2nd half (May, 1953), 171-74.

PURCELL, VICTOR. *The Chinese in Southeast Asia*. London and New York: Oxford University Press, Inc., 1951.

————. *The Colonial Period in South East Asia*. New York: Institute of Pacific Relations, 1953.

RATZELL, FRIEDRICH. *Die Chinesische Auswanderung*. Breslau: J. U. Kern's, 1876.

REMER, C. F. *A Study of Chinese Boycotts, with Special Reference to Their Economic Effectiveness*. Baltimore: The Johns Hopkins Press, 1933.

————. *Foreign Investments in China*. New York: The Macmillan Co., 1933.

————. *The Foreign Trade of China*. Shanghai: The Commercial Press, 1926.

RENO, CLAUDE T. (ed.). *The Manual of the Alpha Tau Omega Fraternity.* 4th ed. Champaign, Illinois, 1946, pp. 155-56.

RHODES, JAMES FORD. *History of the United States from the Compromise of 1850 to the McKinley-Bryan Campaign of 1896.* 8 vols. New York: The Macmillan Co., 1920.

RIGGS, FRED W. *Pressures on Congress: A Study of the Repeal of Chinese Exclusion.* New York: King's Crown Press, 1950.

RIIS, JACOB A. *How the Other Half Lives.* New York: Charles Scribner's Sons, 1890.

ROBEQUAIN, CHARLES. *The Economic Development of French Indo-China.* London and New York: Oxford University Press, Inc., 1944.

———. *Malaya, Indonesia, Borneo, and the Philippines.* London and New York: Longmans, Green, and Co., Inc., 1954.

SANDMEYER, ELMER CLARENCE. *The Anti-Chinese Movement in California.* Urbana: University of Illinois Press, 1939.

———. "California Anti-Chinese Legislation and the Federal Courts: A Study in Federal Relations," *Pacific Historical Review,* V, No. 3 (September, 1936), 189-211.

SCHWARTZ, SHEPARD. "Mate-Selecting Among New York City's Chinese Males, 1931-38," *American Journal of Sociology,* LVI, No. 6 (May, 1951), 562-68.

"Seventh Semi-Annual Report of the Administrator of the Refugee Relief Act of 1953 as Amended," *Interpreter Releases,* XXXIV, No. 7 (February 27, 1957), 40-42.

SEWARD, GEORGE F. *Chinese Immigration in Its Social and Economic Aspects.* New York: Charles Scribner's Sons, 1881.

SIDNEY, KANSAS. *Immigration and Nationality Act* (Annotated with Rules and Regulations). New York: Immigration Publications, 1953.

———. *1954-1959 Cumulative Supplement to Fourth Edition of Immigration and Nationality Act.* Buffalo: Dennis & Co., 1959.

SIMPSON, GEORGE EATON, and J. MILTON YINGER. *Racial and Cultural Minorities.* New York: Harper & Brothers, 1953.

SKINNER, G. WILLIAM. *Chinese Society in Thailand.* Ithaca, New York: Cornell University Press, 1957.

———. *Leadership and Power in the Chinese Community of Thailand.* Ithaca, New York: Cornell University Press, 1958.

SMITH, WILLIAM CARLSON. *The Second Generation Oriental in America.* Honolulu: Institute of Pacific Relations, 1927.

SPENCER, JOSEPH E. *Land and People in the Philippines.* Berkeley: University of California Press, 1952.

STEPHENSON, GEORGE M. *A History of American Immigration, 1820-1924.* Boston: Ginn & Company, 1926.

STEWART, WATT. *Chinese Bondage in Peru: A History of the Chinese Coolie in Peru, 1849-1874.* Durham, N. C.: Duke University Press, 1951.

STRONG, EDWARD K., JR. *Japanese in California.* Stanford: Stanford University Press, 1933.

———. *The Second-Generation Japanese Problem.* Stanford: Stanford University Press, 1934.

A Survey of Chinese Students in American Universities and Colleges in the

Past Hundred Years. New York: National Tsing Hua University Research Fellowship Fund and Chinese Institute in America, 1954.

SUSSMAN, AARON. *The Amateur Photographer's Handbook*. 5th ed. New York: Thomas Y. Crowell Company, 1958.

SWETTENHAM, SIR FRANK A. *British Malay, An Account of the Origin and Progress of British Influence in Malaya* (rev. ed.). London: George Allen & Unwin, Ltd., 1948.

SWISHER, CARL BRENT. *Motivation and Political Technique in the California Constitutional Convention, 1878-1879*. Claremont: Pomona College, 1930.

————. *Stephan J. Field, Craftsman of the Land*. Washington, D.C.: The Brookings Institution, 1930.

TAFT, DONALD R. *Human Migration: A Study of International Movements*. New York: The Ronald Press Company, 1936.

THOMAS, BRINLEY (ed.). *Economics of International Migration: Proceedings of a Conference Held by the International Economic Association*. London: Macmillan & Co., Ltd., 1958.

THOMPSON, WARREN S. *Population and Peace in the Pacific*. Chicago: University of Chicago Press, 1946.

————. *Growth and Changes in California's Population*. Los Angeles: Haynes Foundation, 1955.

THURSTONE, L. L. "The Measurement of Change in Social Attitude," *Journal of Social Psychology*, II, No. 2 (May, 1931), 230-35.

TIEN, JU-K'ANG. *The Chinese of Sarawak: A Study of Social Structure*. London: London School of Economics and Political Science, 1953.

TINKER, HUGH. *The Union of Burma*. London and New York: Oxford University Press, Inc., 1957.

TOW, JULIUS SU. *The Real Chinese in America*. Orange, N. J.: The Academy Press, 1923.

TSU, HSU-HSIEH (ed.). *Hua-Chiao Tze* ("Chinese in Foreign Countries"). Taipei, Taiwan: Overseas Publishing Co., 1956.

TYLER, POYNTZ (ed.). *Immigration and the United States*. (Reference Shelf, Vol. XXVIII, No. 1.) New York: H. W. Wilson Co., 1956.

VANDENBOSCH, AMRY. *The Dutch East Indies, Its Government, Problems, and Politics*. Berkeley and Los Angeles: University of California Press, 1941.

VAN VLECK, WILLIAM C. *The Administrative Control of Aliens*. New York: The Commonwealth Fund, 1958.

VLEKKE, BERNARD H. M. *The Story of the Dutch East Indies*. Cambridge: Harvard University Press, 1945.

WAGLEY, CHARLES, and MARVIN HARRIS. *Minorities in the New World*. New York: Columbia University Press, 1958.

WEHL, DAVID. *The Birth of Indonesia*. London: George Allen & Unwin, Ltd., 1948.

WELLBORN, MILDRED. "The Events Leading to the Chinese Exclusion Acts," Historical Society of Southern California, *Annual Publications*, IX (1914), 49-58.

WHEATON, DONALD W. "Spotlights on the Political History of California from 1887 to 1898," *California Historical Society Quarterly*, V, No. 3 (September, 1926), 283-88.

WILCOX, B. P. "Anti-Chinese Riots in Washington," *Washington Historical Quarterly*, XX, No. 3 (July, 1929), 207-11.

WILDES, LEON. "Review of Denial of Visa," *New York Law Journal*, Vol. CXLII, Nos. 96-98 (November 17-19, 1959).

WILLIAMS, FREDERICK WELLS. *Anson Burlingame and the First Chinese Mission to Foreign Powers*. New York: Charles Scribner's Sons, 1912.

WILLIAMS, S. WELLS. *Chinese Immigration*. New York: Charles Scribner's Sons, 1879.

WITTKE, C. F. *We Who Build America*. New York: Prentice-Hall, Inc., 1939.

WOODSWORTH, CHARLES J. *Canada and the Orient*. Toronto: Macmillan Company of Canada, Ltd., 1941.

WONG, JADE SNOW. *Fifth Chinese Daughter*. New York: Harper & Brothers, 1950.

WOOFTER, T. J. *Races and Ethnic Groups in American Life*. New York: McGraw-Hill Book Co., 1933.

WU, CHARLES LING. Attitudes toward Negroes, Jews, and Orientals in the United States. Unpublished Ph. D. dissertation, Ohio State University, 1927.

WU, CHING CHAO. Chinatown: A Study in Symbiosis and Assimilation. Unpublished Ph. D. dissertation, University of Chicago, 1928.

WU, S. Y. *One Hundred Years of Chinese in the United States and Canada*. Hong Kong: S. Y. Wu, 1954.

YOUNG, DONALD R. *American Minority Peoples: A Study in Racial and Cultural Conflicts in the United States*. New York: Harper & Brothers, 1932.

YU, LIN. "Twin Loyalties in Siam," *Pacific Affairs*, IX, No. 2 (June, 1936), 191-200.

YUNG, WING. *My Life in China and America*. New York: Henry Holt & Co., Inc., 1909.

ZEIGLER, HARLEY H. "Hawaii, Progress in Paradise," in *Concerns of a Continent*, ed. James W. Hoffman. New York: Friendship Press, 1958.

ZIEGLER, B. M. *Immigration, an American Dilemma*. Boston: D. C. Heath & Company, 1953.

Index

Academia Sinica, 325

Acts. *See* Administrative Procedure Act; Chinese Exclusion Act; Displaced Persons Act; Fiancées Act; Geary Act; McCarran-Walter Act; Quota Act of 1921; Quota Act of 1924; Refugee Relief Act of 1953; Restriction Acts of 1882 and 1892; Scott Act; Seven Year Act; War Brides Act

Act of: 1892, 84, 85; 1902, 85; 1924, 64, 85, 94, 217; August 9, 1946, 112; June 16, 1950, 300; June 28, 1951, 300

Adjustment of status: suspension of deportation, 115; general qualifications, 115, 302; Chinese, 300, 300-301

Administrative Procedure Act, 149

Aeronautical engineering, 243-44

Africa, South, 174-75

Age composition, 36-37. *See also* Birth and Death rates

Alien Land Law, 293

American churches, 88

American Coalition, 109, 300

American Council of Learned Societies, 249, 327

American Federation of Labor, 104

American immigration policy, 80-82, 107-8

American Legion, 108, 172

American Security Bank (Honolulu), 190

Anti-Chinese agitation: causes of, 70-71; general, 87-88

Anti-Chinese convention, 73, 88

Anti-Chinese demonstrations, 67-76, 87

Anti-Chinese legislation, 70-74, 183, 316

Anti-Chinese movements: Southeast Asia, 12, 13, 14; Batavia, 15; Canada, 19; Philippines, 25; California, 67-76; bases of, 68-70

Architecture, Chinese in, 246

Arrest: assault, 47; auto theft, 47; burglary, 47; larceny, 47; robbery, 47; rape, 47-48; disorderly conduct, 48; homicide, 48; narcotics, 48-49; drunkenness, 48, 50; gambling, 49-50; vagrancy, 50; juvenile delinquency, 51-52

Arts, Chinese in, 249-50

Asia, Southeast. *See* Southeast Asia

Asiatic Pacific Triangle, 130, 260

Asiatics, exclusion of, 85

Assault, 47

Assimilation: question of, 174-78, 227; suggestion on method of, 315. *See also* Intermarriage; Naturalization

Associations and organizations, Chinese: Chinese Benevolent Association of Canada, 21; Chinese Community Center Association of Ontario, 21; Kipkat Association, 76; Kong Chow Association, 76; Sam Yup Association, 76; Sze Yap Association, 76; Yan Wo Association, 76; Yeung Wo Association, 76; Hop Wo District Association, 77; Ning Yung Association, 77, 221; Shew Hing Association, 77; Yin Hoi Association, 77;

345

Chinese Institute of Engineers, New York, 189; Chee Kung Tang, 216; Chinese United Society, 216; mutual benefit and welfare organizations, 218; list, 218-20; clan and family associations, 219; locality and district organizations, 219-20; Hip Sing Association, 221; On Leong Merchants Association, 221; China Society of America, 222; Chung Hwa Kung So, 222; Fukien Association, 222; Sam Kiang Association, 222; Sino-American Amity, Inc., 222; Wah Pei Association, 222; China Institute in America, 222-23; China Club of Seattle, 223; Chicago Chinese-American Civic Council, 226; Jee Tuck Sam Tuck Association, 320. See also Business, Chinese in: organizations; Chinese American Citizens Alliance; Chinese Consolidated Benevolent Association; Political organizations; Religious organizations; United Parlor of the Native Sons of the Golden State (West)

Attitudes toward Chinese, 66-79, 86-92

Attorney general, discretion of, 123, 149, 150

Attorneys, Chinese, 189-90

Auto theft, 47

Bancroft, H. H., 65

Bank of Canton (San Francisco), 190

Banks, Chinese in, 190

"Barred zones" provisions, 85

Barrio de los chinos, 21

Batavia: import of Chinese, 14; massacre, 15

Beach, Walter G., 45, 46

Bills, private: quota immigration, 110; types of bills, 133; special cases, 135-42; specialists and skilled personnel, 137; qualifications, 138, 142; deportable aliens, 162; deportation, 303; causes, 304; 59th, 85th Congresses, 304; procedure, 305; cost, 306; enumeration, 306

Birth rate, Chinese, 37-39

Blood test, 155, 158-60

Bogardus, Emory S., 167

Britain: crewmen, 161-62; immi-

grants from, 311

Brunsman, Howard G., 287

Buck, Pearl, 166, 231

Buddhism, 54

Burglary, 47

Burlingame, Anson, 74

Burlingame, Fanny Amelia, 233

Burlingame Treaty, 74-75, 236

Business, Chinese in: Southeast Asia, 26; organizations, 183, 186, 194, 218-19; problems, 196; United States, 250-51

California: religion, 54; free immigration, 64-79; school laws, 72; supreme court, 73; Second Constitutional Convention, 73, 88; University of, 192, 327; Alien Land Law, 293. See also Chinese Six Companies; Intermarriage

Callis, Helmut G., 27

Canada, Chinese in: history, 18-20; contemporary professionals, 20-21; population, 284; exclusion, 294

Canadian Pacific Railroad, 18

Canadian pre-examination procedure, 115

Cancer research, 179

Capital Investment Company, 62

Carpenter, Horace W., 234, 324-25

Celler, Emanuel, 144, 301

Census: 1860, 65; 1860-70, 66; 1910, 81; 1950, 39, 42, 288; 1960, 42, 44

Central Pacific Railroad, 41, 64, 229, 230

Chang, F. K., 245

Chatham Square, New York, 319

Chekiang province, 222

Chemical engineering, 244-45

Chen, Lan-pin, 17, 236, 283

Chen, Theodore Hsi-en, 248-49

Chen, Tse-Tuan, 240

Chiang, Kai-shek, Madame, 104

Chicken farm, Chinese in, 186-87

Children, U.S. citizens, 97

China, assimilation with, 175

"China City, The," 205

China Institute in America, 222-23

China quota, 106, 110-12, 260-61

China Toggery-Shoong Company, 250

"Chinatown," 198

Chinatown: characteristics, 36-51, 199-200; family life and pattern, 206-16; women, 208-11; listed, 319. See also Honolulu; Los Angeles;

New York; San Francisco; Tong
wars
Chinatown police squad, 202
Chinatown telephone switches, 203
China Trade and Industrial Service,
186
Chinese, native and foreign-born,
39-41, 288
Chinese American Citizens Alliance,
217, 322
Chinese American Progress, 226
Chinese American Times, 226
Chinese Chamber of Commerce,
217-18, 322
"Chinese confession program," 310
Chinese Consolidated Benevolent Association: New York, 216, 221;
general, 223; Chicago, 319; San
Francisco, *see* Chinese Six Companies
Chinese exclusion: effects of, 34,
91-92, 148, 154; general, 82-85,
123
Chinese Exclusion Act (1904): general, 80, 82-83, 84, 85, 113, 154;
repeal of, 103-5, 299
Chinese Hollywood, 198
Chinese immigrants: characteristics,
30-31, 69-70, 89, 90, 228-30; contributions in language, 231; literature, 231; achievements, 232-34;
science and medicine, 238-41; engineering, 241-46; architecture,
246; social science, 246-49; arts,
249-50; business 250-51; prejudice
against, 253-54
Chinese immigration to United States:
free immigration, 64-79; period of
exclusion, 80-105, 294; recent status of, 106-31; quota, 110-12; nonquota, 112-15; percentage, 295.
See also Coolie trade; Deportation;
Desertion; Hawaii; Illegal entry;
Private bills
Chinese Merchants Associations
Building, 204
Chinese Pacific Weekly, 226
Chinese population, estimate of, 41-
45, 287, 288
Chinese Presbyterian Church, 54
Chinese press, 224-26
Chinese Protective Society, 87
Chinese racial quota, 106-7, 110,
121-22, 144

Chinese Restriction Act: 1882, 75-
76, 80; 1892, 82-83, 84, 296;
amendment, 1884, 83
Chinese Seven Companies, 220. *See
also* Chinese Six Companies
Chinese Six Companies or Chinese
Benevolent Association: organiza-
tion, 67, 76-79, 322, 323; function,
77-78, 216, 309; subpoenas, 156
Chinese students, 235, 294
Chinese students, pioneer of. *See*
Yung Wing
Chinese World, 217, 224, 225
Chou, Wen-Chung, 249
Christian missionaries in China,
255-56, 289
Chu, Ju-Chin, 244
Chung Hwa School, 327
Chung Shan people, 76
Churches and the Chinese. *See* Re-
ligion
Citizenship Act, Canada, 20
Civil engineering, 245-46
Colorado, Chinese in, 319
Columbia University, Chinese Li-
brary, 234
Commodore Stockton School, 90
Confucianism. *See* Religion
Congress: power over deportation,
123-26; power over immigration,
132-47; Chinese in, *see* Fong,
Hiram L.
Congresses: 45th, 74; 47th, 76; 57th,
85; 49th, 91; 78th to 84th, 132-33;
82nd, 137-39, 143; 84th, 140, 143;
81st, 143; 83rd, 143; 59th, 304;
86th, 305
Constitutional Convention of California, 73-88
Contract labor, restriction of, 80.
See also Coolie trade
Coolidge, Mary R., 65, 66, 230
Coolie trade: general, 15-18;
coolie beguilement, 283
Crewmen: awards to Chinese crewmen, 251. *See also* Desertion
Crimes: serious offenses, 45-48;
rural area, 48; other offenses, 48-
50; women, 50-51; by nativity, 51;
juvenile delinquency, 51-52. *See
also* Arrests
Cuba: coolie trade, 17-18; assimilation of Chinese, 21-22; Chinese
business, 284

"Cubic air" ordinance, 72
Cultural associations: general, 219;
  exchange of, 223

Davie, Maurice R., 65, 253
Dean Lung, 234, 258, 324-25
Death, causes of among Chinese, 39
Death rate, Chinese: general, 37-39,
  287; suicide, 53
Delinquency, juvenile, 51-52
Demonstrations against Chinese.
  See Anti-Chinese movements
Denver: Chinatown, 199; riot, 319
Deportation: general, 102-3, 160-62;
  suspension of, 121, 149-52; Congress, 123-26; suspension due to
  fear of physical persecution, 162-
  64; to Communist China, 311; ac-
  tual deportation, 312-13
Desertion: Chinese crewmen, 124,
  126, 161-62, 296, 308; British,
  161-62; remedy, 311
Discrimination: against Chinese,
  general, 85-90; pattern of, 169-74;
  cases, 171-72; employment, 180;
  housing, 171, 313; school, 314. See
  also California: school laws; Chinese exclusion; Legal cases: Gung
  Lum vs. Rice
Disorderly conduct, 48
Displaced Persons Act of 1948, 108,
  110, 117-18, 128, 161, 301
Distinguished Service Crosses, 251
"Don" (cancer treatment), 179
Drunkenness, 48, 50
Dupont, Captain, 7
Dutch (Batavia) massacre, 14-15
Dutch East Indies, 285

Earthquake of 1906, 201
Education, 55-57
Eisenhower, Dwight D., President,
  120, 121, 152, 301
Electronic engineering, 242-43
Emergency legislation. See Dis-
  placed Persons Act; Refugee Relief
  Act
Emigration: from China, 3, 4, 5, 24;
  assimilation with natives, 12; for-
  bidden by Emperor, 290; Chinese
  from U.S., 298. See also Canada;
  Southeast Asia; United States
Employment: general, 57-59; re-
  striction, 180

Engineering: general, 241-46; electronic, 242-43; aeronautical, 243-
  44; mechanical, 244; chemical, 244-
  45; hydraulic, 245; civil, 245-46
Engineers, Chinese, 189. See also
  Engineering
Ethnocentrism, 175
Europe: Chinese in, 95; immigration from, 96, 201; southeastern
  immigration, 80-81, 96
Exclusion. See Chinese exclusion

Family and social life. See China-
  town; Chinese immigrants; Women;
  Wives
Family associations, 219, 222. See
  also Associations
Fiancées Act, 117, 309
Fifteen Passengers Bill, 74, 75
Filipino Federation of America, 322
Filipino intermarriage, 215
Films (movies), Chinese in, 250
Foilcraft Printing Corporation, 318
Folin Wu System, 241
Fong, Hiram L., 63, 228, 237, 238
Foods, Chinese, canned and frozen,
  182-83
Foreign Miner's License Tax Law, 71
Fraser River Valley, 18

Gambling, 49-50
Geary Act, 83-84, 90
General Business Investment Corp.,
  318
Germans, 117, 300
Gold, discovery of, 64, 66
Gold rush of 1849, 18, 66
Gong, Eddie, 209, 232
Goon, Toy Len, 233
Government service, Chinese in, 191
Greater Chinatown, 198
Grocery stores, 184

"Halgoon," 155
Hambro, Eduard I., 5, 282
Harvard University, 192, 232
Hawaii: racial prejudice, 169; intermarriage, 216
Hawaii, Chinese in: general, 4, 32,
  55; occupational, 59, 60, 61, 190-
  91; population, 60, 61, 62, 290;
  exclusion, 84; integration, 169,
  176, 216; social life, 319, 323.
  See also Honolulu

Hayes, Rutherford B., President, 74
Henry Luce Foundation, 222
Herbalists, Chinese, 189
Ho, Chinn, 62
Homicide, 48
Hong Kong, Chinese in: general, 4-5, 28-29; coolie trade, 16; population, 286
Honolulu: Chinatown, 189, 204; Chinese organizations, 216; Chinese press, 224
Hoover, John Edgar, 288
Hop Valley, 319
Hospitals, Chinese, 293
House Immigration Committee, 104
Housing. See Discrimination
Howe, James Wong, 250, 327
Hsiao, Kung-chuan, 249
Hsieh, Chiao-min, 172
Hundred Day Reform Movement, 217, 225
Hungarian refugees, 120
Hydraulic engineering, 245

Illegal entry: problem of, 91, 308, 309; smuggling, 152-53; paper sons, 153, 154-55; immigration slots, 155; fraudulent passports and visas, 155-56, 309; illegal entry through Canada, 157; remedy, 310
Immigrants, Chinese. See Canada; Chinese immigration to U.S.; Southeast Asia
Immigration Act of 1917, 292
Immigration Act of 1923, Canada, 19
Immigration Act of 1924, 85, 97-98, 294, 296, 299
Immigration Act of 1952, 31, 108-10, 157, 162, 217
Immigration and Naturalization Service: fallacies in statistics, 94-96; statistics, 287, 297; changes in attitude, 308. See also Judicial, review of
Immigration laws, state, 292
Immigration policy, 80-82, 107-8
Immigration quotas: preferential, 145; all quota areas, 292; Europe, 292; barred zones, 292; Asia, 328
Income, 59
Indians, American, 37, 170
Indo-China, Chinese in, 9, 25, 285
Indonesia, Chinese in, 283, 285, 286
Industry, Chinese in, 318

Inouye, Daniel K., 325
Insurance brokers, Chinese, 190
Intermarriage: general, 176-77; extent of, 213-16, 320; attitude of Chinese toward, 215; laws barring, 215; Hawaii, 216. See also Assimilation; Hawaii
Italians: general, 81, 116-17, 295; immigrated to U.S., 96; deported, 103

Japanese American Citizens League, 322
Japanese and Korean Exclusion League, 85
Japanese in U.S.: population, 32, 37, 292; characteristics, 45-46, 54, 287; Hawaii, 61; restriction, 85; immigration, 116-17, 292; discrimination in housing, 172-73; press, 225; laundries, 316
Joe Shoong Fellowship, 327
Joe Shoong Foundation, 327
Joe Shoong School in Lodi, 327
Judicial review: in deportation proceedings, 149-50; in immigration cases, 149-52
Jung, Douglas, 21, 325

Kang, Yu-wei, 225
Kearneyism, 68
Keys, Ancel, 287
Kiangsi province, 222
Kiangsu province, 222
Kimlau, Benjamin Ralph, 319
Kimlau Square, 319
Kingman, Dong, 250, 327
Klein, Arthur G., 51
Know-nothingism, 68
Kong Chow Temple, 54
Korean Exclusion League, 85
Korean National Association, 322
Kuomintang, 216
Kwangtung province, 64, 66, 76
Kwong Tai weekly, 226

Labor in California, 80
Lakewood, chicken farm in, 186-87
Lantex Industries, 318
LaPiere, Richard T., 168
Larceny, 47
Latin America, Chinese in: Peru, 16-17; 22-23, 284; Cuba, 21-22; general, 21-23; Jamaica, 22;

Mexico, 22; Panama, 22; Argentina, 23; Brazil, 23; Colombia, 23; Ecuador, 23
Laundry, Chinese: general, 57, 180, 183-84, 196, 316; associations, 183-84
Lee, Gerald, 172
Lee, Rose Hum, 52, 200, 248
Lee, Yuan-Chu'en, 243
Legal cases: *Ho Ah Kow* v. *Matthew Noonan*, 72; *United States* v. *Wong Kim Ark*, 127; *Fong Yue Ting* v. *United States*, 150; *Yick Wo* v. *Hopkins*, 183; *Ham Say Naim* v. *Ruby Elaine Naim*, 215; *Chy Lung* v. *Freeman*, 291; *United States* v. *Mrs. Cue Lim*, 296; *Brownell* v. *Shung*, 307; *Kwock Jan Fat* v. *White*, 307; *Mao* v. *Brownell*, 307; *Quon Quon Poy* v. *Johnson*, 307; *Shaughnessy* v. *Pedreiro*, 307; *Tang Tun* v. *Edsell*, 307; *Yep Suey Ning* v. *Berkshire*, 307; *Rogers* v. *Lu*, 311; *United States* ex rel. *Lee Kum Hoy, Lee Kum Cherk, and Lee Moon Wah, Petitioners* v. *John L. Murff*, 311; *United States* ex rel. *Lee Kum Hoy* v. *Shaughnessy*, 311; *Lim Fong* v. *Brownell*, 311-12; *Chao* v. *Shaughnessy*, 312; *Jay* v. *Boyd*, 312; *Quan* v. *Brownell*, 312; *United States* ex rel. *Chen Ping Zee* v. *Shaughnessy*, 312; *Rogers* v. *Quan*, 312-13; *Gung Lum* v. *Rice*, 314
Li, Cho-Hao, 239, 240
Li, Hung-chang, 57, 236, 237
Li, K. C., 179, 251, 327
Liang, Chi-chao, 217, 225
Liberty Bank of Honolulu, 190
Li Foundation, 327-28
Lin, Hazel, 189
Liu, Frederick Fu, 243
Loo, C. T., Chinese Educational Fund Fellowships, 324
Los Angeles Chinese: riot, 67; Chinatowns, 204, 205-6, 319
Louisiana Purchase Exposition, 90-91
Lue, Gim Gong, 233-34
Lung, Dean, 234, 258, 324-25

Macao: coolie trade, 16-18; Chinese in, 29

McCarran-Walter Act. *See* Immigration Act of 1952
McGreary Amendment of 1893, 84
Maine Mother of the Year, 183, 233
Maintenance of status, failure in, 160-62
Manchu dynasty: ignorance of overseas Chinese, 7-8, 15, 89; coolie trade, 17; overthrow of, 237
Mandarin Heights, 198
Marital status, Chinese, 34
Massachusetts Institute of Technology, 192
Mate selection, 213-14
Mechanical engineering, 244
Medicine, Chinese in, 241, 316
Mental illness, Chinese, 53, 288
Merchants, associations, 221. *See also* Treaty trader
Mexicans, 96, 298-99
Min Chih Journal, 217
Ming: emperor, 6; fall of dynasty, 7
Mining, Chinese in, 69
Ministers and their families, 99
Minnesota, University of, 192
Miss Chinatown contest, 320
Mother of the Year, Maine, 183, 233

Narcotics, 48-49
National Dollar Stores, Ltd., 179, 194, 250-51
National origin system, 81-82, 108, 261
Native and foreign-born Chinese, 39-41; crime rate, 51
Native Sons of the Golden West, The. *See* Chinese American Citizens Alliance
Naturalization: general, 126-29, 177, 302; procedure for, 127; means to assimilation, 127; increasing number, 128-29
Negroes, 69, 167, 170, 173
New China Daily News, 217, 224
"New Chinese" immigrants, 116
New Golden Mountains, 290
"New" immigrants, 11, 165, 171
Newspaper, Chinese, 224-26
New York Chinatown: general, 198, 319; history, 203-4; life, 204; tong wars, 204; organizations, 216; press, 224
New York University, 192, 232
Ning Yung: Association, 77, 221;

(Mr.), 220, 221
Nobel prize, 179, 238, 239
Nonquota immigration, 112-15
Nyctotherus Cheni, 240

Oakland Chinese Community Center, 327
Occupations. *See* Employment
Old age, 213
"Old Chinese" immigrants, 116
Old Golden Mountains, 290
"Old" immigrants, 165, 262
Open-Door Policy, 80
Oregon, University of, 192
Organizations and societies, 216-24. *See also* Associations
Orientals, discrimination against, 170
Overseas Chinese: general, 3-29; contributions from, 8, 11, 27; development, 23-24; population estimate, 282. *See also* Canada; Europe; Hawaii; Indonesia; Indo China; Latin America; Philippines; Southeast Asia

Parity, conservation of, 238-39
Passport rackets, 155-56. *See also* Illegal entry
"Pattern of preference," 167
Pei, I. M., 246, 326-27
Persecution, physical, 162-64
Peru, Chinese in: general, 16-17, 22-23; population enumeration, 284
Pharmacology, Chinese in, 241
Phelps, William Lyon, 236
Philippines, Chinese in: general, 12; restriction, 13-14, 25, 84; business, 285, 286; Retail Trade Nationalization Law, 25
Physicians, Chinese, 188
Pituitary growth hormone, 327
Political organizations, Chinese: Chee Kung Tang, 216; Kuomintang, 217; Hung Man Ming Chi party, 217; list, 218
Population. *See* Overseas Chinese
Presidential citations, 251
Private immigration bills. *See* Bills, private
Profession. *See* Employment
Public Laws: P. L. 85-316, 110, 120-21, 145, 146; P. L. 85-700, 121-22, 145-46; P. L. 86-129, 122; P. L. 86-253, 122; P. L. 86-363, 122-23

Quota Act of 1921, 81
Quota Act of 1924: general, 74, 85, 94; wives, 217
Quota immigration, 110-12
Quotas for Asia, 328. *See also* Immigration quotas

Race homogeneity, 81
Race prejudice: problem of, 166-69; anti-Chinese, 167; in U. S. South, 168; in Hawaii, 169; in Africa, 174-75
Rape, 47-48
Refugee Relief Act (1953), 40, 108, 118-20, 129, 162, 302
Religion, Chinese in, 53-55; organization, 219
Religious organizations, Chinese: Chinese Presbyterian Church, 54; Methodist Episcopal Ministers' Association of Seattle, 87-88; Methodist Mission, asylum for girls, 88; list, 219
"Rescue homes," 54
Residents, returning, 297
Restaurant, Chinese, 57, 180, 181-82
Restriction Act of 1882, 75-76
Retail, import, export, 184-86
Retail Trade Naturalization Laws, 25
Rho Psi fraternity, 56, 286
Right to work, Chinese: prior World War II, 180-81; since World War II, 181
Robbery, 47
Ross, Erskine, 88
Russians, 81, 117-18

San Francisco, Chinese in: Chinatown, 199-203, 319; earthquake, 201, 202; life, 202; tong wars, 202-3; organizations, 216, 217-18, 220, 221-22; press, 225. *See also* California
Schools, Chinese, 220-21
Schwartz, Jean, 318
Scientists, Chinese, 189, 238-41, 316
Scott Act (1888), 83, 84
Seven Companies, The, 220. *See also* Chinese Six Companies
Seven Year Act, 115, 128

Sex distribution, Chinese: in Ja-
    maica, 20; in Canada, 21; in U.S.,
    32-34
Shen, H. J., 194
Sheng, Sing, 171
Shew Hing group, 220
Shipping trade, 187-88
Shoong, Joe, 179, 250, 327
Siam. *See* Thailand
Sino-American Amity, Inc., 222
Sino-Japanese War, 103
Six Companies. *See* Chinese Six
    Companies
Social distance, 167, 213, 313
Social science, Chinese in, 246-49
Societies. *See* Organizations
Soo Hoo, Peter, 205
Southeast Asia, Chinese in: general,
    3, 4, 5, 9, 23-28; population esti-
    mation, 9; anti-Chinese movements,
    12-15, 176, 285; contributions to
    China, 27; assimilation, 175-76;
    against colonial governments, 322
Spanish in Philippines, 12, 13, 14
Status, adjustment of. *See* Adjust-
    ment of status
Sterling, Christine, 205
Stockbrokers, Chinese as, 190-91
Subpoenas, 156, 309
Suicides. *See* Death rate
Summit Industrial Corporation, 186
Sun, Yat-sen, 90, 216, 224
Sung dynasty, 6
"Superior races," 174
Supreme Court, 307
Sutter's Mill, 64
Sze, Yi-Kwei, 249

Taiping Rebellion, 7, 66, 322
Taishan district, 221
Tang dynasty, 5-6
Tang Industries, The, 318
Taoism, 53
Teachers and their families, 99
Teaching profession, Chinese in,
    191-94, 317
Thailand (Siam), 9-10, 12, 285
Tientsin, Treaty of, 7
Tong war, 202-3, 204

Trade guilds, 217
Trader, treaty, 98, 296
Treaties of 1888, unratified, 83
Treaty of 1880, 236
Treaty of Tientsin, 7
Treaty trader, 98, 296
Turks, 170, 314

Unites States citizens, wives of. *See*
    Wives
United States Department of Justice,
    143-44
United States government against
    discrimination, 173-74
United States population, 288
Urbanization, Chinese, 31, 40-41

Vagrancy, 50
Vanguard, 243
Veteran groups, 218
Vietnam. *See* Indo-China
Voluntary departure, 161

Wah Chang Corporation, 179, 194,
    251
Wang, Chi-teh, 326
War Brides Act, 117, 309
Washington, University of, 223-24
Welfare Conference, Chinese, first
    held, 1957, 223
"Wetbacks," 96, 124
Wilder Medal, 233
Wing, Yung. *See* Yung, Wing
Wives: left in China, 12; G.I. brides,
    39, 208, 210; admittance, 97-98,
    112-13
Women, Chinese: general, 89, 94,
    207-8, 211; occupational, 195
Workingmen's party, 70

Yale University, 137, 192, 235, 236,
    237
Yan Wo district, 220
Yang, Chen-Ning, 238, 239, 255,
    325
Young China. 225
Yung, Wing, 17, 18, 103, 214, 229,
    231, 234-37, 283